711 13 EUR

EUROPEAN SUSTAINABLE CIT!ES

Report

Expert Group on the Urban Environment

European Commission

Directorate General XI
Environment, Nuclear Safety and Civil Protection

BRUSSELS, MARCH 1996

European Sustainable Cities-
Report of the Expert Group on the Urban Environment
Published by the European Commission-
DGXI Environment, Nuclear Safety and Civil Protection
With bibliography, with index.
Reference key words: sustainability, urban development,
mobility, environment.
Technical and scientific secretariat provided by Euronet.
Lay-out and cover by Design '88.

March 1996

This report was requested by the European Commission. Any views expressed in this report do not necessarily reflect the views of the European Commission.

A great deal of additional information on the European Union is available on the Internet. It can be accessed through the Europa server (http://europa.eu.int).

Cataloguing data can be found at the end of this publication.

Luxembourg: Office for Official Publications of the European Communities, 1996.

ISBN 92-827-8259-X

Printed in Italy

PREFACE

As we approach the final years of the 20th Century, the increasing urbanisation of the world coupled with global issues of climate change, water shortage, environmental degradation, economic restructuring and social exclusion, demand that we take a deeper look at the future of our cities in Europe. The European Commission Green Paper on the Urban Environment, the Treaty on European Union, the Fifth Environmental Action Programme 'Towards Sustainability', the UN World Earth Summit at Rio, the series of UN conferences concluding with Habitat II, all have common themes and recommendations that invite us to act urgently about sustainability, the future of cities and how these will contribute both locally and globally. The European Sustainable Cities Report expresses how these ideas have been developed and how they should be pursued further in European urban settings.

The Sustainable Cities Project is a combined initiative of DG XI and the Expert Group on the Urban Environment which was established by the European Commission in 1991 following publication of the Green Paper on the Urban Environment. The Expert Group is independent and composed of national representatives and independent experts. Its broad remit, set out in the Council of Ministers resolution on the Green Paper, is to 'consider how future town and land use planning strategies can incorporate environmental objectives' and to 'advise how the Commission could develop the urban environment dimension within Community environment policy'.

In 1993, together with the European Commission, the Expert Group launched the first phase of the Sustainable Cities Project - 1993 to 1996. Its principal aims are to contribute to the development of thinking about sustainability in European urban settings, to foster a wide exchange of experience, to disseminate good practice about sustainability at a local level and to formulate recommendations to influence policy at European Union, Member State, regional and local level, as called for in the Council resolution of 1991.

The contribution of the Expert Group to the Sustainable Cities Project includes two policy reports, the first published in October 1994; a good practice guide; a European Good Practice Information System on Internet; targeted summaries (for different levels of government and different sectors); and a series of dissemination conferences. The exchange of information and experience is being further encouraged through the European Sustainable Cities and Towns Campaign, initiated at the first European Conference on Sustainable Cities and Towns (1994). The second Conference will take place in October 1996 and will act as a reference point on progress on sustainability in Europe and as a catalyst for further development.

The content of this final report represents the conclusion of collective discussions of the independent Expert Group on the Urban Environment and considerable effort has been expended to satisfy different cultural and policy stances. The report takes into account documents published before March 1996.

The preparation of this final report has involved members of the Expert Group supported by the Scientific and Technical Secretariat. It is published within the overall responsibility of the European Commission's Directorate General XI Environment, Nuclear Safety and Civil Protection.

Brussels, February 1996.

Professor Colin Fudge, Chair of the Expert Group on the Urban Environment.
Professor Dr. Roger Smook, Deputy Chair of the Expert Group.
Madame Nedialka Sougareva, Deputy Chair of the Expert Group.

ACKNOWLEDGEMENTS

The European Sustainable Cities Report has been prepared by the European Commission Expert Group on the Urban Environment with the assistance of EURONET in its role as the Scientific and Technical Secretariat.

Over the period 1993 - 1996 much of the work of the Expert Group originated from working groups of experts established to focus on specific topics and themes. This report is based substantially on the work of the following working groups:

- Integration
- Mobility and Access
- Planning and Public Spaces
- Dissemination
- Social Sustainable Systems
- Leisure, Tourism and the Quality of the Built Environment
- Technical Management of Cities
- Holistic Urban Management
- Urban Regeneration

A Core Group, consisting of representatives from the European Commission Expert Group on the Urban Environment under the administrative and managing support of Directorate General XI Environment, Nuclear Safety and Civil Protection, has overseen and coordinated the preparation of this report. Members of the Core Group are Professor Colin Fudge, University of the West of England (Chair); Professor Dr. Roger Smook, Delft University of Technology (Deputy Chair); Nedialka Sougareva, Ministère de l'Environnement, France (Deputy Chair); Ian Clark, DGXI and Eric den Hamer, DGXI (Project Manager). Professor Roger Smook has acted as the coordinator of the production of the final report on behalf of the Expert Group.

The preparation of this report has involved members of the Expert Group on the Urban Environment, supported by the Scientific and Technical Secretariat (editors: David Ludlow, Charlotte Nauta, Susann Pauli and Jan Vogelij), key staff of the European Commission particularly in DGXI, several authors and many others who provided comments and examples. This report builds on the work of the first report prepared by Dr. Liz Mills in cooperation with Professor Colin Fudge, Martin Boddy, Ian Clark, Tony Cross, Roger Levett and Corinne Swain, with the support of the European Academy of the Urban Environment and the technical secretariat. All of these people deserve our thanks for their contributions.

Inputs in the preparation of this report have also been received from representatives of Directorates General including DGIII (Industry), DGV (Employment and Social Affairs), DGVII (Transport), DGX (Information, Communication and Culture), DGXII (Science, Research and Development), DGXVI (Regional Policy and Cohesion), DGXVII (Energy), and DGXXIII (Enterprise Policy).

In 1996 the Expert Group includes the following members as national representatives and independent experts:

BERIATOS Elias - Ministry for the Environment, Physical Planning and Public Works, Greece

BERRINI Maria - Istituto Ricerche Ambiente Italia, representing Legambiente, Italy

BONNEFOY Xavier - World Health Organisation - Regional Office for Europe, Denmark

CATLLA Josep - Conseil des Communes et Régions d'Europe (CCRE-CEMR)

CLINI Corrado - Servizio I.A.R., Direttore Generale, Ministero dell'Ambiente, Italy

CORRAL SAEZ Carlos - Ministerio de Obras Publicas, Transportes y Medio Ambiente, Spain

COX Annemartine - Ministerie van Volkshuisvesting, Ruimtelijke Ordening en Milieubeheer, the Netherlands

CRONIN Michael - Department of the Environment, United Kingdom

CROONENBERGHS Jef - Council of European Municipalities and Regions (CEMR), Belgium

DE LOURDES POEIRA Maria - Direcçao Geral do Ordenamento do Territorio (SEALOT/MPAT), Portugal

FELTGEN Jean-Paul - Ministère de l'Environnement, Luxembourg

FUDGE Colin - University of the West of England, United Kingdom

GASPARINNI Guiliana- Servizio I.A.R., Direttore Generale, Ministero dell'Ambiente, Italy

GONCALVES Bertilia - Direcçao Geral Qualidade do Ambiente, Portugal

HARTOFT-NIELSEN Peter - Miljø- og Energiministeriet, Spatial Planning Department, Denmark

KALLMAYER Herbert - Vertreten der Länder, Bayerisches Staatsministerium des Innern, Germany

KEMPENEERS Serge - Institut Bruxellois pour la gestion de l'Environnement, Belgium

KONUKIEWITZ Manfred - Bundesministeriums für Raumordnung, Bauwesen und Städtebau, Germany

LANGSCHWERT Gabriele - Bundesministerium für Umwelt, Jugend und Familie, Austria

MATTHEWS Finian - Department of the Environment, Urban & Rural Development Section, Ireland

MESSING Susanne - Bundesministeriums für Raumordnung, Bauwesen und Städtebau, Germany

MILLER Michel - Confédération Européenne des Syndicats, Belgium

MONTANARI Armando - European Bureau of Environment, Italy

ONCLINCX Françoise - Institut Bruxellois pour la gestion de l'Environnement, Belgium

OTTO-ZIMMERMAN Konrad - International Council for Local Environmental Initiatives, Germany

PENTTILÄ Hannu - Ministry of the Environment, Land Use Department, Finland

PONS Anne - United Towns Organisation, France

RUEDA PALENZUELA Salvador - Generalitat de Catalunya, Dept de Medi Ambiente, Spain

SEGURA SANZ Rodolfo - Ministerio de Obras Publicas, Transportes y Medio Ambiente, Spain

SMOOK Roger - Delft University of Technology, European Council of Town Planners Representative, the Netherlands

SOUGAREVA Nedialka - Ministère de l'Environnement, Direction Nature Paysage, France

TROEDSON Ulf - Boverket, Division of Urban Management, Sweden

VAN DE VEN Anthony - Eurocities, Belgium

VONHOFF Lubbert-Jan - Eurocities Environment Committee/Gemeentewerken Rotterdam, Afdeling Milieu Beleid, the Netherlands

ZETTER John - Department of the Environment, United Kingdom

In addition, the following individuals have participated in the work of the working groups:

DU BOIS Wolfgang - Stadt Münster Umweltamt, Germany

SCHMITZ Stefan - Bundesforschungsanstalt fur Landeskunde und Raumordnung, Germany

WILLERS Bret - Cardiff City Council, United Kingdom

Observers to the Expert Group include a national representative from Norway, a representative of the Ministry for Urban Development and Environmental Protection in Berlin, and representatives of the following international organisations:

• Committee of the Regions
• Council of Europe
• European Cyclists' Federation
• European Foundation for the Improvement of Living and Working Conditions
• European Parliament
• European Sustainable Cities & Towns Campaign
• OECD (Organisation for Economic Co-operation and Development)

ABSTRACT

The Expert Group on the Urban Environment was established by the European Commission in 1991. In 1993 the Expert Group, which consists of national representatives and independent experts, launched the Sustainable Cities Project focusing on sustainable urban development and the integration of environmental objectives into planning and management strategies. The main output of the project, the European Sustainable Cities Report, is concerned with identifying the principles of sustainable development and the mechanisms needed to pursue it, not only in cities, but at all levels of the urban settlement hierarchy.

The report has an institutional as well as an environmental focus. It is concerned with the capacity of local governments to deliver sustainability. Working towards sustainability requires a fresh look at existing policies and mechanisms and a strong set of principles on which environmentally–sound action may be based. The legal and organisational basis for urban environmental action varies between different Member States, but despite these differences, local governments throughout Europe are, through their various functions (e.g. service provider, regulator, manager), now in a position to advance the goals of sustainability. The report provides a framework for local action and identifies a set of principles to use in setting goals and in evaluating and monitoring progress towards sustainability in urban areas:

1. The principle of urban management
Management for sustainability is essentially a political process which requires planning and has an impact on urban governance. The process of sustainable urban management requires a range of tools addressing environmental, social and economic concerns in order to provide the necessary basis for integration. By applying these tools, urban policy making for sustainability can become broader, more powerful and more ambitious than has been generally recognised.

2. The principle of policy integration
Coordination and integration are to be achieved through the combination of the subsidiarity principle with the wider concept of shared responsibility. Integration should be achieved both horizontally, to stimulate synergetic effects of social, environmental and economic dimensions of sustainability, and vertically, between all levels of the European Union, Member States, regional and local governments to achieve greater coherence of policy and action and to avoid contradicting policies at different levels.

3. The principle of ecosystems thinking
Ecosystems thinking emphasizes the city as a complex system which is characterised by flows as continuous processes of change and development. It regards aspects such as energy, natural resources and waste production as chains of activities that require maintenance, restoration, stimulation and closure in order to contribute to sustainable development. The regulation of traffic and transport is another element of ecosystems thinking. The dual network approach, which provides a framework for urban development at regional or local level, is based on the principles of ecosystems thinking. Ecosystems thinking also includes a social dimension, which considers each city as a social ecosystem.

4. The principle of cooperation and partnership

Sustainability is a shared responsibility. Cooperation and partnership between different levels, organisations and interests is therefore crucial. Sustainable management is a learning process, within which 'learning by doing', sharing experiences, professional education and training, cross–disciplinary working, partnerships and networks, community consultation and participation, innovative educational mechanisms and awareness raising are key elements.

Sustainable urban management should challenge the problems both caused and experienced by cities, recognising that cities themselves provide many potential solutions, instead of shifting problems to other spatial levels or shifting them to future generations. The organisational patterns and administrative systems of municipalities should adopt the holistic approach of ecosystems thinking. Integration, cooperation, homeostasis, subsidiarity and synergy are key concepts for management towards urban sustainability. Existing tools developed in relation to environmental action need to be extended to address the economic and social dimensions of sustainability.

Sustainable management of natural resources requires an integrated approach to closing the cycles of natural resources, energy and waste within cities. The objectives of such an approach should include minimising consumption of natural resources, especially non–renewable and slowly renewable ones; minimising production of waste by reusing and recycling wherever possible; minimising pollution of air, soil and waters; and increasing the proportion of natural areas and biodiversity in cities. These objectives are often easier to achieve on a small scale, which is why local ecological cycles can be ideal for introducing more sustainable policies for urban systems. Local government therefore plays a crucial role.

Sustainability is strongly linked to socio–economic aspects of cities. There is a need for the EU and Member States to create the conditions in which businesses can profit by operating in more environmentally–sound ways. Regional and local authorities should explore ways of creating employment through environmental measures, encourage better environmental performance in existing businesses and encourage industry to adopt an ecosystems approach. Authorities should strengthen the well–being of the population and promote equality and social integration by ensuring that basic services and amenities, education and training, health care, housing and employment are available to all. Resisting recent trends of ignoring environmental and social risks while concentrating on accumulating material wealth requires changes to the underlying values in society, as well as to the basics of economic systems.

Achieving sustainable urban accessibility is a vital step in the overall improvement of the urban environment and maintenance of the economic viability of cities. Meeting environmental and transport objectives requires integrated approaches combining transport, environmental and spatial planning. Achieving sustainable urban accessibility requires the development of sustainability goals and indicators, target setting and monitoring, along with policies aimed at improving accessibility and not simply movement. Reconciliation of accessibility, economic development and environmental objectives should be the primary objective of a city's transport policy. An integrated multi–modal urban transport system is required, where complementarity rather than competition between modes is promoted.

Spatial planning systems are essential for the implementation of city–wide policies for sustainable development. Existing spatial planning systems should be strengthened by encouraging ecologically– based approaches and a move away from a narrow land use focus. The identification of environmental objectives at an early stage in the planning process, the use of targets and indicators, improved forms of public involvement in planning and the potential linkage of spatial planning and Local Agenda 21 processes are encouraged. Environmental carrying capacities at local, regional and global level should be accepted as the guiding principles within which other considerations may be traded off.

Urban regeneration should be used to meet goals of sustainable development through the recycling of previously developed land or existing buildings, the retention of green field sites and protection of countryside and wildlife. Detailed sustainability objectives, including the establishment of ecological links, improved accessibility, energy efficiency and community participation, should also be pursued. Decontamination of polluted soil, a major concern in many urban regeneration projects, should be seen as part of an integrative approach which provides the possibility for achieving cross–subsidy between sites.

Tourism and leisure activities can have significant impacts on the quality of a city's cultural heritage. Planning for tourism, leisure and cultural heritage should be integrated in national guidelines and regional policies addressing economic, social, environmental and cultural aspects. In addition, tourism, leisure and cultural heritage issues should form an integral part of the spatial planning process.

The sustainable city process is about creativity and change. It challenges traditional government responses and seeks new institutional and organising capacities and relationships. This report and its recommendations represent a contribution to this dynamic process, to be refined and consolidated as the Sustainable Cities Project progresses.

TABLE OF CONTENTS

1

Towards sustainability: a long term
commitment to change

1

INTRODUCTION

INTRODUCTION

Driving the sustainability agenda is a shared concern for the future of the planet. However, while the need to change is generally accepted, sustainability is difficult to define and still more difficult to apply. In the long term, meeting the challenge of sustainability requires major changes in attitudes, in society, in the operation of economies and in the influence of economic thought. It is potentially a daunting prospect. However, this report argues that in the short term much can be achieved through practical incremental steps in the right direction - seeking to 'reduce unsustainability' as much as to 'achieve sustainability'. It is already possible to suggest many such steps for cities in Europe. This report provides illustrative policies, programmes and projects and suggests lifestyle changes in the hope of identifying future directions for sustainability.

The Expert Group on the Urban Environment started the work in 1991, since that date the sustainability policy agenda has been broadened

A BROAD AGENDA OF THE EXPERT GROUP ON THE URBAN ENVIRONMENT

1. Since its inception, the work of the **Expert Group on the Urban Environment** has proceeded in the context of developments in environmental policy within the European Community, in the international arena, and at local level, this last through the input of expert members with knowledge of European cities. The independent Expert Group on the Urban Environment was established by the European Commission in 1991 following publication of the *Green Paper on the Urban Environment* (CEC 1990). While the Group retains its original concern with the integration of the urban dimension into environmental policy, the policy agenda has broadened. The remit of the Expert Group is set out in the Council of Ministers Resolution on the Green Paper. The principal environmental policy debates now focus upon sustainable development, and upon sustainable urban development in particular. The *Sustainable Cities Project* is designed to contribute to these debates.

2. The project is not being conducted in isolation, for a number of complementary initiatives have recently been completed, are currently under way or are planned. The Expert Group considers that it is in the best interests of the European Union, Member States, local authorities, NGOs (Non Government Organisations) and other key actors involved in the search for sustainability in cities to draw strength from this positive context, to avoid duplication of work, to share knowledge and ideas, and thus to advance thinking and practice in this important area.

3. While wishing to stress the potential for action in this report, the Expert Group recognises that the context within which cities are located provides challenges as well as opportunities. While small steps towards sustainability are being taken, major problems - such as population growth and poverty in developing countries - remain. Furthermore, the sustainability implications of world events and agreements need to be considered in international policy arenas.

AIMS AND CONTENT OF THIS REPORT; CHAPTER ARRANGEMENT

This is the final version of the Sustainable Cities Report of the Expert Group on the Urban Environment. Its focus is the application of the concept of sustainability in urban areas. Despite its title, the Sustainable Cities Project is concerned not only with cities but with urban settlements at different scales - from city centres and suburbs to small towns. It also embraces the issue of the sustainability of urban regions and of the urban system as a whole. In the view of the Expert Group the principles of sustainable development and the mechanisms needed to pursue it are applicable at all levels of the settlement hierarchy. Nevertheless, the focus of work is upon the city level. The Sustainable Cities Project has an institutional as well as an environmental focus. It is concerned with the capacity of local governments to deliver sustainability. It is important to capitalise upon the good general management practices now increasingly characteristic of local governments in Europe. Working towards sustainability requires a fresh look at existing policies and mechanisms and a strong set of principles on which environmentally-sound action may be based.

The report establishes, in Chapter 2, the changing context within which thinking about sustainable cities is developing and highlights the progress being made at international, European, national and local levels. This is an opportune moment for European cities to take action, playing their part in international processes and debates.

Through the Sustainable Cities Project, the Expert Group aims to develop a set of ecological, socio-economic and organisational principles and tools for urban management which may be applied in a variety of European urban settings. These principles and tools can be used selectively as cities move towards sustainability. Accordingly, the report explores ways in which sustainability concepts may be applied through the adoption of key principles, the setting of objectives, and the use of a range of mechanisms which together amount to a more strategic, integrated and participatory approach to the management of the urban environment. This approach is set out in Chapter 3.

The Expert Group strongly advocates the development of city-wide management strategies for sustainability. However, it is also the intention of the policy report to consider the application of this approach to a range of key policy areas and ultimately to facilitate integration across the policy areas themselves. The policy areas selected as priorities for this report are the sustainable management of natural resources, socio-economic aspects of sustainability, sustainable accessibility, sustainable spatial planning - discussed, respectively, in Chapters 4, 5, 6 and 7.

This report also makes a number of interim recommendations for research and policy related to sustainability in European cities and these are set out in Chapter 8.

The remainder of this introductory chapter outlines particular features of the European urban system, linking economic, social and environmental issues; provides basic definitions of sustainable development; and establishes the key role of cities and of local governments in sustainability.

1.   The Expert Group on the Urban Environment focus on urban areas at city level

Chapter structure
2.   Chapter 2

3.   Chapter 3

4.   Chapter 4, 5, 6 and 7

5.   Chapter 8

6.

4

Social and economic changes have
a great impact on the quality of
the environment

Economic restructuring

Spatial effects of social polarisation
appear in some European cities

EUROPEAN URBAN SYSTEMS

1. Recent changes in the European urban system have been assessed in depth in the study *Urbanisation and the Function of Cities in the European Community* (European Institute of Urban Affairs, 1992). The share of Europe's population living in all settlements defined as urban continues to increase, with the largest cities continuing to house a very significant proportion of the population. The European Union is the most urbanised region in the world, with 79% of the total population in 1992 living in urban areas (CEC, 1994a).

2. It is possible to identify a clear cycle of urban change in the European system during the post-war period, from urbanisation to suburbanisation, then de-urbanisation (also called counter-urbanisation) and, most recently, re-urbanisation, with close links between population shifts and changing economic fortunes. The largest industrial cities of the north and west experienced outward shifts in population and employment early on, while smaller towns and cities - especially those located in the south and west - grew. The period since the mid 1980s has witnessed a slowing of these population shifts in a period of economic recession, and, most recently, a revival of population growth in some of the largest cities, linked in part to programmes of public and private investment in historic city centres. In the early 1990s the urban system is more demographically stable than in the period from the 1950s to the late 1980s but cities are still vulnerable to change, especially from migration from eastern and central European countries. The Single Market and the enlargement of the European Union are further forces for urban change.

3. Economic restructuring within the European urban system reflects the decline of areas with economies dependent on heavy industry and port functions and the growth of areas whose economies are based on favoured sectors such as research and development in manufacturing, or financial, producer or consumer services. Sectoral changes have resulted in the emergence of three broad areas, referred to as the 'old core' (the older urban areas of the UK, Belgium, north and east France, Luxembourg, the Netherlands, northern Germany and Denmark), the 'new core' (southern Germany, northern Italy, south east France, central and eastern Spain) and the 'periphery' (the rest of Spain, Greece, southern Italy, Portugal, western France and Ireland). The impact of economic restructuring upon cities reflects their location in core or peripheral areas.

4. The social structure of European cities has been deeply affected by economic restructuring through the mediating role of the labour market (Van Weesep & Dieleman, 1993). The spatial effects of social polarisation are in some cities so marked that commentators have begun to speak of 'divided' or 'dual' cities (Mollenkopf & Castells, 1991). The problems of the inner city, closely linked to the selective nature of migration and to employment loss, are well known. However, in many cities it is the peripheral areas and post 1960s settlements on the urban fringe which are now home to the most disadvantaged urban residents and the location of the lowest quality environments. In some cities there is a direct link between urban regeneration schemes fostering central area re-urbanisation and social problems; low income residents and low value-added economic activities have been squeezed from city centres. Most of Europe's poor quality neighbourhoods house a mix of unemployed people, the elderly poor, single young people and minority ethnic groups. For many of these people lives are not sustainable now. For the excluded and the marginalised there is an inevitable focus on current personal survival rather than on global issues. This understanding underlines both the significance of equity in sustainable development definitions and the tension between providing for the urban residents of the future and addressing the economic, social and environmental needs of those living in our cities today.

Greater economic integration is likely to have far-reaching impacts upon the economies of cities. Under the Single European Market, barriers to trade between Member States have been substantially removed. An important feature of the convergence trend is the diminishing role of national boundaries and the emergence of the 'super regions' which transcend them (CEC, 1991a). Additionally, unification may boost the importance of capital cities, eroding the competitive position of smaller cities and towns. All regions of the EU are intended to benefit from economic growth facilitated by the Single Market. In reality, however, new patterns of economic advantage and disadvantage are emerging, since the Single Market is only one factor amongst many influencing trends in local economies (Hogarth et al, 1993).

Moreover, it is becoming increasingly apparent that the Single Market - as it currently operates -presents challenges for sustainability. In particular, too little attention is being paid to the environmental impact of the increased movement of goods and people, and to the adverse effects on local economies and, more generally, on local ways of life. Expansion of the EU as new Member States join, together with growth in the number of affiliated countries, affects the nature and role of individual cities, as well as the shape of urban Europe as a whole. Several of the countries that have recently joined the EU have more stringent environmental control regimes than required within the EU. The effects of the enlargement of the Union on common environment policy, with associated implications for cities, are as yet unresolved. New links between the post-communist societies of Eastern and Central Europe and the EU are already affecting the urban system. The effects are particularly visible, for example, in re-unified Germany where the city of Berlin is acquiring a new prominence.

The success or failure of cities to adapt as economic restructuring and unification proceed depends in many ways upon the cities themselves, and in particular upon visionary political leadership and sound management. Parkinson (1992) has described the emergence of the *entrepreneurial city*, characterised by strong civic leadership and by the establishment of effective local partnerships between the public, private and voluntary sectors. It is likely that the sustainable city will initially share many of the organisational attributes of the entrepreneurial city. However, the environmental quality of the sustainable city will be substantially better, and there will be a stronger focus on reducing the use of resources, waste minimisation, equity and social welfare. Cities perceived as sustainable will in future come to be seen as attractive locations for investment as well as pleasant places in which to live and work.

A comprehensive review of the state of the built and natural environment in European cities is provided in the Urban Environment chapter of *Europe's Environment: The Dobris Assessment* (European Environment Agency, 1995a. The statistical tables underlying the urban environment chapter are available in the accompanying volume '*Europe's Environment: Statistical Compendium for the Dobris Assessment*' (European Environment Agency, 1995b). This chapter in many ways complements the analysis of economic and social trends, for the links between urbanisation and economic change and environmental conditions are firmly established. Different patterns and stages of economic development generate different kinds of environmental problem and distribute them unequally both within and between cities. In areas of both growth and decline the development and re-development of buildings and infrastructure have direct impacts upon natural ecosystems. Congestion, pollution from traffic, stress and noise have major consequences for health, and, more generally, for the quality of life.

5. In member state economies more attention should be paid to local ways of life

6.

7. Visionary political leadership and sound management will influence the success or failure of the city as a living organism

8. A review of the state of the built and natural environment in European cities

9. Europe's Environment analyses the quality of the physical environment in 51 European cities using data on 20 indicators, focusing on urban patterns (population, land use cover, areas of dereliction and urban renewal and urban mobility), urban flows (water consumption and waste, energy, transport of goods, waste production, treatment and disposal, and recycling) and urban environmental quality (air and water quality, noise, traffic safety, housing conditions, accessibility to green space and wildlife quality). Most of these issues are touched upon in this report.

10. Poor quality of the urban environment is a key concern for both city managers and the public. However, environmental conditions vary greatly between cities and regions in Europe, partly as a result of the variable implementation of standards and guidelines. In addition, there is a great deal that individual municipalities can do to improve conditions in their localities.

11. Basic planning principles like those formulated in the Charter of Athens will be influenced by new sustainable planning goals. The European Council of Town Planners aims at a revision of planning principles, promoting the mix of urban functions.

5   CITIES AND SUSTAINABILITY

Definitions of sustainable development used in the report

1. In developing its approach to urban sustainability the Expert Group endorses the following well-accepted definition of sustainable development set out in the *Brundtland Report* (World Commission on Environment and Development, 1987 p.43):

"Sustainable development is development that meets the needs of the present without compromising the ability of future generations to meet their own needs."

2. The following definition by the **World Conservation Union, UN Environment Programme and World Wide Fund for Nature** (1991) is regarded as complementary:

"Sustainable development means improving the quality of life while living within the carrying capacity of supporting ecosystems."

3. Sustainable development is thus a much broader concept than environmental protection. It implies a concern for future generations and for the long-term health and integrity of the environment. It embraces concerns for the quality of life (not just income growth), for equity between people in the present (including the prevention of poverty), for inter-generational equity (people in the future deserve an environment which is at least as good as the one we currently enjoy, if not better), and for the social and ethical dimensions of human welfare. It also implies that further development should only take place as long as it is within the carrying capacity of natural systems. Clearly, addressing the sustainable development agenda provides new challenges for urban policy integration within holistic frameworks.

Future generations

4. The following more practical and local interpretation of sustainable development, provided by the **International Council for Local Environmental Initiatives** (1994), is helpful as we seek to apply the concept in Europe's urban areas:

"Sustainable development is development that delivers basic environmental, social and economic services to all residents of a community without threatening the viability of the natural, built and social systems upon which the delivery of these services depends."

This report explores the core meanings of sustainability by thinking of the city in ecosystems terms. The role of cities in solving global environmental problems is acknowledged in the Green Paper on the Urban Environment. Cities affect the global system through, for example, energy and resource use, waste and polluting emissions. They affect regional systems though river catchments and flows, patterns of land use and stresses on surrounding rural areas which are subject to pollution, development and recreational pressures. Within the city itself it is possible to speak of ecology in the literal sense: the habitats cities provide and the plants and animals that live in them. We may also conceive of the human ecology of cities - the way cities provide for human needs and wants, the qualities and options of human life they make possible, and the relationships between planning, design and service provision and human behaviour and welfare. Finally, and of most relevance in this policy report, ecology may be used as a metaphor or model for the social and economic as well as physical processes of cities, viewing the city itself as a complex, interconnected and dynamic system. Cities are both a threat to the natural environment and an important resource in their own right. The challenge of urban sustainability is to solve both the problems experienced within the cities themselves (the focus of action in the past) and the problems caused by cities.

WORKING TOWARDS MANAGEMENT FOR URBAN SUSTAINABILITY

There is no single set of policies which can be applied equally to all European cities. Cities experience a range of problems relating, for example, to geographical location, demographic profile and sectoral mix. Clearly, the legal and organisational basis for urban environmental action varies between Member States, in part reflecting differences in the responsibilities assigned to different tiers of government. Additionally, though the EU as a whole has no specific urban policy, a few Member States (such as Britain, France, Germany and the Netherlands) have explicit urban policies targeted at selected urban areas, and these may offer practical opportunities for the application of sustainable development principles.

Although not explicitly examined in this report, there are clearly likely to be relationships between the structure of municipal government and the prospects for urban management for sustainability.

Whatever their competencies and responsibilities, local governments throughout Europe, through the many and varied roles which they perform, are now in a strong position to advance the goals of sustainability. As a direct or indirect service provider, regulator, leader by example, community informer, advocate, adviser, partner, mobiliser of community resources, initiator of dialogue and debate, the local authority is ideally placed to formulate a multi-levelled corporate strategy for the sustainable management of the local environment. Such action reinforces and complements global initiatives.

5.   Cities are both a threat to the natural environment and an important resource in their own right

6

1.   Variety of Member States urban policy

2.

3.   Local governments have a key role in advancing the goals of sustainability

This report sets out the context
within which local authorities can
develop policies and actions for
sustainable development

4.   Since the goal of sustainable development involves significant choices between conflicting objectives and major change in the way of life of communities, it cannot merely be imposed from above. It must be built by, through and with the commitment of local communities. Individual routes to sustainable development must be worked out at the local level. The local authority's role should be as manager of the local eco-system, committed to ensuring that the linear flow of natural resources into wastes and pollutants is transformed into the circular, self-adjusting flow of an eco-system (LGMB, 1992a).

5.   Within the EU there now exists a common framework of both regulation and more general environmental policy at both European and Member State levels. This report seeks to provide a fuller development of this supportive framework, stressing traditions of respect for human rights, social justice and democracy, as the context within which European local governments and municipalities can develop innovative policies and action, in the longer term facilitating the development of a more sustainable urban Europe.

2

A POSITIVE CONTEXT FOR SUSTAINABLE CITIES

THE EUROPEAN UNION CONTEXT

1. Since 1991 the European Community, now the European Union, has sought consolidation of its actions for environmental protection and re-orientation of environment policy to promote the objectives of sustainable development. These policy shifts have key implications for the urban environment. The principal developments are summarised here.

The Treaty on European Union

2. The *Treaty on European Union* agreed at Maastricht in 1992 marks an important shift in the ethos of the Community away from the pursuit of economic growth regardless of the environmental consequences (CEC, 1992d). It introduces the promotion of 'sustainable growth' as a major policy objective. Article 2 states that **"the Community shall have as its task...to promote...sustainable and non inflationary growth respecting the environment"**. While the term 'sustainable growth' is problematic, environmental protection and economic concerns are, in effect, to be given equal weight. Additionally, Article 130b requires that environmental policy should contribute to the strengthening of economic and social cohesion. However, it remains the case that environmental solutions adopted by Member States must not threaten the internal market (Article 100a).

3. Evidence of the recent shift in policy emphasis, following Maastricht, regarding the relationships between the economy and the environment is contained in the *White Paper Growth, Competitiveness, Employment* (CEC, 1993b). Early sections of the White Paper contain a reminder of the need to ensure that environmental legislation affecting businesses is consistent between Member States, a proposition for increased use of eco-technologies which aim at environmental efficiency through the product cycle, and a suggestion that new jobs can be created in various aspects of environmental protection. Chapter 10 of the White Paper is more radical. It proposes a new development model in which economic growth would be achieved through measures designed to achieve increased employment and a better quality of life alongside lower consumption of energy and natural resources. The paper goes on to propose a re-fashioning of existing policy instruments, with the ultimate aim of 'reversing the present negative relationship between environmental conditions and the quality of life on the one hand and economic prosperity on the other'.

4. The specific environment provisions of the Maastricht Treaty are contained in Title XVI Articles 130r to 130t (CEC, 1992d). Article 130r states:

"Community policy on the environment shall aim at a high level of protection taking into account the diversity of situations in the various regions of the Community. It shall be based on the precautionary principle and on the principles that preventative action should be taken, that environmental damage should as a priority be rectified at source and that the polluter should pay. Environmental protection requirements must be integrated into the definition and implementation of other policies."

5. The Commission is seeking to ensure the integration of environmental protection requirements into the definition and implementation of Community policies, as required by the Single Act, by evaluating the environmental impact of all proposals, including legislation.

6.

In line with the *Resolution of the Parliament on the Fifth Environmental Action Programme* (see below), the Commission is also taking account of the requirement in Article 130r in its own work by assessing the environmental impact of its actions, strengthening internal mechanisms (an officer has been designated in each Directorate General and a coordination unit established in DG XI), reporting progress on internal integration and preparing a code of conduct concerning its own practices, for example in purchasing, waste prevention and energy saving. Additionally, EU environment policy is required to contribute to the promotion at international level of measures to deal with regional or global problems (Article 130r.1). This requirement underpins European inputs and follow-up actions to the Rio conference, discussed below.

7.   The significance of spatial planning
for sustainability is recognised

The Maastricht Treaty also makes provision for the first time for Europe-wide measures in spatial planning. This is significant for sustainability, since it is widely acknowledged that spatial planning systems have an important role in delivering sustainable development. According to Article 130s.2:

"...the Council, acting unanimously on a proposal from the Commission and after consulting the European Parliament and the Economic and Social Committee, shall adopt:

- provisions primarily of a fiscal nature;

- measures concerning town and country planning, land use with the exception of waste management and measures of a general nature, and management of water resources;

- measures significantly affecting a Member State's choice between different energy sources and the general structure of its energy supply."

8.   Formalisation of the subsidiarity
principle

The Maastricht Treaty is also particularly significant for its formalisation of the subsidiarity principle contained in Article 3b and for its requirement, in Article A, that decisions should be taken as closely as possible to the citizen. Through the Treaty, local authorities have gained a specific role in the implementation of legislation and initiatives. The Treaty also formally provides for direct links between the European Commission and local authorities and the formulation of environmental policy and actions at city level has been given a firmer basis in EU law.

'Towards Sustainability': The Fifth Environmental Action Programme

'Towards Sustainability':
The Fifth Environmental
Action Programme

9.

Recognition of the need to develop 'bottom-up' approaches in pursuit of sustainable development is built in to the EU's main framework for environment policy, the Fifth Environmental Action Programme (CEC, 1992a). Through the Fifth Environmental Action Programme the EU recognises that the top-down approach to environment policy based on legislation, on which the EU has long relied, is characterised by a considerable gap between policy formulation and implementation inhibiting the achievement of sustainable development objectives. The Programme therefore adopts a new approach to tackling environmental problems and proposes new instruments. The key elements of the new approach involve integration - both internal integration between the various environmental

Significance of land use planning

issues and external integration of environmental objectives into other EU policies - and the concept of joint and shared responsibility for the environment between the EU and Member States, along with other relevant partners, including local governments and municipalities.

10. The Fifth Environmental Action Programme constitutes a turning point for the Community. Just as the challenge of the 1980s was completion of the Internal Market, the reconciliation of environment and development is one of the principal challenges facing the Community and the world at large in the 1990s. 'Towards Sustainability' is not a programme for the Commission alone, nor one geared towards environmentalists alone. It provides a framework for a new approach to the environment and to economic and social activity and development, and requires positive will at all levels of the political and corporate spectrums, and the involvement of all members of the public active as citizens and consumers in order to make it work (CEC 1992a, Executive Summary).

11. The Fifth Environmental Action Programme, which sets the environmental agenda for the period 1993 to 2000 and beyond, was officially adopted in February 1993. It was accompanied by a report on the *State of Europe's Environment* (CEC, 1992e). In contrast to previous environment programmes, the Fifth Programme seeks to address the root causes of environmental problems rather than treating the symptoms. It seeks to initiate change in current trends and practices and ultimately to achieve change in patterns of human consumption and behaviour. Significantly for the policy areas highlighted for detailed analysis in this report, Towards Sustainability identifies transport and industry amongst key sectors in which integrated approaches to sustainable development must be adopted. The Action Programme also places considerable emphasis on the role of land use and strategic planning to achieve many of the Programme objectives.

The Fifth Environmental Action Programme is a strategic programme, addressing root causes of environmental problems

12. In many ways the Fifth Environmental Action Programme exemplifies an approach to sustainable development which is coming to be widely accepted and which is set out in detail in Chapter 3 of this report. It is a strategic programme, setting objectives and targets, identifying those responsible for implementation, and indicating a range of techniques (including, for example, strategic environmental assessment, environmental audit and life cycle analysis), originally targeted at manufacturing industry, but which may also have an application in the management of cities for sustainability.

13. The *Progress Report from the Commission on the Implementation of the European Community Programme 'Towards Environmental Sustainability'* (CEC, 1996a) constitutes a comprehensive appraisal of the influence of the Fifth Action Programme on the environment and on progress towards sustainable development since 1992 when the Fifth Action Programme was published. The Progress Report is complemented by the updated State of the Environment Report *Environment in the European Union 1995* (European Environment Agency, 1995c). On the basis of the analysis set out in both documents, the European Commission will put forward proposals for the direction to be followed up to the end of the century. These proposals are expected by the end of 1996.

14. The Progress Report shows that the spirit of the Fifth Action Programme has been taken on board and developed in a variety of ways by the range of actors involved and with increasing sense of shared responsibility. It concludes that the future aim is to ensure that sustainable development is seen for what it is, a development within the environmental limits of which we have the knowledge at a particular point in time. Furthermore, the report identifies the need to set priorities, the key elements to move the process along,

the need to develop indicators to allow progress to be measured and above all the need to ensure a better integration of environmental requirements into other policy areas in line with the Treaty.

The Progress Report also identified the urban environment as a cross-cutting theme for which local and regional authorities in the first instance have competence. One of the key tools in this respect is land use planning. The report acknowledges that cities are the point at which implementation of environmental policy must start. There is evidence of increasing recognition of this fact because of the success of cities in communicating via networking. In relation to the urban environment, the Progress Report concludes that there is increasing attention within the EU on the role of cities in the transition to a new development model. Furthermore, the report recognises the inadequacy of the sectoral approach at EU level, to face the complex nature of urban problems. Sectoral EU strategies which lack an overall framework fail to consider the interdependence of urban problems and to take full advantage of the capacity of cities to create synergies.

The financial instrument LIFE is intended to promote and demonstrate models of behaviour consistent with sustainable development within the policy context provided by the Fifth Environmental Action Programme. All the LIFE fields of action have some relevance to the Sustainable Cities Project, but it is worth singling out here the promotion of sustainable development and the quality of the environment; education and training and, in the context of Rio commitments, actions outside the EU, including the provision of technical assistance for environment policies, action programmes and technology transfer. In keeping with the new emphasis on partnership approaches in tackling environmental problems LIFE gives preference to joint ventures involving many actors.

European Urban Focus

The subsidiarity principle indicates that most urban policies and programmes are most appropriately developed and implemented by Member States and the cities themselves. Some Member States regard it as particularly crucial that cities continue to have the prime responsibility for policy and action in their local areas and that the identification of appropriate forms of action at different governmental levels should be further debated. However, the Commission, reflecting the wishes of the European Parliament, has now formally recognised the need to give more attention at European Union level to the problems of cities, especially since, with a heavy concentration of the EU's population in urban areas, there is already a strong urban dimension to many of the EU's actions.

Lobbying for Europe-wide action for cities is by no means new. For example, the **Council of Europe** (COE), of which all EU Member States are members, began an Urban Programme in the early 1980s. The *European Urban Renaissance Campaign* (A Better Life in Towns) ran from 1980 to 1982. This was followed, between 1982 and 1986, by an urban policy programme which in 1986 became the responsibility of the *COE's Standing Conference of Local and Regional Authorities of Europe* (CLRAE). In March 1992 the CLRAE adopted the European Urban Charter, designed as a practical - although not very detailed - urban management handbook for local authorities (CLRAE, 1992). The Charter also provides the basis for a possible future convention on urban rights and for an annual award scheme for towns subscribing to its principles. Many of these principles have relevance for sustainability and are re-visited in the present report.

15.   Implementation of environmental policies should start at the urban level

16.

European Urban Focus

17.   The subsidiarity principle emphasizes the responsibility of Member States and cities for urban environmental policies

18.   Europe-wide action for cities has been an issue since the early 1980 's

19.

In its 1989-92 programme the **European Foundation for the Improvement of Living and Working Conditions** broadened its remit to include urban environment issues, having previously concentrated on the economic and social aspects of urban life. In 1993 the Foundation extended this work by initiating a programme on urban innovations contributing to the sustainable city. The programme covers economic and social aspects of sustainability, including questions of social justice, as well as environmental issues. It examines processes and mechanisms - such as environmental auditing and community participation - as well as physical innovations. The Foundation's four year work programme for 1993-1996 includes further projects on urban issues with a strong sustainability component. These cover, for example, the quality of urban life, sustainability indicators for medium sized cities and a range of projects on economic development and employment.

Only recently has the urban dimension of EU policies explicitly been recognised

20.

Explicit recognition of an urban dimension in various EU policies and programmes is relatively recent. (The full range of actions is reviewed in *Community Actions in Urban Matters* (CEC, 1993a)). Examples include the *THERMIE* and *SAVE* energy programmes, and *URBAN (Community Initiative concerning Urban Areas* (CEC, 1994b) which the Commission announced in March 1994 as an additional component of Regional Policy. URBAN proposes a more ambitious and better coordinated approach through which cities may benefit from EU actions in the period 1994-1999, along with a specific initiative to promote innovative actions and networks for the exchange of experience and cooperation. This initiative is targeted at areas of urban deprivation within large cities, as measured by, for example, high unemployment and environmental decay. The initiative gives priority to innovative projects forming part of long term urban integration strategies being implemented by the cities concerned.

21.

The **Committee on Spatial Development,** established in 1991 following a meeting of Ministers on Regional Policy and Planning, regularly discusses urban issues. Currently the Committee is overseeing the work contained in the report *Europe 2000+: Cooperation for European Territorial Development* (CEC, 1994a) in which strengthening of the European urban system and sustainable development are central objectives.
The **Committee of the Regions** has recently established an Urban Affairs Committee which will provide an important political lobby for greater integration of urban policy at EU level.

22.

In the field of environment policy, integration of the urban dimension has been extensively pursued. An integrated approach was first advocated in the Fourth Environmental Action Programme 1987-92, and this led to the publication of the consultative *Green Paper on the Urban Environment* (CEC, 1990) and to the establishment of the Expert Group on the Urban Environment in 1991.

The Green Paper on the Urban Environment identifies many aspects of the urban problem

23.

The rationale for detailed consideration of the urban environment is set out in the Green Paper, which was a response to pressure from three sources - the concern on the part of several European cities that a preoccupation with rural development within the European Commission was overshadowing the interests of urban areas, the commitment of the then Environment Commissioner, Carlo Ripa di Meana, and a resolution tabled in December 1988 by Ken Collins, Member of the European Parliament, urging that the problems facing the urban environment be studied in greater detail. This Green Paper is regarded as a milestone in thinking about the urban environment, principally because it advocated a holistic view of urban problems and an integrated approach to their solution.

24.

The Green Paper discussed the key role of cities as the home of increasing proportions of Europe's population and their role as the organising units of the urban system and the foci of economic, social, cultural and political life. It examined the many and varied problems facing the urban environment and discussed the root causes of urban degradation, seen as linked to the structural changes in the economy, to population shifts, and to changes in patterns of communication, transport and consumption. Questions of economic activity and the health of urban residents were also considered, along with the quality of life, seen as an essential component of the diverse, multi-functional European city.
The improvement of the urban environment contributes both to the quality of life and to the development of the urban economy. The Green Paper also sparked a number of debates. The most heated, perhaps, concerned the views on urban form and land use expressed in the Green Paper. While the shape of the built up and natural areas of cities is clearly important, this report seeks to extend the discussion to consider ways in which urban society is managed. For the shape of the sustainable city will ultimately reflect the priorities for action identified by urban governments and their communities.

25.

As the Green Paper acknowledged, each European city is to some extent unique.
The principles and mechanisms advocated for urban management for sustainability in this report must be applicable in diverse urban settings, for example in the historic city centres of the north and west as well as in the new settlements of the Mediterranean region. However, the European urban system has characteristics which distinguish it from urban systems elsewhere. In North America, for example, the urban system is more expansive and has a much shorter history, while cities in the developing world are still experiencing very rapid urbanisation. A further feature distinguishing European cities from cities elsewhere relates to the progressive political and economic integration of the European Union, although it is important to recognise that cities world-wide are increasingly affected by the globalisation of economies and operate in the context of trade area agreements.

° The Green Paper acknowledges the unique features of European cities

26.

As moves towards a possible Europe-wide urban policy progress, it seems increasingly likely that sustainable development will be seen as essential for integrating economic, social and environmental policy objectives. The approach to urban management for sustainability set out in this report, with its emphasis on integration and partnership mechanisms, clearly has much to offer in this context.

Common Transport Policy

27.

Common Transport Policy

The European Union's evolving strategy for transport, expounded in the White Paper *The Future Development of the Common Transport Policy: A Global Framework for Sustainable Mobility* (CEC, 1992b), makes the essential observation that transport is never environmentally neutral and that if the EU is to achieve its wider objectives for the environment as set out in the Fifth Environmental Action Programme all transport approaches must have regard to environmental consequences. The communication from the Commission on *The Common Transport Policy Action Programme 1995-2000* (CEC, 1995a) identifies policies and initiatives in three fundamental areas, and includes environmental and safety objectives.

Transport is never environmentally neutral

28. The White Paper has recently been followed by two Green Papers. The first, *Towards fair and efficient pricing policy in transport* (CEC, 1995b), explores ways of making transport pricing systems fairer and more efficient, by giving users and manufacturers incentives to adjust their transport behaviour. The aim is to reduce congestion, accidents and environmental problems as part of a response to current unsustainable transport trends. Urban areas especially are seen as a target for a new comprehensive policy responses to ensure that prices reflect underlying scarcities which would otherwise not be sufficiently taken into account. Rural areas and peripheral regions are already operating within the appropriate financial frameworks.

29. The Green Paper *Citizens' Network - Fulfilling the potential of public transport in Europe* (CEC, 1996b) states that the development of public passenger transport systems must be given greater priority as part of an integrated approach if further adverse consequences for our quality of life and for the environment are to be avoided. The paper suggests ways of making public passenger transport more attractive and usable, through the establishment of the "Citizens' Network".

European Spatial Development Perspective and Regional Policy

European Spatial
Development Perspective
and Regional Policy

30. A detailed discussion of the changes to European regional policy and the emergence of a European spatial policy is beyond the scope of this report. However, of particular significance for debates about whether urban development can ever be made environmentally-sound are the changes to regional policy heralded in the publication *Europe 2000: Outlook for the development of the Community's territory - a preliminary overview* (CEC, 1991a), measures taken in 1993 to green the Structural Funds, and the more recent work on *Europe 2000+ : Cooperation for European Territorial Development* (CEC, 1994a).

Europe 2000+ stresses the
important role of all urban areas in
achieving social and economic
cohesion and sustainability

31. Europe 2000+ provides up to date evidence of changes in the European urban system. It reflects concerns about the impacts on urban areas of the Single Market and of the enlargement of the EU at a time of recession, highlighting the increase rather than the desired decrease in regional disparities. The document makes a strong commitment to social and economic cohesion and to sustainability. It stresses the important role of all urban areas, regardless of size, in achieving these goals.

32. Europe 2000 and Europe 2000+ both form the basis for the emerging European spatial policy. An informal Council of Ministers Meeting in November 1993 considered that the Member States and the Commission should prepare a strategy document entitled a European Spatial Development Perspective, in accordance with a strategy for sustainable development, and instructed the Committee on Spatial Development to prepare it. The document, which will not be binding on Member States, is intended to cover the territorial aspects of various Community sectoral policies and set out basic objectives and principles. It will therefore represent the political extension of the Europe 2000+ document (CEC, 1994a).

Transport in urban areas

In the application of Regional Policy the influence of quality of life and environmental factors on the location and success of economic activity is now explicitly recognised. As the Commission states:

"a more integrated Community over the next decades must increasingly set its economic objectives in terms of sustainable growth... Without a reversal of the environmental degradation of the past, the older industrial regions will be bypassed by regions encouraging modern, cleaner forms of activity. Similarly, in the regions lagging behind, environmentally insensitive development will damage their economic prospects at a time when many firms are actively seeking out environmentally attractive locations. For the stronger regions, the failure of the Community to achieve improved regional balance implies further congestion with all its associated environmental costs" (CEC, 1991a).

The Structural Funds can have an impact upon the physical environment in three main ways - by inflicting environmental damage, especially through large scale infrastructure projects, and, more positively, by financing environmental improvements and by ensuring that development programmes and projects take account of sustainable development aims.

The revised *Structural Fund Regulations* adopted in July 1993 address all three issues. The most significant new requirement is that Member States should include environmental profiles of the regions for which they seek Structural Funds support in their Regional Development Plans which form the basis of bids to the Commission. Each profile is expected to contain a state of the environment report, an evaluation of the environmental impact of the plan, details of the arrangements for participation of 'environmental authorities' in plan preparation, implementation and monitoring, and details of the arrangements to ensure compliance with EU environmental legislation. The Regulation is worded as follows:

"Development plans for Objectives 1, 2 and 5b must include an appraisal of the environmental situation of the region concerned and an evaluation of the environmental impact of the strategy and operations planned, in accordance with the principles of sustainable development and in agreement with the provisions of Community law in force" (Regulation 2081/93 20.7.93 OJ L193 31.7.93).

'These changes should lead to the more effective integration of environment within the funding process. They also highlight the importance of taking a strategic perspective with respect to economic growth and the environment, reflecting the importance of environment for a functioning and sustainable economy' (Bradley, 1993). However, more effective enforcement of the Structural Fund Regulations than has previously occurred will also be required if environmental performance is to be improved. There continues to be a high degree of decentralisation in the operation of the Structural Funds, and the principle of partnership, giving responsibility to national, regional and local authorities and other relevant agencies, has been re-iterated in the revised Regulations.

Significantly for the Sustainable Cities Project, Europe 2000 emphasised the role of cities in the implementation of the more environmentally-sound regional policy. Although the Structural Funds have until recently been targeted at regions rather than particular urban

33.   Regional policy is an important instrument for achieving environmental objectives

34.   The Structural Funds can affect the environment both positively and negatively

35.

36.   Improvement of environmental performance requires more effective enforcement of Structural Fund regulations

37.

areas, cities within eligible regions have received substantial funding, often for projects with an environmental, as well as economic, dimension. In addition, under Article 10 of the *ERDF* regulation, 32 urban pilot projects, some with environmental actions linked to economic goals, were carried out in the period 1989-1993. Article 10 has also provided for the financing of 15 networks between cities under the *RECITE* inter-regional cooperation programme.

38.   The most recent changes to the Structural Fund Regulations have broadened the scope for addressing urban issues. In July 1994 the Commission defined four priorities which will share the 395 million ECU available for Article 10 in the period 1995-1999. These include spatial planning at the European level and urban policy. The programme for pilot projects in spatial planning has a budget allocation of 45 million ECU, and the programme for urban pilot projects 80 million ECU (CEC, 1995c).

Cohesion Policy

Cohesion Policy

Cohesion Policy

Social and economic cohesion as promoted in the Maastricht Treaty can conflict with environmental objectives

39.   The Treaty on European Union establishes social and economic cohesion as one of the main pillars of the European Union (Title XIV, Articles 130a to 130e) and as an element in all other Community policies. In addition, the Treaty promotes the development of trans-European networks in transport, telecommunications and energy (Title XIV, Articles 129b to 129d) with the explicit **"need to link island, landlocked and peripheral regions with the central regions of the Community"** (CEC, 1994a, p.11). The potential conflict between these two objectives and the environmental objectives of the Treaty discussed earlier in this chapter is apparent. The European Parliament has in its resolution of 5 April 1995 expressed the need to make the budget expenditure more sensitive to environmental issues.

40.   The Community's cohesion policy is principally implemented through the Structural Funds and the *Cohesion Fund*. The Cohesion Fund is aimed at assisting transport projects and environmental projects (45%). The environmental projects are in themselves seen as a means of operationalising sustainable development. These projects constitute either direct investments in environmental measures or investment in measures with a positive impact on the environment. Examples of the former group include collection, treatment and recycling of waste, treatment and rehabilitation of industrial sites as well as upgrading of deprived urban areas. An example of the latter group is investment in public transport which strengthens the basis for indigenous regional development and at the same time improves the competitive situation of public transport against other less environmentally friendly transport systems.

41.   The positive environmental implications of the revised Structural Fund Regulations have been discussed above. In addition, a communication from the Commission to the European Parliament (CEC, 1995d) examines the developing relationship between cohesion and environmental policies and illustrates options for achieving greater synergy between them in the implementation of Structural Fund Programmes and Cohesion Fund Projects. The Commission considers that should be environmental a minimum of 50% of all projects. That projects funded by the Cohesion Fund will comply with environmental legislation and standards, and that the highest environmental quality is achieved within the projects. Further development of project eligibility and selection criteria which not only reflect the need of compliance with environmental rules but also reflect economic, social and environmental sustainability will be undertaken.

Directives with relevance to urban environments

The Commission has for some time been considering the extension of the principle of environmental assessment to the preparation of policies, plans and programmes. Currently the *Environmental Impact Assessment* (EIA) Directive (85/337) applies only to certain development projects. This is one of only three pieces of EU legislation to protect land from the untoward consequences of development (the others being the Directive to protect wild birds and their biotopes, and the Directive to protect scarce habitats and threatened or endangered species of plants and animals). *Strategic Environmental Assessment* (SEA) - in which the environmental impacts of policies and plans is assessed at the policy making stage, already compulsory in some countries, is also advocated.

The *Directive on the Freedom of Access to Environmental Information* (90/313) which requires that information for example on air and water quality, flora, fauna, soil and natural sites is available to persons requesting it, is also assisting State of the Environment reporting by local authorities.

The *Report from the Commission on the State of Implementation of Ambient Air Quality Directives* (CEC, 1995e) highlights the experiences with the implementation of existing ambient air quality Directives. The Council of Ministers are currently in the process of adopting a *Directive on Ambient Air Quality Assessment and Management,* which will attempt to overcome the difficulties experienced with earlier legislation in this field both by the Commission and Member States. The proposed Directive (CEC, 1995f) will, through daughter Directives to be adopted between 1996 and 2000, set standards for 13 substances and define the responsibilities of Member States in reaching these standards. Part of the requirement will be that areas, including agglomerations with more than 150,000 inhabitants or that are unlikely to meet set standards by the deadline set in the daughter Directive, will be required to draw up an action plan to tackle the air pollution. The plans, which must list the measures to be implemented to improve the situation, will be evaluated by the Commission in terms of the suitability of the measures chosen and their effectiveness in improving air quality.

Mechanisms for consultation and exchange of views at the European Union level

The **Environment Policy Review Group**, comprising representatives of the European Commission and Member States, has been established to develop mutual understanding and exchange views on environment policies and measures.

The Fifth Environmental Action Programme identifies a number of non-governmental groups, individuals, voluntary groups and industry, as able to play a part in the implementation and enforcement of environment policy. In 1994 the Commission established a **Consultative Forum on the Environment** to facilitate consultation with the various sectors involved in environmental policy, although there is no formal mechanism obliging the Commission to respond to the Forum's recommendations. Included on the Forum are representatives from local and regional authorities, trades unions, community and environmental protection organisations and businesses.

Public participation is necessary   47.

The involvement of individual members of the public in the Fifth Environmental Action Programme is problematic since it relies on individuals being aware of their rights and responsibilities, and on the provision of mechanisms to facilitate their involvement. The process by which complaints can be made direct to the Commission is one such mechanism, but it requires a high level of knowledge on the part of individuals. Implementation of the Directive on the Freedom of Access to Environmental Information may go some way towards filling information gaps and providing basic rights. However, the development of local participatory mechanisms for citizen involvement is likely to prove more effective. Currently, the non-governmental environmental organisations, most of them members of the **European Environmental Bureau**, satisfy much of the strong public demand for environmental information.

48.

The **European Environment Agency** in Copenhagen plays a key role in providing the Union and Member States with the reliable and comparable information needed for effective monitoring of environment policy, building on the work previously undertaken through the *CORINE* database. This work is carried out in close conjunction with the European Commission, and in particular with Eurostat which has responsibility for providing information on urban areas involving both environmental and non-environmental aspects.

International action for sustainable cities

2.

THE GLOBAL DIMENSION

International action for sustainable cities

In developing recommendations based on examples of good practice in sustainable urban development relevant to the European context, it is important to learn from experience in other parts of the world.

Worldwide initiatives for urban sustainability   1.

- In 1987 eleven European cities became the founding members of the **World Health Organisation's** *Healthy Cities Project*. 35 European cities now lead a much extended Healthy Cities movement, the European principal aim of which is the improvement of living conditions in cities. Of particular relevance for the Sustainable Cities Project are the strategic management approaches and mechanisms developed by Healthy Cities, with their strong emphasis on community partnership, networking and the innovative use of indicators and targets (Draper et al, 1993). The *WHO Global Strategy for Health and Environment* (WHO, 1993), closely linked to Agenda 21 (see below), makes strong links between health, the environment and development.

- In 1990 the **United Nations Centre for Human Settlements** (Habitat) launched its *Sustainable Cities Programme*. Its principal goal is to provide municipal authorities in developing countries 'with an improved environmental planning and management capacity which will strengthen their ability to define the most critical environmental issues, to identify available instruments to address these issues, and to involve all those whose cooperation is required in concerted and practical action.' (UNCHS, 1990). The Programme is designed to promote the sharing of expertise between cities in different regions of the world.

- In September 1990, representatives of more than 200 local authorities from all parts of the world founded the **International Council for Local Environmental Initiatives** (ICLEI) at the UNEP- and IULA- sponsored World Congress of Local Governments for a Sustainable Future held at the United Nations in New York. As a network of local authorities, ICLEI facilitates the exchange of experience between cities, towns and counties and disseminates examples of good environmental practice world-wide. ICLEI is also facilitating the Local Agenda 21 Model Communities Programme.

- In August 1991, 130 cities signed the *Toronto Declaration on World Cities and their Environment,* committing their cities to the preparation of sustainable development plans.

- In May 1992, 45 cities taking part in the **World Urban Forum,** one of the events associated with the UNCED conference, signed the *Curitiba Commitment* for sustainable urban development. In many ways the Curitiba Commitment provides a blueprint for action which individual cities can follow in drawing up action plans for sustainable development in consultation with their local communities.

The European Sustainable Cities Project is closely linked to other ongoing programmes addressing urban environment/development relationships, including, for example, the **UNDP/World Bank/UNCHS** *'Urban Management Programme'* and the UNDP/World Bank *'Metropolitan Environmental Improvement Programme'.* One output likely to be of particular interest to the European Sustainable Cities Project is the guide to the preparation of city environmental strategies currently being prepared by the World Bank in cooperation with UNDP and UNCHS, as outlined in the paper *Toward Environmental Strategies for Cities* (World Bank, 1993).

2.

The **OECD**'s *Urban Programme* aims to enhance understanding of the ecosystems of urban areas, to evaluate examples of good practice in urban environmental improvement, and to assess the effectiveness of integrative policies by local authorities and by other agencies in the public, private and voluntary sectors at various levels of government. A number of general policy principles and guidelines have emerged from this programme, all of them of relevance to this report.

3. Several policy principles have emerged from OECD's Urban Programme

The OECD publication *Environmental Policies for Cities in the 1990s* (OECD, 1990), significant for demonstrating the strength of international concern for environmental issues in cities, also went some way towards developing a set of operational principles for environmentally-sound urban management. More recently, and of particular relevance for the European Sustainable Cities Project, the **OECD Environment Group on Urban Affairs** has agreed a programme of work in the period 1994-95 on *The Ecological City.* This project is concerned principally with policy development and processes. Among the objectives are clarification of the meaning of sustainability for cities and methods by which it can be pursued. Results of this programme so far suggest approaches in line with the proposals in this report (see for example OECD, 1994).

4.

The UN Conference on Environment and Development, Rio 1992

The *UN Conference on Environment and Development* (UNCED) held in June 1992 in Rio de Janeiro focused the world's attention on the need to promote sustainable development on a global scale. The EU took a leading role in the negotiations at Rio, and the EU and all Member States signed the *Framework Convention on Climate Change,* which commits them to take actions aimed at returning emissions of carbon dioxide and other 'greenhouse gases' to their 1990 levels by 2000, and the *UN Convention on Biodiversity* which establishes a framework for international co-operation to protect the world's species and their habitats.

In June 1993, the European Council of Ministers adopted a *Decision for a monitoring mechanism of Community carbon dioxide and other greenhouse gas emissions.* The Decision requires all Member States to devise, publish and implement national programmes for limiting their emissions of carbon dioxide in order to contribute to the fulfilment of the commitment relating to the limitation of carbon dioxide and other greenhouse gas emissions in the UN Framework Convention on Climate Change, as well as the Community's own objective to stabilise carbon dioxide emissions in the year 2000. The Commission is responsible for the evaluation of the national programmes in order to assess whether progress in the Community as a whole is sufficient to ensure fulfilment of the two above mentioned commitments (CEC, 1994c).

In addition, all Member States committed themselves to the *Rio Declaration on Environment and Development* (The Earth Charter) and to *Agenda 21,* a detailed action plan setting out specific initiatives which nations should undertake. It calls on governments to prepare national strategies for sustainable development and requires them to submit progress reports to the **UN Commission on Sustainable Development** (CSD), established in 1993 to monitor progress in implementing the agreements reached at Rio. An overview of the CSD and of work on sustainable development by international agencies (including, for example, the World Bank, the World Health Organisation and the Food and Agriculture Organisation) is provided in Bigg (1993).

As part of their follow-up to UNCED, Member States made a commitment at the European Council meeting in Lisbon in June 1992 to produce national action plans for the implementation of Agenda 21. This is in addition to the commitment to prepare national reports to the CSD. In their sustainable development plans, Member States need to have regard to the *Fifth Environmental Action Programme* which provides many of the policy and fiscal instruments needed to meet the Rio commitments.

Unlike the Conventions, which become legally binding on the signatories once ratified, Agenda 21 is not a legally-binding agreement but its influence is considerable and there is not space in this report to do justice to the large volume of work now going on worldwide under its auspices. Within Agenda 21 concern is not limited to the physical environment. World trade, poverty, population growth, health, and international cooperation and coordination are among the topics addressed. There are 40 chapters, each of which includes a statement of objectives, an outline of required actions, guidelines for developing a framework for action, necessary institutional conditions, and the means of implementation, including finance.

Much of Agenda 21 has relevance for the urban environment. For example, the promotion of sustainable urban economies and land use and management are strongly featured, and there is a requirement to integrate transport and spatial planning. Local governments are given a key role in ensuring implementation of the Agenda 21 commitments. A summary of the main points of interest to local government is contained in LGMB, 1992b. Chapters 7 (Sustainable Human Settlements) and 28 (Local Authorities) are of particular importance, the latter setting out targets for local authorities, that by 1994, 'representatives of associations of cities and other local authorities should have increased levels of cooperation and coordination with the goal of enhancing the exchange of information and experience among local authorities' (28.2.c), and by 1996 local authorities should have 'undertaken a consultative process with their populations and achieved a consensus on local Agenda 21' (28.2.a).

Institutional capacity-building to ensure the delivery of sustainable development is a major theme of Agenda 21. Capacity building includes the processes and means for national governments and local communities to develop the skills and expertise needed to manage their environment and natural resources in a sustainable manner. Capacity is embodied in human resources, institutions, and an enabling environment - and has as its essential elements a legal framework, enforcement mechanisms, technical skills, and individuals' basic knowledge of the natural environment (UNDP brochure on Capacity 21). Capacity at the local level is being developed through the *Local Agenda 21 Initiative* facilitated by ICLEI (1993, and see also LGMB, 1994a). Local Agenda 21 is essentially the process of developing partnerships between local governments and other sectors.

Strategic action is required to coordinate and integrate environmental and development concerns. Advice is now available for local governments in Europe on the mechanisms that are likely to be required to achieve strategic action (see for example LGMB (1993a) for the UK). In Chapter 3, below, these mechanisms are explored in some detail.

A further fund, the *Global Environment Facility* (GEF) was established by the World Bank, UNDP and UNEP to facilitate projects considered to be of global benefit. Through this fund financial help will be provided to developing countries to assist them in implementing the agreements reached at UNCED. Several Member States have already contributed to the GEF.

PROGRESS TOWARDS SUSTAINABILITY IN MEMBER STATES

Member States vary in the extent to which they have begun to incorporate sustainable development objectives into national environmental policy. This in part reflects diverse approaches to environmental policy generally and the extent to which responsibility for implementing environmental policy is decentralised to regional or local government level. As the following paragraphs reveal, however, most progress has occurred in the area of environmental policy. Economic and social sustainability dimensions are much less developed.

10.   Agenda 21 and the urban environment: a key role for local government

11.   Capacity building to insure the delivery of sustainable development

12.

The urban environment

13.

3.

1.   Differences exist between environmental policies of Member States

2.   Most Member States have produced national reports on environment and development as part of the UNCED process. Local level action for sustainability varies from country to country, but real progress is evident, especially through both formal and informal city networking. Processes such as The Local Agenda 21 process are important vehicles for policy development and progress. Specific examples of city action are given later. The following paragraphs provide a brief selective review of recent progress in Member States based on information provided by the national representatives of the Expert Group up to December 1995.

Austria

3.   In **Austria**, an advisory body, the Austrian Regional Planning Conference (OROK) provides policy guidance at state level for regional, Land and local authorities. The OROK developed the Austrian Regional Planning Concept entitled 'Österreichische Raumordnungskonzept 1991' in 1991. The 'Österreichische Raumordnungskonzept 1991' and 'Nationaler Umweltplan 1995' provide national planning policy and strategies.

4.   An important focus of activity for regional planning in Austria is the development of possible frameworks for settlement provision. The key issues concern uneconomical use of space, excessive dedication of land for building, and the inelasticity of the land market, all of which have consequenses for nature and the environment. The Regional Planning concept encourages forms of settlements economical in their use of space, and places restrictions on the erection of second and holiday homes.

5.   The national and regional plans also contains a number of proposals for improvement in the current legal system. Links between legal instruments and measures such as housing subsidies, business subsidies and expansion of public transport facilities are considered.

6.   In respect of open space, the goal is to maintain functionality of the natural environment and multi-functionality of the cultural landscape; to improve protection against natural hazards and to preserve endangered areas from the encroachment of urban development.

Belgium

7.   In **Belgium**, each level of power (Federal, regional, and municipal) is empowered to establish its own structures of coordination to achieve the purposes of Agenda 21. A Federal government programme explicitly refers to the concept of sustainable development when aiming at 'a viable society strengthening sustainable development, quality of life ... all this being summarized in a dynamic policy of urban revival.' A Federal Plan for Sustainable Development is currently being prepared.

8.   At the regional level, state of the environment reports have been prepared for many years. The regions have also developed sectoral plans focusing on topics such as waste, protection of nature, and water management, and have now moved to preparing integrated strategies. These are presented in the 'Environment and Nature Report' for Flanders, the 'Environmental Plan for Sustainable Development' for Wallonia, and the 'Regional Development Plan' for Brussels. All these strategies emphasize urban problems or urban aspects of problems such as mobility and air pollution, energy management, and demography. Each region is also responsible for ensuring coherence between the so called Territory Disposition Plans and the transport plans.

9.   At the local level, several cities and communes have developed strategies or specific plans focusing on sustainable development. Examples include Charleroi, Mons, and Bruges.

Various consultative organs have been set up both at the Federal (National Council for Sustainable Development) and regional levels (MINARAAD, CEWOD, CERBC). Several cities and communes have established their own local consultative organs to focus on issues related to sustainable development and the environment. Related to this are the various methods being developed at each level, and especially at the local level, for improving opportunities for public participation, transparency of information, evaluation processes and interactions between different sectors.

Environmental policy in **Denmark** is in a period of transition as clean up gives way to integration of environmental care into all aspects of society. Sustainable development objectives are now explicit in national legislation for planning and environmental protection. Throughout Denmark there is a strong emphasis on environmental monitoring and the freedom of environmental information.

Denmark proposed one of the first national plans for environment and development in 1988 as a follow up to the Brundtland Report, and this Action Plan for the Environment and Development has since provided the framework for environmental policy. Implementation is by means of more detailed action plans, on the sustainable development of energy, transport, agriculture and the aquatic environment. Each contains firm environmental goals and targets and requires participation at the local level and amongst citizens.

The Danish government has decided to implement continuing strategic environmental planning. The two key elements of this policy are an environmental progress report and a White Paper setting out priorities, targets and specific initiatives. The White Paper will principally draw together strategies on environmental issues already in place. The first progress report was published in December 1993 and the first White Paper was published in 1995 and introduces the concept of ecological scope. Both the Progress Report and the White Paper will be updated at intervals of four years.

Denmark's report to the UN Commission on Sustainable Development, published in April 1994, is notable for its emphasis on support for initiatives in developing countries, for example through a new Environment and Development Fund set up in 1993, through the transfer of environmentally-sound technologies and through capacity-building programmes.

In Denmark, statutory environment and planning powers are highly decentralised. National environmental policy stresses the key role of cities in achieving national and international sustainability targets. For example, all municipalities with populations greater than 10,000 are encouraged to prepare local action plans on transport and the environment as part of the national policy to reduce transport-related CO_2 emissions.

The principal tools for developing sustainability regionally and locally are the regional and municipal plans. Local initiatives towards sustainable development are exemplified by the Green Municipalities Project, involving many pilot projects in nine municipalities, and by pilot projects established as follow-up to the national plan 'Denmark Towards the Year 2018'. One aim of these pilot projects, in which municipalities and the Ministry of the Environment work cooperatively, is to develop the municipal plan as a tool for implementing a local environmental action plan or a Local Agenda 21 process. A Local Agenda 21 campaign will be launched jointly by the Ministry of Environment and the National Association of Local Authorities.

10.

11.   Denmark

12.

13.

14.

15.

16.

Finland   17.   In **Finland**, the Building Act was revised in 1990 to incorporate sustainable development into the Act as a goal for all land use plans: "Plans shall be drawn up for land, or its use otherwise planned, in a manner contributing to sustainable development of natural resources and the environment..."(§1). In 1994 new legislation introduced the requirement for Environmental Impact Assessment, not only for projects but also for all land use plans as well as any plans, policies or programmes which may have a significant impact on the environment.

18.   In 1992, prior to Rio, a pilot project was launched to promote sustainable development at the municipal level in Finland. The goal of the project was to discover and encourage activities which support sustainable development in various sections of municipal government. Altogether 14 municipalities of different size and from different parts of the country participated in the pilot phase, which was supported by the Ministry of the Interior and the Association of Finnish Local Authorities. Each municipality in the pilot project chose its own priority areas, main activities and measures according to its needs and resources. These included sustainable purchasing policies, improving waste management or water protection, sustainable energy policies and development of decision making systems.

19.   A follow-up project was launched in 1995 by the Association of Finnish Local Authorities. This project aims at the further strengthening of sustainable development in all Finnish municipalities. In addition to this project, sustainable development is also included as an important theme in all documents, publications and practices of the Association of Finnish Local Authorities. Local Agenda 21 - projects are under preparation in all major cities and in over forty municipalities.

20.   The Finnish Association of Architects (SAFA), the Ministry of the Environment and the Technology Development Centre (TEKES) started the Eco-Community Project in the beginning of 1994. The main aim is to study and implement a comprehensive, sustainable urban housing environment. Discussions, seminars and design competitions are planned under the auspices of the project to function as multi-disciplinary co-operation and training forums.

21.   The planning competition for an Ecological Housing Area in Viikki, Helsinki formed a major part of the Eco-Community Project. The area will also be used for demonstration and experimental purposes of the TEKES 'Environmental Technology in Building' Programme. The competition produced several good town planning solutions which also realised the deep integration of the built and natural environment. It resulted in ideas supporting the ecological goals of energy and water management of the area, recycling of materials, microclimate and the design of the landscape and the immediate surroundings.

France   22   In developing its contribution to UNCED, prepared by the Ministry of Environment, the government of **France** approved eight action principles relevant for sustainability, including, for example, the promotion of environmental quality as an element of economic competitiveness, partnership with local organisations, and decentralisation of environmental responsibilities.

23.   The administrative decentralisation which has occurred since 1983 has transferred powers of urban management, along with some public finance, to local communities. French local authorities are extensively involved in environmental action, but until recently relatively

few had attempted to establish a holistic approach to environmental management, strong divisions between functional departments being more typical (Barraque, 1994). During the 1980s it became increasingly clear that the technical solutions available were insufficient, given the complexity of urban environmental problems.

In 1983 the Ministry of the Environment and local authorities established the first consultative initiative for the development of true local environmental policy. Under this programme - the 'Protocoles d'accord pour la prise en compte de l'environnement urbain' - which ran from 1983 to 1989, the towns of Angers, Besancon, Bourges, Poitiers, Reze and Toulouse established local frameworks within which experimental projects were carried out.

24.

In September 1990, the Ministry of the Environment set out the National Plan for the Environment, defining objectives, action principles and a range of implementation mechanisms for sustainable development. Building on the earlier 'protocoles' programme, this plan advocates the preparation of local environmental plans (PLE) for towns with backing from the state. The PLE approach - with its emphasis on local understanding of the urban environment - was an immediate success - around 100 local authorities took part between 1990 and 1992.

25.

The gradual acquisition of experience by both national and local partners led to the next stage in green plan development - Charters for the Environment (CPE), first proposed in 1992. The CPE, partnership programmes for sustainable development in towns, are established according to the same principles as the PLEs but are firmer in their requirements for strategies and action programmes. The charter is a contractual and financial commitment made by each of the partners involved (local and national). Through this programme the state has redefined and strengthened its involvement in innovative local environmental action. About 20 charters have already been signed (examples are those of Aurillac, Cherbourg, Issy-les-Moulineaux, Mulhouse and Strasbourg), a further 10 are under negotiation and others are at an embryonic stage. It is anticipated that the evaluation of recently-signed charters will show the potential for long-term application of partnerships and joint approaches to local environmental action. Environmental plans and charters are essential features of the Local Agenda 21 movement in France.

26.

In **Germany** environmental concerns have become increasingly important for urban policies and town planning, and have tested the ability of planning systems at various levels to negotiate conflicting concerns effectively. Environmental concerns expressed by local communities and citizens' groups, together with corresponding adjustments in the relevant town planning laws, have strengthened the environmental and sustainability aspects of urban development.

27.   Germany

Already the Town Planning Code of 1987 introduced the essential elements of environmental assessment for town planning as part of the local planning process. Pilot projects supported by the Federal Government have provided valuable methodologies and tools for environmental assessment.

28.

An important priority has been given to consultation and environmentally sound land use practice through town planning. The Planning Law of 1993 requires local communities to limit new claims on open space and to compensate losses in natural resources wherever such losses are unavoidable.

29.

30. Urban development and renewal policies at federal, state and local levels have 'urban ecology' as one of their priorities. In many cities and towns, federal and state governments support local actors in making cities more energy-efficient, more environmentally friendly and more habitable.

31. A large number of experimental projects - from projects using recycled building material to large scale ecological renewal projects - have used Federal funds to guide communities down the path of urban sustainability. The Federal Government has selected the towns of Schwabach and Altenburg as ecological model cities to test comprehensive local programmes for ecological towns and cities. A growing number of towns and cities are engaging in the Local Agenda 21 process or use other methods for involving local enterprises, households and interest groups in campaigns for sustainable cities.

Greece

32. In **Greece**, environmental issues have been vigorously examined over the last 15 years, with a view to solve existing problems but also preventing future problems. In the national report (May 1994) to the United Nations Committee on Sustainable Development, the national strategy is elaborated to create sustainable options for production and consumption in every economic and social area.

33. In cities the quality of life is promoted by means of spatial planning, improvement of infrastructure, collection of waste, energy management and the promotion of the use of public transport. Furthermore these actions are supported by administrative reorganisation in 1994 which provided local administrations new competencies in the fields of spatial planning and the protection of the environment.

34. Spatial plans and environmental plans are principal means of achieving the aims of sustainable development in both urban and rural areas. Funding is provided from the regional development funds and a series of studies have been funded by the Interreg programme, directed at the protection of coastal zones under tourist or urban pressures.

35. In the national action plan on the environment a series of actions is envisaged to reduce air pollution in cities. Moreover a study programme on spatial planning of about 74 MECU has been launched for 13 regions in the country, to identify and manage vulnerable zones, the preparation of urban plans in secondary residential zones, the rehabilitation and renovation of downgraded urban quarters, the restoration of historic centres, etc. Specific programmes and projects are envisaged for both metropolitan areas of Athens and Thessaloniki. The responsible minister is reforming the institutions and legislation for spatial planning to meet the requirements of sustainable development.

Addressing both urban and rural areas

Ireland

36. In **Ireland** an Environment Action Programme based on the principles of sustainable development, precautionary action and the integration of environmental considerations into all policy areas was published by the government in January 1990. This aims to provide a comprehensive and systematic framework for environmental protection, and it is through this Programme that the environmental aspects of Agenda 21 will be implemented. Sustainability objectives are also set out in other policy documents, notably the pivotal Programme for Partnership Government and the National Development Plan, submitted to Brussels in connection with Structural Fund spending for the period 1994 to 1999.

37.

Overall responsibility for the implementation of environmental policy rests with the Minister for the Environment, and the Department of the Environment will prepare progress reports on the Environment Action Programme. However, the government is further committed to the integration of environmental considerations in other key policy areas - notably industry, transport, energy, tourism and agriculture - and Environmental Units have been established in the relevant government departments to facilitate this process.

38.

The main mechanisms for meeting sustainable development objectives in Ireland are contained within the spatial planning system. Environmental Impact Assessment is widely used. Separate environmental control systems have been developed in relation to water, air pollution and waste. An Environmental Protection Agency was established in 1993. With responsibilities including, the operation of an integrated system of pollution control, the preparation of reports on the state of the environment in Ireland, Environmental Impact Assessment of projects such as those assisted by the Structural Funds, and the supervision of local authority activities affecting environmental quality.

39.

In Ireland the concept of sustainable development is built into urban policy. Cities such as Galway and Limerick are notable for the extent to which they have achieved environmental progress through renewal of the physical urban fabric.

40.   Italy

Italy established a Ministry of Environment in 1986. In 1993 the competencies of this ministry were integrated with those of the Ministry for Urban Areas, reflecting the increased salience of urban environmental issues at national level. However, the development of strategies, administrative arrangements, technical coordination and financial measures to deal with environmental problems is still at an early stage.

41.

In 1989 and 1992 the Ministry produced general reports of the state of the environment which included national and regional statistical data, but no data were available for urban areas. In 1990 the Ministry of Environment set out two three-year Programmes for Environmental Protection which defined a number of fields of action and priority areas for intervention. The Programmes for the period 1992-96 set out specific actions in the 56 major Italian urban areas, focusing on monitoring air quality and noise pollution; reduction and control of traffic; implementation of new urban transportation systems and of new vehicles with low environmental impact; and safety of urban areas affected by industrial risks connected to plants and ports. The Ministry of Environment is funding the programmes, with some, especially the new transportation systems co-financed by the private sector and the EU (URBAN, THERMIE, LIFE, SAVE).

42.

In December 1993, Italy formally adopted a National Plan for Sustainable Development which sets out measures for the implementation of Agenda 21. This document identifies strategies for energy, industry, agriculture, transport and tourism, but it does not contain clearly defined tasks or timetables for action.

43. The Ministry of Environment has established a number of directives for cities which set out what local administrations can do to reduce traffic impacts and air pollution. These are broadly in line with EU guidelines, and air quality standards are fixed. A few local municipalities are voluntarily engaged in international partnerships for sustainability, especially in the field of energy. The city of Bologna, for example, is active in the ICLEI CO_2 reduction project. A campaign against greenhouse gas emissions has recently been promoted by the environmental association Legambiente, and some 30 cities of different sizes participate.

The Netherlands

44. Environmental policy in the **Netherlands** aims to solve environmental problems within one generation and to achieve sustainable development, seen as dependent upon maintaining the carrying capacity of the environment. The general principles and approach are set out in the 1989 National Environmental Policy Plan (NEPP). The plan adopts an integrated approach based on themes (such as climate change, acidification and groundwater depletion) and target groups (such as industry, agriculture, waste disposal companies and consumers) who are given responsibilities in relation to each of the themes. The plan sets clear targets and time-scales for each theme (for example, the reduction of CO_2, NO_x and SO_2 emissions, elimination of the use of CFCs and reduction in the percentage of population seriously affected by noise by the years 2000 and 2010).

45. Implementation measures are contained within the Fourth Report on Spatial Planning and the Structure Scheme on Traffic and Transport. Implementation is based upon a mix of legal requirements and financial incentives. However, the government also seeks to encourage a change of behaviour on the part of individuals through a range of 'social instruments'. State, province and municipality all have responsibilities for policy implementation, depending on the policy area.

46. The second National Environmental Policy Plan (NEPP2), published in December 1993, covers the planning period to 1998. The environmental targets contained in NEPP2 are more stringent than in the first Policy Plan and it stresses the need for more effective implementation of existing policies rather than the setting of new goals and objectives. NEPP2 proposes adjustments to policy mechanisms and greater support of target groups - especially those which have been difficult to reach in the period since the first Plan - to enable them to exercise their environmental responsibilities and change their behaviour. In addition, NEPP2 requires all policy proposals submitted to Cabinet to include environmental impact assessments.

47. To assist in monitoring the progress of national policies for sustainable development, indicators for both environmental themes and target groups have been developed and published in a handbook commissioned by the Ministry of Housing, Physical Planning and Environment (Adriaanse, 1993).

48. An examination of environment policy in the Netherlands in the light of Agenda 21, set in motion by the Netherlands government in August 1992, has revealed that many - although not all - aspects of Agenda 21 have been incorporated into Dutch environment policy or practice. Significant progress has also been made in taking forward links with developing countries. Debate on the social aspects of sustainable development within the Netherlands is facilitated by the Platform on Sustainable Development established by the Ministry of Housing, Physical Planning and Environment in which a wide range of organisations participate.

49.

In the Netherlands it is difficult to identify 'leading cities' in the field of environmental policy and action. Most local authorities seek to implement environmental objectives through the town planning process, some cities paying particular attention to energy saving or seeking to encourage sustainable building techniques.

50.   Portugal

In **Portugal**, the Ministry of Environment and Natural Resources has taken the lead in the follow-up to the Rio conference, including the preparation of a proposal for Agenda 21. Other departments of central government, NGOs and private institutions have had an opportunity to comment upon and add to the proposal. In general, policy development for sustainability is at a relatively early stage, but it is being facilitated by new legal frameworks concerning special areas and by the new instruments following from EU membership.

51.

At city level, Evora is regarded as a leader for its capacity to take a global view of urban issues, although it is not yet possible to identify a Portuguese city which has achieved a truly integrated city-wide strategy. Local authorities vary a great deal in the methods they use to involve local communities in policy making and implementation for sustainable development, typically working with a range of partners.

52.   Spain

Policy objectives for the environment in **Spain** are set out in the Plan Nacional de Medio Ambiente (the National Environment Plan). The plan has been prepared in the context of four national policy objectives: the integration of environmental objectives into sectoral policies, participation of citizens at relevant levels, the improvement of environmental impact assessment procedures and the reorganisation of market mechanisms to achieve environmental aims. A new approach to environmental management is based on the coordination with target groups such as industries, agricultural producers, consumers etc. An environmental strategy at the national level is being developed through three specific action lines; the reduction of major environmental deficits, the integration of environmental objectives in other national policies, and international cooperation and participation in supra-national environment policies.

53.

In the National Environment Plan, four priorities have been clearly defined: the fight against desertification and the restoration of forest resources; the improvement of water quality and the efficient management of water resources; the treatment and management of urban, industrial and agricultural waste; and the improvement of the quality of the urban environment. Each of these will be addressed by means of specific programmes or action plans. In 1995 the Spanish Government gave its approval to several action plans referring to hazardous waste (Plan Nacional de Gestion de Residuos Peligrosos), contaminated land recovery (Plan Nacional de Recuperacion de Suelos Contaminados), and water resource treatment (Plan Nacional de Saneamiento de Aguas). Programmes related to urban environmental improvement include measures to increase the use of public transport and to reduce the use of the car, promotion of less polluting fuels, the reduction of domestic air pollution and control of noise in cities. Further programmes relate to integrated urban rehabilitation and renewal, preservation and recovery of the cultural heritage, the promotion of open and green space within and surrounding cities, and environmental education. Some of these plans and programmes are currently being implemented by the Ministry of Public Works, Transport and Environment through specific agreements with regional and local authorities (Comunidades Autonomas y Ayuntamientos).

Promotion of open space

54. The Spanish Progress Report submitted in 1994 to the UN Commission on Sustainable Development listed and described the different objectives and priorities on environmental strategy at the national level. Since then, representatives of national and regional departments have met several times to establish a basis for coordinated action to develop policies based on the EU Fifth Environmental Action Programme and to take forward Local Agenda 21 initiatives.

Sweden

55. In **Sweden**, policies for environment and planning have undergone a period of transition since 1987 from conservation to sustainability. Sustainable development objectives are implicit in both the Natural Resources Act and the Planning and Building Act. Several government bills on environmental issues and sustainability have been presented during the 1990s. Environmental impact assessment is now mandatory for many projects and in most planning situations. National environmental policy is implemented through Regional Action Plans on sustainable development.

56. Statutory environment and planning powers are now highly decentralised, and local authorities have direct responsibilities for, for example, water supply and waste disposal. However, there is currently a significant trend towards privatisation. All Swedish local authorities have environmental strategies which include provision for waste minimisation and recycling. Several communities, such as Göteborg, have sought to develop integrated programmes for sustainability. Of 286 municipalities, some 200 have started, or decided to start, Local Agenda 21 work. A consultation document, 'National Vision for Sweden 2009', which addresses sustainability principles, eco-cycles as applied to transport, networking and competitiveness between cities, has recently been published.

United Kingdom

57. The most comprehensive statement of environment policy in the **United Kingdom** is the third report on the 1990 Environment White Paper published in May 1994. This reports on commitments to action from earlier years and adds new ones, providing a baseline for future monitoring. Information about the state of the UK's environment is contained in the report The UK Environment, the first edition of which was published in 1992.

58. The UK government advocates a range of measures for policy implementation. In the 1992 update of the White Paper the government expressed a general presumption in favour of using economic instruments, although regulation remains important. Responsibility for implementation is shared, with central government, local authorities, industry, voluntary groups and the public all being seen as having a role to play. The spatial planning system is a major vehicle for policy implementation, and the government has issued Planning Policy Guidance instructing local authorities to include sustainable development objectives in Development Plans and in transport planning.

59. In response to the commitments at Rio the government has prepared the 'UK Strategy for Sustainable Development', along with plans on biodiversity, climate change and forest principles. Three new forums for discussion have been set up - a Panel on Sustainable Development to advise central government, a UK Round Table for Sustainable Development, with representation from various interest groups, and the 'Going for Green' public initiative, an awareness-raising campaign aimed at individuals.

Agenda 21 is being taken forward at local government level, with support from the Department of the Environment. This work is facilitated by a Central and Local Government Environment Forum. Local authorities in the United Kingdom are committed to preparing Local Agenda 21 plans by 1996. A national programme to steer local authorities in this task is being coordinated by the Local Government Management Board. The Local Agenda 21 Initiative is developing guidelines to assist local authorities in the UK in drawing up sustainable development plans (LGMB, 1994a). Examples of other activities include the development of indicators of sustainable development, training programmes for local government staff, and the promotion of links with selected African countries as an input to Capacity 21. The Local Agenda 21 Initiative has also convened a series of round tables to examine particular aspects of sustainable development. The UK Local Government Declaration on Sustainable Development was launched in September 1993, and a set of operational principles and guidelines published in 'A Framework for Local Sustainability' (LGMB, 1993a).

The formal environmental protection role of UK local authorities has recently been strengthened. However, all of the most radical environmental activity undertaken by UK local authorities, including the production of environmental strategies, audits, state of the environment reports and, most recently, Local Agenda 21 work, is non-statutory (Mills, 1994a,b) and, in contrast to the situation in some other Member States, undertaken without financial support from central government. By mid 1992 around three quarters of UK local authorities had in place some kind of authority-wide green plan (Wilson & Raemaekers, 1992), although in only a few places could the plan be described as a fully-developed strategy for action. Certain UK local authorities - such as Cardiff, Kirklees, Lancashire, Leicester, Newcastle, Sheffield and the London Borough of Sutton - have achieved an international reputation for their environmental policy work. Partnership approaches - strongly featured in, for example, the Environment City and Recycling City programmes - are increasingly facilitated through environmental forums, which also seek to involve local communities in policy formulation and implementation.

NETWORKING FOR SUSTAINABILITY

Ideas and experience in the development, management and implementation of policies and projects for cities and towns are increasingly being shared through both informal and more formal networking at local, regional, national and international levels, with the encouragement, and in some cases financial support, of national governments, EU and international agencies. Networks now link both distant and neighbouring cities. Some have been established to link cities with common characteristics and problems. As well as facilitating the transfer of knowledge and best practice, networks act as catalysts for cooperation between cities and lobby for resources.

Networking is long-established amongst European cities, often growing out of traditional municipal twinning arrangements. Municipal twinning provides a sound framework for the exchange of environmental good practice since it is usually based on long-standing and intensive contact between local authorities (Van der Bie, 1993). Recently there has been a particular increase in twinning between local authorities in the EU and municipalities in Central and Eastern Europe, principally to support the build up of democratic society in these countries, to provide technical expertise and to develop and implement

60.

61.

4.

1.

2.   Municipal twinning for the
      exchange of good practice

environmental policies. Examples include the joint working between Helsinki in Finland and Tallinn in Estonia to improve water quality in the Gulf of Finland, and development of ecologically-sound energy supply in a residential district of L'viv in the Ukraine through a twinning contract with Freiburg in Germany. In general, however, traditional twinning is much less prevalent in the peripheral areas of the EU (Ireland, Portugal, Spain, southern Italy and Greece) than elsewhere, and environmental twinning is accordingly less well developed in these areas.

3.   Municipal twinning is encouraged by a number of umbrella organisations such as **the Council of European Municipalities and Regions** (CEMR) and the **United Towns Organisation** (UTO) which supports several specifically environmental networks. The European Parliament provides funding to assist twinned municipalities in overcoming problems which limit their twinning activities. The Exchange of Experience Programme provides financial support for, for example, seminars and technical exchanges. These activities have been extended to municipalities in Central and Eastern Europe through the ECOS programme. Both programmes are managed by the CEMR.

Networking is encouraged by the
European Commission

4.   Networking acquired a higher profile during the 1980s with the encouragement of the European Commission as part of the efforts to foster economic and social cohesion between regions. Commission support has particularly increased with the development of the *RECITE initiative* (Regions and Cities for Europe) since 1991.

5.   Several existing European local government networks have an environmental dimension or have been established in the policy areas picked out for detailed examination in this report. The **Eurocities** network (representing large cities) and the **Commission de Villes** (representing smaller and medium sized cities and towns) are wide-ranging, fostering initiatives in, for example, environmental action, transport, economic development and urban renewal. More specialised networks include, for example, **Energy Cities** in the field of urban energy management, **Environet** in the field of economic development; **ECOS, POLIS, Public Transport Inter-change** and the **Car Free Cities Club** in transport; and **ROBIS,** which deals with the recycling of land for residential and commercial development, in the area of spatial planning.

Networking is supported by
Agenda 21

6.   Networking for sustainable development is specifically mentioned in Agenda 21, and relevant examples of international cooperation between cities were outlined earlier in this chapter. Building institutional capacity as well as sharing ideas and technical know-how is an important facet of networking for sustainability. Some existing European networks, such as Eurocities, have recently taken steps to focus on sustainability objectives. New networking arrangements are also being established. For example, as an input to the implementation of the Climate Change Convention, ICLEI has launched a *Cities for Climate Protection Campaign.* To join, cities must commit to a local action plan to reduce emissions of greenhouse gases. In March 1993, 83 European cities launched the European Cities for Climate Protection Campaign in Amsterdam. Some 360 European cities are members of the **Climate Alliance of European Cities with the Indigenous Rainforest Peoples of the Amazon.** This commits member cities to reducing CO_2 emissions and ending their use of CFCs and tropical timber.

The *European Sustainable Cities and Towns Campaign* based on the *Aalborg Charter* was launched in May 1994 and is supported by major European networks of local authorities including CEMR, Eurocities, ICLEI, UTO and WHO. Its objectives are to promote development towards sustainability at the local level by encouraging cities to enter into Local Agenda 21 and similar processes and to provide assistance to cities in developing their long-term environmental action plans towards sustainability. Activities of the Campaign together with the work of Expert group on the Urban Environment on policy for sustainable cities form the principal components of this European Sustainable Cities Project funded by the Environment Directorate of the European Commission.
A second European Conference on Sustainable Cities and Towns will be held in Lisbon, Portugal, in October 1996.

A CONTEXT FOR LOCAL ACTION

This chapter has examined policy developments and initiatives for urban sustainability and the urban environment internationally, within the European Union and in individual Member States. It is impossible to cover all activities in this context, particularly as new initiatives are emerging at a rapid rate as a result of activities undertaken at the local level, for example by the environmental movement. In developing approaches for urban management for sustainable cities, European cities are therefore able to draw upon an accumulating body of experience and action.

This broad review of progress suggests that there is an emerging consensus about the approaches required to move towards sustainable development in cities. Policy frameworks within the European Union and individual Member States are increasingly supportive of actions for sustainability at local government level. However, national strategies for sustainability do not necessarily have a strong urban dimension, nor do urban policies, in countries where these have been put in place, have explicit sustainability goals. There is a need for a clear set of principles to use in setting goals and in evaluating and monitoring our progress towards sustainability in urban settings and, building on international good practice. These issues are discussed in Chapter 3.

Emerging consensus on the
required approaches to sustainable
development

3

SUSTAINABLE URBAN MANAGEMENT

PRINCIPLES FOR SUSTAINABLE URBAN MANAGEMENT

INTRODUCTION

The first half of this section is a review, based on previous work, of what sustainable development means in a European urban context, and why cities and urban life are crucial for sustainability. The second part seeks to develop an understanding of why cities currently often fail to live up to their promise of sustainable development. The problem is diagnosed by applying concepts of systems ecology to cities. These concepts provide strategies for sustainability by incorporating ecological aspects into the development of the built environment.

PRINCIPLES OF SUSTAINABILITY AND SUSTAINABLE DEVELOPMENT

1. As chapter 1 pointed out, sustainable development is a much broader concept than environmental protection. This report could develop at length a philosophical debate about the definition of 'sustainable development' bringing together social, economic, moral and political considerations. While these are important they can also distract us from our main purpose of exploring and disseminating ways of working towards sustainability in urban areas. However, the particular nature of sustainability as a policy goal calls for particular ways of working towards it. It is therefore necessary to understand certain features of the concept of sustainability before moving on to discuss how to achieve it. The purpose of this section is to examine these features. It draws upon and further develops the reasoning in the UK Local Government Management Board's *Framework for Local Sustainability* (LGMB, 1993a).

Environmental limits

Firstly it is important to recognise that the environment can impose thresholds for certain human activities, and that there are circumstances in which 'trade offs' should not be made of environmental resources or harm against any other potential advantages or benefits. The continuing ability of the environment to provide resources, absorb wastes, and provide basic 'life support' services such as temperature maintenance and protection against radiation are of critical importance for human well-being and existence. If we do not have adequately clean air to breathe, enough water to drink, an atmosphere that shields us from harmful radiation, and soils and climate which enable us to grow sufficient food, we are unlikely to regard any combination of other benefits as compensating us for their loss. There is increasing evidence to suggest that we are breaking, or risking breaking, some important global carrying capacity thresholds (UNEP, 1994).

3. Determining where environmental thresholds lie - the earth's 'carrying capacity' - will not be easy. Even where (as in the case of greenhouse gases) there is evidence that an important threshold is being exceeded, scientific knowledge may not allow the precise threshold to be set. There may be many more thresholds which we are not even aware of yet, because the consequences have not yet forced themselves into our awareness and scientists have not yet asked the questions which would reveal them. In cases of uncertainty, the avoidance of potentially critical risks to the physical ecosystem must be given a very substantial weight in decision taking. This is usually called the precautionary principle, and is explicitly endorsed in the Maastricht Treaty.

Demand management

The precautionary principle means that human activities must be carried out within limits imposed by the natural environment. This calls for policy processes which are designed to manage - that is, reduce or redirect - certain demands, rather than to meet them (which has been the traditional public service approach) or to find an optimum trade-off point between opposing demands (as in many systems of spatial planning). Sustainable development is concerned with reconciling this with the aspirations of human societies to develop, progress and improve wealth and living standards. At the level of municipal government, this overall aim is mirrored in the need to reconcile the pursuit of sustainability with day to day service delivery objectives and pressures, and the expectations of local people. Achieving this aim invokes two further principles - environmental efficiency and welfare efficiency.

4.   Demand management

Sustainable development requires the management of demands, rather than meeting demands

Environmental efficiency

The 'principle of environmental efficiency' means the achievement of the maximum benefit for each unit of resources used and wastes produced. Environmental efficiency can be increased in several ways (European Sustainable Cities and Towns Campaign, 1994):

- increasing durability, so that environmental costs are spread over a longer useful life;

- increasing the technical efficiency of resource conversion, for example through greater energy efficiency or recovery of waste heat;

- avoiding the consumption of renewable natural resources, water and energy faster than the natural system can replenish them;

- closing resource loops, for example by increasing reuse, recycling and salvage (and avoiding pollution);

- simplifying and avoiding the need for resource use (non-renewable resources). We have a cultural tendency to multiply complexity - to pile elaborate solutions on to simple problems. In environmental terms it is often better to simplify productive processes and avoid the use of resources.

Strongly related to these principles are the aims to sustain human life and well being, as well as animal and plant life and to maintain and increase biodiversity and biomass.

All of these, but especially the last, are related to what can be called the 'principle of elegance' (Brugmann, 1992). This is the principle of solving problems through simple, economical means. It is the principle according to which, for short distance personal transport, a bicycle is more elegant than a car because it provides essentially the same result with 20kg of material, converting the rider's motive power at 98 per cent efficiency, rather than with 800kg of material and a fossil fuel engine operating at around 20 per cent efficiency.

Environmental efficiency

5.   Reducing the use of natural resources, increasing durability and closing resource loops will contribute to sustainability

Closing resource loops

6.

PRINCIPLES OF
SUSTAINABILITY AND
SUSTAINABLE DEVELOPMENT

Welfare efficiency

Multiple use and social and
economic diversity are key
elements of sustainable
development

Welfare efficiency

The 'principle of welfare efficiency' is a social equivalent to the principle of environmental efficiency. It is concerned with obtaining the greatest human benefit from each unit of economic activity. This can be increased through:

8.

- multiple use - putting economic assets to the greatest possible range of social uses;

- increasing economic and social diversity, to provide the greatest possible range of activities and means of exploiting economic assets through their life cycles.

These points anticipate the 'ecosystem' model of cities which is described later.

Equity

Social solidarity is a key principle
of sustainable development

9.

Equity

Equitable distribution of wealth is also closely related to sustainability. The poor are worst affected by environmental problems and least able to solve them. Wealth, on the other hand, enables people to consume more goods, travel more, live in larger dwellings etc, resulting in increased consumption of natural resources and energy, and increased production of waste. Furthermore, the wealthy can afford to ignore or escape some of the environmental consequences of their actions. So inequitable distribution of wealth both causes unsustainable behaviour and makes it more difficult to change. Equity for people now living must accompany sustainability's concern for equity for future generations. In other words social solidarity is an important principle for sustainability, as recognised by the Brundtland Report (World Commission on Environment and Development, 1987, p.43):

"Even the narrow notion of physical sustainability implies a concern for social equity between generations, a concern that must logically be extended to equity within each generation."

**Implications of these
principles for
development policy**

Implications of these principles for development policy

These principles - demand management, environmental efficiency, welfare efficiency and equity - have significant implications for our model of development:

- to reconcile continuing development with environmental limits we must choose certain types of development rather than others;

- 'efficiency' has meanings beyond maximising the economic output of each human being;

- human benefit is not necessarily identical to utility as measured by neo-classical economics;

- quantity of goods should be replaced with quality of life;

- environmental sustainability is closely connected to social equity.

These points mean that to make development sustainable (or, indeed, less unsustainable), we must define indices of development which relate directly to human wants and needs and to environmental capacities, and then design policy instruments to intervene consciously to achieve them. This is a major theme of Agenda 21:

To make sustainable development happen, explicit plans and strategies at all levels are needed

"Agenda 21 insists that sustainable development will only happen if it is explicitly planned for. On almost every major question it specifies a patient and thorough process of considering a wide range of issues together, making explicit decisions about priorities, trade-offs and sacrifices, and creating and refining long term frameworks of control, incentives and motivation complete with quantitative, dated targets in order to achieve what has been decided.

Plans and strategies are called for at a wide range of levels: international strategies for biotechnology and health, national ones for resource use, ones based on watersheds for ecosystem protection, city level strategies for sustainable transport, and so on. Agenda 21 firmly rejects the notion that 'market forces' or any other unconscious and undirected phenomena can solve the serious problems of integrating environmental, economic and social concerns" (LGMB, 1993a).

EUROPEAN CITIES AND SUSTAINABILITY

1.3

Cities are the major loci of production, consumption and civilised creativity as well as the source and site of much environmental damage. Many problems and issues arise because of the particular features of cities and urban life. Conversely, many solutions are specific to cities and urban management.

Problems of and solutions for sustainable development are located in European cities

This section explores the specifically urban dimensions of sustainability. It considers first how cities relate to several different dimensions of environmental, or physical, sustainability, and then the urban aspects of the quality of life and equity dimensions of sustainability discussed above.

Cities and global environmental sustainability

Urban activities have great impacts on global carrying capacity thresholds through:

Cities and global environmental sustainability

Consumption and pollution represent impacts of cities on global environmental sustainability

- the use of fossil energy in urban buildings, economic activities and transport, and corresponding emissions of 'greenhouse gases' and other pollutants;

- consumption of physical resources and production of wastes (which should be seen as two sides of the same coin);

- releases of globally-damaging pollutants such as ozone depleters and heavy metals.

The size, population and high per capita consumption levels of Europe's cities mean they are together responsible for a significant proportion of the global sustainability crisis. They must reduce these global sustainability impacts. These are all cases where the principle of demand management should apply.

EUROPEAN CITIES AND
SUSTAINABILITY

Cities and regional/local
environmental
sustainability

Cities have substantial impacts on
regional ecosystems

Resource depletion generates waste

Cities and regional/local environmental sustainability

Cities are large entities in their regional ecosystems. They can have substantial impacts on regional carrying capacity thresholds through their concentration of activity. Depletion of resources is one facet of this. For example, the combination of industrial, institutional and personal water use in a large city can create such demand for water that regional water tables are lowered, causing drought, subsidence, vegetation change and intrusion of polluted or saline water into aquifers. Historically the demand for timber for building and fuel has resulted in deforestation in and around many cities.

As at the global level, resource depletion is mirrored in waste generation. Environmental systems have been swamped by human waste arising from increasing levels of consumption concentrated in urban areas. For example:

- the volume of liquid wastes from cities has frequently overwhelmed the carrying capacity of rivers, causing loss of fish and other species, eutrophication and accumulation of toxic residues;

- urban air pollution has frequently formed a health hazard;

- disposal of urban solid wastes has consumed large areas of land and resulted in leachate and methane problems.

7.

Cities also exert a powerful 'gravitational pull' on surrounding areas. They have always had a tendency to draw resources in from far afield. As local carrying capacity thresholds are reached, as urban administrations become more aware of them and fastidious about not breaking them, and as long distance transport becomes cheaper and easier, the ecological 'shadow' of cities - the hinterland affected by urban demands - rapidly grows. For example:

- mines, quarries and power stations in rural areas increasingly service urban resource and energy demands;

- urban waste is exported further and further to rural dumps;

- farming is increasingly geared to urban demands for highly processed, permanently available, packaged food. Ease of transport, consistency and standardisation take precedence over nutrition, animal welfare, resource efficiency, diversity, regional differentiation and even taste;

The ecological shadow of cities

Ecological footprints of European
cities cover the whole planet

- the volume of city dwellers seeking rural recreation impose stresses on the countryside.

Urban life also brings a cosmopolitanism which, coupled with a concentration of wealth, gives many European urban consumers both the appetite and the economic power to reach out to the most remote and exotic parts of the world in search of new consumer experiences. The ecological 'footprint' of Northern cities now extends to cover the whole planet (Rees, 1992). Cities in the North increasingly 'appropriate the carrying capacities of distant elsewheres'. Sustainability therefore requires urban policies to be complementary to rural and regional policies.

Cities are themselves ecological habitats. Urban development usually reduces biomass and biodiversity by building over land and displacing animal and plant populations. However, it can also create new habitats and niches. The character and structure of urban green spaces, the connections between them, their interactions with buildings, the ways they are managed, levels of noise disturbance and pollution, and patterns of human behaviour such as recreation will all influence the habitat qualities of cities.

Cities are ecological habitats

Quality of life

Quality of life

Preserving the integrity of the global environment is a precondition of all other aspects of the quality of life. The Brundtland, 'Caring for The Earth' and ICLEI definitions of sustainability mentioned in Chapter 1 all start from human needs rather than the environment. In all of them, the overall point of sustainable development is to safeguard and improve the quality of human life. This is why the precautionary principle and the principle of demand management apply to global sustainability impacts. But people value many aspects of the environment which are unconnected with sheer physical survival, such as the aesthetic and cultural quality of surroundings, access to countryside and tranquillity. People also, of course, value many things which are not 'environmental' at all. Material living standards, public health and safety, access to education, health care, fulfilling occupations, opportunities for personal development and advancement, community, culture, social life and recreation are among the many things which contribute to the quality of human life.

10.   Global sustainability is a precondition for quality of life

People will only choose to live in cities if cities offer them what they regard as a good quality of life, and in that sense, cities will only be sustainable in the sense of their own survival if they can provide this. However, in a sustainability context it is necessary to distinguish between quality of life in terms of basic needs on the one hand, and on the other more luxurious desires which cannot be sustained in the long term, on the other. A shift towards more environment-oriented priorities is therefore required, and as a consequence, an adaptation to more sustainable lifestyles.

Cities have the potential to offer a sustainable quality of life

The potential of cities and failure to reach their potential

The potential of cities and failure to reach their potential

To provide both good quality of life and environmental sustainability, cities must offer people the option of living sustainably. The concept of availability of sustainable patterns of life links environmental sustainability, quality of life and the future success of cities.

As the Green Paper on the Urban Environment (CEC, 1990) suggested, cities have great potential to reconcile the various dimensions of sustainability. The population density which characterises cities can bring immense variety and choice of work, goods, services, recreations and society within easy reach. The same density also enables a large proportion of travel to be carried out by environmentally efficient public transport, supports more efficient environmental services (such as reuse and recycling of wastes), and promotes more energy efficient built forms. Density is discussed further in Chapter 5.1.

The rest of this section argues against defeatism in respect of the failure of policy interventions. It uses an ecosystems approach to probe some reasons for the failure of cities to live up to their sustainability potential and to confirm the possibility of doing better. It sets the context for discussion of the policy tools needed to manage urban areas for sustainability which follows in section 2 of this chapter.

THE ECOSYSTEMS APPROACH

Brugmann (1992) and Tjallingii (1992) propose that a city can be considered as an ecosystem, and that ecological concepts can be used for understanding the problems of urban sustainability and for choosing approaches to solving them. There are three interrelated strands to this idea.

The *first strand* recognises that each city is, literally, a physical ecosystem in a similar way to a wetland or a forest. Techniques of empirical ecology can be applied to analyse cities in terms of flows of energy, nutrients and physical materials and to study effects on other physical ecosystems such as the surrounding countryside. This is the sense in which ecological concepts have already been, in the first half of this section, used to describe the physical impacts of cities. Perhaps the most important insights which this sense of ecology offers to urban environmental management are those concerned with carrying capacities, thresholds, natural capital and the progressive closing of resource loops as a way for cities to continue developing after reaching resource limits.

Within the ecosystem approach as proposed by the Dutch Institute for Forestry and Nature Research (Tjallingii et al, 1994), ecodevice models are developed. The ecosystems approach has been elaborated for the Ministry of Housing, Spatial Planning and the Environment in the Netherlands (Tjallingii et al, 1994) into the dual network strategy, discussed in chapter 7 section 1. The figure below illustrates the ecodevice model applied to environmental problems.

FIGURE - The ecodevice model applied to environmental problems

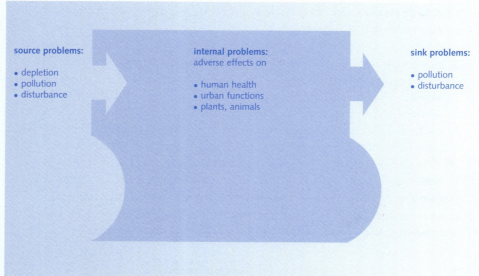

source problems:

- depletion
- pollution
- disturbance

internal problems:
adverse effects on

- human health
- urban functions
- plants, animals

sink problems:

- pollution
- disturbance

Side notes:

1. The ecosystems approach enables cities to reach their potential in offering their citizens a sustainable quality of life

2. The ecosystems approach consists of three strands: physical, social, and systems

Source: Tjallingii, S. (1995), p.42.

The model can help policy makers to understand why and how cities fail to live up to their promise. The essential problem is that the more complex a system is, the more its overall behaviour depends upon interactions between different elements, and the more difficult it becomes to understand or model these within the frame of reference of traditional disciplines.

The *second strand* of the ecosystems approach is to apply the concepts of physical ecology metaphorically to the social dimension of cities - as it were to think of each city as a social ecosystem. Ecological concepts such as niches (for different kinds of people, lifestyles, activities), diversity, and different kinds of dependence (parasitism, symbiosis) can illuminate the 'human ecology' (itself a revealing phrase) of cities.

Each city can be viewed as a physical ecosystem, and metaphorically as a social ecosystem

The concept of carrying capacity takes on an important meaning here. It refers to the ability of a city as a social system to accommodate social demands and stresses. The breakdown of social order in cities can be seen as analogous to the breakdown of physical ecosystems - as a result of stresses (such as pollution in one case, or poverty in the other) overwhelming the ability of mechanisms (such as digestion and recycling of pollutants in one case, or community support and self-help mechanisms in the other) to assimilate the stress.

6.

The *third strand* of the ecosystems approach emphasises the 'systems' rather than the 'eco' aspect. This seeks to understand the *continuous processes* of change and development in cities by treating cities as complex systems to which concepts of systems theory can be applied. This is the strand which informs much of the discussion of management later in this section.

7.

Together with the systems dimension, the physical and social strands lead to concepts that enable policy makers to integrate different elements in their decisions

Some of the key ecosystems concepts are:

- negative feedback, or 'damping', where the system reacts to change in such a way as to limit or contain it. An example might be the way that a local authority will respond to increasing development pressures on urban green space by strengthening its protection in the development plan;

- positive feedback, or 'snowballing', where the system reacts to change in such a way as to reinforce it. An example might be the way that the choice by some well-off households to move out from an inner city area prompts others to follow, contributing to a cycle of decline;

- homeostasis, or change within stability, where negative feedback loops keep the overall system much the same while elements within it alter considerably. An example might be a city which accommodates a complete change in its main industries without changing its overall character;

- state transition, or 'step' change, where the way the components of a system mesh together alters fundamentally and irreversibly. An example might be the change, which in many European cities probably occurred between 1950 and 1970, from homeostasis in travel patterns to positive feedback encouraging car use;

- closure versus openness - the degree to which a system is insulated from, or vulnerable to, external changes. For example the Single Market and increasing requirements for tendering and restrictions on 'anti-competitive' practices have in recent years opened both the private and public sectors to the vagaries of world markets, so that 'the local economy' may mean little more than the enterprises which happen to be located in a particular area;

- emergence - the ability of a complex system to develop characteristics and behaviour which are 'greater than the sum of its parts' and cannot necessarily be predicted or managed in terms of the behaviour of its constituent elements.

9.   The three strands making up the ecosystems approach as outlined above are closely linked. In the following discussion the term 'ecosystems approach' is used where the general approach is being considered. Where it is necessary to distinguish the three senses, the terms 'ecological', 'human ecology' and 'systems' are used.

10.   As the examples suggest, the Expert Group believe that these three strands of the ecosystems approach can help policy makers to consider the interrelationships between disparate elements - the physical environment, the economy and welfare. One of the most important benefits of the ecological approach is to illuminate the relationships between individual behavioural choices and the contexts in which they occur.

Processes of positive and negative feedback and of step change may be consciously designed and 'engineered' in order to achieve policy goals. Much of the following discussion places emphasis on strengthening processes of negative feedback. This is not because homeostasis is 'natural' or automatically desirable, but simply because many of the problems of European cities at present seem to be caused by uncontrolled (and often unrecognised) positive feedback effects.

Urban ecosystems are not closed like natural ecosystems

An important difference in principle between a natural ecosystem and a city is that natural systems tend to maintain their equilibrium by circulating resources and wastes internally. In urban systems, in contrast, problems of supply and waste disposal have generally been solved by increasing both supply and discharge and thus the flows into and out of the system, exacerbating both internal and external environmental problems.

Reducing environmental problems requires the development of strategies at several levels and for several themes

In order to tackle environmental problems, such as depletion, pollution, and disturbance, and to reach more sustainable development, strategies have to be developed at several levels and for several themes:

- the regulation of flows or chain management for factors such as traffic and mobility, water, energy, and waste;

- a translation into practice for both built-up and open areas;

- participation, in order to influence individual lifestyles and operation of industries.

Transport is a good example of systems effects:

- each time an urban resident chooses to make a particular journey by car instead of bus, the bus service receives marginally less revenue, and the buses are marginally more delayed by car congestion. Both effects make the bus service marginally less attractive to its remaining users, encouraging them too to swap to car use - and so on;

- the more people use cars, the more important it becomes for employers, shops and other services to be accessible by car, and the less important to be accessible by bus. Services tend to relocate to sites more accessible to cars than to public transport. This in turn encourages more people to switch from bus to car - and so on;

- as the number of people using buses at night drops, women begin to feel unsafe and try to avoid them - further reducing the number of people on the buses and reducing the perceived and actual safety of the service for those who still use it;

- similarly, as the number of parents dropping children at school by car increases, other parents worry more about the danger of traffic, and start to drive their children to school too to protect them - further increasing the traffic and the perceived danger (Hillman, Adams & Whitelegg 1990, Hillman 1993);

- life without a car becomes increasingly restricted and inconvenient, encouraging more people to opt into owning a car. Owning a car involves substantial fixed costs, such as the capital and depreciation on the car itself, tax, insurance and garaging. But, once these costs have been committed, the marginal cost of each journey is low. At the point of use, public transport appears more expensive because the fare must cover a substantial proportion of the service's fixed costs. Thus once a household owns a car, it is cost effective to use it for as much of the household's travel as possible.

This example demonstrates some of the systems effects described above:

- positive feedback - each move to more car use changes the situation in ways that encourage still more use of the car;

- step change - at the level of individuals and households, buying a car makes a discontinuous change in the attractiveness of car use. At the level of the whole city, the eventual effect of the move to car transport is to replace a strong pull towards the centre of the city with a strong pull away from the centre;

- emergence - few would wish to move from a city with low traffic levels and high accessibility of basic amenities to one with high traffic and low access. Indeed most people, if asked, would state the opposite preference. Yet the overall effect of all individual behavioural choices is to produce the high traffic, low access city. The system as a whole exhibits a dynamic which is different from - in this case opposite to - the wishes of the majority of its constituents.

Transport as an example of systems effects

Less people use buses

SUSTAINABLE CITIES

50

PITFALLS OF CONVENTIONAL
GOOD MANAGEMENT
PRACTICE

Systems approach to
management

Systems approaches to management

After popularity in the 1970s, systems approaches to management problems were eclipsed through the 1980s but are now coming back into fashion. At the *analytical* level, systems approaches - well accepted by both physical and social scientists - treat organisations as more than the sum of their parts, and emphasise the fact that they have aims and values which cannot be described purely in terms of their constituents. At the *practical* level, systems approaches are of most use in enabling organisations to understand change and then to manage it through processes of consensus and consent.

The 1980s belief, wide spread in Europe, that market interactions could provide a full and satisfactory model of how organisations worked made the 'analytical holism' of systems models redundant. Likewise the belief that market-motivated decisions by individuals were sufficient for the effective management of large organisations undermined the consensus-seeking collectivism of systems solutions. The market approach fell down precisely where 'systems' interactions are most significant, for example where social or environmental consequences of market-driven decisions are significant and are interrelated in complex ways. This report argues that understanding and managing these complex interactions is at the heart of the urban sustainability agenda. The inability of market reductionism to provide adequate tools for this is one factor motivating a return to systems approaches.

1.5 PITFALLS OF CONVENTIONAL GOOD MANAGEMENT PRACTICE

The 'ecological rationality' perspective in political science (see for example Dryzek, 1987) argues that traditional hierarchical bureaucratic structures are intrinsically poor at dealing with the complexity and speed of development of environmental and sustainability issues, and argues for a new management approach. The remainder of this section seeks to apply this general insight to European cities. Section 2 of this chapter goes on to suggest some practical policy tools to move towards the new management approach suggested.

Ironically, four of the most highly regarded forms of conventional management-methods in which urban governments have excelled - have tended to make problems rooted in the complexity of systems harder to understand and solve. The four are sectoral specialisation of individuals, and of organisations; quantified performance measurement; and the application of market mechanisms.

Pitfall 1: Sectoral specialisation of individuals

Feedback loops of the type described above thread in and out of different disciplines. The more strongly sectoral, departmentalised and specialised policy and implementation become, the more difficult it becomes for one individual to gain a complete overview. In the example used above, there is a risk that:

- Transport planners will perceive only the rise in car traffic, and respond to it by building roads without acknowledging that this will reinforce the problem.
  Land use planners will see only pressure for development on greenfield sites, and will at best be able only to damp and retard it, and at worst encourage it to solve problems of city centre access.

- Local economic development managers will see only the preference of potential business investors for road access, and will argue for road building and against planning restrictions to facilitate development, without appreciating that this may undermine the future attractiveness of the city.

- Professionals concerned with urban health will see only a local air pollution problem, and tackle it as best they can through mitigating measures.

- Providers of social services will see only the dispossession of people left in inner areas without cars, and seek to palliate these - perhaps by organising buses or lift rotas to take carless people to out of town shops, thus reinforcing the pressure for car-accessible development.

Pitfall 2: Sectoral specialisation of organisations

Personal specialisation is of course closely related to the specialisation of remit and activities of different organisations. In the example above there may be separate local authority departments or other agencies for road building, spatial planning, economic development, health and social services. Each will be competing (more or less explicitly) with the others for funding, influence and prestige, by seeking to show that the problems *it* can deal with are the most pressing, and the methods *it* can apply are the most effective.

Pitfall 2:
Sectoral specialisation of
4. organisations

This dynamic gives all these organisations a vested interest in the sectoral definition of both problems and solutions. Attempts to define problems in broader terms, or to seek solutions at a different level, go against the career interests of most of the people involved. Cross-sectoral problems may provoke debilitating struggles between departmental interests rather than collaborative problem-solving. The 'solutions' implemented by particular departmental interests, such as road building, may compound problems rather than contribute to their solution.

Pitfall 3: Quantification of performance

Pitfall 3:
Quantification of
performance

A second current orthodoxy of good practice is the drive to measure performance. It is widely stated that 'you cannot manage what you cannot measure'. However indices of performance often seem unconnected with, or even negatively related to, sustainability goals.

In the example above, measures of service provision such as kilometres of road, numbers of parking spaces, levels of car ownership, and measures of mobility such as numbers of journeys or household expenditure on travel may seem indices of difficulty rather than success. Even measures of public transport subsidy or special needs transport provision seem to measure problems rather than solutions.

The measurement of environmental performance raises some specific methodological problems. Conceptually it is necessary to know the full environmental consequences of each decision or action from 'cradle to grave' in order to evaluate performance or compare options. Thus 'life cycle analysis' ought, in theory, to form the basis of all environmental decision taking and performance measurement.

Life cycle analysis may be useful in describing different costs and benefits in the long term, and thus it provides a better background for political decisions about which costs and benefits to choose. However, full, reliable and objective life cycle analysis is impossible because:

- even the simplest action has an 'infinite regress' of environmental consequences. A decision always has to be taken as to where to stop considering them - and this decision always introduces potential bias and leaves uncertainty;

- assumptions about the 'additionality' of particular actions - the difference they make to what would have happened anyway - are required at every stage. For example, the question of whether disposable or washable nappies are the more environmentally damaging depends on questions such as whether a washing machine is run more frequently to wash nappies, or whether extra capacity in the waste collection system is needed to handle disposable nappies;

- there is no objective basis for comparing and offsetting different kinds of environmental costs and benefits. For example the question of whether diesel or petrol vehicles are environmentally worse depends on whether the extra health problems caused by diesels are more or less important than the extra global warming caused by petrol. There is no 'right' answer to this question.

Pitfall 4: Application of market mechanisms to public services and policies

Pitfall 4:
Application of market
mechanisms to public
services and policies

A further management trend is the application of market methods and disciplines. Markets operate through price signals. Commercial success is compromised by attention to 'externalities' - anything not priced in the market. Several aspects of the 'marketisation' of decision taking can reinforce the problems of departmentalism and quantification already mentioned. These include financial targets for service provision; discounting and investment appraisal; and the 'invisible hand' or 'invisible elbow' question. These are discussed in turn.

Financial targets for service provision

The setting of financial performance targets for public services militates against broader policy thinking. For example, in many British cities, the newly privatised hospital trusts are seeking to sell city centre hospital sites and move to peripheral locations. From the point of view of the hospital trusts this is a rational, indeed an unavoidable, decision. The proceeds of the land sales will pay for better medical treatment facilities, which the trusts exist to provide. The trusts cannot, and should not, be expected to take responsibility for the resulting social and environmental damage through loss of public transport accessibility, public transport revenue, extra traffic and difficulty and expense for non-car-owning visitors.

The more rigorously performance is measured on a cost centre basis, the less managers are able to afford to consider broader impacts. The definition of service delivery contracts and the separation of 'purchasers' from 'providers' of services can reinforce these problems. If 'purchasers' see their role as defining service requirements as tightly as possible, and 'providers' have to deliver those requirements as cost-effectively as possible, broader public service objectives are liable to disappear down the gap between the two.

Investment appraisal

Any company has to discount the future - give less weight to costs and benefits the further ahead they are likely to occur - because in the commercial world 'time is money'. Money now is worth more than in the future because it could be earning interest. Discounting is equivalent to saying that benefits or costs to people next year matter 5 per cent (or whatever the discount rate is) less than current benefits or costs. This contradicts the most basic principle of sustainability, that the rights of future generations are as important as those of the present.

13.

On a discounting basis it is not 'rational' to spend slightly more now to secure even large benefits a long way into the future - for example to spend a little more to increase the design life of a building from 50 to 100 years. Discounting therefore leads directly to cheap and flimsy urban buildings and infrastructure. Their low construction standards and requirements for constant repair and early replacement result in inefficient use of both environmental and financial resources. Their low design standards and obvious impermanence undermine urban character and sense of place; their short life erodes continuity and identity; and the resulting incessant building and demolition activities constitute a major nuisance in many urban areas.

'Invisible hand' or 'invisible elbow'

Adam Smith described the market as an 'invisible hand' which would optimise the distribution of resources. It can just as easily function as an 'invisible elbow' producing a result which none of the market agents intended, and which leaves them all worse off (Jacobs 1991). For example, as shown above, a whole series of individually rational decisions to travel by car instead of public transport can leave everyone - car-users included - worse off.

Research indicates that in London bus passengers would have shorter door-to-door commuting times than car drivers do now if fewer people drove. This is a 'prisoner's dilemma'. No individual can alter the cumulative dynamic. It is still rational for each individual to change to using a car. Altruistic behaviour simply disadvantages the individual concerned.

There is no necessary relationship   19.
between the structure and
dynamics of markets and urban
sustainability

The whole city is more than the
sum of its parts

Reasons conventional good management practice fails

The reason these management methods fail is that they all attempt to make complex problems manageable by slicing them down into narrower frames of reference. However, sustainability requires integrated approaches horizontally (through departments) as well as vertically (through levels).

Both professional value systems and sets of conventional performance indicators seek to establish a very tightly closed loop between behaviour and reward. They succeed in providing hard, unambiguous rules of conduct and criteria of success by the exclusion of complicating contextual factors. But this is exactly the reason why they are inadequate to cope with complex systems, where these 'complications' are often the key questions.

Market economies are themselves complex systems. The interactions of land prices, development finance decisions, rents and incomes of residents can be as complex as the interactions of physical development and infrastructure changes, environmental quality and quality of life. The reason markets fail to deliver sustainability is that there is no necessary relationship between the structure and dynamics of markets and those of urban sustainability. The simplest reason for this is that money values often do not reflect what economists revealingly call environmental 'externalities'. A deeper problem is that markets are intrinsically incapable of managing 'public goods' - goods which are not tradable, which are not 'consumed' by one person to the exclusion of others, but can be enjoyed simultaneously by any number of people with no diminution.

It follows from this that a whole city cannot be assumed to be just the sum of its parts - and that problems of the whole cannot necessarily be solved simply by broader or wholesale application of the solutions which 'work' at the level of parts. Specifically:

* well-being or welfare of the whole city is not automatically or necessarily advanced by better practice in any one sector. For example better roads can make a city as a whole more difficult to travel around;

* the wealth of a city is not just the sum of the incomes of all the people. Increasing overall economic prosperity may impoverish and restrict the lives of the less well off more than it increases the welfare of the better off. The 'trickle- down' of wealth expected by advocates of free market policies does not generally seem to have reached the urban poor;

* a whole set of individually 'rational' decisions in a market will not necessarily leave everyone well off.

1.6   ## INSTITUTIONAL ARRANGEMENTS

An Ecosystems Approach to urban sustainability requires certain patterns of organisational management. This in turn implies organisational patterns and administrative systems which address issues in a holistic way. Drawing on the ecosystems metaphor and the goals of sustainable development, the following principles are advocated:

- integration:- The vertical and horizontal integration of organisations, policies, plans and programmes; integration of the external environment with the internal policy making process; integration of time and space dimensions; integration of values and behaviour; integration of personal need and institutional capacity;

- co-operation:- Recognising the mutual dependence between all agents in the system; equal access to power and resources; a proactive approach to consensus building; mobilising action through empowerment; networking;

- homeostasis:- The management of dynamic change within a flexible but broadly stable system. This implies: developing an organisational culture which accommodates change; recognising the incremental nature of policy processes; feedback systems to regulate change; addressing issues of values, motivations and ownership;

- subsidiarity:- Making decisions and implementing action at the lowest level consistent with the achievement of the desired goals. This implies: matching rights with responsibilities and powers with resources; accepting diverse conceptions of problems; creating organisational frameworks which manage complex dependency and promote agreement; building new relationships between different levels of government and between local authorities and the community;

- synergy:- 'Create a whole that is either greater than or qualitatively different from the sum of the parts' (Brugmann, 1992). This implies providing strategic direction for incremental actions; outlining a vision of the possible; adopting cyclic rather than linear planning.

CONCLUSIONS

Cities and urban life hold the key to sustainable development. Europe's cities can and should be not only highly resource efficient but also safe, healthy, pleasant, fulfilling and inspiring places to live. Too often they fail to be either physically or socially sustainable. This is at least partly because current management approaches often fail to recognise and respond to the complexity of the links between physical, economic and social processes within cities.

The section has suggested that ecological and systems approaches can help both to elucidate the complexity of urban management problems and to guide the choice and application of policy tools to tackle them, enabling European cities to live up to their full potential for environmental, social and economic sustainability. Ecological and systems insights offer a distinctive approach to urban policy making and require a distinctive set of policy tools.

There is no such thing as one overall strict method to meet the aim of sustainable development. The ecosystems approach as recently expounded in Ecopolis (Tjallingii, 1995) offers ways to tackle problems within their contexts. In relation to this, section 2 explores policy tools that can be applied in various combinations to manage change in practice.

1.7

New approaches are needed to achieve urban sustainability

TOOLS FOR SUSTAINABLE
URBAN MANAGEMENT   2

INTRODUCTION   2.1

New approaches to urban
sustainability require cities to apply
conventional management
methods more knowingly and
within a broader framework

3

2.

Ecosystems management tools for
integration

*Solve problems at all spatial
scales*

TOOLS FOR SUSTAINABLE URBAN MANAGEMENT

INTRODUCTION

The application of tools for sustainable urban management requires cities to apply conventional management approaches more knowingly, with a more sophisticated understanding of their limits, and within a broader framework informed by systems thinking. The key challenge for urban policy making implied by this is to find means of pursuing urban sustainability objectives which:

- help to solve problems at all spatial scales (rather than moving problems to different scales or locations);

- support (or at least avoid obstructing) the achievement of other essential goals of urban policy such as economic and social welfare;

- promote widespread involvement and gain legitimacy through participative processes;

- influence positive change at different policy levels and in different areas of activity; and

- result in the effective implementation of goals in the most efficient manner.

The fundamental challenge is to achieve integration: integration between different levels (vertical) and between different actors in the policy process (horizontal). It is important to distinguish this from 'balance'. It is not enough to try to optimise trade-offs between different goals - for example to decide how far environmental aims justify compromising other goals. Instead the aim, as far as possible, should be to find ways of achieving different goals together, thus striving for multi-objective projects within a dynamic process. A project in the UK provides an example. Municipal investment in energy efficiency has not only reduced energy consumption and air pollution, but it has also reduced poverty, improved quality of life and appears to have improved health status in a poor inner-city district in Sheffield (Green, 1995).

The ecosystems approaches outlined in section 1 of this chapter leads to the identification of a set of management tools. This section considers these tools under five main headings - collaboration and partnership, policy integration, market mechanisms, information management and measuring and monitoring. Many of them are not new. In some cases the discussion simply confirms the importance of existing methods (such as city-wide environmental strategies) or implies a need for them to be applied more widely (environmental management systems) or given more weight (environmental considerations in budgeting). In other cases it shows a need to reappraise and develop established tools in a more sustainability-conscious way, better informed by ecosystems thinking. This applies, for example, to environmental impact assessment and utility regulation. Other tools are either completely new (environmental budgeting), radical developments of previously familiar ones (environmental indicators) or direct familiar methods to achieve new policy aims (environmental tax reform). This report focuses on the environmental tools available to urban management processes.

The use of explicit environmental management systems is likely to become more widespread. The UK government has sponsored an adaptation for local authorities of the *Eco-Management and Audit Regulation*, originally for manufacturing industry. This is already being applied in a range of local authorities in the UK and could be used throughout the EU.

The discussion in each sub-section is designed to give an overview of the principal tools and to highlight their importance for sustainable urban management. Each tool in this section is considered as an element within an integrated system of environmental management. In this regard they may be viewed as a 'toolbox' which can be drawn on as and when needed. There can be no prescriptions for how to use or combine these tools; there are many ways of moving towards sustainability. The toolkit concept is based on the idea that all institutional and environmental contexts are different and each therefore requires a novel approach. The fundamental goal is to achieve an integrated environmental management process, but the elements in that process will evolve through the interplay of different interests. The section 'Strategic framework and incremental steps', first, gives some guidance for integrating tools within a strategic framework.

Strategic framework and incremental steps

2.2

1.

The principle of integration is never more important than for combining the goals of sustainability with the realities of urban management. On a strategic level, a comprehensive and broad-ranging plan is necessary to define the vision of what a sustainable society will look like. This represents the framework within which actions can be formulated and implemented. What is needed is a process which allows for practical incremental steps, guided by the general goals in a strategic framework.

The management tools presented in this section offer advice for an integrated process of environmental management at both strategic and operational levels. These tools represent various options which can be combined and applied in different ways. Apart from the overriding importance of seeking integration, there are no prescriptions offered. Each community must choose its own path. What is most important is that the journey begins.

The choice of the most appropriate management tools can be guided by the sustainability objectives outlined in the 'Introduction'. Three additional criteria may help in directing this choice: define problems at the right level; use composite instruments to achieve multiple aims; seek to build capacity.

Define problems at the right level

Define problems at the
right level

In seeking new management approaches it is essential that problems are defined at the appropriate *conceptual* level. Most non-trivial problems can be defined in several different ways. Each definition implies a different kind of solution. For example, traffic in towns can be seen:

- as a local noise and odour nuisance, the solution to which might be double glazing in homes, catalytic converters or electric cars;

- as a local congestion nuisance, in which case a solution might be to increase road capacity;

- as damaging to the urban fabric, suggesting the removal of traffic from sensitive areas by ring roads or bypasses;

STRATEGIC FRAMEWORK AND
INCREMENTAL STEPS

Problems need solving, not moving

Manage problems at the right
spatial level

Management of water

Use composite instruments
to achieve multiple
objectives

- as damaging to 'liveability', possibly solved by routing traffic underground; or

- as excessive mobility demand, to be addressed by reducing the need to travel (Institution of Environmental Health Officers, 1993).

The more parochial a definition of a problem, the more danger there is that the corresponding solutions will, by neglect of feedback loops, make the underlying problem worse. The more broadly and strategically a problem is defined, the more chance there is of finding a solution. This will often entail defining problems at a higher - that is to say more abstract or generic -level than technical specialists have been accustomed to. In particular it requires problems to be solved rather than moved.

6.   This is the key to reconciling the pursuit of sustainability with delivering day to day services. Indeed it will often help with the achievement of service objectives which are not necessarily related to sustainability, since unrecognised and unmanaged systems effects do not only frustrate sustainability goals.

7.   Similarly, it is necessary to manage problems at the right *spatial* level. The structure and responsibilities of local and regional government vary greatly between Member States. There is no one 'correct' pattern. However, urban management for sustainability does require that attention is paid to the concept in Agenda 21 of the appropriate scale of decision taking. Agenda 21 repeatedly points out that effective planning of resources such as water is far easier if the units of planning correspond to natural domains such as river catchments. Agenda 21 applies the same logic to human settlements, although they are not literally 'natural domains'. For example, urban transport needs to be planned at the level of the 'commutershed' - usually the whole city and a substantial area around it.

Most European countries have tiered systems of regional and local government in which responsibilities, powers and resources are distributed amongst the tiers. Cities rarely have complete governmental jurisdiction over their geographical areas making policy integration more difficult, especially for services which need to be provided at a strategic level.

The structure and organisation of local government are therefore important factors in determining the ease or difficulty of formulating and implementing sustainable development policies.

Use composite instruments to achieve multiple objectives

In addition, when devising new policy approaches for sustainability it is generally necessary to devise composite instruments to achieve multiple objectives. Much policy thinking is based on the doctrine that policy instruments should be designed to solve one problem at a time. This is obviously attractive as a way of imposing some clarity and accountability on policy processes. But the ecosystems model requires recognition that this pattern is so exceptional as to be almost unknown.

Instead, it should be assumed that any problem will require a combination of policy instruments to solve it - and that each of these components should in turn help to solve more than one problem. Composite instruments to achieve multiple objectives must be the standard approach to policy making.

Seek to build capacity

All the tools described in this section have an additional purpose. They are significant for the development of the *capacity* of city administrations and other partners to deliver sustainability. This was described in Chapters 1 and 2 in terms of adopting an institutional as well as an environmental focus.

Capacity is more than technical competence, knowledge and methods; it is also crucially dependent on the confidence and motivation of individuals, the flexibility and openness of structures, the commitment and leadership of elected representatives and the credibility and goodwill which an administration commands in the broader community - that is, with aspects of organisational culture. These may be hard to measure, but they are essential to success. The tools set out should be used with these broader objectives in mind.

13.

The need for political process

It has been emphasised that management tools do not exist to provide objective, 'technical', solutions to urban environment problems. Management for sustainability is essentially a political process. This section explores some of the implications for urban governance of the use of management tools. Issues related to political process are also discussed in chapter 5 section 2 in relation to social aspects of sustainability.

2.3

What all the management tools have in common is a knowing, or even manipulative, approach to matters sometimes thought to be authoritatively or objectively 'given':

- standards of professional excellence and good practice cannot be left solely to the professions, but must be informed by broader views of the function of each discipline;

- likewise, the aims of individual departments and sectors cannot be assumed to promote the general good, but must be actively co-ordinated through processes of consultation and partnership;

- performance measurement is not just a technical problem. Conscious decisions about the purpose of the activities being assessed must guide the choice of performance indicators;

Common features of the tools

- markets do not establish values in a neutral and impersonal way. Instead, they may (or indeed may not) be useful ways of distributing goods according to value relationships settled from outside.

The tools described are all means of modifying or constraining the operation of professions, performance monitoring, and markets within sustainability objectives set from outside. By applying these tools, urban policy making for sustainability can become much broader, more powerful and more ambitious than has hitherto been generally recognised. However, this raises two related problems. Firstly, there is the problem of legitimisation. How can the application of sustainability concerns as guides and constraints to what have previously been seen as autonomous systems be justified and legitimated? Secondly, there is the problem of implementation. How can this process be implemented by cities-in other words,what are the conditions under which cities can use the tools?

Legitimisation

Legitimisation

Democratic choice is a key theme
of Local Agenda 21   4.

Whatever their limitations, markets provide a neutral, impersonal arbiter of value. Similarly, professional hierarchies have been seen as reliable guarantors of good practice and values. Other criteria can be legitimated through the political process. Democratic choice can legitimate both sustainability objectives and the means to achieve them - provided people are educated and accurately informed about the consequences of their choices. This is a key theme of Local Agenda 21. It means that professions, performance measures and markets are all tools within civil society, and serve its ends rather than their own.

The political process legitimises the
limitations on personal freedom

There is a stronger point about the need for political process. Two linked features of the traffic example discussed in section 1 illustrate the limitations of markets: the way that a series of individually rational choices to use cars can add up to a situation where everyone is worse off than before (the 'invisible elbow'); and the way no individual alone can overcome many cumulative actions. Problems like this are soluble only if all accept limits on their own freedoms. These limitations can only be acceptable if people choose or at least consent to them. The 'social contract' model of politics, in which civil society is created through individuals voluntarily agreeing to collective limitations on their own actions in order to make them all better off, holds the solution to sustainable urban management.

3.1 Historical and contemporary examples of 'social contracts'

When the New Town of Edinburgh was being developed in the 18th century, the landowners imposed elaborate restrictions on design, materials, common services and local impacts. It was the guaranteed universal observance of these standards - the certainty any prospective resident could have that his or her neighbours would be required to observe them - which made the New Town attractive to those who invested in building houses there.

In Bremen the council is building a car-free development. The development is heavily oversubscribed. Evidently there are plenty of people willing to forgo the option of having a car themselves in return for knowing their neighbours have done so too and that the whole neighbourhood will be free of traffic noise, danger and fumes.

This social contract tradition can be reinterpreted in systems terms as the recognition that 'emergence' in problems - the kinds of complex interactions in cities which have been discussed above - call for 'emergence' in solutions: the creation of a new level of human organisation, civil political society, instead of relying on the 'war of all against all' (even in the limited form of a free market economy). An insistence on trying to solve social problems using only individualistic means - which is what an insistence on market mechanisms and a denial of the political level means - can be seen as a deliberate refusal to understand the problem or to use tools commensurate with the task.

Implementation

Much of the previous discussion has assumed that cities are closed, autonomous systems. Of course they are not. People, money, physical resources, ideas and techniques move in and out of them all the time. Degrees of 'closure' affect the ability of cities to use the tools described. For example, at one extreme any city administration can apply Eco-Management and Audit (see section 'Tools for formulating, integrating and implementing local environmental processes'), or an analogous approach, within its own activities. At the opposite extreme, few city authorities can have much impact on the overall balance of taxation between resources and labour. Even where powers exist at a municipal level to levy local taxes on, for example, labour and energy, exercising them to any significant extent will cause movements of people and businesses into or out of the city more than changes in behaviour. Thus this is a tool which needs to be applied at a national level. Indeed, so far as national economies are 'open', it may be a tool which can only be applied at EU or global level. This theme is further explored in chapter 5 section 1.

Between the two extremes, the availability of options depends on the context set by national politics. For example:

- a 'positive feedback' response by central government - such as reacting to urban congestion by further road building - can undermine local government efforts to impose negative feedback;

- municipal action to promote environmentally preferable businesses such as recycling will be frustrated if there is a national or international glut of recycled materials and no action is taken by governments to create markets;

- promotion by a city of waste minimisation will have limited effects on industry if there are cheap disposal sites elsewhere and 'free trade' provisions mean companies are free to use them;

- rules against favouring local suppliers in purchasing and tendering encourage increased transport of goods and services. This is obviously bad for global sustainability, but it also militates against the implementation of integrated solutions at the local level.

Implementation

7.   Degrees of 'closure' affect the ability of cities to use the tools

National politics can put constraints on the use of tools

Use of local and renewable energy

TOOLS FOR COLLABORATION AND PARTNERSHIP: LEARNING BY DOING

One of the most important groups of tools is concerned with building collaboration and partnerships between different organisations and interests. This is essential for two reasons. First, it reduces the tendency of individual organisations and agencies to pursue their own agendas in isolation from the broader public interest. Second, most problems can only be solved through co-ordinated action by a range of actors and agencies. This point is strongly emphasised in both Agenda 21 and the Fifth Environmental Action Programme which is based around the concept of shared responsibility.

A theme running throughout this section is 'learning by doing'. Involvement in decision making and management means that organisations and individuals engage in a process of mutual betterment. Viewing environmental management as a learning process both reinforces the point made earlier about taking the first step towards sustainability and highlights the importance of experimentation.

Two categories of tools are discussed in this sub-section. The first category focuses on the operations of local authorities. The tools here are:

* professional education and training;

* cross - disciplinary working;

* partnerships and networks.

The second category of tools deals with the relationship between a local authority and its community. These are:

* community consultation and participation;

* Innovative educational mechanisms and awareness raising.

Professional education and training

Professional education
and training

Professional education and training
should emphasize that there is no
'one best way' of solving
problems

Establishing and implementing strategies for sustainability, whether or not the formal mechanisms described in the previous section are applied, requires city managers and sectoral specialists to adopt broader frames of reference than have been typical in the past. An ability to see issues in the round and to empathise with other perspectives is also a prerequisite for successful partnership. To achieve this it is necessary to increase the knowledge, competence and confidence of *all* local authority staff in dealing with the environmental aspects of their work. Appropriate training should be a high priority.

The role of technical and professional specialists is particularly significant for policy integration. Many senior local government staff have specialised early in (for example) an engineering discipline such as landfill management or road construction and risen to senior positions by being outstandingly effective in this context. Their professional position and prestige depend on being in charge of large amounts of landfilling or road building. It is not reasonable to expect such people to be instantly enthusiastic about minimising waste or obviating traffic.

Some senior officers have made such transitions. But this should be seen as an achievement of personal development despite, rather than because of, career dynamics. It is necessary to make it easier for specialists to treat their technical skills as one of a number of tools to solve problems rather than the only one - and to prosper personally and professionally by doing so.

Methods for doing this include:

- inclusion of sustainability and systems ecology in the curriculum of professional training, and requirements for understanding of them at an appropriate level in all professional examinations and qualifications;

- definition by professional bodies and institutes of the profession's mission and values at a 'functional' rather than 'technical' level (Brugmann, 1992), that is, in terms of the human challenges or problems the profession seeks to address, rather than the technical means of doing so;

- management structures that break down technical barriers. These are considered below;

- incorporating sustainability issues in the induction courses for new employees. (Cardiff City Council in the UK has found that this has been a strong motivator for people and has been instrumental in building-up a sense of corporate ownership);

- placement schemes in organisations which work for sustainable development. This is a way of supporting the organisation's work and of raising the trainee's overall awareness. Because most placement schemes are directed at young people, this also serves a long term educational role.

The requirement for training in sustainability issues, tools and mechanisms is immense. This applies at all levels and in all sectors. In the same way that information has to be made accessible to its audience, so too training programmes should be developed to suit particular groups - age groups, professions and occupations, ethnic groups, etc..

It is of course ultimately for elected politicians, or political nominees, to lead and manage each organisation. Many of the best initiatives described in this report derive ultimately from the vision and commitment of local politicians. A strong commitment from the top to openness and consensus can transform a previously unsupportive organisational culture. It is therefore crucial for elected members and nominees to public office to have the best possible understanding of both urban sustainability issues and the tools for tackling them. Training and awareness programmes for local politicians are therefore at least as important as those for administrators and technical specialists.

Cross-disciplinary working

The grouping of technical specialisms into broader management units oriented to delivery of services, and multi-disciplinary, task-oriented teams, offer possible models for working across professional boundaries. Specialists can potentially achieve a broader outlook without losing relevant technical expertise.

Methods for overcoming
professional barriers

Cross-disciplinary working

Cross-disciplinary working can
broaden a specialist view

Partnerships and
networks

Partnerships and networks can
combine all the expertise needed
for sustainable development

Local governments may seek to re-organise their formal internal management structures as part of a more strategic approach to the management of environmental issues. Structures for both officials and elected politicians may be set up.

Alternatively, or in combination with this last approach, cities have established cross-sectoral working groups to address environmental issues (such as energy or recycling). Membership of these groups may include both professional employees of the local authority and elected politicians. Additionally, corporately-based posts of environmental co-ordinator or animator to promote integration may be created. Over 300 UK local authorities now have an environmental co-ordinator or equivalent post.

Partnerships and networks

13.   Chapter 2 introduced the issue of networking. This emphasised that because the actions needed are diverse, implementing sustainable development requires the active support and co-operation of a range of actors and agencies, and therefore approaches based on partnership.

14.   Networks represent a participative approach to planning and implementation which seeks to mobilise the skills, resources and commitment of all parties, ensuring joint ownership of solutions. Both Agenda 21 and the Fifth Environmental Action Programme repeatedly emphasise the need for such arrangements, often termed multi-stakeholder partnerships. Municipalities have an important role in orchestrating partnerships.

The establishment of formal multi-agency partnerships to develop strategic approaches to solve locally-identified problems in a specified geographical area is now common practice in Europe. These often aim to lever funds to support projects from national governments or the European Commission. The integrated rural development partnerships which are fundamental to the LEADER programme are of this type, and urban regeneration initiatives such as the Contrats de Villes in France and the Single Regeneration Budget in the UK follow this pattern. Effective involvement of local communities and voluntary agencies in formal partnerships remains problematic, however.

Another type of partnership arrangement is the formation of a network to promote common commitment to a particular cause. A whole range of networks, both formal and informal, exist which promote sustainable development. They aim to outline and promote a set of common objectives, and to share experience and information. They therefore perform the functions of communication, education and dissemination. At the European level, some of the more important urban sustainability networks are: Eurocities; ICLEI; UTO; Car Free Cities; WHO Healthy Cities; European Sustainable Cities and Towns Campaign. At the individual Member State level, most countries are also active in developing networks. Examples are: The Danish Association of Sustainable Communities; The Finnish Municipal Sustainable Development Project; Communes pour L'environnement (France); Municipalities Against Global Warming (Italy); Eco-Municipalities (Sweden); Environment City (UK).

The success of a network depends on it being able to maintain active involvement of its members. This means that a network must take a proactive stance in relation to marketing its message and must have a strong co-ordination structure.

Community consultation and participation

All groups in society must have a voice in deciding what sustainable development requires and in working towards it. Some requirements of sustainable development are dictated by facts about the planet's ecology, such as the need to reduce fossil fuel use to avert global warming. But even aims of this sort can be achieved only if people accept and adopt them. Processes of securing agreement on, and commitment to, sustainability aims are indispensable even where a sustainability imperative is determined independently of what any group in society thinks.

At smaller scales, the aims themselves - the 'content' of sustainable development - can only be established through social processes. There is no 'objective' scientific answer to questions about which amenities and qualities matter for human development. These are a matter of the beliefs, values and aspirations of the people concerned, and can only be established through their involvement. Consultation and community involvement are therefore essential for establishing the meaning and content of sustainable development, at both global and local levels.

There has been increasing recognition in recent years of the importance of generating widespread ownership and involvement in environmental management processes. This has brought a resurgence in the development of mechanisms. The emphasis has been on developing consensual approaches to environmental problem resolution. These mechanisms have got a number of characteristics in common. First, they involve a new approach and outlook. For the local authority this often means adopting a more flexible approach to management processes and the setting of objectives. Second, decisions are arrived at through negotiation and bargaining. This emphasises the importance of process rather than the 'look' of the final product. Third, a cultural shift is needed by all participants in the environmental management process. For the public this might mean adopting a less confrontational stance, for the private sector it might mean sacrificing some of their economic objectives in favour of sustainability goals, and for the local authority it might mean a greater re-allocation of their resources and more power sharing. Finally, consensual approaches are by their very nature opposed to hierarchical structures and sectoral divisions. Professional, academic, cultural, sectoral and economic barriers need to be overcome (see above).

All segments of the community will gain from a positive approach to collaboration and partnership. Environmental and community groups, the private sector and the general public gain from greater access to the processes that shape their environment. The local authority gains legitimisation for its activities and ensures that it is pursuing the public's mandate. In addition, the local authority obtains access to information and expertise that it might otherwise be excluded from. Most importantly, the whole community gains from joining together to implement the recommendations that emerge from an integrated environmental management process.

A key is to create the conditions that enable collaboration and participation to take place. This is another facet to institutional capacity building. Rather than producing an exhaustive list of mechanisms this section will outline a number of objectives and discuss various actions that can be taken in pursuit of these objectives.

20.

TOOLS FOR COLLABORATION
AND PARTNERSHIP:
LEARNING BY DOING

Policy option:
Promote and facilitate
public involvement in
decision making processes

Conditions for enabling
collaboration and participation

Mechanisms for facilitating greater
public involvement in decision-
making processes

Policy option: Promote and facilitate public involvement in decision making processes

A key objective should be to promote community involvement within collaborative networks for environmental management. Involvement in framing and implementing processes will lead to greater ownership of those processes. This in turn will serve to empower those who are involved. The imperative of greater community involvement is currently being highlighted by the requirements of Local Agenda 21, with its emphasis on defining sustainable development in terms that people can relate to and be part of.

There are a number of specific mechanisms that can be used to facilitate greater public involvement in decision making processes.

- Environmental Fora. An environmental forum brings together the various segments of a community to debate issues, decide on agendas and feed into the decision making process. There is no standard model for an environmental forum. Some fora are issue specific and some adopt a strategic guidance role. The most important characteristic is that a discursive and consensual approach is maintained, thereby facilitating liaison between the local authority and the community and between different interests within the community.

3.2 An example of an environmental forum, Lahti, Finland

The city of Lahti in southern Finland established an Environmental Forum in 1993 with the aim of promoting sustainable development in the Lahti area. The need to work towards Local Agenda 21 provided a catalyst for consolidating existing initiatives in environmental conservation, and work on the state of the environment. Although environmental protection measures have had some success, it is recognised that the achievement of further improvements depends upon the more sustainable actions of many individuals in everyday life. The Forum, an initiative of the city council, brings together communities, organisations, businesses and the public in the greater Lahti area. In all, some 40 organisations are represented by around 90 active participants. The first stage in the Agenda 21 process is an audit of present environmental conditions in relation to the objectives of Agenda 21. Forum participants are developing sustainable development objectives for the Lahti area and mechanisms for achieving them, along with proposals for monitoring the implementation of objectives. The aim is to complete the Local Agenda 21 process during 1996, when implementation will begin. Since unemployment has recently increased in Lahti, leading to changes in social as well as economic life, the Environmental Forum is especially concerned with the economic and social aspects of sustainability, seeking to green the local economy.

- Roundtables. First developed in Canada to provide a platform for addressing cross-sectoral and cross-jurisdictional issues. They are a type of environmental forum but are expressly designed to serve three particular functions: to act as a catalyst in promoting policies and processes which contribute to sustainable development; to base their decisions on consensus, and to have broad-based representation from key interest groups. There is no standard form; they can operate at national and local level, can focus on either specific or general issues and can have varying levels of political and resource support.

- The Natural Step. A mechanism for consensus building, education and empowerment developed by the Swedish doctor Karl-Hendrik Robert. It is based on a process of enlisting support for a 'consensus' set of principles or decisions through co-opting established interests and building support from below. Once the basic set of principles have been agreed there is a much stronger basis for generating further involvement.

- The Environment City Model. A UK partnership programme involving the cities of Leicester, Leeds, Middlesborough and Peterborough which developed a 'model' for how to harness public support. At the core is an environmental forum similar to that described above. In support of the forum there are a number of Specialist Working Groups (SWGs) - focusing on key environmental subject areas that serve to develop strategic policy, monitor the state of the environment and plan and manage specific projects. In some cases there is also an executive committee to bridge the gap between strategic planning and operational management. The whole process is supported by a central co-ordination and information point. Although the model is still undergoing refinement, it has been extremely successful in generating partnership, co-operation and consensus.

- Eco-villages. In Denmark a National Association for Sustainable Communities was established in 1993. Members include individuals, housing and tenants associations and groups seeking to promote sustainable lifestyles through the development of sustainable communities (or eco-villages) in both urban and rural settings. A national campaign for ecological lifestyles - Green Lifestyle -began in 1994. This programme - part of the international Global Action Programme - aims to help individuals to make environmentally beneficial changes to daily life. Information is provided through a workbook, covering different aspects of life, designed to be used by eco teams - families, communities, schools or workplaces - advised by facilitators from the Danish network of Energy and Environment Offices.

Policy option: Seek to assess and reflect public attitudes, values and priorities

The key theme here is that it is no longer sufficient to rely solely on abstract notions of 'democracy' and 'community development'. The community consists of a plurality of groups, systems, perspectives, etc. which should all be actively harnessed for the purposes of environmental management. This means that segments of the community should be identified and a range of approaches adopted for each different segment. This entails breaking down stereotypical notions of class, profession, culture, etc. in order to arrive at a realistic mosaic of society. Once this has been achieved, the local authority is in a much stronger position to assess the factors which will influence behaviour and encourage involvement. To a large extent the mechanisms will overlap with those identified above for promoting and facilitating public involvement.

There is a need for public consultation which broadens the participation base and allows input to policy formulation. Traditional methods, where the public is invited to comment on published documents, may fail to reach groups who are less articulate, confident or familiar with bureaucratic processes. Community empowerment is an important aspect of social sustainability. Methods for achieving this include, for example:

Eco-building

Policy option:
Seek to assess and
reflect public attitudes,
values and priorities

Development of a realistic view
of the segments of the
community

Development of realistic ways of
reaching the different segments
in the community

- Focus groups, where six to eight people with particular characteristics (for example members of minority ethnic groups, or people without cars, or on low incomes) are invited and helped by a facilitator to discuss their views on selected topics - for example provision of public transport. Focus groups will not produce statistically representative views. But they can reach minority groups and achieve a deeper and more illuminating response than traditional survey techniques.

- 'Planning for real' exercises, where small groups, with expert facilitators 'on tap not on top', try out different approaches to real planning problems affecting their own lives, often using pictures or models rather than words. The advantages are immediacy, practicality, and accessibility.

27.   Many cities have been energetic in developing and applying these new mechanisms.

3.3 Mechanisms for community involvement

Rhondda Borough Council, with the Welsh Development Agency, commissioned the Community Design Service (CDS), a Cardiff-based community technical aid centre, to bring together the residents of Tylorstown Ward in the Rhondda Fach valley in South Wales. The aim was to identify major areas of environmental concern to the residents, to develop solutions and to demonstrate how local people could be involved in environmental change. A series of meetings and workshops facilitated by the staff of CDS, together with a publicity campaign, resulted in the preparation of a community environmental action plan for the area, now linked to the statutory development plan prepared by the local authority. The exercise also led to the designation of the upper Rhondda Fach valley as a Strategic Area for the receipt of government funding under the Welsh Office's Urban Programme (now the Strategic Development Scheme), and most of the schemes proposed under the plan (including, for example, the enhancement of derelict sites, traffic calming and the renovation of community meeting places) have now been implemented.

Address motivational factors

Address motivational factors

Attempts at collaboration and partnership are often hampered due to an apparent reluctance on the part of key interest groups to get involved. What often seems to be a lack of interest and inertia, is in fact a reaction from the public to the intractability of environmental problems and the impenetrability of many institutions to outside influence. An integrated environmental management process must therefore explicitly address motivational factors.

Factors which motivate public involvement

The factors which motivate involvement are specific to the context and much will depend on the mechanisms used to facilitate this involvement. There are, however, a number of general criteria:

- develop solutions from the bottom-up rather than imposing predetermined programmes from the top;

- relate sustainability issues to aspects of local life;

- use terminology that the public can understand and relate to;

- emphasise the difference that each person can make, both in causing the problems and contributing to the solutions;

- outline a 'vision' of the possible - the benefits to be gained from moving towards a sustainable society;

- if one approach does not work, then adopt an alternative strategy, but do not give up.

Policy option: encourage involvement by being open and transparent in process; use mechanisms that encourage active participation

30.

The overriding concern should be to make decision making processes accessible. Too often a local authority will only fulfil its mandatory consultation regardless of whether this is sufficient to encourage involvement or not. Typically this is limited to the presentation of a range of predetermined alternative solutions in order to meet goals which the public have had no say in deciding. The form of presentation is also often through a rather static and one-way means of communication (for example, consultation documents, exhibitions, public meetings).

Rather than seeking involvement towards the end of the process, there should be encouragement for the public to become active partners *in* the process. Although lack of powers and resources limit what a local authority can do, involvement can be facilitated by using mechanisms that emphasise the principles of openness and transparency. Openness refers to access to information and decision making systems, the ability and the means to influence these systems, and the removal of disciplinary barriers so that issues are highlighted rather than obscured. Transparency means that every attempt is made to explain the operation of the process so that the method and the management are amenable to scrutiny.

Policy option: focus on generating 'ownership' through building commitment

Ownership is a product of values, perceptions, motivations and involvement. A great deal of work still has to be done on identifying the conditions which promote public ownership of environmental management processes. It is widely recognised, however, that without this sense of public ownership, a local authority's scope for action will always be limited. Pursuing the objectives mentioned earlier in this section should go a long way to ensuring widespread commitment. Direct involvement and empowerment will then help turn this commitment into a sense of ownership.

Policy option: encourage
involvement by being
open and transparent in
process

Open and transparent decision
making processes encourage
participation

Policy option:
focus on generating
'ownership' through
building commitment

Each person can make a difference

Policy option:
innovative educational
mechanisms and
awareness raising

Policies should address the
people's own perceptions

Policy option: innovative educational mechanisms and awareness raising

While traditional education and training methods can be used within local authorities, these will often be inappropriate for use in the wider community. A range of innovative mechanisms should therefore be explored. These may require experimentation on the part of the local authority and may also demand a flexible approach to management and control. They will be likely to involve forging partnerships with environmental and community groups. Innovative mechanisms include systems of information exchange that are more interactive, use a range of senses and are usually informal and voluntary. Rather than imparting information in a sterile way they focus on interpreting issues in a way that finds resonance with the audience. Two particularly successful innovative mechanisms are EcoFeedback and *Global Action Plan*.

34.   'EcoFeedback' is a Dutch initiative which aims to help people reduce the impact of their household on the environment, particularly in relation to energy and waste. It uses simple monitoring systems and established information media to help households reduce their energy consumption and waste production. A quarter of all households in the Netherlands now participate in the scheme and this success has led to it being launched in other countries.

35.   Global Action Plan (GAP) is an international campaign, supported by the UN, which aims to involve households in practical programmes of action. Participating households are sent an action pack each month for six months on water, waste, energy, transport and shopping and 'next steps'. Each pack contains readable, approachable, information, a checklist of actions for the household to take, and a monitoring card with instructions on how to assess and record the effect of the actions. The idea is much the same as EcoFeedback but the range of issues is greater and there is more emphasis on improving the quality of life than on cost savings.

Public opinion surveys consistently show a very high level of interest in sustainability issues. Equally, however, there is a prevailing gap between expressing interest and taking action to bring about change. Filling this gap is just as much about raising awareness as it is about devising efficient mechanisms and tools. Indeed, in the long term, it is only through widespread awareness of the problems and the solutions that lasting change can be sustained.

Awareness raising requires that attention be paid to factors which motivate people, especially that sustainability issues are shown to be relevant to people's everyday lives. Awareness raising should occur on all levels simultaneously. Thus specific actions in relation to education and training might be backed by a programme of popular activities, such as advertisements, a television and radio campaign, music events, etc.. Often it is a simple message that has most impact. In this regard, there needs to be more attention paid to marketing the ideas of sustainability (see section 'Systems for managing information').

Empowerment is a key-concept in
raising awareness

There are innumerable ways in which awareness of sustainability issues can be raised. Examples include:

- promoting high profile environmental initiatives. Activities such as recycling serve the dual function of reusing materials and promoting beneficial environmental action. The simple act of recycling helps show people that they can and do make a difference and encourages them to be more responsible in other areas of life also;

- launching 'flagship' projects to facilitate large-scale public involvement and lead to visible environmental improvements. Examples are the creation of a wildlife park, the removal of graffiti from public spaces, a river clean-up, tree planting and an environmental festival;

- highlighting the role of networks in generating awareness. Most networks produce and distribute material on their activities. Many also have information systems to encourage transfer and dissemination;

- canvassing politicians, public bodies and businesses on their environmental views is a tactic that has been used for many years by campaigning groups to help 'force' issues onto the agenda.

Awareness raising must be accompanied by a process of empowerment. After awakening a desire to take action, the means by which this can be brought about need to be made available. Otherwise the sense of powerlessness that many people already feel will be made worse with long term harm for sustainable development. The tools discussed in this section should help ensure that awareness can be translated into positive action.

39.

TOOLS FOR FORMULATING, INTEGRATING AND IMPLEMENTING LOCAL ENVIRONMENTAL POLICIES

2.5

The largest group of tools for sustainable urban management helps the city to set overall goals within which professional excellence and the pursuit of sectoral objectives are firmly lodged. These tools have been developed in relation to environmental policy and action. It is now necessary to extend them so as to address all dimensions of sustainability. In particular, this will require integration of economic and social considerations with environmental concerns and the adoption of longer time horizons in policy formulation.

Each tool discussed here combines with the others; they should all be viewed as elements in an integrated environmental management process. Some focus on policy formation (for example, the production of statements and charters) while others focus on implementation of these policies (for example action plans and strategies). The remaining tools lie on a spectrum between policy and implementation, seeking to influence the way that decisions are made and systems operated.

Analysis of these tools and recommendations for their use should seek to encompass the entire environmental management process. This requires a consideration of the actors, stages and institutional context which influence the process.

The principal tools are:

- city-wide environmental statements and charters;

- city-wide environmental strategies or action plans;

- local Agenda 21 strategies;

- environmental budgeting;

City-wide environmental
statements and charters

City-wide environmental
strategies or action plans can
be designed in accordance
with ecosystems principles

- environmental management systems;

- environmental impact assessment;

- strategic environmental assessment.

City-wide environmental statements and charters

5.   An overall statement of a local authority's environmental values and aims can perform several important functions. First, it articulates a vision and sets an agenda for all the different specialisms within the authority and for the wider community. Second, it provides a justification and basis for the development of environmentally-directed policies and actions within different functional areas. Third, it provides criteria by which the environmental effects of non-environmental actions can be judged, both within the authority and by others in the community. Finally, the process of initiating, drafting, agreeing and adopting such a corporate statement necessarily involves a range of people. Participation helps raise their awareness and encourages them to take ownership of the resulting statement. Many municipalities have adopted environmental declarations, charters or statements of varying levels of detail.

6.   A number of important characteristics of these statements and charters need to be emphasised:

- they are expressions of intent to act in a certain way, but on their own do not help in defining or implementing this action. The aspirations of a statement or charter must be integrated into other levels of the environmental management process if they are to be achieved. The practicality and usefulness must also be assessed through monitoring and feedback;

- statements and charters need not be detailed or exact to begin with. If they are intended as the first stage in a process, there will be opportunities to revise and up-date them later;

- as with all management tools, application must be considered within a particular organisational context. An environmental statement or charter must have the support of all agencies that will have a role in putting the goals into practice.

City-wide environmental strategies or action plans can be designed in accordance with ecosystems principles

Translating corporate statements of environmental commitment into action requires the establishment of a strategy or action plan containing explicit policy goals and targets, a clear statement of responsibilities, details about how the strategy is to be resourced and implemented in terms of legal powers, finance and staffing, a timetable for implementation and, ideally, arrangements for monitoring progress. Preparation of such a strategy will usually include a review of environmental conditions in the local area and some assessment of the environmental impacts of current policies. Effective political leadership is essential. The aim is to promote convergence of sectoral actions on agreed overall environmental aims, bringing various environmental measures into a coherent policy framework. These plans should become the basis for on-going monitoring of action programmes. The Expert Group strongly advocates the development of city-wide strategies for urban management as a central tool for policy integration.

The design of city-wide environmental strategies and action plans may be enhanced through the explicit application of ecosystems principles, as in the development of integrated environmental plans. These plans are further discussed in Chapter 7.

3.4 Examples of city-wide environmental strategies

Sweden has 15 'eco-municipalities' which have adopted a holistic and strategic view of environment and development. All began by formulating environmental goals which are followed up and revised at regular intervals. Most set up an environmental committee or made other changes to conventional work practices to further the eco-municipality objectives. Examples of towns declaring themselves 'eco-municipalities' include Overtornea and Orebro.

The Environmental Protection Plan being developed in Münster in Germany is designed to parallel the land use plan, including environmental baseline information, an analysis of quality, and the problems and opportunities associated with further development. In order to reflect and accommodate the dynamic nature of city systems, the process is supported by a computer information system.

The Area Sustainability Study of Ettrick and Lauderdale in the south east of Scotland aims to interpret and apply the principles of sustainability and thereby identify the scope and feasibility of action. As part of the process there was an attempt to assess the interactions between the key economic sectors and between the natural, community and economic assets of the area. Although the study is quite conceptual it should prove useful to other authorities aiming to apply the principles of sustainability. The intention is to build on the findings of the study in helping to develop a Local Agenda 21 strategy.

The Baden-Wurttemburg Region's Framework for Environmental Planning (FEP) is an overall planning tool created to integrate environmental objectives into all policy fields of local government. It defines general environmental guidelines for policies which are relevant for the different sectors.

The ultimate aim of an environmental management process is that it evolves as an integral part of a local authority's working practices. In this way, environmental management is not seen as an adjunct to other policy processes, but is integrated into the culture and day-to-day functioning of the organisation. The term 'evolves' is central to understanding how this process of integration is to come about. The complexity is such that it would be extremely difficult to proceed in any way other than incrementally.

TOOLS FOR FORMULATING, INTEGRATING AND IMPLEMENTING LOCAL ENVIRONMENTAL POLICIES

Local Agenda 21

Local authorities need all the skills and tools available to implement Local Agenda 21

Steps in developing a local agenda: Action in the local authority

The development and implementation of city-wide environmental strategies and action plans require effective community participation and partnership mechanisms, as called for in the Local Agenda 21 programme.

Local Agenda 21

Local Agenda 21 is essentially a strategic process of encouraging and controlling sustainable development. The development, management and implementation of this process requires all the skills and tools that can be brought to bear by a local authority and its community. Given the lack of expertise with this type of holistic process and the imperative of producing an initial strategy by the end of 1996, it is clear that local authorities need advice in defining the tools and management systems most appropriate for making progress.

12.   The initial strategy or plan is to be produced through a process of widespread public consultation and in a spirit which encourages a lasting consensus. The United Nations Association Sustainable Communities Project identify five basic principles for facilitating community involvement in the process:

• consultation should go well beyond established groups;

• the process should be non-adversarial;

• consultations should be mediated by external advisors;

• new groups should be continually encouraged to contribute;

• local interests and priorities should be reflected.

Local authorities and communities throughout Europe are now in the process of evolving their Local Agenda 21 strategies and a good deal of guidance has emerged on approaches and content. Advice available in the UK suggests the following steps (LGMB, 1994a):

Steps in developing a local agenda: Action in the local authority

• Managing and improving the local authority's own environmental performance.

• Integrating sustainable development aims into the local authority's policies and activities.

75

TOOLS FOR FORMULATING,
INTEGRATING AND
IMPLEMENTING LOCAL
ENVIRONMENTAL POLICIES

Steps in developing a
local agenda: Action in
the wider community

Steps in developing a local agenda: Action in the wider community

- Awareness raising and education.

- Consulting and involving the general public.

- Creating partnerships.

- Measuring, monitoring, evaluating and reporting on progress towards sustainability.

These steps are clearly in line with this Report - Local Agenda 21 presents an excellent opportunity for integrating and implementing the themes of the Sustainable Cities Project.

Policy option: environmental budgeting

15.

Ecological ideas such as natural capital, carrying capacity and constant natural assets already use the language and concepts of financial accountancy. Environmental budgeting develops this metaphor into a practical tool for environmental management. Techniques of financial accounting and budget management can help a city to manage its environmental 'wealth', 'income' and 'expenditure' with the same care and prudence as it manages its financial resources.

Environmental budgeting is an example of a new function for a traditional management tool

16.

Communities should establish a 'budget' of annual permissible levels of pollution, resource extraction, conversion of open space into development, and so on, and monitor and control activities in relation to these levels. The environmental budget must be brought into balance each year. In other words, the local authority must plan its actions each year to make sure that none of the 'accounts' in the environmental budget is 'overspent', and must monitor and report on their state (Storksdieck & Otto-Zimmerman, 1994).

Environmental budgeting in this sense does not involve any attempt to 'monetise' environmental costs or benefits. Instead, it applies techniques of financial accountancy - budget setting, measuring, monitoring, expenditure control and reporting - to non-financial stocks and flows. These are chosen through scientific and political processes because of their environmental significance. ICLEI recommend that the environmental budget is debated and approved in a public forum or council meeting.

Environmental budgeting is a management rather than a financial tool. It is different from what this report calls 'environmental factors in budgeting', which is a tool for reflecting environmental implications in financial budgeting. This is discussed below.

The development of an environmental budget is part of the target setting element of a wider environmental management process. The main benefit of this tool is that it facilitates access to decision making processes by making the issues more understandable to the general public. This access should then further promote involvement. As an inventory of environmental resources, a 'budget' also has a major role as a system for monitoring (see section 'Tools for measuring and monitoring sustainability impacts').

Local agenda 21:
Involving the public

TOOLS FOR FORMULATING,
INTEGRATING AND
IMPLEMENTING LOCAL
ENVIRONMENTAL POLICIES

Policy option:
Environmental
Management Systems

Environmental Management
Systems can help local
governments to implement their
commitments to sustainability as
stated in charters and strategies

Policy option: Environmental Management Systems

Standardised approaches to the preparation and implementation of environmental strategies are provided by environmental management systems such as the EU's Eco-Management and Audit (EMA) scheme. These require organisations to:

- adopt corporate environmental policies;

- identify significant environmental impacts;

- define and carry out 'programmes' of action to work towards the aims in ways consistent with the principles;

- monitor and report on progress towards explicit targets; and

- update policies and programmes in the light of the results of monitoring.

21.   Management systems specify procedures rather than the levels of performance that must be reached. The EMA scheme includes some safeguards against triviality, including requirements to work towards relevant best practice, to 'address' all 'significant' environmental effects of activities, and periodically to publish an accessible and externally verified statement of performance. However, a management system should be seen as a tool which can help a city authority to implement commitments to sustainability, rather than as itself part of those commitments. It can help to ensure that an environmental statement or charter is put into effect - but the environmental benefits achieved will depend on the contents of the charter (see Morphet et al, 1994).

As Chapter 2 indicated, the UK has adapted the Eco-Management scheme specifically for local authorities (Department of the Environment 1993a). This version promotes policy integration by:

- providing for corporate overview and co-ordination of environmental performance across the authority;

- requiring consideration of the environmental effects of the authority's policies and services as well as the direct effects of its own activities;

- giving guidance on the use of several of the 'tools' discussed in this section.

Work is under way to help define sustainability aims, and definitions of good practice can be adopted by users to ensure that the management system does indeed promote sustainable development.

Policy option:
Environmental Impact
Assessment (EIA)

Environmental Impact Assessment
is a tool for predicting the
environmental effects of a activity

Policy option: Environmental Impact Assessment (EIA)

As the name would suggest, Environmental Impact Assessment means the assessment of the effects of a proposed new activity or development on the environment. The EIA Directive 85/337/EEC (CEC, 1985) requires EIA to be carried out for many types of mainly large development project. While it is undoubtedly a useful tool, there are several problems with this mandatory form of EIA.

Some assessments concentrate on minor aesthetic issues and fail to address environmental questions adequately. Some procedures lack independent scrutiny by competent authorities with both environmental and development expertise, or a critical system of accreditation for consultants wishing to carry out assessments.

There are more fundamental problems. EIA is not carried out until a project proposal is well defined is after serious policy choices have already been made. Generally therefore EIA can influence cosmetic and palliative measures more effectively than fundamental choices. EIA only applies to a limited number of projects depending on factors such as the nature, size and location of the project, and not to the majority of local projects. In many countries statutory EIAs are carried out or supervised by regional agencies of national authorities and local authorities have little involvement.

Several hundred Germany municipalities have developed voluntary procedures for EIA and applied them to activities including strategic planning, development planning, procurement, and the construction of roads and buildings. These have filled gaps in the coverage of statutory EIA, notably for construction. Bologna in Italy has also developed procedures for EIA applied to strategic planning and projects at urban level. Some cities in eastern and central Europe where EIA is not mandatory have also developed voluntary schemes.

The five year review of the EIA Directive published by the European Commission in 1993 (CEC 1993c), covering the period to 1991, concluded that the full potential of the Directive had not yet been realised. It revealed that not all Member States had by then fully implemented the requirements of the Directive into national laws, and that there was considerable variation in practical compliance. In addition, practice has shown variation in the use of scoping provisions and methods, and in the effectiveness of public consultation. The diversity of approaches 'raises questions as to whether the Directive is really achieving its wider harmonisation objectives' (Sheate 1993). In order to produce greater benefits from the application of the EIA procedure, the Commission will propose amendments to the 1985 Directive including improvements to information and consultation requirements as is mentioned in the 1996 Work Programme of the Commission, and new project categories (CEC, 1994e). The Commission's review of the EIA Directive fails to address what is probably the greatest weakness of the present system - it generally applies only to project-level decision making and not to policies, programmes or plans.

Policy option: Strategic Environmental Assessment (SEA)

Assessment should now be applied to policies, programmes and plans. Strategic Environmental Assessment (SEA) should be undertaken as part of the policy design process. It requires that overall objectives should be stated, a variety of policy options to meet them considered, and their relative environmental impacts assessed. SEA needs to be undertaken early enough to influence the decision making process which determines which option to adopt, and indeed whether the policy, plan or programme should go ahead at all.

Environmental Impact Assessment should be modified in order to reach its full potential

27.

28.

Policy option: Strategic Environmental Assessment (SEA)

Strategic Environmental Assessment should be integrated into the policy process]

SUSTAINABLE CITIES

78

TOOLS FOR FORMULATING,
INTEGRATING AND
IMPLEMENTING LOCAL
ENVIRONMENTAL POLICIES

3   SUSTAINABLE URBAN MANAGEMENT

SEA offers a system of integrated environmental planning which could help achieve many of the objectives of the European Sustainable Cities Project. The difficulties with applying SEA are, however, quite substantial. They include technical complexity, lack of methodological experience, institutional inflexibility and a good deal of political misgiving. Despite these difficulties the European Commission are working on a proposal for SEA and several countries have introduced aspects of SEA.

Developing workable and consistent methods of SEA is a considerable challenge. As with EIA, standard guidelines are needed to ensure that assessments give sufficient weight to global and strategic impacts, and the quality of assessments should be policed by a specialist agency independent of developer interests.

32.   Because of the different scales at which SEA operates, there is a particular need to engender a spirit of co-operation among all actors in the environmental management process. The incorporation of environmental concerns into policies, plans and programmes should be integrated vertically between different levels of government and horizontally between agencies and segments of the community.

33.   Some progress on SEA is already being made. EIA of policies is obligatory in Denmark, Finland and the Netherlands. France, Germany and Sweden make some provision for SEA, largely within the framework of their existing EIA legislation. In the UK, there is a requirement that all development plans are subject to an environmental appraisal (Department of the Environment, 1993b).

3.5 Examples of SEA in practice

In the UK, Lancashire County Council is assessing the impacts of its existing Structure Plan policies on environmental resources in the county, to use the results as a 'filter' on policies being carried through into the next version of the plan, to use the County's state of the environment report to identify and formulate new policies, and to subject revised policies to the same assessment.

Alternative systems of Strategic Environmental Assessment

Most of the existing and proposed systems of SEA apply the provisions of EIA to other levels of decision making. These types of systems could be described as 'incremental'. They derive from the same conceptual base as EIA but recognise that more influence can be exerted at higher levels of decision making. However, a study published by the United Nations Economic Commission for Europe in 1992, which included case studies from Germany, Finland, Norway and the Netherlands, illustrated the difficulties of transferring mechanisms used in EIA of projects to strategic decision-making (UNECE, 1992). An alternative system, in place in the Netherlands, involves the installation of sustainable development objectives at the policy level and then the 'trickle down' of these objectives to lower levels (Glasson et al, 1994).

In the longer term, consideration should be given to extending the scope of EIA and SEA to consider all issues relevant to sustainability and not simply environmental effects (see for example Werrett 1994 and Glasson & Heaney 1993 who argue the need to improve the coverage of socio-economic impacts within the EIA process in the UK context).

TOOLS FOR GREENING THE MARKET

2.6

The purpose of these tools is to help reconcile the use of market mechanisms with the requirements of sustainability. The tools discussed are:

1.   Reconcile the market

- local environmental taxes, charges and levies;

- pricing structures;

- utility regulation;

- investment appraisal;

- environmental considerations in budgeting;

- environmental criteria in purchasing and tendering.

These are considered in turn. (For a fuller discussion see LGMB 1993b.) Section 1 in chapter 5 discusses the economic aspects of sustainability in more detail and provides illustrative examples of many of the tools.

Local government's ability to apply these tools varies between Member States. Where local government's influence is least, central government's responsibility is greatest.

Application of these tools depends upon the autonomy of local government

The most important tool of all in this area will generally be outside the scope of local government. This is ecological tax reform, which is concerned with shifting the balance of taxation from socially desirable factors such as employment on to undesirable environmental factors such as energy use and waste generation. This is discussed in chapter 5 section 1. A coherent policy of ecological tax reform at EU level could greatly reduce the need for the following tools to be applied at regional and local levels. This section is therefore to a certain extent reliant on the 'residuarity principle', that less well known counterpart to the 'subsidiarity principle', which states that where one level of government is unable or unwilling to take action appropriate to it, other levels have a responsibility to try to fill the gap, however incompletely.

Where powers exist, local authorities can raise taxes or charges on environmentally undesirable activities. Chapter 6 gives some examples of charging for road use and parking.

3

Policy option:
pricing structures

Price structures can be an
incentive for sustainability, as long
as the sustainable option is
cheaper

An elegant way to combine an environmental tax with other measures to promote behaviour change is hypothecation - earmarking the money raised by the tax directly for spending on measures to counter the damage, rather than treating it as general revenue. For example, if a city authority recycles car parking receipts into measures to reduce the need for parking (and thus driving), such as public transport subsidies, more money will be spent where the problem is most evident, and both the tax revenue and the need to spend it should decrease together over time. Similarly a local waste disposal levy could be used to subsidise recycling and waste reduction initiatives.

7.   Environmental charges directly linked to environmental spending in this way can be called levies rather than taxes. Levies alter environmental behaviour at both the taxing and the spending stage. They are attractive from the systems viewpoint because they connect problem and solution. Spending on the solution is linked automatically to the size of the problem: a negative feedback loop. Clearly this only works if the scope of the spending is tightly restricted. Spending parking levies on more generally defined 'environmental improvements' will not have this desirable feedback effect. Spending them on further parking provision will have the opposite, positive feedback effect!

Policy option: pricing structures

8.   Price structures often give no incentive, or even a disincentive, to sustainable behaviour. For example:

- flat rate charges for services such as water and sewerage, or payment for services such as waste collection out of local taxation, give no incentive to users to conserve resources;

- lower energy tariffs for large users can make it worthwhile for customers just below the qualifying threshold to waste energy in order to qualify;

- as argued above, the high fixed costs of car ownership and low marginal costs per mile driven mean that once a household has a car it will save money by using it whenever possible in preference to public transport, which looks more expensive at the point of use because the ticket price includes a share of the fixed costs.

Sustainable behaviour can be made more attractive by changing the structure of prices to ensure that reducing environmental impact always saves money, and that sustainable options are cheaper at the point of use. For example:

- resource charges should increase with the amount used. Water supply can be metered In many German cities, waste collection charges depend on the size of a household's bin;

- utility tariffs should be designed so there is never a point where using *more* costs *less;*

- the cost at the point of use of environmentally undesirable options such as car use can be increased by tolls, road pricing, local fuel taxation and parking charges. At the same time the cost at the point of use of more sustainable options such as public transport can be reduced by municipal subsidy supported by local taxation (which should be regarded simply as the 'fixed cost' of the city infrastructure).

Charging for basic services can disadvantage people on low incomes. They can be protected through special measures such as grants to install energy efficiency measures. Alternatively, pricing structures can be designed to meet equity as well as environmental objectives. For example the Sri Lankan electricity tariff has three bands. Every household can buy a 'subsistence' level of consumption at a very cheap rate. For higher levels of consumption there is a higher 'standard' tariff rate, and then a very high 'luxury' rate. Under this tariff, everyone can afford a basic level of provision and everyone has an incentive to avoid waste. Such a structure could be adapted for energy in Europe. The same principle could be applied to avoid conflict between conservation and equity in other 'resource pricing' areas:

Price structures designed to meet equity objectives

- metering of domestic water supplies need not deprive lower-income families of the freedom to wash if the 'subsistence level' - enough water for cooking and hygiene - is free or sold at a very low tariff;

- 'smart' technologies for road pricing could differentiate between different categories of user, and (for example) give elderly or disabled users cheaper rates, or a certain number of free trips, or toll-free access to certain amenities;

- Freiburg was the first city in Germany to introduce a linear time-variable charge index for electricity. There is no standing charge, so that those using less energy also pay less. Electricity meters have been modified so consumption can be measured according to three different time periods.

Policy option: utility regulation

In many US states, regulators only allow gas and electricity companies to charge their customers for investments which can be shown to be the most cost-effective way of responding to demand. In many cases it is cheaper for the energy company to reduce demand by selling, or even giving away, insulation, heating controls and other energy-saving measures, than to meet demand by building a power station. In such cases the regulator will not allow the company to pass the cost of the power station on to its customers, but will allow it to add the cost of the insulation programme onto fuel bills.

Policy option:
utility regulation

Under this system, energy companies routinely run substantial energy conservation programmes - and make profits out of doing so. 'Least cost planning' as it is called resolves the contradiction between conservation and commerce by making conservation activities themselves a source of profit (Association for the Conservation of Energy, 1991).

Where least cost planning has not been introduced, some of its benefits can be achieved through an 'energy services' approach, where the end user buys the services provided through energy - for example warm space or levels of lighting rather than energy itself - from an intermediary 'energy service company' or ESCO which makes its profit by providing the contracted level of *service* with the minimum amount of *energy*. An example is contract energy management, where a specialist company provides the capital and the technical expertise to install energy-saving measures, recoups its investment from the savings in fuel bills over an agreed period, and then hands the equipment over to the 'host' organisation. Local authorities should be encouraged to apply energy service approaches in their own operations and promote them in the wider community.

Inherent in any approach to utility regulation must be a programme of consumer advice. The benefits of least cost planning, for example, can only be realised if consumers can be persuaded to adopt energy saving measures. This can partly be achieved through market mechanisms (grants, subsidies, pricing levels, etc.) but of equal importance will be the availability of information and advice. Energy saving trusts and advice centres should therefore be supported and the message of energy conservation effectively marketed.

Policy option: investment
appraisal

Whole life asset management should be a guiding principle in investment appraisal

Policy option: investment appraisal

15. The anti-sustainability results of conventional investment appraisal methods were discussed in section 1. There is an alternative method for appraising investments, 'whole life asset management'. As the name suggests, it is based on the idea of seeking the best ratio of benefits to costs over the whole life of an asset, rather than a quick payback. As a rule it will result in more durable, adaptable and resource-efficient designs of capital assets such as buildings and equipment.

16. Establishing whole-life asset management as standard practice in local government would require changes to both investment appraisal guidelines and funding patterns. For example, it would be necessary for reductions in likely longer term revenue costs to be reflected in levels of initial capital expenditure. It can be facilitated by financial control regimes which do not separate 'revenue' from 'capital' budgets.

'Whole life' approaches should be seen not as a novelty but as a return to the intuitively sensible approach to durability which guided most public works investment throughout Europe until the recent decades, and which made possible the construction of Europe's urban architectural heritage. The take-over of public service investment by commercial methods of appraisal is a recent and transient phenomenon, most of whose results are likely to decay and disappear before earlier buildings built to higher standards.

The introduction of environmental considerations into the economic decision making of a local authority is an essential component of any environmental management process. This is in fact not a single tool but an element that overlaps with many of the others discussed in this section and encompasses the environmental consideration of budgeting. Thus, ensuring that policy decisions are appraised for their environmental implications is a form of SEA and incorporating environmental assessment into an authority's investment strategy is an element of environmental plan making and EMAS.

Because of the wide-ranging implications of this tool, it is an aspect of environmental management that has hitherto received little attention. It strikes at the very heart of the prevailing power interests both inside and outside local government.

Policy option: environmental considerations in budgeting

Budgetary and project appraisal processes must recognise costs and benefits beyond separate sectoral or functional interests. For example, decisions about whether to maintain small schools should not be taken purely in terms of efficiency of delivery of the service concerned, but must also take into account the broader environmental and social implications, such as patterns of travel, viability of small communities, and effects on disadvantaged groups.

Understanding of the environmental efficiency of expenditure - the environmental benefit or cost of each unit of money spent or saved - must permeate all public service decision taking. This does not mean, as is sometimes assumed, that environmental costs and benefits must be converted into monetary terms - a very contentious issue - but only that some mechanism exists to identify and quantify environmental costs and benefits and include them together with financial factors in the considerations guiding the decision. The relative weighting of the different types of cost and benefit can be carried out through multi-variate techniques such as Sustainability Assessment Maps (Clayton & Radcliffe 1993).

Polciy option: environmental considerations in purchasing and tendering

As large consumers of goods and services, city authorities can have significant buying power and the signals they give about purchasing priorities can be very influential. Inclusion of environmental criteria in specifications can both support manufacturers of sustainable products directly and give a valuable signal to both suppliers and other purchasers. Wherever a city authority is buying goods or obtaining services through a commercial contracting or tendering process, environmental criteria should be included in the tender specifications. This can ensure that contracted-out services meet the same environmental standards as provision in-house. This is becoming increasingly important as de-regulation and privatisation of local government services increases the role of the private sector. Inclusion of explicit environmental requirements in internal service level agreements can likewise ensure that separation of 'purchaser' and 'provider' functions helps rather than hinders improvement in environmental performance. This presupposes a firm commitment to the view that good environmental performance is an integral part of the service being delivered, rather than an extraneous distraction.

The degree of flexibility that local authorities have in introducing environmental criteria into purchasing and tendering policies is governed by their legal mandate. Provided environmental requirements are expressed in generic terms and care is taken to avoid restriction of competition (for example by giving competitive bidders a reasonable time to obtain or achieve a requirement currently only held by one), environmental purchasing will generally be consistent with EU procurement directives. A general rule is that when requirements are expressed generally and where restrictions on competition are avoided, then there is considerable scope for specifying minimum environmental standards. However, a specific preference for local manufacture, which would be highly desirable on sustainability grounds to reduce transport of goods, would not be consistent with the principles of the Single European Market.

Local authority purchasing and
tendering can be a powerful tool
for greening the market

Of all the issues related to 'greening' economic activity this is probably the one where
a local authority can have greatest immediate impact. It is also one where experience has
shown that vast improvements in environmental performance can be achieved with little
disruption and with the possibility of cost savings. It is firstly an issue of awareness and
then an issue of information, assimilation and dissemination.

3.6 An environmental purchasing policy, Woking, UK

Woking Borough Council is a local authority that has adopted a purchasing policy based
on the specification of minimum environmental standards. Their policy contains an analysis
of the issues and a set of eight product category 'Guides' for use by purchasing managers.
The policy also includes an analysis of the cost implications, concluding that if the
recommendations are developed alongside a strategic approach to waste reduction (based
on the 4-R's: reduce, reuse, repair, recycle), there are clear opportunities for cost savings.

3.7 Integration in practice, Helsingor, Denmark

As an example, the town of Helsingor has achieved an integrated approach to energy and
waste management through the combination of a number of policy instruments and
institutional features, including some of the market mechanisms discussed in the preceding
section.

Waste collection charging. Municipalities are required to cover the costs of collecting and
disposing of waste in their charges to householders and other waste producers. Waste
collection charges are required by law to be completely separate from other local authority
funding, and completely transparent. This means that methods of collection and disposal
are under local democratic control. Voters in Helsingor voted for more recycling and the
slightly higher household waste collection charges needed to fund it.

Local authority powers over waste collection. Municipalities have legal power to specify
how householders present their waste for collection. Helsingor ran careful trials and broad
consultations to establish the most convenient and acceptable way to collect organic
waste. But having decided on a method, they can require all households to conform.

Local authority powers to run enterprises. Helsingor could choose whether to build and
own the plant itself, or contract a private company to do so, or to work in partnership
with other agencies including municipalities or companies as convenient.

The plant took advantage of Government 'soft loans' for sustainable energy projects.

The Danish government has invested in the heat distribution network which allows the
plant to sell its waste heat, doubling the overall energy conversion efficiency.

The national electricity grid gives a standard premium price for all electricity generated
from renewable sources. Projects can be designed around this.

A further step towards the 'greening' of purchasing and contracting can be taken by developing co-operative ventures with other organisations and product and service providers. An environmental purchasing consortium, for example, would help rationalise the work of participatory organisations and achieve economies of scale.

Another aspect of this issue is the 'greening' of a local authority's own investment funds. In the UK, the London Boroughs of Richmond and Sutton have both taken steps to ensure that their pension funds are invested in companies with a proven ethical and environmental code. In some EU Member States, pension fund trustees are under a legal duty to maximise the financial return on funds but even then a certain amount of social or environmental proactiveness can be justified on prudential grounds. There is considerable scope for making a tangible contribution with what are often very large sums of money. At the same time, the authority is sending out a message of environmental responsibility to the business community.

Systems for managing information

2.7

1.

Systems of environmental information are formalised ways of getting access to data, manipulating this data and then communicating with the intended audiences. These systems have always existed but recent technological advances have meant that more sophisticated mechanisms are now widely available. This in turn has lead to an information 'explosion' whereby the amount and accessibility of data has grown exponentially. The main concern now is not, in most cases, the lack of data but where to look for it and how to handle it. Indeed, many of the management tools discussed in this section are attempts to apply a systematic process so as to make more efficient use of the available data.

While the need to improve existing information systems and incorporate new technology is still an important concern, it is equally important to ensure that the systems are performing their functions satisfactorily. This is largely an issue of human behaviour and organisational culture. The behavioural factors relate to with the capacity of individuals to absorb information and to accept new technology. All too often information technology develops faster than the ability of individuals to use it. The problems faced by individuals are accumulated and expressed at the organisation level. Typically an organisation's culture is very slow to accommodate change. Thus an improved system for handling information may not be matched with new structures for using it. Likewise, hierarchical control might discourage dissemination of information in an attempt to maintain the existing order.

Green investments

Information systems are now entering a new phase of development where the emphasis is on promoting interest and making the technology more user-friendly. Advances in the application of multi-media, interactive CD Roms, etc. should help ensure that innovation is accompanied by widespread acceptance. Another area of current interest is in the development of higher level information co-ordination systems. This recognises that the management of information is of crucial importance and that mechanisms need to be devised to ensure most effective use.

Methods of data
collection

Consistent and comparable
methods of data collection are
necessary to order information
chaos

Methods of data collection

Some of the tools for data collection are discussed in other sub-sections in relation to the technical management of data. Another dimension concerns the characteristics of data and the uses to which it is put.

On a technical level data must be consistent and comparable. It must therefore be collected for a defined purpose and must be in a form that facilitates up-dating and contributes to decision making. While it is taken for granted that the data should be accurate, of equal importance is that the data is *seen* to be accurate and that the collection methods are transparent. This is what might be termed the 'political' dimension of data collection. Questions must be asked about who is collecting the data, the purpose that it is deemed to serve, the definition of data needs and, most importantly, who has access to the data (and this is not just physical access - see below). Asking these questions is a recognition that information is a political tool and must therefore be seen to be serving democratic ends. Also of importance is the definition of targets and indicators (see 'Tools for measuring and monitoring sustainability impacts and successes'). Data should be collected for a purpose and that purpose should be defined in terms of measurable targets. The iterative process of target setting and indicator identification must therefore be conducted with the involvement of all interested groups.

6.   A good deal of work still needs to be done on the integration of data collection at different scales - local, regional, national and European. All these levels are involved in data collection but their systems are not always co-ordinated and this can lead to duplication of effort and lack of comparability.

Access to and dissemination of information serves democratic ends

Information should be made accessible and then disseminated as widely as possible. Accessibility is not simply a physical issue - it is a matter of interest and resonance. Far too often, information for a non-professional audience is neither understandable nor of direct relevance to large sections of the community. Similarly, detailed reports with complicated technical data are rarely of interest to the public and there is often no attempt to adapt the information for a wider audience. Information is often disseminated through traditional, static, media such as reports and exhibitions. Advances in technology, such as multi-media presentation, use of the Internet, interactive displays, modelling and visioning offer the opportunity for information to be made more interesting and therefore more accessible.

Access to and
dissemination of
information should
be user defined

Access to and dissemination of information should be user defined

The public audience will consist of many sub-groups each with their own requirements, levels of competence and interests. Many of these sub-groups are clearly definable, such as ethnic minorities, specialist interest groups, age groups, etc.. Others, however, might require a good deal of effort to identify. Social and economic groupings might exist where not even the members of the groups realise that they share common characteristics. An example of this is the classification used by sociologists whereby groups are defined according to age, sex, education, income, etc.. All groups, both tangible and intangible, have got different information needs and effective communication will depend on these needs being met.

Finally, the European legislation on Freedom of Access to Environmental Information requires that public bodies make most information which they hold accessible to the public. In order for this legislation to be effective there needs to a concerted effort in informing people what is available and training provided on retrieval and use.

Marketing

Marketing and public relations are often a relatively weak area of expertise among urban environment managers, trained as they are in specialist professions rather than in communication techniques. However, the imperative of generating community involvement and raising awareness demands that attention is paid to marketing the sustainability message. All the mechanisms mentioned in this section can be of use and marketing experts might need to be brought in at various stages, such as the launch of an initiative, the publication of a report, etc.

TOOLS FOR MEASURING AND MONITORING SUSTAINABILITY IMPACTS AND SUCCESS

This group of tools attempt to reconcile the search for quantifiable policy objectives and measures of success with sustainability aims. The key is to define sustainability indicators, establish clear operational targets and monitor the effectiveness of management processes.

Policy option: the usefulness of sustainability indicators

Sustainability indicators are definable, measurable features of the world whose absolute levels or rate and direction of change are intended to reveal whether the world (or a city) is becoming more or less sustainable.

There is always a two-way process. Indicators are implied by policy aims, but they also help define and mould them. Per capita GDP was implied as an indicator by a certain view of economic progress. However it has since come to embody and constitute progress, to the virtual exclusion of other indicators.

The choice of indicators is therefore never a purely technical matter, but always and inescapably a matter of policy choice with important consequences. It should therefore always be open to, and accountable to, policy processes.

Policy option:
the usefulness of
sustainability
indicators

Sustainability indicators help to
define policy aims, and are in turn
defined by policy objectives

Sustainability indicators should be
defined by open, transparent, and
democratic processes

Advantages of sustainability
indicators

This is particularly true of sustainability indicators. Because sustainability is a new and unfamiliar topic, the process of defining indicators is playing a very influential role in constituting notions of what is sustainable development. In many policy areas, practitioners and other interested parties can judge new proposed indicators against a clear and secure prior understanding of the subject. Few people feel that they have such an understanding of sustainability. A deficient or unbalanced set of sustainability indicators may therefore impoverish or distort our understanding of sustainable development, rather than provoking rejection of the indicators.

6. It is therefore especially important that any process of choosing sustainability indicators should be explicit, open and transparent, and that the reasoning behind the choice should be made clear to all those with an interest. Another important response to the problem of choice in sustainability indicators is to involve local communities.

7. A second, related problem is the tension between ease of measurement and policy significance. Indicators have to be both practically useful and related to policy aims. Hard-pressed practitioners will very reasonably prefer indicators which can be measured easily and which bear a clear and direct relationship to their work. But the indicators which are easiest to measure will not necessarily capture whatever is most important in a particular policy area - or even important at all. In many fields, the quantity of activity or change - which is most straightforward to measure - is much less significant than its quality, which is harder to measure. It is important to guard against giving too much weight to minor or irrelevant factors simply because they are easy to measure.

In summary, the advantages of indicators are:

- directing information collection and making it accessible to decision-makers and the public;

- helping decision making by providing quantifiable measures to guide the application of institutional mechanisms and operational tools, particularly in relation to specifying targets;

- allowing for comparison over time and space;

- allowing effectiveness to be measured and progress to be assessed;

- if combined into indices, providing a convenient summary of data;

- enabling the assessment of environmental components which cannot be measured directly but instead measuring variables which indicate the presence or condition of that component.

- allowing for integration and comparability between issues within the conception of the urban ecosystem;

- providing a vision and a range of signposts for a desired future state;

- monitoring conditions, changes, performance, actions, activity and attitudes.

Typology of Sustainability Indicators

The first thing to note when discussing types of indicators is that they are synthetic. They have no meaning other than that defined by the purpose for which they have been selected. There is therefore no universal set of indicators, and they can be chosen and combined in any form that most suits the conceptual purposes involved. In relation to local government environmental policies, for example, indicators will be defined according to goals and objectives in a plan or strategy. At national level they could be defined by government policies and international agreements.

The typology presented below focuses first on environmental indicators and then on quality of life indicators. The links between the two will also be explored. The topic of indicators is extensive and impossible to cover comprehensively in this context. Further information on these indicators and other types of indicators can be found in the report Indicators for Urban Policies (Ville de Rennes, 1995).

Environmental Indicators

Broadly speaking environmental indicators can be divided into two types: environmental quality indicators and environmental performance indicators.

- Environmental Quality Indicators

    Often referred to as primary indicators, these are used to measure the condition of key environmental features. The features chosen should either be significant in terms of level of impact or scarcity or they could be indicative in that they represent an overall measure of quality or basic trends. Examples of the former are emissions of gases like CO_2 and SO_2 and of the latter, chemical oxygen demand (COD) in water and quantity of waste generated. Environmental Quality Indicators provide a tool to help quantify sustainability impacts.

- Environmental Performance Indicators

    These do not measure the condition of the environment directly but rather the influence of human activities on the environment. They include both secondary indicators which measure basic quality by proxy and the general effectiveness of policy and tertiary indicators which assess the direct effect of particular policies. Examples include the level of economic activity, public opinion, number of protected areas and amount of energy generated. Environmental Performance Indicators are tools for monitoring the outcome of policy decisions.

    A point to note is the difference between Direct and Indirect Performance Indicators. An organisation's practices, over which there is direct control, can be measured using objective and clearly defined indicators. The amount of energy consumed or waste produced are examples of such direct performance indicators. In the case of policies, a public sector body can establish indicators and set targets but does not have direct control over the activities of others. A more indirect performance indicator is therefore required, one which measures the activities of the public sector authority but recognises that these only influence the actions of others. An example of this would be the level of response to a campaign promoting energy conservation.

11.

Another type of indicator which is related to the two already mentioned but of a different order, concerns the integration of environmental concerns in economic policies. For the want of a convenient title, these may be called Environmental Accounting Indicators. There are two broad forms that these indicators can take: putting an economic valuation on environmental costs and benefits is a means to measure performance, while a system of natural resource accounts can be used to measure quality. Environmental accounting indicators are therefore not intrinsically different to the other two but are used for a fundamentally different purpose.

A final distinction is between indicators for purely *internal use* in an organisation and those for *external use*. This is an important distinction because the two sets need not correspond to each other. Internal indicators are designed to review policies and practices and thereby provide information and feedback to decision-makers. They should therefore be chosen for their ease, reliability and representativeness in measuring operational procedures, outcomes, levels of satisfaction, achievement against standards, etc.. External indicators should be derived from those used internally but have an overriding requirement of providing information in a digestible form. Essential qualities are therefore accessibility, clarity and brevity. Clearly, internal and external indicators perform different tasks and it would be a mistake to misuse them.

- Environmental Pressure Indices

Eurostat (the Statistical Office of the European Communities) is currently investigating the possibility of establishing an environmental pressure index for urban areas, as part of the 'European System of Environmental Pressure Indices'. The development of such indices, and their eventual integration into a system of green national accounts, was at the core of a Communication from the Commission to Council and European Parliament in 1994 (CEC, 1994f).

Environmental Pressure Indices

Quality indicators

Within the typology of sustainability indicators the second main category comprises those which address quality of life. The concept of quality of life is quite vague but it can be usefully interpreted as a means to describe the attributes of sustainability to the general public. Quality of life indicators are therefore not always different from environmental indicators but they are more user-friendly, and should be widely recognisable and meaningful to a broad cross section of the community. They translate 'technical' environmental indicators into visible and emotive indicators which will help generate and facilitate community involvement. In terms of Local Agenda 21 Strategies, it is quality of life rather than environmental indicators which will be of most interest to the public.

Two principal types of quality of life indicators can be identified. Provocative Indicators are designed to stimulate thought and concern by interpreting environmental factors in terms that people can easily relate to. The purpose is literally to provoke a response and thereby bring about positive change. Issues include open space, urban form, health, amenity, noise, security and communication. Examples of provocative indicators are the length of time a car is owned and the number of people who grow their own food. Indicators of

Quality indicators

Quality of life indicators facilitate community involvement

The surface makes the difference

Sustainable Lifestyle Options attempt to measure some of the more qualitative elements of sustainability incorporating subjective values into the policy making arena. Some of the factors are personal growth, education, aesthetics, play and leisure, creativity and imagination.

3.8 Examples of European experience with indicators

At the European level, one of the most influential projects is being conducted by the Strategies for Sustainability working group of the Eurocities Environment Committee. They have initiated a project to develop a common set of indicators based on the same methodologies, standards and measurements. The aim is to facilitate comparison between different locations and contexts. Cities involved are Amsterdam, Bilbao, Bradford, Bristol, Cardiff, Lyon, Munich, Nurnberg, Rotterdam and Strasbourg.

At the national level, Norway, the UK and the Netherlands have been making considerable progress. *Norway* is at the forefront of developments in natural resource accounting. More recently a programme of environmental quality indicators has been initiated to complement the resource accounts and to contribute to the policy making process. Three categories of indicators have been developed to reflect primary environmental quality, non-renewable resources and renewable resources. The Ministry of the Environment have published a discussion paper with suggestions on how the indicators may be used.

In the *UK*, the main work on sustainability indicators has been organised by the UK Local Government Management Board (LGMB). In 1994 they published a report of the first phase of work designed to arrive at a common set of indicators for use by local authorities. Criteria used to choose indicators are that they are relevant, build on rather than supplant existing reporting mechanisms, reflect a range of scales, encourage political commitment and community participation, and that they incorporate the concept of environmental carrying capacity. A menu of 101 indicators have been identified under 13 different headings or themes. These were then piloted in selected local authorities and the lessons from their practical application have also been published.

The process of developing indicators in *The Netherlands* is quite well advanced. The Government's National Environmental Policy Plan is seeking to apply indicators in the pursuit of sustainable development. At the same time, a number of other agencies are pushing forward the agenda of sustainability. In particular, the pressure group Milieudefensie have attempted to define what a future sustainable society would look like by calculating the availability of essential resources.

Targets

Indicators guide action through the setting of targets. This is a crucial part of the mechanism of the Eco-Management and Audit scheme and similar approaches. Part of the way they ensure that commitments are implemented is to require explicit targets to be set for all actions, and the people responsible for reaching the targets to be identified, and then monitor and report progress in terms of those targets.

Targets

Indicators guide action through target setting

Targets for environment indicators
are set in relation to carrying
capacity

17.

Vertical and horizontal integration
requires specification of targets at
each level

18.

Organisations and individuals can also set targets for indicators of environmental performance level. These may well be 'instrumental' targets - set to secure a commitment to a direction of change - rather than attempting to reflect any ultimately desirable level.

Targets for environment indicators are of a different kind. They are determined not by human choice but by the physical realities of global carrying capacity thresholds and human impacts on them. There is still considerable uncertainty about these at a global level. However at regional and smaller scales it is often possible to identify cases where a carrying capacity threshold is being broken, and to estimate the change in human activity needed to bring pressure back within it.

This distinction is important because it helps to clarify the relationship between targets and indicators. In relation to measures of environmental quality, the indicator will be chosen to reflect a politically defined target. This target will in turn be an operational objective emanating from a scientific assessment of environmental carrying capacities. Environmental performance indicators can, but do not necessarily, reflect a predetermined target. There are many cases where the indicator can be chosen and then an appropriate target assigned (for example, measures of public opinion and level of economic activity). The most important thing to bear in mind is that the relationship between targets and indicators is iterative, each helping to define the other.

Targets are useful only in so far as they help in the achievement of policy goals. They must therefore be meaningful and measurable. Systems for monitoring should be employed to ensure that information is continually fed back and that progress is kept under review. There should be a target setting process from the national to the local level. Targets should be defined according to the aims and objectives of sustainable development. This implies a tiered system of sustainability strategies (vertical integration) and co-operation within sectors (horizontal integration).

Vertical integration requires further development of the various national and international sustainability strategies. These range from Agenda 21 to the EU's 'Towards Sustainability' and the national strategies now being developed throughout Europe. National and international strategies will require local implementation, so more effort needs to be put into defining the actions that need to take place at the local level. Specification of actions will also require the detailing of powers and resources.

With regard to horizontal integration, there are three interrelated areas of activity where a target setting approach should be introduced. The first relates to the management tools discussed in 'Tools for formulating, integrating and implementing local environmental policies'. As experience is gained with using these tools, more opportunities will arise for introducing a higher degree of specification. This will allow targets to be defined at a local level and procedures to be put in place to measure achievement. The second area of activity is in the development of Local Agenda 21 strategies. This is related to the first, but involves a more explicit recognition of the role of a local community in the formation of goals and specification of objectives. The targets emanating from this

(Inter)national policies require
local implementation

process are likely to be implemented through the tools identified in section 'Tools for formulating, integrating and implementing local environmental policies', but will be of a different order from those which a local authority acting on its own would specify. The third area of activity involves the introduction of sustainability targets into all other sectors of local authority policy. This relates in particular to local economic development plans. Sustainability targets must be integrated with all other areas of activity and not developed within a separate process.

The more developed and localised a target, the easier it is to attach indicators. There are two issues of particular importance here. The first is a re-emphasis of the point made above that the implementation of sustainability goals will take place at the local level and therefore this is the level where effort, power and resources need to be concentrated. This means that targets must be defined at the lowest level possible and that the target characteristics are detailed as precisely as possible (for example in terms of priority, cost, timespan, etc.). The second issue relates to the sequence of activities involved in defining targets and identifying indicators. The importance of targets is that they provide 'staging posts' against which performance can be measured.

Targets need to be defined according to the subsidiarity principle

Important characteristics of targets

There are a number of important characteristics of targets which should be noted. First, targets must be defined in terms of measurable indicators. Targets defined in relation to environmental performance will have the objective of achieving goals defined in terms of environmental quality. Reducing CO_2 emissions from transport, for example, will be designed to achieve a predetermined target so as to contribute towards the control of global warming. Second, there may be a range of targets for each indicator and these must be set at the level of that indicator. Thus a target for improving air quality in a city may be set using levels of carbon monoxide while a national air quality target may be measured using carbon dioxide (although CO_2 also can be used at city level). Third, no target may be totally accurate. Scientific uncertainty dictates that the 'precautionary principle' should be evoked and targets defined according to 'safe minimum standards'. Finally, and following from the above, all targets must be recognised for being ultimately political. Though informed by science, decisions will be made through the political process. Targets should therefore be set on a consensus basis, with widespread involvement.

Environmental budgeting is a useful tool in both helping to define targets and as an element in a system for monitoring progress.

SYSTEMS FOR MONITORING

Policy option: Systems for monitoring sustainable development must be integrated in all policy processes

2.9

Policy option: Systems for monitoring sustainable development must be integrated in all policy processes

The importance of monitoring systems in delivering sustainable development means that they should receive special attention. Systems for monitoring must be built into all processes and linked to the use of all other management tools. Monitoring must be a key part of the policy process and of plan making. It should be borne in mind, however, that monitoring systems are only one element in a comprehensive process and must therefore be dealt with in this way. This section discusses some of the essential elements of a monitoring system.

Policy option:
Sustainability indicators
are an integral part of
any monitoring system

Policy option:
SoE reporting should be
undertaken on a regular
basis   4.

5.

SoE reporting can be used for
developing and formulating
policies or for reviewing policies

Policy option: Sustainability indicators are an integral part of any monitoring system

The ultimate purpose of indicators is that they measure environmental conditions and trends and thereby allow an assessment of the effectiveness of policy. If the indicators are not continually monitored, then they serve no useful purpose.

The elements in a monitoring system will be determined by the type of indicator that is being measured. Environmental quality indicators can be monitored through a process of state of the environment reporting (see below). Environmental performance indicators will be monitored through an on-going environmental management process. To be useful, the results of the monitoring will need to be communicated. This requires the integration of the monitoring system with a management system such as EMAS.

Policy option: SoE reporting should be undertaken on a regular basis

This should not just assess current state but also desired future states. It should help determine the capacity of different locations for different purposes. SoE reporting can also be used to compare situations in different cities and to create a climate of competition between cities in their work towards sustainability. SoE reports are used in this way in both Germany and Italy.

SoE reporting is a process of environmental monitoring that has gradually developed over the last two decades. It has its origins in the 1969 US National Environmental Policy Act (NEPA) and has since spread throughout the world. Local authorities in Europe have for a long time undertaken many of the tasks of SoE reporting but it was not until the late 1980's that the systematic SoE process became widely used. It is this systematic process that is crucial in understanding the purpose of SoE reporting. Local authorities and other organisations collect and process vast amounts of environmental data. SoE reporting aims to ensure that this information is comprehensive in that it covers all essential issues and that it is put to use by feeding it into the policy making process.

Two principal types of SoE reporting may be distinguished. The first is a comprehensive review of environmental quality. This is an attempt at a synoptic process, looking to assess the overall condition of a wide range of environmental parameters and to evaluate key environmental quality indicators. This type of review is of course potentially endless, and part of the SoE process will be to prioritise issues. Where information is hard to find or where the quality of the information is poor, this may be noted for further action.

The second type of SoE reporting is the policy-orientated SoE. This is where the SoE process links up with the environmental management tools discussed in section 'Tools for formulating, integrating and implementing local environmental policies'. Instead of attempting to be comprehensive, the SoE aims to collect information that specifically relates to setting or assessing policy goals. These policy goals can be measured using a range of environmental performance indicators. This approach is, therefore, far more pragmatic, but risks defining environmental quality in purely functional terms and thereby losing the broader picture. In reality, some kind of balance between the comprehensive SoE and the policy-orientated SoE processes should be struck. The scope and effectiveness of SoE reporting can be judged by referring to the quality of decisions and policies made as a result.

There are currently two major problems with SoE reporting. The first is that the quality of environmental monitoring is very variable across Europe. Inconsistencies in definition, different sampling frequencies, uncertainties in classification, etc. result in problems of comparison both at the local level and between different regions. The second major problem arises out of the lack of consensus on a single set of environmental indicators. This makes it difficult to introduce findings into the policy process.

The quality of environmental monitoring varies between Member States and there is no consensus on a single set of environmental indicators

As it stands, SoE reporting is essentially a reactive process, seeking to assess the quality of the environment that results from various human impacts. There is considerable scope for introducing an element of proactive planning into the process by evaluating a range of desired future states. This could begin by assessing the capacity of different locations for different purposes. This type of capacity planning already takes place in many areas but has not yet been systematically incorporated into the SoE process. A further phase of development could be to use the SoE report to help outline a vision of a sustainable society. This vision could become an important element in goal setting and could be a tool of community involvement. This is the approach adopted in Helsinki where the SoE report is an integral part of the municipality's programme of public awareness raising.

On the one hand, an environmental budget is a systematic process of community target setting. At the same time, it aims to monitor achievement against these targets and to communicate the findings in an accessible form to decision makers and the public. There would appear to be merit in using an environmental budget alongside a SoE report. The information gathered from the SoE surveying could be presented to the public as a budget and thereby help stimulate debate and gain more community involvement in the policy formation and implementation process.

10.   Environmental budgeting is both a decision making tool and a monitoring system

Policy option: Community profiling can help the community to define itself and the value of the local environment

Policy option: Community profiling can help the community to define itself and the value of the local environment

In addition to monitoring the state of the local environment in scientific terms, effort should be directed towards gauging the public's perceptions of the environment and needs in relation to health, social services and community development. A range of community profiling techniques have been developed for this purpose. These techniques work to help a community define both itself and what they consider valuable in their locality. This can serve to empower the community by getting them involved in the environmental management process and in addition helps ensure that the local authority is addressing all the relevant issues. Once a profile has been established it can be used to monitor progress by assessing the actual and perceived changes in quality of life.

Policy option:
Public involvement in
monitoring systems

Policy option: 13.
Technology can assist
environmental
monitoring

A range of tools exists to integrate
sustainable development in policy
making processes at all levels

Supranational and national
governments have a major role in
developing and using tools for
sustainable development

Diversity and experiment with
tools is needed

Policy option: Public involvement in monitoring systems

Ultimately it will be the public, and not simply objective measures of environmental performance, that will decide whether sustainable development is being achieved or not. Two important measures of sustainability are environmental quality and public awareness. Both of these aspects are directly related to people's everyday lives, and the public's co-operation in deciding whether change has occurred is therefore essential. Mechanisms for public involvement were discussed above.

Policy option: Technology can assist environmental monitoring

Technological issues are beyond the scope of this report. Suffice it to say that the technical methods and equipment of environmental monitoring are continually developing and have expanded the scope for more detailed and comprehensive analysis. Significant advances have been made in the areas of remote sensing, geographic information systems, thermographic imaging and pollution measurement. Within resource constraints, local authorities should endeavour to keep up-to-date with the technology and to maintain the necessary professional expertise.

3   CONCLUSIONS

This section has addressed the challenge of policy integration for sustainability and reviewed a range of environmental management tools which cities can use in seeking to manage their areas in more sustainable ways. Some of these are already familiar, or are developments from familiar ones. Others are new.

At city level, local strategies for sustainability which have the commitment and active participation of the local community can provide frameworks for effective action and experiment.

If Europe's cities are to achieve their sustainability promise, governments must also allow cities maximum freedom to apply suitable tools at local level. Municipal and regional governments must be granted appropriate powers and resources, for example for taxation, subsidy, regulation and investment.

National governments and the EU should also consider application of the integrative tools set out above. Indeed some of them, especially those concerned with the economic framework, can only be applied at national and supranational level.

National governments should define, disseminate, promote and monitor good practice in the integrative management tools, for example Eco-Management and Audit, EIA, SEA and sustainability indicators. More effective application of existing legislative frameworks is needed.

By recognising the 'systems' level, the tools set out in this section should help urban environmental policy to become more sophisticated and effective. But it follows from the discussion of complexity that none of these tools is a panacea and that the ways in which these tools interrelate are complex and difficult to predict.

There is an urgent need for experiment and diversity in sustainability policy and practice. Cities are complex enough to display the full range of problems, yet small enough to make changes relatively quickly - and for problems to be containable. Many European cities have already developed innovative approaches, as the examples quoted in this report show. The environmental problems linked to global sustainability, in particular, have diverse causes and require diverse solutions at the level of the individual or household. Many innovative projects have been developed at local community level, and it is important that cities establish policy frameworks to foster these. It will be immensely valuable for policy makers to be able to compare (say) a city which keeps building roads to a similar one which actively restricts traffic; one which landfills its rubbish with one which charges households more to set up closed loops for energy and materials recovery (as in the example of Helsingor described in Box 3.7).

Cities will not be able to follow different paths if the socio-economic system is too open, or if their powers are arbitrarily restricted, or if policies at other levels cut action by cities. Thus the need for experimentation requires cities to have the powers to be, up to a point, 'closed' systems - to have the power to manage resource and financial flows. This may require some reconsideration of other policy goals such as free trade. These issues should be explored openly and pragmatically; no one policy objective should be taken as absolute or inviolable.

8.   The benefits of cities 'closed' systems

This pragmatic argument - that the search for solutions to the sustainability crisis will be helped if cities are allowed more freedom to be 'systems laboratories' - is bolstered by both the political principle of subsidiarity and a moral argument about choice. According to the social contract theory summarised above, 'choice' and 'compulsion' are not opposites but concomitants. People may choose to live within frameworks of restrictions if they give collective benefits which outweigh their personal freedoms.

9.

This explains the apparent paradox of people voting for the restriction of freedoms which they themselves exercise. However it leads to a fresh paradox. Central government restrictions on local government powers and finance, sometimes imposed in the name of protecting individual freedoms, can reduce choice and freedom by depriving individuals of the option of living in cities which are actively managed and regulated in pursuit of their own conceptions of the public good.

The overall message of this section is that cities should use the ecosystems approach to help understand environmental problems and treat the suggested policy instruments as a toolkit. Every city will have different circumstances, and find different tools appropriate, but together they offer a powerful set of approaches to the sustainable management of the urban environment. The following chapters explore sustainability issues and the application of the principles and tools discussed in Chapter 3 in a number of important policy areas.

4

This report adopts the Ecosystems
Approach for defining problems
and finding solutions

4

A holistic view and an integrated
approach are crucial for
sustainable management of natural
resources, energy and waste

*Recycling bin from recycled
plastic*

SUSTAINABLE MANAGEMENT OF NATURAL RESOURCES, ENERGY, WASTE

INTRODUCTION

The objective of this chapter is to address the problems of consumption of non-renewable or slowly renewable natural resources and energy that exceed the capacity of the natural system, and the related waste accumulation that characterises today's urban lifestyles.

The Ecosystems Approach is used, both to provide an understanding of the underlying causes of excessive consumption of stock or flow-limited resources (i.e. where the flow of the resource is not constant, for example seasonal rainfall), and to help focus on the policy options available for minimising the problems and achieving more sustainable management systems. The Ecosystems Approach implies that the essential concepts that should form the basis for policy options for sustainable management of natural resources are those of flow management and the closing of loops in which materials and energy are circulated.

2. As mentioned in chapter 3, natural systems tend to maintain their equilibrium by circulating resources and wastes internally. Any unused energy and material end up as waste, but only as part of a stage in the overall circulation process. This waste supports vast amounts of organisms which in turn transform the waste into substances that are again useful in the ecosystem.

3. In the urban system, waste is accumulated, but rather than being transformed into useful substances, it largely remains outside the circulation process (Flander, 1994). This is the major difference between the operation of the natural system and the urban system. It is a cause of unsustainability that must be addressed urgently. City managers, planners, architects, builders etc. should consider the lessons that nature can teach about ecological and economical flow management. These lessons are vital and can result in significant improvements in efficiency. It has been shown that urban management based on ecology can actually achieve a saving of up to 50% of electricity, heating energy, drinking water and wastes (Hahn, 1993).

This chapter provides a policy-level discussion aimed at influencing the way cities manage flows of natural resources (including water), energy and waste. The aim is to identify policy options that introduce principles of the natural systems into the management of urban systems, thereby achieving a more efficient and sustainable urban environment. Ideally, these policy options should be based on the multiplier effect, whereby one solution addresses several problems at a time. The multiplier effect can only be achieved by taking a holistic view of society and nature.

Inevitably, the plethora of issues which constitute the direct concerns of flow management cannot be examined separately or in great detail in this chapter. Instead, this chapter concentrates on natural resources, energy and waste as three broad issues under which the majority of the management issues can be grouped and specific policy options provided, which apply to all the sub-issues. In other words, aspects which concern particular land-uses, activities and their inter-relationships are not tackled separately in terms of their specific effects on natural resources, energy, waste production and pollutants.

This facilitates explanation of the basic assumption that sustainable management should be based on the Ecosystems Approach. It also stresses the need for the integrated approach to sustainable management whether in terms of land-uses, activities or flows of energy. An integrated approach is vital, especially due to the highly interactive relationship between the key parameters of natural resources, energy and waste. When a state of sustainability is sought, an integrated approach is required in order to maintain a balanced and socially equitable relationship between the parameters. The policy discussion is therefore based on the principles of an integrated approach to closing the circulation of natural resources, energy and waste. Measures such as minimising consumption of natural resources, increasing efficiency of energy production, utilisation of renewable sources, re-use of waste and recovery of heat, and the implementation of decentralised efficient management systems will be explored.

All the policy options discussed in this chapter provide a useful step towards sustainability. However, no single policy option has the power to achieve sustainable development as such. Each problem has its range of solutions which depend on the level of sustainability aimed for. In addition, every region, district or city has its own state of development in relation to sustainability, so that it is not always logical to attempt to move from one "ambition level" to another step by step. Sometimes it is as cheap to choose a solution at a higher level of sustainability as the one below it. For example, in relation to waste water treatment in a settlement without a sewerage system, it is as cheap to build autonomous local area waste systems as it is to construct traditional sewerage and a sewage farm.

NATURAL RESOURCES

2

1.

The presence of natural resources is fundamental to every human activity, irrespective of scale and intensity, and indeed to life as a whole, both within natural systems and urban systems. In large cities, enormous amounts of natural resources are needed to satisfy the needs and desires of their inhabitants and their activities. Consumption of natural resources produces waste of all kinds, and creates far-reaching adverse effects on the planet's ecosystem.

Today the main cause of malfunctioning is the manner in which natural resources are exploited and consumed. Apart from exceeding the capacity of the natural system, consumption is extremely inefficient. Natural resources are consumed without regard to the balance of the natural systems, and without ensuring equilibrium within the urban system. Excessive consumption is allowed to continue without an overall strategy for sustainable waste management. In other words, natural resources are extracted from the natural system to support the life of cities, but hardly anything is returned to the natural system in a useful form, or in a form which elements of the natural system could transform into useful substances for re-entering the circulation process. Instead, useless and/or harmful substances are dumped into the environment thus placing pressure on the carrying capacity and assimilative functions of the natural system. Despite general awareness of huge inefficiencies in production techniques, distribution and end-use, this irresponsible consumption of natural resources is stimulated, at least indirectly, by accommodating for increased production. This is in conflict with principles of sustainability and the Ecosystems Approach.

Excessive exploitation and consumption of natural resources highlights the urgency for adoption of management principles

AIR

Working towards closed systems of natural resources is working towards sustainability

In order to address this problem, cities should move towards the adoption of management principles comparable to those within natural systems. Currently cities are not self-sufficient closed systems, they are highly dependent on surrounding areas. In a sense, cities can be defined as systems surviving on their ability to import most of what they need (Ministry of the Environment and Natural Resources, 1992). There are very few needs that cities satisfy internally. Natural resources are imported into cities, consumed and then exported in the form of air pollution, water pollution and solid waste. The flows are therefore directed into cities, but instead of returning flows back to the original sources, the waste products are stored in the soil or spread to the air and water. The circulation is therefore far from complete. Working towards a closing of cycles by integrating flows into the ecological cycle and returning waste products to the original source helps to achieve a more sustainable urban environment. These principles are often easier to achieve on a small scale, which is why local ecological cycles can be ideal for moving towards sustainable cities as a whole. However, the appropriate level at which cycles ideally should be closed is not fixed, but could be the neighbourhood level, local or regional levels depending on circumstances.

4.   Natural resources can be divided into two main categories, biotic and abiotic. They consist of flora, fauna, air, soil, water, minerals, renewable and non-renewable materials and forms of energy. The interaction of the biotic and abiotic features, in the presence of various forms of energy, contribute to the formation of climate, which is another important factor for life as a whole. This section will deal with those natural resource aspects of the urban system which are in urgent need of sustainable management. They are air, soil, flora, fauna, and water. The sub-issues of energy and waste are treated separately in sections 3 and 4 in this chapter.

2.1   **AIR**

Both humankind and natural phenomena affect air quality

There can be no doubt that air, and specifically good quality and sufficient supply of air, is one of the most valuable sources for the maintenance of life on the planet, whether or not one adopts an anthropocentric view. This resource, which can no longer be considered as a free commodity, is associated today more than ever before in the history of humankind, with a host of problems. These problems can be categorised into two main sources. The first concerns the sum total of the productive activities of the primary, secondary and tertiary sectors which deplete the qualitative features of this resource as well as the processes which generate it. Thus agriculture, mining and quarrying, manufacturing, transport and communications, construction, energy production, etc. all contribute to a greater or lesser extent, in combination with a host of other activities (recreation, health, education, tourism), to the supply and quality of air, especially in urban areas. The second source concerns natural phenomena, such as volcanic action, forest fires and other natural volatile substances, which also affect air quality either directly or indirectly, and in combination with other factors (climatic conditions) which are nonetheless valuable for life on the planet.

Burning waste

Sustainable management of cities and the alleviation of atmospheric problems is concentrated mainly on pollution sources which originate in the city, but nevertheless affect adversely both the biotic and abiotic parts of the ecosystem within and outside the city. Other secondary effects of polluted air, such as global warming, ozone depletion, photochemical smog, etc. should also be of concern for sustainable management.

These secondary effects originate mostly from the city, but they also directly affect climatic, microclimatic and atmospheric conditions generally. These are important factors for the sustainable functioning of both the urban and the natural systems.

The main goal of sustainable management in relation to air is to ensure quality and supply. As far as the objectives of sustainable management are concerned, two main issues can be identified:

- to reduce pollution sources and quantities;

- to promote the re-generation and filtering of air.

The main goal in relation to air is to ensure quality and supply

The first issue is related to production and consumption. The second issue is directly related to the protection of green features.

Energy production and consumption are the main sources of air pollution, although evaporative loss of solvents has become an increasingly important source of photochemically reactive materials. Inevitably, a large number of issues which are associated with air and its management therefore overlap with the sub-issues of energy, waste and transport in the city. Several policy options available for reducing pollution sources and quantities have a multiplier effect by coinciding with policy options that serve the purposes of minimising energy consumption, increasing efficiency of energy production, utilising renewable energy sources etc. These policy options are discussed in section 3. Policy options directed at reducing pollution from the transport sector are discussed in chapter 6. In addition to these, there are others which serve the objectives of air pollution more directly. These include:

4.

Policy option: action plan for air quality

Drawing up an action plan to achieve air quality targets is a way of aiding the implementation of actions geared specifically towards increasing the quality of the air. The Council of Ministers is currently in the process of adopting a Directive on Ambient Air Quality Assessment and Management, which through daughter Directives to be adopted during 1996, sets standards for 13 substances and defines the responsibility of Member States in reaching these standards. Part of the requirement will be that areas, including cities that are unlikely to meet set standards by the deadline set in the daughter Directives, will be required to draw up action plans to tackle air pollution. See chapter 3 section 2 for discussion of Action Plans.

Policy option:
action plan for air quality

Policy option: greening the city

The capacity for air re-generation and filtering can be increased by providing more green elements and selecting suitable plant species that maximise the transformation of CO_2 into oxygen. This helps to counter urban emissions, particularly from road traffic. Greening the city is a policy option with a multiplier effect. Apart from cleaning the air, green elements also serve to reduce noise pollution, to assist the formation of suitable micro-climatic conditions by reducing the impact of wind, balancing temperature variations and hydrating the air. The wider benefits of green space are discussed in chapter 7 section 1.

Policy option:
greening the city

4.1 The use of fresh air channels in German planning practice

Planning practice in Germany considers fresh air channels that provide city centres with fresh air from the urban fringes. This also helps in equalising differences in temperature between cities and the surrounding landscape. The fresh air channels are essentially green corridors, but with vegetation that does not obstruct the wind and therefore the air flow into the city. Fresh air is directed into the city through the fresh air channels and rises upwards as it warms up in the centre of the city. The fresh air channels have a multiplier effect by providing excellent routes for footpaths and cycleways.

7.   Furthermore, there are areas that the city should attempt to influence through the spatial planning system, environmental legislation at local level, information and awareness raising. These include supporting energy efficient and 'clean' industries; and promoting the use of energy efficient appliances and services (e.g. type of refrigeration unit, goods which have been finished with electrostatic paints, services which minimise the need for travel, both public and private).

8.   Another important objective of sustainable management in relation to air could be that of alleviating problems created by natural phenomena which have affected air quality, such as, for example, the replanting of dépleted woodlands on the urban fringe.

2.2   ## WATER

Water: crucial resource for humankind, vegetation and fauna

Water is a natural resource on which all life is dependent. For humankind water is indispensable for basic functions (drinking, washing and cleaning), for industrial processes and for agriculture. Water is a renewable and a re-usable natural resource. In principle, water is not scarce in European countries. Water is part of a cyclical process of the natural system - rainfall is stored as groundwater and in rivers, lakes and seas, then evaporates and forms clouds which in turn result in rainfall.

Problems concerning water quantity: availability of water

The quantitative state of water sources can vary geographically with significant regional differences, seasonally and as a result of climatic factors such as droughts or heavy rainfall, but also as a direct result of human intervention which can lead to both shortage and flooding.

Water is extracted in huge amounts to support human activities, and although water shortage, at least at a large scale, is often associated with developing countries with extreme climatic characteristics, it is also a problem that periodically occurs in some European countries. The consequences of water shortage, and especially the measures taken by the water industry to secure a supply of water even during prolonged droughts, are harmful to the natural system. A common solution is to extract water from rivers to the extent that the level falls, thereby slowing the flow. The slower the flow, the less oxygen the river can contain. Lower oxygen levels cause direct suffering to fish, even death, and affect the quality of fish spawning areas. Furthermore, lower water levels in rivers reduce the diluting capacity of the river in handling permitted levels of effluent, and levels which normally are considered harmless can become harmful.

Focus on water quantity

The January 1995 floods in north western Europe were the legacy of an unsustainable past. The principal causes ranged from excessively fast rain to surface water flow and river beds too narrow to accommodate the quantity of water. The accumulation of relatively modest human interventions in river basins, such as cutting down small areas of woodland, urban expansion and the building of new settlements, straightening the courses of streams, laying drains for agricultural field improvement, waste disposal from factories and the use of herbicides by local authorities, all contributed to the floods and their environmental consequences. This example highlights the need for sustainable management of the water system. Attention needs to focus on the quantity of water, including the relative amounts of permeable surface, retention, infiltration, river bed resistance, on the problems of polluted agricultural land and city parks following floods, and on questions of water quality, all part of the general water management problem.

Human intervention does not only affect the quantitative state of water sources, but also the qualitative state. All water used by humans is returned to the natural system in some form. This in itself is good, because it completes the cycle or the flow of water. The problem is that used water is polluted in various ways and no amount or level of waste water treatment will return the water back into the natural system in its original qualitative state.

Furthermore, water which is not directly used by humans is also affected by urban systems. Rainwater is normally infiltrated into the ground in the natural system. However, in urban systems rainwater gets trapped on impermeable surfaces and is transported by a fast waste water system. The amount of rainwater that is infiltrated is greatly reduced. Instead, the rainwater is polluted by dirt and chemicals which pollute the groundwater. Eventually, drinking water supplies are contaminated.

5.   Problems concerning water quality: polluted used water

6.

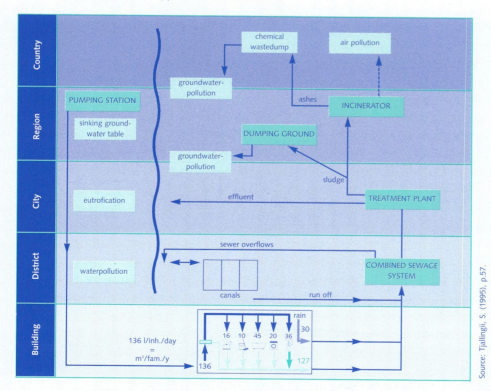

Source: Tjallingii, S. (1995), p.57.

FIGURE - The Water Chain, existing systems and environmental problems

Minimising impacts on the natural system in respect of water

7. From both a quantitative and a qualitative point of view, it makes sense to apply the principles of sustainability to water management, so as to cause the least possible impact on the natural system in respect of water, while securing a basic service for all citizens including access to pressurised water and sewage networks. The basic service implies that household water should pose no health hazard, should be inoffensive in terms of appearance (both looks and smell) and should not pose any technical obstacles to basic usage.

8. An integrated vision for the future management of the water system is required. Urban land forms part of the water system, and urban water management can be a major influence in managing the system as a whole.

9. The principles of sustainable water management are related to water conservation and minimising the impact of all water related functions on the natural system. It is important to take into account the complete cycle of urban water systems including water extraction, treatment, distribution, and consumption, sewerage, waste water treatment, and waste water disposal. All these functions have an impact on the quantitative and/or qualitative state of water resources. They also affect other aspects of the natural system. The aim of sustainable water management should be not only to secure the availability of a basic level of service, but also to ensure the protection of habitats, flora and fauna, to preserve the water's capacity to dilute and remove pollutants, and to safeguard the aesthetic and recreational values of water elements in the landscape.

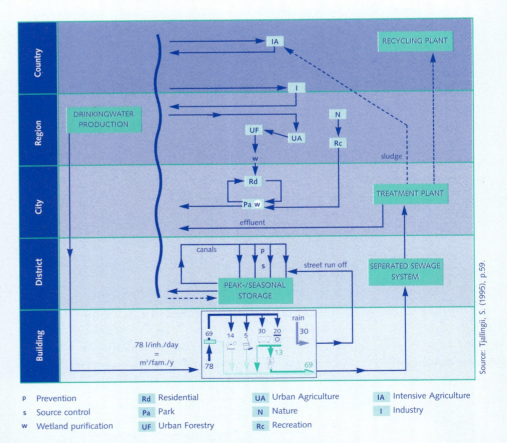

Source: Tjallingii, S. (1995), p.59.

P	Prevention	Rd	Residential	UA	Urban Agriculture	IA	Intensive Agriculture
S	Source control	Pa	Park	N	Nature	I	Industry
W	Wetland purification	UF	Urban Forestry	Rc	Recreation		

FIGURE - The Water Chain - guiding models for the long term

Conservation as a principle is important, although it is recognised that the relationship between behaviour and physical and climatic conditions is affected by the specific situation in different countries. Conservation may therefore seem to be more of an issue in one national or regional context than another, but the fact remains that whether or not water resources are abundant, consumption results in pollution and waste and, if for no other reason, should be minimised.

10.   Conservation as a guiding principle

Policy options for sustainable water management include:

Policy option: collecting storm water

Policy option: collecting storm water

11.

Storm water is relatively clean if collected before it touches the ground and mixes with various surface pollutants. It can be utilised for purposes where drinking water quality is not required, thus cutting down consumption of valuable drinking water which undergoes substantial treatment processes. Storm water can be collected from roofs of buildings, as is often the case in rural areas. It can be utilised for watering lawns and other green spaces, for cleaning public spaces such as streets, pavements etc.

Policy option: facilitating the infiltration of storm water

Policy option: facilitating the infiltration of storm water

The infiltration of storm water into the ground is the ecosystem's way of handling new supplies of water and incorporating it into the natural system. Vegetation and soil can purify water, by binding its pollutants and utilising its nutrients. The use of impermeable surfaces prevents storm water from being infiltrated into the ground. Apart from mixing with pollutants such as oil and heavy metals and transporting them to the waste water system, this disturbs the ground water balance and affects the vegetation. Cities can, through the spatial planning system, promote the use of permeable surfaces wherever possible. Car parks are an example of areas that function equally well with well designed permeable surfaces as with impermeable.

12.

Stormwater infiltration

Policy option: facilitating the retention of storm water

Policy option: facilitating the retention of storm water

The high proportion of impermeable surfaces in cities can also be counterbalanced by creating ponds, ditches and wetlands which allow the retention of storm water, rather than eliminating it as quickly as possible through the waste water systems. Retention of storm water is a multiplier solution which reduces the additional pressure that storm water otherwise places on capital intensive waste water treatment systems, while it enhances the natural purification of the water and enriches the flora and fauna. Storm water retention facilities also have a social impact through the recreational value that water elements add to the environment.

13.

Reuse of rainwater

4.2 Green structures and nitrogen purification, Halmstad, Sweden

The city of Halmstad is affected by nitrogen leaching. Most of the pollution is airborne, or comes from fertilisation of farmland, and a small part from waste treatment plants. The improvement of nitrogen purification at waste water treatment plants and in farming, is being reinforced by biological measures. The city parks administration has made park land available for management and purification of storm water. The municipality is running various projects in which storm water is held in ponds and wetland before being conducted into the receiving waters. In return, the citizens of Halmstad can enjoy aqueous environments where plants and animals thrive. One pond in a residential area has been used as a basin for short-term storage of storm water since the 1970s. The pond is now fully integrated into the environment. Swans and other birds nest there, and there are numerous frogs. To improve the nitrogen treatment and increase the ecological variation, a wetland area was developed downstream of the pond. The people in the neighbourhood, including school children, helped the park staff to create the wetland, which is now becoming an area with a wealth of flora and fauna. The schools use the area to provide children experience of the natural environment (Ministry of the Environment and Natural Resources, 1992).

4.3 An ecological solution for management of rain water, Marne la Vallee, France

The new town of Marne la Vallee within Val Maubuée incorporates existing areas of forest and other green spaces. A network of streams and ponds has been utilised to provide an ecological solution for the control and treatment of rain water. These spaces also have recreational and landscape functions. The management approach has included the preparation of an inventory of landscape, fauna, flora and habitats, and public surveys to assess the recreational pressures exerted on these spaces and public expectations regarding their use. The spaces have been classified according to their type, social function and ecological value, and appropriate conservation and management strategies have been devised for each. Particular importance is placed upon the maintenance or creation of links between open spaces within the town and with natural areas outside it.

Policy option: recycling grey water

Policy option: recycling grey water

14.

The issue of water use efficiency raises the question whether it is efficient to use drinking water for purposes where there is no need for water that meets such high standards. Two separate water supply systems, one carrying drinking water and the other recycled washing water, i.e. grey water, is an option that addresses this issue. It is costly to implement such a system in existing urban areas, except in areas of urban regeneration and other large scale reconstruction sites. These are suitable urban targets for this policy.

They can be designed to include internal recycling systems for grey water. Water that has been used for washing purposes can be circulated through a small scale recycling facility and fed into the water system for use in toilets, outdoor taps etc. Attention has to be paid to health issues (i.e. all water must meet minimum standards to minimise health risks and to ensure that no technical harm is caused to appliances). The two-water supply systems also have to be designed in a way that minimise risk of misuse, i.e. preventing grey water being used for drinking purposes by mistake (children especially).

Cities can promote the use of two-water supply systems through the spatial planning system, and by incorporating such requirements into building regulations. Where the installation of complete two-water supply systems is considered unfeasible, the option of installing double sewerage networks may provide a compromise. This involves the separation of waste water into two categories, washing water and toilet waste. The washing water could be treated separately (to remove harmful substances such as phosphorus) and then reused, for example, for agricultural purposes.

15.

Policy option: promoting more environmentally friendly sewerage solutions

It is important not only to conserve water, but also to improve the quality of the waste water which is returned to the water system. The use of biological treatment plants has increased, especially the ones based on methods of activated sludge, trickling filters and biorotors (Santala, 1994). Other forms of more environmentally friendly ways of treating and disposing waste water are also being introduced. These are passive methods which make use of ecological functions and require no technical installations or monitoring of operation and maintenance. These include biological ponds, aqua culture methods, reed beds, artificial wetlands, infiltration etc. The use of this type of ecological treatment method is dependent on the specific features of the site and, especially in dense urban areas, can be constrained by limited space available. The use of such treatment systems, wherever possible, should be encouraged through a series of incentives, subsidies, grants, tax reduction, etc. Legislation in the form of a new Directive on the construction and operation of biological treatment plants for urban waste at tertiary levels may be required.

16.

Policy option: promoting
more environmentally
friendly sewerage
solutions

Policy option: controlling pollution sources

The importance of controlling chemical and other industrial pollution sources cannot be over emphasised. Water is very receptive to pollution, and can transport pollution long distances from its original source, thereby spreading harmful substances throughout the ecosystem. It is therefore important not only for air quality, but also for the quality of water sources, that appropriate pollution control/emission legislation regulations are in place and enforced. The European Commission's new Directive on Ambient Air Quality Assessment and Management will, once adopted, make a significant contribution to this issue.

17.

Policy option:
controlling pollution
sources

Policy option:
controlling mineral
extraction

Land is a resource for
development, that is threatened

Policy option: controlling mineral extraction

18. Most construction activities include the use of stone material in some form. Apart from stone being a limited natural resource, the extraction of stone material affects not only landscapes but also groundwater areas. The recycling of stone material should be promoted so that the effect of minerals extraction on groundwater quality and balance is minimised. Where the spatial planning system covers mineral extraction, it is important that cities exercise their right to influence rates of extraction, for example by making sure that permits are given only where there is an absolute need. Environmental impact assessments should be given proper weight when considering applications, and the use of environmental taxes can also assist in ensuring that extraction keeps within reasonable limits. A raw materials charge on extraction and import of materials including sand, gravel, clay and chalk is in operation in Denmark.

19. There are a number of additional measures that can enhance water conservation and reduce pollution sources. These include the introduction of water metering to provide a direct financial incentives to save water; the promotion of awareness raising initiatives and labelling systems to influence behaviour and increase the use of water-saving appliances. Financial incentives such as subsidy can also be used to promote water- or energy-saving technology. The role of physical/practical measures such as proper maintenance of water and sewerage networks to minimise leakages, and restricting the use of salt on icy or snowy roads to minimise the pollution of soil and groundwater, should also be stressed.

2.3   SOIL, FLORA AND FAUNA

1. Land has been treated as a infinite resource, while the Ecosystems Approach demands that land, whether sub-soil or surface, is accorded the status of a natural resource, to be managed sustainably.

2. Sustainable management should treat land as a resource for development; as a regulating factor in climate, air and water and adverse weather conditions such as flooding, frost, high winds, etc.; as a natural element which supports complex living ecosystems of flora and fauna; as a raw material source; and as a natural element of which today's city-dwellers are in greater need than ever before for their recreation and psychological well-being.

3. Associated with soil in the city - apart from tremendous losses through development, and to a lesser extent through erosion - are pollution and general soil and habitat degradation. Major sources of these problems are the ever-increasing need for development, a large number of activities which create various degrees of pollution (e.g. toxic waste from industry, run-off from road surface) weather erosion, the dumping of waste in liquid and solid form and activities connected with mineral extraction. As a direct result of these problems, the biotic elements for which land provides the basis, such as flora and fauna, are also degraded.

4. The general aim should be an increase in the size of natural areas and their conservation. Given that the condition of flora and fauna today represent two of the most important indicators of the state of the ecosystem, and as land, flora and fauna in combination with the presence of water and suitable climatic conditions are some of the most important ingredients for a healthy ecosystem, it is apparent that sustainable management should aim at the following:

- the safeguarding of a necessary quantity of land for the development of natural and human-made ecosystems, green structures for the city and the surrounding areas;

- the provision of an adequate area of land for this green structure to be self-regenerative; this would also have a catalytic effect for the development of biodiversity.

Major steps for the achievement of these aims, and the comprehensive management of what might be described as natural resources, could include the following:

Policy option: developing a green structure

The development of a green structure for the city provides crucial links between the city and the surrounding countryside. These can include existing green spaces such as agricultural land, parks, tree plantations and natural forests. Although green belts at intervals encircling the city provide recreational value to citizens, they do not provide the vital interconnection of the green areas which ensures the viability of flora and fauna. Green corridors which actually link countryside to green elements within cities provide the best ecological frameworks for habitats, thus combining an increase in biodiversity with recreational value. This is increasingly being recognised by cities. Many are actively seeking to improve the linkage between separate areas of open space, to create green corridors, allowing plants and animals to colonise new niches.

4.4 Development of interconnected nature areas, Aarhus, Denmark

Aarhus describes itself as a green city. The city itself is regarded as an ecosystem. In physical planning strong emphasis is given to the protection and development of nature areas within the city and to connections between these and surrounding countryside, in accordance with the city's ecological plan. An important feature is the creation of forest areas close to the city. In addition to their role as recreational facilities and as barriers to urban sprawl, the new forests are intended to become corridors for wildlife, to act as filters for air pollution and to improve groundwater quality. A more ambitious plan involves the uncovering of the river which previously connected the valley to the west of the city with Aarhus Bay to the east.

Policy option: restoration and enrichment of soil and flora

The improvement of soil and plant-life can be brought about through the upgrading of areas which have fallen into disuse by urban activities, as well as land unsuitable for development due to slopes, instability, flooding and other similar characteristics, by reclaiming and rehabilitating soil and sub-soil. This can be enriched by the greening of unbuilt areas on private property, road networks and open spaces, both public and private.

5.

6.

Policy option: developing a green structure

Green corridors

7.

Policy option: restoration and enrichment of soil and flora

Policy option: increasing bio-diversity

The move away from mono-culture towards increased bio-diversity is an important aspect in the sustainable management of cities. Formal parks and lawns contribute only in a limited way to the natural system, although their contribution to the quality of life of citizens is significant. The natural system consists of a multitude of species of both flora and fauna that are mutually supportive and reinforcing. Mono-cultural green areas in urban systems cannot provide the complex support that a healthy ecosystem requires. The number and size of green spaces that are maintained in a natural state should therefore be optimised.

Policy option: setting up city farms

Bringing the natural system into cities through small-scale city farms contributes to greening the city and providing educational value. The inhabitants of cities, especially children, know little about ecosystems and where their food comes from. Large scale farming practice, a centralised food processing industry, transportation and the retail market have become essentially incomprehensible. By setting up small city farms to run on the basis of traditional agriculture, municipalities can make their local environment richer and healthier while raising the awareness of citizens. Furthermore, it is important that where high quality agricultural land is adjacent to urban areas, it is protected from development, for example when the city expands. It should rather be maintained in agricultural use, thereby retaining its functional value while providing the benefits of city farms.

4.5 Aspö city farm, Skövde, Sweden

The municipal housing company of the Swedish town of Skövde has set up a city farm adjacent to three residential areas. The city farm has cows, pigs, chickens, and small fields of grain and other crops. Day nursery and school classes frequently visit the farm, and anyone who is interested may join in the work. Children can help look after the animals, although the animals are sent to the slaughterhouse as with normal farming practice. The services of a farmer are hired for the management of the farm, and a recreational teacher is hired to lead study tours and other activities. The farm makes a small profit (Ministry of the Environment and Natural Resources, 1992).

The development of a green structure which consists of some of the most important resource elements in the city, i.e. soil and habitats developed both in natural and human-made ecosystems, should, in order to fulfill its purpose, be based on the following planning and management principles:

- it should provide safe habitats of a high quality for a diversity of species;

- it should delineate clearly the nature and intensity of the various activities that it accommodates;

- it should create a feeling of identity and familiarity in its users and, as a result, respect for its conservation needs;

- it should provide an opportunity for education and enlightenment regarding both the sustaining of such a resource and the innovative techniques used in achieving this;

- it should provide mechanisms for monitoring progress towards attainment of the original goals (quantitative indicators).

11.

Finally, the policy options which characterise the holistic approach to sustainable management of natural resources, as well as the other concerns of sustainable management, should follow basic principles. These are identification and quantification of the present state of resources and their value in terms of rarity and availability; and a detailed understanding of the causes of the problems involved, based on an understanding of the interaction and relationships of key parameters, in order to solve the problems of the past, produce action for conservation and preservation, and control those activities and processes associated with the exploitation of resources which act detrimentally both in the city and its resource catchment area.

ENERGY

3

In recent years, current energy policies reflect the dramatic consequences of former energy policies which have led to the depletion of resources, increased pollution, and climatic effects. The adoption of the principles of sustainable development has highlighted the necessity of energy conservation, suggesting intervention at different spatial scales of planning and the use of renewable sources which are more compatible with environmental protection and conservation of natural resources.

1.   Energy policies and environmental problems

The urban population consumes energy, and therefore natural resources, at a much faster rate than ever before and urban populations consume more energy than non-urban populations. Due to their population density and the activities concentrated in them, cities account for 75-80 % of energy consumption from less than 10% of the European Union's surface area (CEC, undated). Energy is not only consumed for necessary activities and the satisfaction of needs, but it is also wasted during the production process and subsequently during both distribution and use.

2.   Energy consumption is concentrated in urban areas

This excessive energy consumption, which requires increasing external inputs of natural resources and gives rise to a growing discharge of wastes outside the urban system, causes serious internal and external environmental problems. The problems are concerned with depletion of natural resources, pollution and disruptions of natural systems. In short, the balance within the urban system is highly distorted, and this is a serious threat to the functioning of the natural system. The amount of energy which is being directly wasted through inefficient production techniques and heat losses is significant. Similarly the amount of energy indirectly wasted through under-utilisation of renewable energy sources, which potentially could make a significant contribution towards reducing air pollution and climatic change, while ensuring security of energy supply into the future is substantial.

3.

FIGURE - The Energy Chain, existing systems and environmental problems

Source: Tjallingii, S. (1995), p.64.

4.

Theoretically energy supply should not be a matter of concern. Energy constitutes the only resource which can penetrate the otherwise closed system of the earth. Provided the necessary logistical problems are solved, and the necessary scientific research and practice application is made, energy availability should be secure. Nevertheless, the issue of energy is a matter of tremendous concern today due to inefficient and wasteful production, transportation, distribution and consumption, as well as secondary negative effects from these activities upon all the constituent parts of the ecosystem, mainly in the form of gaseous and heat pollution.

5.

Given the high energy intensity of cities, a primary concern is to influence the behaviour of citizens as well as industry towards a more energy efficient and 'cleaner' operation of the urban system. Although it may be an obvious point, it is important to emphasise that consumers do not demand energy as such, rather they demand energy services, such as heating for buildings, industrial processes and cooking, light, transport etc. The delivery of these services requires energy, and the amount of energy required depends on the efficiency with which that energy is converted into the desired service (Jackson, 1992). This efficiency rate is in turn dependent on various issues, including available technology, management system, land use patterns, etc. The land use pattern is pre-determined to a large extent in existing urban systems, but it is possible to influence the technology and management system applied.

6.

It is important to recognise that cities can through sustainable energy management play a crucial role in influencing energy consumption and pollution levels. The consumption of energy, i.e. the demand for energy is local by nature, although the production and supply of energy is often centralised. The city is therefore an ideal focus for the targeting of energy policy, and cities can make specific contributions to energy saving, utilising local energy sources and reducing environmental impacts (CEC, undated).

The inefficient and wasteful production, transportation, distribution, and consumption of energy are threats to sustainability

In recognition of this, DGXVII of the European Commission has financed the creation of local energy agencies since 1992. The pilot programme Energy Management for Regions and Cities has created 22 urban agencies to deal with energy management and to contribute to the environmental protection and sustainable development of those cities. Activities include publicity campaigns and other means of influencing the behaviour of businesses and consumers. The involvement of elected members in the management of the urban energy agencies provides the political will that helps the agencies to attain their targets and local employment is created in response to the specific professional skills that are required to implement plans. One condition for granting Community aid at the urban level for agencies, is co-operation between different Member States, the transfer of know-how and the dissemination of results. The cities that have benefitted from this action can serve as examples to the neighbouring ones or to ones that face similar problems.

In practice, the involvement of cities in the management of their energy systems varies considerably between the Member States and within countries or even regions. There are sometimes institutional, political, financial and even technical obstacles to the development of urban energy policies. These may include:

- restrictive national institutional frameworks within which the production, transport and distribution of energy have to operate;

- insufficient financial resources;

- lack of professional specialist skills within the city to prepare and implement energy policies;

- lack of political motivation within the city.

In addition, many European cities lack the innovation and will to address energy problems. It is therefore important that cities are made to understand the importance of their involvement, and that they are provided with the information and the frameworks needed to engage proactively in the development of sustainable urban energy policies (CEC, undated).

Urban energy policy can be targeted at several levels including the provision of municipal public services, the operation of internal municipal activities, the behaviour of businesses and individuals, and the operation of the energy industry. Influencing energy use in municipal activities (external and internal) is clearly easier than influencing local businesses, individual citizens or the energy industry. Nevertheless, cities can and should take action in one form or another to promote and facilitate energy conservation at all levels.

Urban energy policy can also be targeted at various sectors. Energy consumption in European cities is roughly divided into the residential and tertiary sectors (40%), industry (30%) and the transport sector (30%) (CEC, undated).

In the residential and tertiary sectors, fields of activity such as health, education, recreation, housing, services etc. consume substantial amounts of energy. This occurs not only during the construction phase but also for the heating, lighting, ventilation and cooling of spaces. Other important energy needs have to be satisfied for the provision and functioning of infrastructure, including the lighting and maintenance of public spaces, the supply of water and the treatment of all kinds of waste.

115

ENERGY

7. Cities can play a crucial role in influencing energy consumption

8.

9.

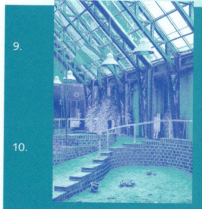

10.

Closed veranda in child day care centre

11. Cities can promote and facilitate energy conservation at all levels

12.

13. In the industrial sector, manufacturing and other production activities have expanded and intensified in an effort to satisfy an ever-increasing demand for consumer and luxury goods. This has resulted in the consumption of vast amounts of energy for the extraction of raw materials, for the production processes and for the transportation of goods.

14. The ever-growing need for mobility and the dependence of the city on increasingly remote areas for transportation of material goods and people, has caused transportation to be another main energy consumer, especially of non-renewable fuels, and a major polluting factor.

15. The discussion in this section is focused on energy consumption for stationary purposes, rather than for transport which is addressed in chapter 6 (accessibility) and chapter 7 section 1 (spatial planning). It will focus on ways of improving city management in relation to minimising energy consumption and increasing energy efficiency.

16. It is inevitable that the policy options for sustainable management are numerous and multifaceted. This is a result of the large number of issues which concern energy, e.g. sources, production, distribution, pollution, etc., and the fact that it is arguably the most important factor in the functioning and development of every human activity and ecosystem component.

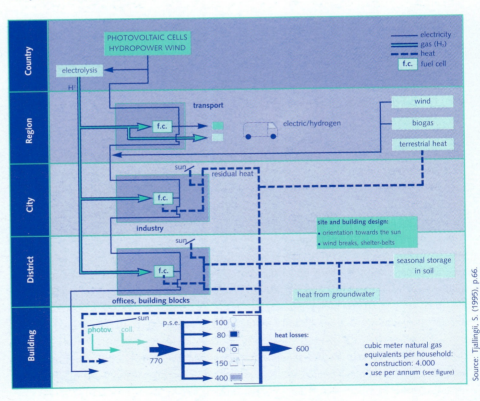

Source: Tjallingii, S. (1995). p.66.

FIGURE - The Energy Chain, guiding models for the long term

Policy option: energy conservation as a basic aim

The basic aim of sustainable energy management is concerned with energy conservation. The Brundtland Report recommends a 'low energy future' as the only viable strategy (World Commission on Environment and Development, 1987). This aim can be addressed through a number of both general and more specific policy options.
The general ones include the role of information and awareness raising, addressed in chapter 3 section 2, to motivate actors to conserve energy; the role of cities in supporting small scale applied research and facilitating the setting up of demonstration projects to develop technological applications regarding the use of renewable resources and energy conservation measures; and the importance of applying a fair 'pricing system' based on the principle of the 'thermodynamic efficient city', as opposed to the conventional economic efficiency principles applied today, to bring about social equity in the sustainable management of the city.

Sustainable energy management has an important role to play in relation to over-production, transportation, distribution, consumption and general environmental impact. The undesirable consequences of these activities have far-reaching effects that extend well beyond city boundaries. While sustainable energy management cannot effectively control all these aspects, it should attempt to influence decisions on behalf of the consumers it represents. This includes the place of energy production as well as the means and safety of production. The same applies to matters of transportation and distribution. Lengthy and potentially dangerous networks can be shortened and made safer through planning and design. Aspects of safety relating to energy consumption range from stricter guidelines for the siting and mix of land use, and activities to control emissions from the use of various energy sources. Specific policy options include:

Policy option: introducing local energy management systems

The environmental, financial and social consequences of centralised energy management are evident in all European cities. The adverse effects of energy use have resulted in substantial rehabilitation costs, and forcing cities to adopt policies on energy saving and substitution in order to try to improve the local environment. Cities should actively engage in developing a decentralised energy management strategy whereby clear aims and actions are defined, and influence is exercised upon the various public or private operators involved. It is important that the efforts of the various actors involved are organised, co-ordinated and monitored in an attempt to attain higher levels of energy conservation. This can be achieved through the development of an overall strategy for reducing energy demand and the adoption of energy management conservation standards. The overall energy management strategy may be developed within the framework of a Local Action Plan (see chapter 3 section 2). For example, Italian national law (n: 10/1991) requires municipalities with over 50,000 inhabitants to prepare an Energy Action Plan and integrate it with the land use plan. Several cities including Rome, Livorno, Rovigo, and Padova have already prepared such Action Plans. Alternatively, urban energy agencies (referred to above) can be set up for this purpose.

17. Policy option: energy conservation as a basic aim

18.

4

19. Policy option: introducing local energy management systems

4.6 Integrated approach to local energy management, Newcastle upon Tyne, UK

With financial support from the European Commission the city of Newcastle upon Tyne has prepared an Urban Energy Plan. The plan was prepared by a team involving the city council's Development Department, major energy suppliers, the city's two universities and the public transport operators. The plan was prepared in parallel with the formulation of a major land use and transportation plan. By involving many of the key players, the city has been able to go well beyond its normal role and seeks to influence the balance of energy use in the city and its effect on the environment. The plan was prepared in two stages: establishing base year information and preparing alternative scenarios. New policy initiatives were examined and an Action Plan produced drawing together the main components under four headings: combined heat and power, renewable energy sources, energy efficiency and transport. A target of 30% reduction of CO_2 emissions by the year 2006 was established. As a consequence the city council must regularly monitor progress achieved in each of the main areas of action, energy consumption and the levels of pollutant emissions (Energie Cités, 1994).

4.7 Integrated approach to city management, Brescia, Italy

The city of Brescia is actively involved in technical energy management through its municipal service company which is responsible for production, transport and distribution of electricity and heat, distribution of gas and water, maintenance of public outdoor lighting and traffic lights, management of public transport systems as well as collection and disposal of household waste. The company operates an energy loss reduction plan and several energy saving programmes. The vertical integration, i.e. the ability to monitor activities from production to distribution, contributes to the success of these programmes. Cogeneration has permitted substantial savings and provides half of the city's council housing with heating (Energie Cites, 1994).

Policy option:
promoting local energy
production   20.

Policy option: promoting local energy production

Centralised energy production requires fuel to be transported long distances involving substantial energy use for transportation. Similarly, the lengthy energy distribution networks incur increased risk of leakage and energy loss. Energy production at the local level can minimise these problems and has other benefits in environmental, economic and social terms. It facilitates utilisation of local energy sources, enhances the efficiency of local energy management systems, provides local employment and contributes to the development of local skills in the energy technology field. Local, or decentralised, energy production not only enhances the overall efficiency of energy production, but also its flexibility, by allowing for the detailed adjustment of production in relation to local demand.

4.8 Decentralised energy production, Amsterdam, the Netherlands

In 1988 the city of Amsterdam launched a programme for decentralised cogeneration units and district heating using emissions from nearby power plants. The municipal energy company is responsible for implementing the programme and 22 small installations were operational in 1994, with an additional 16 under construction. The locally produced electricity is distributed to the grid belonging to the municipal energy company, whereas the heat is used on site in council housing, hospitals, hotels and other large buildings. The programme has led to energy savings of 30% and has proved the economic viability of such projects. In addition, local organisations produce and consume their own energy, and the city's waste incineration plant produces electricity that is fed into the municipal distribution system. Decentralised electricity production meets nearly 20% of Amsterdam's electricity demand.

Policy option: promoting least cost planning

By applying the concept of least cost planning (see chapter 3 section 2) to energy suppliers it is possible to motivate them to adopt substantial energy conservation programmes while still making profits. The aim should be to sell and charge for a service to the consumer, i.e. a specific level of warmth or light for a room, rather than units of energy. This approach motivates the energy supplier to provide the specified service level using as little energy as possible, thereby conserving energy. The energy saving may be a result of introducing insulation measures for example, the costs of which the energy supplier can transfer to the consumer according to the principles of least cost planning.

21.

Policy option: promoting least cost planning

Policy option: replacing non-renewable energy sources with renewable ones

Most of the energy produced in Europe is reliant on fossil and nuclear fuels. These fuels raise problems concerning scarcity and pollution, and safety. Sustainable management should stress the importance of alternatives in energy production, emphasising renewable and environmentally friendly energy sources such as solar, wind, water, geothermal, plant oil, bio-gas etc. which minimise the impact on the ecosystem of production, transportation, distribution and consumption of energy by reducing air pollution and climatic change, ensuring safety of production and security of supply into the future. The production of solar energy is increasing in the southern European countries and the production of wind energy is widespread in Denmark and the Netherlands.

22.

Policy option: replacing non-renewable energy sources with renewable ones

Wind as energy resource

4.9 Development of renewable energy sources, Mallow, Ireland

County Cork is working with several municipalities to develop local energy production projects. The County has worked with Mallow municipality to develop the use of geothermal energy from a water source to the east of Mallow Town. Parts of these resources are used to heat Mallow swimming pool by means of a heat pump. The County is now aiming to develop alternative energy in all possible forms. Several feasibility studies have been undertaken with financial support from the European Commission, and a project for the promotion and use of renewable energy has been defined. The project will potentially benefit up to 700,000 inhabitants, and will have environmental, as well as social and economic benefits (Energie Cités, 1994).

Policy option:
co-generation of
electricity and heat

Policy option: co-generation of electricity and heat

23.   Despite the substantial technical development programmes to improve the efficiency of electricity generation, the efficiency of approximately 30% is generally low. The remaining energy is wasted in the form of heat which often is expelled through cooling towers or into rivers. The utilisation of this waste heat should be maximised through co-generation of electricity and heat. Co-generation of power and heat can increase the production efficiency to around 90%, thereby significantly reducing the quantity of fuel needed to provide a given amount of useful energy. The city of Helsinki produces 84% of its energy via combined heat and power generation at an efficiency level of 90%. The introduction of heat-power generators in building complexes is also successful in the Netherlands (see example in Box 4.7).

Policy option:
recovery of industrial
waste heat

Policy option: recovery of industrial waste heat

24.   Heat, generated in huge quantities by industrial processes, is often wasted in the form of liquid or hot gases. This waste heat could be used to provide heating for factories, schools, hospitals, and other buildings directly or as feeds to local district heating networks. This option is beneficial both to the industry making an income from selling waste heat, and for the city purchasing cheap energy to feed into local networks. Re-use of waste heat reduces the overall demand for energy, by replacing energy which would otherwise have to be generated. This more efficient utilisation of fuel for energy provides a step towards the achievement of balance between the inputs and outputs in the urban system. In the Netherlands, for example, industrial waste heat is often used for heating green houses.

Policy option: production of energy from waste

The careful design of waste processing plants, the use of biomass and the production of biogas from landfill sites and sewage treatment processes are examples of ways of making use of the waste that urban systems accumulate, for the purposes of reducing energy demand from other sources. However, biogas plants are very investment intensive and large amounts of material are needed to make it viable and it may be difficult to collect enough household waste locally. Co-operation with industrial or agricultural producers of biological waste, or with farmers cultivating bio-energy crops, may overcome these problems. The utilisation of waste for energy production is further discussed in section 3 in this chapter which also includes an example (Box 4.14) of co-operation between municipality and industry for bio-energy.

25. Policy option: production of energy from waste

Grass roof

Policy option: using sustainable design principles

Cities can use the spatial planning system to harness design and planning to secure significant energy savings. Options such as bio-climatic architectural design, layout, construction materials, insulation techniques, siting of activities, densities, orientation of buildings, provision of green structures, microclimate etc. can play an important role, either directly or indirectly, in the achievement of increased energy efficiency of urban systems. For example, high density implies lower energy use in buildings, because apartments and townhouses require less energy for heating and cooling than detached single-family houses. Admittedly, a high overall density may also imply that sites with unfavourable microclimatic conditions are developed, but this loss is more than outweighed by the savings due to lower requirements of space heating or cooling. Requirements in relation to the above issues can be incorporated into the building regulations of cities. The question of ecological principles in urban renewal is discussed in chapter 7 section 2.

26.   Policy option: using sustainable design principles

4

4.10 Bioclimatic architecture, Sikies, Greece

In order to increase the efficiency of a national law on energy saving which was passed in 1979, the town of Sikies decided to upgrade dwellings and to commission the drafting of a bioclimatic architectural guide from the University of Thessalonici. The guide contains simple principles that can be applied by the building industry in urban development schemes, the design of new buildings and the renovation of existing buildings. The guide has resulted in building schemes which make efficient use of the sun and reduce overall energy consumption (Energie Cités, 1994).

27. The development of ecological housing estates in new settlements is being examined in the New Sustainable Settlements Project co-ordinated by the European Academy of the Urban Environment, Berlin (Kennedy & Haas, 1993). Seven estates in five European countries have been examined and although the projects differ in their aims and approaches, all stress the application of green building techniques, energy efficiency, the recycling of waste and the multiple use of open space. Although the initiatives examined in this study are small scale, it has been concluded that these developments are capable of implementation on a larger scale, for example in public sector housing. Furthermore, these developments do not necessarily involve substantially increased costs. Participation of the residents has been variable in the projects examined in these studies, but it is regarded as highly significant and in the final analysis, building ecological estates depends upon the extent to which residents are prepared to change their behaviour.

28. A partly EU funded project (DGXVII PERU Programme), involving a shared feasibility study, is being undertaken by the cities of Athens, Graz, Madrid and Rome based on a set of actions to reduce energy consumption in building cooling. The results of the project are expected by the end of 1996.

Policy option:
energy audit

Policy option: energy audit

29. An energy audit of the city's internal and external activities, and of their own building stock, can be the basis for introducing suitable energy efficiency measures such as recovery of waste heat and increasing the thermal efficiency of the city's own building stock. An energy audit could be undertaken as part of the application of an Environmental Management System or SoE reporting, which are discussed in chapter 3 section 2.

4.11 Energy management in municipal buildings, Odense, Denmark

In 1979 the municipality of Odense initiated a process to reduce energy consumption in municipal buildings. A systematic survey of energy consumption was carried out, followed by a heat audit whereby possible energy savings were assessed. Modifications to buildings and installations were made on the basis of these audits. This was supported by information which was disseminated to both decision-makers and end-users. A total investment of 10m ECU has generated savings of 22m ECU between 1981 and 1993. The annual saving is currently 2.3m ECU. The above measures are being complemented by various building management systems and monitoring systems (Energie Cités, 1994).

Policy option:
financial incentives/
environmental taxes

Policy option: financial incentives/environmental taxes

30. These can be used to direct implementation in accordance with specific policy aims. A CO_2 tax, from which biomass fuels are exempt, is applied in Denmark, as are various grant schemes for renewable energy including wind, straw, biogas and hydro power.

incentives can also support the installation of insulation measures, in the Netherlands for
the municipality can give grants for this purpose. Also in the Netherlands, levies on the
energy are being considered to make conventional energy more expensive to create funds
e and stimulate research on the application of renewable and environmentally friendly
ources. This will reduce price differences between the use of conventional energy and more
le forms of energy. The use of energy taxes is also being considered by central
ent in Finland. In Italy, developers producing energy from renewables can sell it to the
utility at a favourable price for the initial eight-year period of the investment.

4.12 Involvement by third parties, Charleroi, Belgium

The city of Charleroi undertook a survey in 1985 which showed that the modernisation of
heating installations in municipal buildings would result in a one third reduction of the
energy bill. However, the city could not afford to finance the required investment but
brought in third parties to finance it. They were repaid out of the savings made by the
city. Ownership of the equipment was transferred to the city on termination of the
contracts. This approach enabled the city to undertake large-scale energy-saving actions
with no increase in debt, no impact on operating costs and investment financed by energy
savings. The overall annual saving generated by these actions is estimated at 23% of
overall expenditure on heating and lighting of all buildings in Charleroi, and a saving of
33% in the volume of fuel (Energie Cités, 1994).

WASTE

This section addresses the issues of liquid and solid waste. Toxic waste is not discussed in
this report. Major problems in the past have been associated mainly with liquid waste.
That is because solid waste consisted mostly of organic and non-toxic substances, with the
exception of sites around metal works - which produced toxic sludge and probably
discharged it into sewage networks.

LIQUID WASTE

Waste with a biological load, discharged waste-water, final washes from metal works,
refineries, food processing plants, tanneries, textile plants and shipyards along with the
waste from urban homes, hospitals, universities, schools and businesses make up the basis
of the liquid waste of the European city. The problems arising from the production of
liquid waste are connected with the discharge of incompatible substances in large, and
therefore difficult to assimilate, quantities into aquatic receptors. Eutrophy in lakes, coastal
regions and rivers is the most common phenomenon resulting from the uncontrolled
discharge of waste. The simple, older type of sewage network in European cities cannot
provide the answer to the problem.

4

4.1

1. Older types of sewage networks
    and problems of liquid wast

LIQUID WASTE

4

Control is needed to maximise the efficiency of Integrated Waste Management Systems

Policy option: regular control and monitoring of waste water receptors

Policy option: integration with other restrictive policies

2.   As far as domestic, industrial and hospital waste is concerned, the chemical and biological treatment of such waste, which has been in effect since the 1960s, has proved to be fairly successful. Community legislation and the directives which Member States have incorporated into their legal systems have made a very positive contribution. However, despite the pioneering nature of EU legislation, state controls have sometimes proved to be rather lax, with the result that there are major urban centres which today still do not operate biological treatment plants to deal with urban waste, or which have obsolete industrial concentrations where waste processing plants are almost impossible to install due to lack of space.

3.   The specific policy options for liquid waste management are largely those discussed in section 2 of this chapter under waste water treatment. Briefly they include water conserving measures such as recycling grey water, minimising leakages, installing water meters, and the utilisation of environmentally friendly sewerage solutions.

4.   At a broader level, what is needed today, is the adoption of an integrated system of waste management that can be implemented in all Member States. A plan could be drawn up by the European Commission for an umbrella approach, which allows for context specific implementation. Although centralisation is generally not the best solution, since policies required vary greatly from city to city, it is nevertheless likely to be the most appropriate solution. Strict control should be exercised by a European Commission body in order to maximise the efficiency of an Integrated Waste Management System. This body could be the European Environment Agency, which could be given special powers to control and monitor treatment plants, impose fines, withhold or remove operating licences from industries that do not comply with conditions, etc. even though this may conflict with the principle of subsidiarity.

5.   In addition to the policy options presented in section 2 (Water), the following principles could function as effective tools in a policy aimed at a sustainable waste management system, and could therefore support an integrated liquid waste management system:

Policy option: regular control and monitoring of waste water receptors

6.   Regular checks and monitoring of waste water receptors should be carried out including measurement of the quality of aquatic receptors and surrounding ground area, where waste is discharged. The results of these checks should be the basis for determining priority actions.

Policy option: integration with other restrictive policies

7.   Integrating the liquid waste management system with restrictive policies such as a ban on the production of chlophen would result in the immediate removal of toxic waste associated with the production process of this chemical and its disposal after use.

SOLID WASTE

4.2

1.

Like liquid waste, solid waste can also be divided up into categories. Domestic and commercial refuse, hospital waste, industrial by-products, reused industrial products, rubble produced by construction activities, waste that consists, for the most part, of non-biodegradable materials, is encountered in all European cities. The composition of the waste differs only slightly from city to city or from country to country. Organic waste, that is the biodegradable part of the waste material, represents a greater proportion of waste produced by the cities of southern Europe than of those in the north. This is waste that is decomposed either in rubbish tips or in waste processing plants, sewage networks and aquatic receptors, and is in fact the least of the problems involved in waste management.

2.

Non-biodegradable materials, mainly plastic of all kinds but particularly PVC, are the biggest problem because of their continuous accumulation and the dioxins that are emitted if PVC mixed with other waste is incinerated at a low temperature. The shortage of space for waste disposal is also aggravated by the rapid increase in the dumping of materials that are biodegradable, but which take a long time to decompose (e.g. metals). Paper, aluminium, tin and glass make up 30-40 % of the volume of waste at waste tips arriving within a short time of their manufacture and disposal on the market.

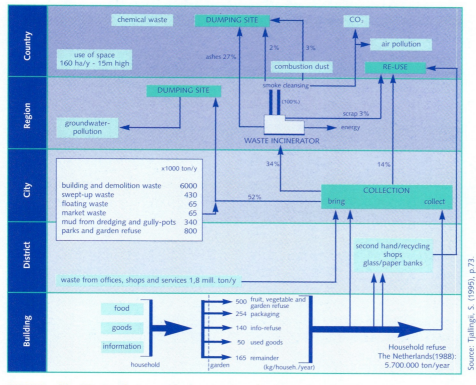

FIGURE - The Waste Chain, existing systems and environmental problems

3.   Incineration contributes to the greenhouse effect and releases toxic substances

Simple landfill or even sanitary burial cannot provide the answer to the problem of solid waste management. The wisdom of incineration has been called into question, backed by scientific arguments, since it contributes to the greenhouse effect and releases toxic substances such as dioxins into the air. The solution to this difficult problem would appear to lie in mixed systems which advocate multiple use, the reuse and recycling of materials in conjunction with the sanitary burial of rapidly biodegradable materials.

The need for integrated
Community legislation

4. The evolution of policies for solid waste management over the past 30 years shows that integration, avoidance of the production of solid waste and disposal through waste sorting (in whatever form), aimed at saving materials for recycling, appear to be gaining ground at local, regional and national level. However, there is a clear lack of any bold, integrated Community legislation. Present regulations seem to conflict with issues concerning the harmonisation of national economies and statutory obligations of the Treaty of Rome (e.g. precedence of the principle of 'fair competition').

5. Scientific institutions, local authorities, federal states, national authorities and even the EU, have invested and continue to invest in countless studies on more rational and environmentally friendly management of urban waste. The EU co-sponsors initiatives by local agencies for the separation and recycling of waste. However, in practice policies vary greatly from city to city, even within the same nation, and can in no way be considered as unified throughout the EU.

Three main aims for sustainable
waste management: (1) reduction
of waste production, (2) making
the best use of waste as a
resource, (3) avoidance of hazards
to the environment and health

6. Sustainable waste management should include three main aims: reduction of waste production, making the best use of waste as a resource, and avoidance of hazards to the environment and health. These aims are not easy to achieve within today's waste management systems which often are centralised and difficult to comprehend. Individuals cannot easily see the consequences of their behaviour, or any results from changing it. Sustainable waste management should therefore be localised whenever appropriate, involving the efforts of all actors within the city. There are, however, matters that do require centralised treatment, for example at the macro-industrial level. A rational, functional proposal for ordering priorities in solid waste management has been formulated as follows:

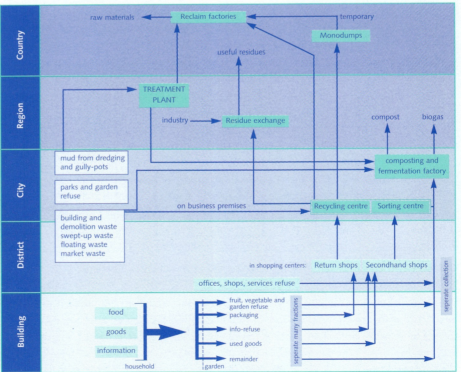

FIGURE - The Waste Chain, guiding models for the long term

Source: Tjallingii, S. (1995), p.75.

"The smallest possible waste production, primarily non-biodegradable and secondly biodegradable over a long period of time, is preferable to the irrational use and dumping of valuable and increasingly scarce resources such as metals, paper and petroleum by-products".

This could be supplemented by the following statement:

"The problem of waste management is not a local or even a regional one; on the contrary, it is a composite socio-economic and cultural issue which in many ways characterises contemporary urban culture and depicts life in the European city".

The most important persistent problem, a multi-faceted and difficult issue concerning production and consumption, is packaging - which industry, and activities such as transport and commerce, have been conditioned to produce and the citizen to consume.

The arguments put forward by European industries revolve around the immense investments made, possible job losses - 12% to 15% of the workforce is engaged in the production of packaging, and if the number of people indirectly employed in the packaging industry is also taken into account, from the server in the fast-food restaurant to the supermarket employee who opens boxes and puts tins on the shelves, then the percentage rises to between 45% and 50% - and quality of products, which according to the industries themselves are produced using the latest packaging technology.

These arguments are accepted by the majority of the labour unions which do not want to see unemployment rise. The arguments are supplemented by consumers who, despite the development of environmental awareness, cannot function both as purchasers of products and as producers of waste operating the rational approach referred to earlier, especially in those cities where no integrated system of waste management has been established and where there are no incentives for reuse and recycling. Unfortunately, this situation applies to the greater part of Europe. Exceptions to the rule are Austria, Denmark, Finland, Germany, the Netherlands and Sweden.

Thus when the government of a European Member State sets restrictions on packaging, industry and the governments of other Member States appeal to the European Court on the grounds that the principle of free market competition is being violated. Unified Community legislation designed to tackle the management of waste and deal with matters of production, consumption and distribution is therefore now even more urgent.

The three-pronged tenet of "no waste - reusable materials - recyclable materials" should be the basic ordering of priorities in waste management. Repair and reuse of goods should be emphasised. Reduction of transport requirements in the management of waste is another important aim of waste management. Transport of waste is extensive and consumes enormous amounts of energy. It is expensive and it has direct environmental consequences. Waste minimisation is therefore important not only in relation to the problems that waste disposal creates, but also in terms of energy consumption. The smaller the cycles of materials are, the easier it is to deal with the problems, and to generate responsible behaviour. The basic principles of such a sustainable policy ought to be as follows:

7.

8. Addressing the problem of packaging

9.

10.

11.

12. Three tenets of waste management

Maximum seperation at source

Policy option: reduction of packaging, and increased use of recyclable and reusable packaging

Excessive packaging should be banned. Reclaiming materials for reuse provides a greater number of jobs than would be lost in the production of packaging. There should be incentives for biodegradable, reusable or recyclable packaging, and imposition of a tax on plastics and other non-biodegradable packaging and materials. A further reduction of waste and energy consumption can be achieved through reduction of recyclable waste and increase in the use of reusable packaging. Levying of a smaller tax on recyclable packaging and materials is appropriate, as they require greater expenditure of energy and water than that needed for reusable packaging and materials. The use of deposits on bottles, crates etc. provides a financial incentive to consumers to bring back reusable packaging to the collection centre (which often is the store where the product was bought).

Policy option: maximum separation at source

Recovery of materials through the separation of waste at the source of waste production or by mechanical sorter (or other means) at a later stage in the waste disposal chain should be encouraged. The earlier the separation takes place the more efficient and appropriate the waste treatment can be due to the lesser extent of waste contamination. Incentives for local agents who produce less waste and manage the recyclable materials at source, e.g. reduction of municipal taxes, could be introduced. Appropriate collection facilities for various types of waste should be provided to encourage individuals to separate waste.

Policy option: local composting of household and garden waste

This local waste treatment reduces the overall amount of household waste to be collected and treated at municipal level, while providing high quality soil for the individual, and a valuable insight into the natural system. Composting therefore constitutes an important part of awareness raising and can have several additional multiplier effects, both environmentally, socially and economically. The spatial planning system and building regulations should be used to ensure that appropriate facilities are incorporated into the design and construction of neighbourhoods and buildings.

Policy option: regulations on use, reuse and recycling of building materials

Construction materials should be selected based on thorough knowledge of their impact on waste during construction, use and demolition. The lifetime and the reusability/recyclability of the construction materials are important indicators of how sustainable they are. The lifetime is very much dependent upon the ability to repair and maintain the material /construction. Many materials and installations today are manufactured in a way which makes repair impossible. Such things should be avoided as far as possible. Practice has shown that 70% of waste generated at construction sites can be reused or recycled if separated at the site (Heino, 1994). It is possible to make future use of all soil and stone material, wood, cardboard, metal and plasterboard. Only plastic materials prove difficult to recycle.

4.13 Full ecological cycles, Västerås, Sweden

Composting biological household waste is a key to good source separation. An example of this is a condominium block with 69 apartments in the town of Västerås. Source separation begins in the kitchens, which have been designed to make room for several waste containers. All biological waste is composted in thermally-insulated composters. There is a composting room alongside every entrance hall to the block. In the courtyard there is a compost corner where composted material ages before being used in the block's garden allotments. In addition to the composting rooms, there are also recycling rooms where inhabitants put all their recyclable waste. As a result of this waste separation and composting, the local sanitation department only collects 40% as much waste from this particular block as it does from other comparable blocks that have not been designed with similar composting facilities. The inhabitants also return twice as much paper and nearly four times as much glass for recycling as other people in Västerås (Ministry of the Environment and Natural Resources, 1992).

Policy option: environmentally friendly waste disposal systems

17.

Energy recovery through the use of biogas from landfill sites using systems which reduce air pollution makes efficient use of waste. Sanitary burial of non-usable materials and other technological developments compatible with an integrated and sustainable waste management policy should be developed and promoted. Charges can deter the use of landfill and incineration, thus encouraging reuse, recycling and minimisation of waste production. In Italy, a new law is about to be passed which introduces a tax on landfill treatment of solid waste.

4.14 Co-operation between municipality and industry for bio-energy, Eslöv, Sweden

The municipality of Eslöv has constructed a sedimentation chamber for waste water. It is used in collaboration with a food processing business which produces large amounts of vegetable and other food waste. Municipal waste water accounts for 15% of the sedimentation material, and the vegetable and food waste for 85%. The extracted bio-gas is conducted to a heating centre which services 450 one-family houses. The profit generated from the sale of the bio-gas covers the waste treatment costs. The sedimentation residue is spread on fields. Previously the waste water treatment plant produced 20,000 tonnes of sludge annually. The sedimentation chamber has reduced this quantity to 6,000 tonnes annually (Ministry of the Environment and Natural Resources, 1992).

Natural resources,
energy and waste are
inter-related

Adopt integrated and
ecological approaches

Maximise the
involvement of key
players in resource
management

Marginalised area

5

CONCLUSIONS

1.   The chapter emphasises that a more sustainable functioning of urban systems requires a move towards management of cities that makes use of the lessons nature can teach about ecological and economical flow management, which contrary to common belief often go hand in hand, so that the goals of the economy can be allied with those of environmental protection.

Natural resources, energy and waste are inter-related

2.   The issues of natural resources, energy and waste are closely interconnected. Cities are places of high energy intensity; the more energy consumed, the higher the need for natural resources to support the energy production. Similarly, the higher the consumption of natural resources and energy, the more waste is accumulated. Due to this inter-relationship it is logical that several of the relevant policy options have multiplier effects. So by addressing one particular problem, the policy options may simultaneously solve one or more other problems.

Adopt integrated and ecological approaches

3.   An integrated approach to closing the cycles of natural resources, energy and waste should be adopted within cities. The objectives of such an approach should include minimising consumption of natural resources, especially non-renewable and slowly renewable ones; minimising production of waste by reusing and recycling wherever possible; minimising pollution of air, soil and waters; and increasing the proportion of natural areas and biodiversity in cities. These objectives will be easier to work towards on a small scale, which is why local ecological cycles often, but not always, are the ideal basis for introducing more sustainable policies for urban systems.

Maximise the involvement of key players in resource management

4.   Cities should develop the integrated approach to natural resource management within a framework of co-operation and involvement of as many key players as possible. Cities should take an overall co-ordinating and directing role and aim to increase understanding of the relevant issues. To be most effective, the city should develop its natural resource management strategy in co-operation with the utilities, local businesses, construction companies and individuals. Some initiatives inevitably require the co-operation of the national government, whose role it is to provide the necessary frameworks for facilitating the implementation of energy conservation policies. Such frameworks may include fiscal measures (both in the form of taxes and grants), regulatory changes, new powers for municipalities etc.

CONCLUSIONS

Key role for cities in local energy management systems

For example, it is important to the success of local energy management systems, that the energy industry and the local politicians are involved. It is recognised that it is easier to influence the city's internal and external activities in relation to energy efficiency, than to influence conventional energy supply industries which make money by selling energy to consumers, not by improving energy efficiency. However, it is not impossible. In some countries like the Netherlands, municipalities are stake holders in independent energy production industries. In these cases they should use their rights as stakeholders to influence the boards of those industries. However, where cities cannot act directly, they should use their prominent position in society to deliver the important messages of sustainable energy management and the means of working towards it to national governments, the energy supply industry and the consumers. Cities can influence all these levels, especially by joining forces with other cities, lobbying and putting pressure on the relevant actors.

5.   Key role for cities in local energy management systems

Tools for sustainable management of natural resources

Cities have a significant role in influencing sustainable management of natural resources. Through spatial planning, building regulations, management of municipal public services and internal activities combined with innovation and dedication, cities can achieve improvements in water conservation, energy conservation, waste minimisation, biodiversity and biomass, and air quality. Tremendous gains can be achieved through the rational design and planning of spaces, activities and flows of resources.

Tools for sustainable management of natural resources

6.

Information and education as a key factor in sustainable urban systems

Influencing behaviour through education, information and practical example is a key factor in achieving more sustainable urban systems. The relationship between influencing behaviour and sustainable management of natural resources is particularly evident. It is an area where people's behaviour affects the level of sustainability very directly. Often it is also an area where people can see the results of changed behaviour in a very transparent way.

Information and education as a key factor in sustainable urban systems

7.

Another important factor which sustainable management should attempt to utilise is the effect that efficient and effective communications systems have (for data and information) on energy savings. These gains are particularly spectacular when applied to large cities which suffer from compound administrative and bureaucratic problems. They are heavily congested because of the lack of efficient public transport and effective networks.

8.

5

An understanding of the economic
policy context is necessary for the
consideration of urban
environment and economy

Socio-economic
sustainability

Economic policy should be placed
in a context of equity and social
distribution

SOCIO-ECONOMIC ASPECTS OF SUSTAINABILITY

ECONOMIC ASPECTS OF SUSTAINABILITY

The discussion of urban environment and economy must start from an understanding
of the economic policy context. European cities and national economies are now firmly
linked in a global system of production, capital movement, trade and investment. Policy
initiatives at local, regional and national scale have to work within the limits set by global
markets.

Global competitive pressures have caused a massive economic restructuring in European
cities. Manufacturing industry has rapidly declined as investment and production have
moved away from Europe towards new markets, lower input costs and cheap labour.
The remaining manufacturing is generally capital intensive, focused on mass consumer
industries, using more technologically advanced and flexible production systems and fewer
and more highly skilled workers.

Overall employment has shifted to a wide range of service industries. However there
has also been rapid restructuring within these, with selective job losses and geographical
shifts as well as dynamic growth in some sectors. Within cities, sectoral shifts have often
been accompanied by de-urbanisation of economic activity and employment, with growth
concentrated on the periphery of major cities and in smaller cities and towns.

4.   The traditional industrial regions of northern Europe have seen the greatest employment
losses and have had mixed success in restructuring and diversifying. A new core area has
benefited from recent growth. Peripheral regions remain economically as well as
geographically marginalised.

Socio-economic sustainability

5.   Economic policy at city and regional level has focused on achieving economic growth
and job creation - frequently in the face of the adverse impacts of economic restructuring.
This policy could be more effective if issues of equity and the social distribution of
unemployment, employment in general or employment at certain qualification levels, were
addressed more directly.

Economic growth in itself, and growth-based strategies, do not address issues of
distributional impact, equity or social justice. Indeed, there is evidence that patterns of
economic growth have in some cases deepened social polarisation and inequalities
between different sections of the labour force and between different social groups. In
many cities these are manifested in increases of social unrest, lawlessness and fear, even
where policing has been increased. These raise serious questions about the *social*
sustainability of many cities - their ability to continue to function as coherent communities
with at least some sense of shared identity and destiny, standards of behaviour, and
collective provision of basic amenities. These concerns which are discussed in section 2 of
this chapter have stimulated interest from economic development organisations in labour
market processes and policy, and in the way economic measures affect different social
groups.

The sustainability movement's interest in the quality of life has broadened the appraisal of economic activities. Clearly, economic activities also make a crucial contribution to welfare, not only providing jobs and income but also opportunities for personal development and benefits for local communities. On the other hand, they can detract from community well-being by providing only an impoverished and unsatisfying work experience, imposing burdens on publicly-provided infrastructure and services, and disrupting communities through excessively rapid growth or decline (section 2 of this chapter discusses other aspects of welfare). These factors are increasingly recognised in the EU's economic programmes. Funding for structural adjustment programmes increasingly pays attention to social and equity concerns.

Environmental sustainability and economic activity

Economic activity, in essence, involves adding value through the transformation of inputs such as labour, energy and materials, into outputs, plus waste or by-products. Economic activities have major impacts on sustainability issues. First and most obviously, their consumption of energy and materials and production of wastes and by-products are the main way that humanity affects global sustainability issues.

Economic activities may also have regional sustainability impacts. They may consume resources (such as biomass or water) for which there are regional carrying capacity limits, or produce emissions which overload the assimilative capacity of the environment at local or regional level, or occupy buildings and land making them unavailable for other uses. Economic activities must therefore play a key role in achievement of the aims for environmental sustainability set out in chapter 3.

This is recognised by the Fifth Environmental Action Programme. Most obviously, industry is the first of the five 'target sectors' singled out as crucial for the move towards sustainability. However the other four target sectors - energy, transport, agriculture and tourism are all also concerned with economic activities. In all these sectors the Programme emphasises the need to minimise resource use and waste production, to move to cleaner processes, and to avoid breaching carrying capacity limits.

Environmental changes will increasingly shape economic trends. After a point, environmental degradation and economic decline reinforce each other. This downward spiral could spread to large areas of the world (Brown, 1991).

The current indicator for economic progress is the gross domestic product (GDP). Bymeasuring flows of goods and services, GDP undervalues qualities that sustainable societies strive for, such as durability and resource protection and overvalues planned obsolescence and waste. Indicator for economic progress would measure economic and social advances by sustainability criteria rather than simply growth in short-term output.

Urban effects

Location of economic activities in cities has some significant implications for environmental and social sustainability.

Environmental
sustainability and
economic activity

Economic activities have major
impacts on sustainability issues

9.

10.

GDP is not a good indicator of
sustainability

Urban effects

Location of economic activities in
cities can reduce impacts on global
sustainability

The global sustainability impacts of many kinds of economic activity can be reduced by locating them in cities. As Chapter 3 argued, the high density of a city means, at least potentially, shorter average distances to workers' homes and consumer markets, reducing transport impacts. A study for the UK Department of the Environment found that density was the most important single factor in determining the average distance people travelled.

Higher density also means that infrastructure services can be provided more efficiently because of shorter distances. Perhaps most importantly, there are better opportunities for closing resource loops. Heat distribution, waste reuse and recycling are more viable because the concentration of economic activities provides enough business to support specialist activities which could not otherwise achieve economies of scale. Many Scandinavian cities have heat distribution networks: in a dense area, the levels of use justify the infrastructure cost. This integration is facilitated by municipal control of energy supply as well as waste management. High urban land values encourage more compact and energy-efficient built forms (see Chapter 4).

For regional sustainability effects, dense cities pose a problem rather than an opportunity. The higher the concentration of economic activities of a particular type, the sooner regional carrying capacity thresholds are reached. For example, the concentration of textile companies in the Aire and Calder rivers in greater Manchester has resulted in a lower toleration of pollution from any one of them than if they were more spread out. The severity of air pollution in Bilbao is a consequence of the concentration of industry there as well as the high emissions from each factory.

Location of economic activities in cities can increase impacts on regional and local sustainability

17.   Density is thus the factor which can make cities positive for the global sustainability impacts of economic activity and negative for the regional and local impacts. There is thus a paradox. Economic activities may cause less environmental damage in cities than elsewhere per capita or per unit of production. But they may appear more damaging because of their greater concentration per hectare.

18.   Density and scale also have both positive and negative implications for the social and welfare consequences of economic activity. The larger a local economy, the more it is able to support pools of specialists in particular skills. A city can provide specialists with the best technical education, a professional 'peer group' and a range of employers with whom to develop a career path without having to relocate.

The larger an economic region, the more it is able to support a cluster of companies specialising in a particular business without distorting the economy and reducing the range of alternative employment available. The collapse of a major industry is less disastrous in a major city, where it is only one among many sources of employment and wealth, than where it is the dominant economic force.

However, high density also accentuates negative social and welfare effects of economic activities, such as pollution from production and transport. The poorest and most disadvantaged residents of cities often also live in the worst local environmental conditions, while those who can afford to will buy a better local environment elsewhere. The locational concentration of these social and economic problems increases the risk of self-reinforcing cycles of deprivation, dereliction and disadvantage.

Environmental quality in cities is unequally distributed

Policy options for sustainability

The urban economy is perhaps the area where policy integration is most crucial. European cities need to meet economic needs while also responding to the social and environmental sustainability agendas. Failure to reconcile these three aims will result in cities failing to provide the material prosperity their residents expect, or failing to provide social well-being for their residents, or continuing to pose a major threat to the environment.

The White Paper *'Growth, Competitiveness and Employment'* (CEC 1993b) points to ways of reconciling employment and competitiveness with sustainability. Fields for job creation identified in a survey conducted by the European Commission (CEC 1995h) include daily life, quality of life, leisure, protection of the environment, housing improvements, security, local public transport, redevelopment of public urban areas, cultural heritage, and waste management. Chapter 10 of the White Paper proposes a shift in development away from maximising the productivity of *labour* - of which there is a surplus throughout the EU - and towards maximising the efficiency of the use of *resources* through increasing the use of labour. This could simultaneously relieve pressures on environmental sustainability, reduce unemployment and inequity, and reduce the high labour costs which disadvantage the EU compared to its economic competitors.

**Policy options for
sustainability**

Policy for urban economy must
also address social, and
environmental needs

Labour policies can serve as a tool
for the greening of the economy

Policy option: improving the environmental efficiency of each economic activity

There is enormous scope for reducing the environmental cost of each unit of economic utility. A number of changes can help with this:

- increasing the durability and reparability of products so that the resource 'costs' are spread over a longer useful life;

- increasing the efficiency with which resources (especially energy) are used, in both manufacture and use;

- simplifying production processes, avoiding over-specification, redundant elaboration and levels or dimensions of 'quality' which do not increase a product's usefulness or fitness for its purpose;

- minimising packaging and transport;

- using reclaimed and recycled materials in production, and in turn making products reusable and recyclable;

- using renewable instead of finite resources, and producing wastes in biodegradable forms.

Cities can encourage and help businesses of all types to adopt and apply these approaches. They can also encourage development of a specific 'sustainability business' sector to provide the equipment, products, services and expertise to help the broader business community apply them.

23.   **Policy option: improving
the environmental
efficiency of each
economic activity**

Policy option: developing an
environmentally sustainable
'industrial ecology' at city
and regional level

Methods to avoid relocation to
areas of low environmental
standards

Policy option: developing an environmentally sustainable 'industrial ecology' at city and regional level

As well as improving the environmental efficiency of individual businesses, cities can gain further benefits from the interconnection of activities. Wastes produced by one business can be recycled by another into products used by a third. Surplus or exhaust heat from one process can be used in others. A concentration of potential users can make a specialist environmental service viable.

An ecosystems approach to industry is required, involving:

• conscious mapping of resource flows at a city and regional level;

• co-ordinated development of industry sectors, technologies and individual companies to maximise resource synergies;

• minimisation of imports of materials, exports of wastes and long distance movement of part-finished goods;

• provision of sustainability infrastructure such as energy and waste distribution and recovery services, public transport and railheads for goods;

• encouraging businesses to locate near their workforces, suppliers, customers and other businesses with synergies. Density of development, and urban location, will generally help.

27. This approach will help to realise the potential *global* sustainability benefits of urban location of economic activities discussed earlier. However it must avoid the *local* and *regional* sustainability disbenefits of economic activities in cities. Hitherto dirty, dangerous and 'bad neighbour' activities have been kept away from residential and recreational areas. This zoning of land uses works against global sustainability and needs to be replaced with making as much economic activity as possible sufficiently safe, clean, quiet and benign to be acceptable neighbours within cities. The question of mixed uses in cities is further discussed in Chapter 7.

In encouraging businesses to locate within cities, stringent standards for emissions and impacts should be based not only on point loads but also on ambient environmental quality. This will mean that the acceptable level of emissions from a new plant will be affected by the level of emissions already being produced by others in the region.

This approach creates the further danger of encouraging economic activities to move to regions, or countries, with lower environmental standards, or where lower density of industry allows each source to produce more pollution without breaching carrying capacity limits. Methods to avoid this include:

• harmonisation of standards for pollution control, and a common ecologically-grounded framework for spatial planning and land use throughout the EU;

• progressive raising of environmental standards internationally, and international agreements to prevent 'dumping' of dirty developments;

- a collaborative problem-solving approach by city authorities to industrial environmental problems, rather than the punitive regulatory one encouraged by traditional regulatory frameworks;

- an overall economic framework which makes sustainable business profitable.

Policy option: ensuring that economic activities support social sustainability

This involves ensuring that the benefits of economic activities, and the chance to participate in economic life, are spread fairly through society, so that the economy aids rather than erodes social cohesion. This will be helped by an emphasis on ensuring that local production (of goods and services) provides employment for local people in satisfying local needs. Free trade and globalisation of markets are not automatically beneficial to social sustainability.

This may imply a need to reconsider and redefine the aims of local economic policy. For example conventional employment and unemployment statistics may not be a reliable measure of the ability of people to participate actively and fulfillingly in the local economy: they do not reflect the extent to which the technically 'unemployed' can participate to their own satisfaction through informal and 'third sector' activities; or the degree to which formal jobs are meaningless, boring and alienating.

Policy option: Creating jobs through greening the economy

Both sectoral studies and macro-economic modelling have indicated that greening the economy will generally result in a net gain in employment (Jacobs 1994). However much of the 'green business' employment involved in most of the studies to date is concerned with pollution control and clean-up.

A *sustainable* economy would prevent environmental problems through clean technologies, requiring less employment in environmental remediation rather than more. It is therefore not clear that an *environmentally* more sustainable economy will necessarily involve higher employment - although one of the latest 'jobs from the environment' studies (Ecotec, 1994) indicates that sample measures leading to sustainable development in the Fifth Environmental Action Programme's five priority areas will generally lead to job creation.

'First mover advantage' in developing green technologies has enabled some countries, notably Germany and Denmark, to develop lucrative new industry sectors. Economic regeneration is more likely to achieve economic objectives if local communities are actively involved in ensuring that proposals meet social as well as economic objectives, and that environmental quality improves both well-being and an area's attractiveness for developers.

Policy option:
ensuring that economic
activities support
social sustainability

5

Policy option: Creating
jobs through greening
the economy

32.

Green business: recycling of building material

ECONOMIC ASPECTS OF SUSTAINABILITY

Three options for cleaner technology

There is a continuous and increasingly urgent demand for sustainable technology. Fortunately various contributions to more environmentally efficient techniques and energy efficient techniques have already been made, usually as a result of economic conditions, and lately because of environmental considerations as well. Current technology development should be reoriented and future development directed with respect to sustainability.

Technology's contribution toward the realisation of the prospect of sustainable development can be optimised through three approaches:

- environmental care - streamlining the current production systems;

- environmental technology - short-term improvement and application of existing technology;

- sustainable technology - the long-term improvement of technology and finding new technology.

'Backcasting' and a new techno-economic paradigm

37.   A new approach was introduced for energy by Goldenberg et al. (1985) and is expressed by the term 'backcasting'. This implies directing and determining the process that technological development must take and possibly also the pace at which this development process must be put into effect. This goal-directed approach is based on an inter-connecting picture of demands which technology has to meet in the future, especially sustainability criteria.

38.   In the coming decades a rapidly decreasing eco-capacity will undoubtedly result in a fundamental shift in relative costs of the dominant production factors (energy-environment versus capital and labour) and might thus induce a new techno-economic paradigm. Such a shift might redirect the development of economy and technology towards an optimum with lower energy and environment intensities (Jansen, 1994). The European Commission (CEC 1995h) summarise the following opportunities for the creation of jobs:

Job creation in the field of local public transport

The employment trend in the urban public transport sector is currently stable if not negative, due to gains in productivity, the application of new information technology and the limitations of public budgets. However, there is an alternative option which should enable substantial numbers of jobs to be created. Based on a more locally-oriented strategy of development and on public/private partnership, this consists of enlarging the concept of the service provided by public transport and attempting to respond more effectively to the changing requirements of users.

The creation of new jobs in this field depends largely on the national context, with less discrimination against public forms of transport being a key issue. In particular, the proper allocation of external costs (e.g. pollution and road and track maintenance) for *all* forms of transport would place public transport on an equal footing, economically speaking. Work regulations should be adapted to the need for multiple skills; and new legal instruments adopted to encourage delegated and integrated management of all forms of transport in urban and rural areas.

Building projects employ large numbers of workers. But the maintenance of public areas, street furniture, street signs and cleansing services could also generate new jobs. A continuing flow of jobs derives from the improvement of the quality of life once an area becomes more attractive with the re-stimulation of economic activity mainly in the service sector: commerce, tourism, arts etc.

In encouraging exchanges of experience and deepening of inter-national links, the EU should put greater emphasis on methods for the improvement of urban public areas and the consequent creation of jobs. Similarly, it should take greater advantage of the full range of instruments for local development which it possesses. Financial and legal instruments should foster co-operation between the public and private sectors in local projects and medium or long-term contracts between the various public authorities concerned. The search for new modes of financing may well be facilitated by tax reforms and by restructuring the current distribution of national wealth between towns and regions.

Urban renovation provides opportunities for a wider variety of job-skills and more scope for using smaller businesses and other bodies. A study on urban renovation programmes carried out in Portugal shows that, on average for the same budgetary expenditure, twice as many people are employed for rehabilitation work (90-120 man-days) as for new building work (50 man-days).

Housing maintenance and associated services may seem to be more promising in terms of job creation, because they are highly labour-intensive and respond to a new, largely unsatisfied demand for the services. However, they tend to be small-scale and operate on small budgets and do not provide a significant contribution to job creation.

Job creation in the field of redevelopment of public urban areas

Job creation in the field or property renovation and housing maintenance

44.

5.1   Job creation by minimising heat-loss in individual houses, Denmark

Since 1974 Denmark has successfully pursued a policy of improving housing to save energy. By 1980, the number of jobs created by this policy was estimated to be 10,000, most of them permanent. For individual houses, which constitute the priority target for this measure, it is calculated that the investment will pay off in less than 9 years, through savings on heating bills. A programme aimed to reduce energy consumption used in heating by 30% throughout Denmark would create 5,800 regular jobs over 20 years, given the number of properties to be treated.

National policies facilitate the creation of jobs for renovating the housing stock, for maintenance and for caretaking. These policies combine the following aspects:

• promotion of integrated neighbourhood renovation projects, bringing in multi-trade partnerships (incorporating various skills) and multi-sector partnerships (small business, starter enterprises, non-governmental organisations, local authorities, etc.) the idea being to promote a better relationship between residents and suppliers;

Job creation

Job creation in the field of
cultural heritage

Job creation in the field of waste
management

Job creation in the field of security

- organisation of a 'one-stop housing assistance system', with the ability to coordinate the full range of housing problems from financing and construction up to and including maintenance, cleaning and services to residents;

- guaranteed stability over time of financial and legal arrangements, given that building firms are very sensitive to this aspect in the light of long repayment periods;

- diversification of public aid for both supply and demand to take into account all subsectors of the construction business. This improvement should be accompanied by an information and counselling policy (e.g. approval of advisers who have contracted to observe a code of professional ethics, and collaboration between different welfare workers).

There is growing need for the various skills involved in the creation, restoration and maintenance of cultural heritage sites, the management of the sites, and reception of visitors, plus those involved in dissemination of information about cultural heritage. Such work should be stimulated by national governments through fiscal policy.

47. There is employment in all parts of the chain of waste management: from sorting and recovery of waste to research in the field of technical improvement. The area of ecological waste treatment also offers new employment opportunities. The national authorities must continue their action to stimulate waste recovery and recycling, which basically means taxation.

5.2   Job creation by the reduction of building waste and energy, Copenhagen, Denmark, Amsterdam, the Netherlands

In Copenhagen efforts have been made over the last five years to reduce waste from the demolition of buildings (40,000 tonnes in 1989 fell to 2,000 tonnes in 1994). Bricks and cement are converted into gravel, sawn wood is incinerated. The greater the care taken to preserve materials during demolition, the greater the amount of work and labour required. 'Selective' demolition reduces waste by almost 95% and the cost of access to the rubbish tip. Extrapolating the Copenhagen experience to the whole of Denmark, 850 long-term jobs would be guaranteed by this method of selective demolition, 130 of which are linked to the re-use of bricks.

In Amsterdam Energy Teams have been set up to help residents with energy saving in their homes. They offer advice and carry out practical work. In a four-year period about 40 jobs were created and 7000 homes were visited.

Currently, TV-monitoring, scanning and surveillance techniques, together with data processing and communication technologies, open up possibilities for new types of services, generally for relatively moderate operating costs. These policies are all the more effective if followed up at local level by measures designed to:

- promote preventive behaviour by residents, e.g. improving information on the real
  risks and providing financial incentives for certain forms of security equipment (a solution
  is suggested for each specific need in an explanatory catalogue);

- make provision for integrated security policies, with co-ordination between the various
  departments or services concerned (justice, police, housing, health) and a partnership
  with private or semi-private small firms providing a service for the general good and
  receiving start-up aid or job creation assistance on a decreasing scale (for example
  50% public funding in the first year, 20% in the second year, 0% in the third year).

Policy option: spatial planning and transport planning

Spatial planning clearly has a crucial role in achieving the spatial relationships between
economic activities, infrastructure, populations, markets and resources implied by the policy
directions stated above. The role of spatial planning is discussed in detail in Chapter 7.

50.

Similarly, urban policies for the maintenance and development of infrastructure for
walking, cycling and mass public transport, and for rail and water transport of goods have
a crucial role in allowing cities to increase the sustainability of economic activity. Some of
these issues are considered in Chapter 6.

Policy option: advice and support for local businesses in improving environmental performance

Policy option: advice
and support for local
businesses in improving
environmental
performance

51.

Cities and other authorities already provide advice and support to businesses in a
variety of ways. *(see box 5.3, next page)*

Policy option: promotion of green consumerism

'Green consumerism' is an important influence on business. Cities can encourage and
enable both corporate and individual consumers to identify and to value products and
services generated more sustainably so as to give them market advantage. Research in the
UK (Worcester 1994) indicates that 'consumers are voting with their pocketbooks. Half or
more of the British public report that because of concern for the environment they buy
'ozone friendly' aerosols or avoid them altogether (71%), buy products which are made
from recycled material (54%) or packaged in recycled materials (50%), and half say they
... minimise the amount of electricity and fuel their household uses.' Moreover these
percentages have been rising since 1990. This work also indicates that 'people in Britain
seem to want more information on the environmental risks posed by everyday products
(87%), ways of disposing of waste (86%), and the potential risks of nuclear radiation
(84%).' Providing this type of information can have an important effect on consumer
behaviour. The growth of ethical funds and ethical banking indicate that many people are
prepared to accept the possibility of lower financial gains in return for the guarantee that
their money is not supporting industries and activities which they regard as inappropriate.

5.3 Support and advice to businesses, Gelderland in the Netherlands, Cork in Ireland and Berlin in Germany

The Internal Environmental Care System project in the Gelderland province of the Netherlands helped to establish formal environmental management systems in small enterprises. Public authorities both assisted in improving the environmental performance of smaller companies in the region and established a closer dialogue with them over environmental issues, by providing training for company managers, carrying out assessments of production processes and advising companies on environmental management procedures (Ecotec 1994).

The Clean Technology Centre in Cork is an independent non-profit organisation providing research, information and educational material on clean technologies to subscriber companies, carrying out pollution abatement studies and trials in their premises, and contributing to the development of standards and legislation at national level.

The Berlin Senate's Environmental Support Programme offers small and medium sized enterprises subsidies of up to 50 per cent of the cost of environmentally sound investments and innovations. The programme aims to reduce pollution, disseminate new technologies and innovative solutions, and raise environmental awareness in smaller companies. Funded by the European Regional Development Fund, the programme was launched in 1990 in West Berlin and has been extended to the eastern part of the city.

5.4 Minimising the use of packaging, Lothian Regional Council, Scotland

Lothian Regional Council invited Friends of the Earth Scotland to mount an exhibition in its consumer advice shopfront on the environmental consequences of packaging and consumer action to avoid over-packaging. The display material was based on Friends of the Earth Netherlands' packaging campaign.

Policy option: targeted inward investment strategy

A number of cities are targeting inward investment strategies on types of economic activity which are more favourable in terms of sustainability. This has implications not only for marketing but also for strategic and physical planning and for the provision of sites and premises, infrastructure, financial support and support services.

Policy option: building competitive advantage

Cities and regions can gain advantage in competing for inward investment from a
pleasant living environment and high quality of life. These will also help an area to retain
existing economic activity. Cities must however take care that the businesses they attract
do not undermine the quality of life which attracted them.

Initiatives like this can be seen as implementations of the Regional Environmental

5.5 Business and quality of life, Emscher Park, Germany

The Emscher Park International Building Exhibition is a programme conceived by the state
of Nord-Rhine-Westphalia in 1988 to promote structural change in the Emscher region, an
area of industrial dereliction in the Ruhr valley. The main objective is the ecological
renewal of the region - a corridor some 80km long - to create a new basis for economic
development. Within the region there are several projects for the development of business
or science parks which aim to encourage environmentally friendly businesses or firms
specialising in environmental technologies and which also make provision for other uses
such as housing and child care facilities. Several involve the redevelopment of redundant
colliery sites. For example, the site of the former Arenberg-Fortzetsung colliery in Bottrop is
being reclaimed to provide a green commercial park for small and medium sized local firms
and for the promotion of local employment opportunities, especially for women.

Building competitive advantage

Management approach put forward in Welford 1993. This is based on a region-wide plan
for environmental improvement, agreed between public agencies and companies, as a
source of comparative advantage at both company and regional level.

55.

Policy option: promoting the environmental business sector

Defining the 'environmental business sector' is not straightforward. 'Sustainability
businesses' can encompass everything from low-technology but highly skilled craft
activities to low-skill, labour-intensive collection and sorting of recyclable materials. On a
larger scale, some Member States now have a major 'clean technology' sector which is
actively promoted at national and regional levels as well as in cities. Local economic
development agencies and programmes can target support mechanisms such as the
provision of premises, infrastructure, grants, loans, advice and development work so as
to encourage businesses of this type.

ECONOMIC ASPECTS OF
SUSTAINABILITY

5

5.6 Support for 'sustainability businesses', Edinburgh (Scotland), Kolding, Fredericia and Vejle (Denmark) and Herning, Ikast, Videbaek and Silkeborg (Denmark)

Lothian and Edinburgh Environmental Partnership, is a not-for-profit company funded by Edinburgh City Council to develop sustainability businesses in the fields of energy, transport and recycling. It has successfully launched an office paper and aluminium can recycling enterprise, helped establish a number of businesses including a cycle courier company, a nappy laundry and an agency providing energy conservation measures to low income householders, and is developing a range of further projects.

The 'Triangle Region' of southern Denmark, which encompasses eight municipalities including, for example, Kolding, Fredericia and Vejle, describes itself as an 'open green town' or 'green city network'. Within this region efforts have been made to foster commercial activities favouring environmental and clean technology and resource saving. Local authorities and private companies have worked together in pioneering approaches to waste treatment and combined heat and power, reducing both energy consumption and emissions in the local area.

Green City Denmark is a partnership between four municipalities in central Jutland: Herning, Ikast, Videbaek and Silkeborg. With the support of the two counties (Ringkobing and Aarhus) within which these towns are located, these were the first Danish municipalities to endorse the International Chamber of Commerce's Business Charter for Sustainable Development. The partnership, which involves co-operation between the local authorities and leading-edge private companies, is designed to provide a shop window for Danish expertise in environmental technology.

Policy option:
linking economic
development and labour
market policy

Policy option: linking economic development and labour market policy

The need to link economic development with labour market policy in order to secure distributional goals rather than relying on the 'trickle down effects' of economic growth is now well recognised. Research for the UK Department of the Environment (Department of the Environment, 1994) has tended to confirm doubts about the effectiveness of 'trickle down'. This relates directly to social sustainability arguments as identified earlier in this Chapter.

Local labour market measures on recruitment and training can be directly linked to environmental goals, thus linking social and environmental sustainability issues. The French government has made 400 million francs available to regions and, from May 1994, to a wide range of local bodies and associations to co-fund 'green employment' initiatives (Ministere de l'Environnement, 1994). These also cover training, including professional training. Typical projects include waste management, river treatment and improvement, measures to safeguard biodiversity and landscape quality and other forms of environmental protection and improvement. Stimulating partnership at local level among bodies with an interest in employment and the environment is an explicit aim.

5.7 Training, job creation and environmental sustainability, Berlin, Germany

In 1991 the Berlin Senate launched the Berlin Ecological Renovation Programme for East Berlin to meet both labour market and environmental objectives. It co-funds employment and training initiatives in the environmental field and investments directed towards environmental protection and urban renewal. While immediate employment initiatives create short term jobs, investments in environmental infrastructure promote and safeguard jobs in the longer term.

Community enterprises can meet economic, social and environmental needs simultaneously. They are better able to raise capital where investment institutions are able to include social and environmental benefits in their lending criteria. Successful community enterprise and an ethical dimension to funding therefore tend to come together.

Community enterprises can integrate economic, social and environmental concerns

Measures of this sort need not be limited to the formal economy. In the UK there are 300 Local Employment and Trading (LETS) schemes. These provide a mechanism for people within a locality to exchange goods and services through a local currency. The aim is to allow people to provide and receive socially useful services whether or not they are in conventional employment or have disposable income.

60.

5.8 Local employment and trading systems, Cardiff, UK

Cardiff City Council is supporting the development of LET systems alongside credit unions, non-profit local associations for pooling resources to provide members with credit.
The hope is that the combination of labour exchanged through the LET scheme and access to affordable credit for raw materials from the credit union will together enable low income and marginalised people to provide each other with goods and services. Cardiff also has community businesses which repair and resell unwanted furniture and provide gardening services for the elderly; both have important elements of skills training.

Policy option: partnerships between urban government and industry

Partnership approaches have already been commended in Chapter 3. They are particularly valuable in the greening of industry. Far more can be achieved through collaboration between city agencies and the business community than through confrontation.

Policy option:
partnerships between
urban government and
industry

5.9 Partnership in action, Bilbao, Spain

Bilbao's economy is based on traditional sectors - steel, metals, chemicals and energy. These are characterised by substantial air pollutions, especially SO2. Development is concentrated along a narrow river valley, resulting in levels of air pollution well above permissible limits. The pollution reduces the quality of life in the city and damages the city economy. The city's port has been losing car export business to Santander because air pollution in Bilbao has damaged the paint on cars waiting for shipping. New businesses avoid locating to Bilbao because of the perceived environmental problems. Bilbao Metropoli-30 is an initiative of the Basque government which seeks to engage the private and public sectors in finding a strategy for the revitalisation of the city. It accepts that environmental degradation is one of the most severe problems facing the city, and that economic development - and a reversal of the current industrial decline - depends upon environmental improvement. The 19 founding partners of the initiative included the Basque Government, the Provincial Government, the Municipality of Bilbao, public agencies including two universities and the chamber of commerce, and major local enterprises. Over the three years the initiative has been in operation the number of partners has increased to 94.

62.   It is too early to attempt a full assessment of the initiative in Bilbao. However, it has engaged the active involvement and support of several sectors of local industry and helped to create markets for a fledgling environmental management industry in the region. More importantly, environmental issues are increasingly viewed not as a peripheral distraction but as part of normal business management (Ecotec, 1993). Many examples of partnership now exist.

5.10 Examples of partnership, Coventry and Sheffield in the UK

A forum, Coventry Regional Environmental Management Panel, initially set up over 20 years ago to discuss and resolve pollution issues, has developed a wider environmental management role and created a climate of co-operation and trust which has made possible an impressive range of other joint local authority/business initiatives on the environment.

Sheffield Heat and Power, a joint venture between the city council and a Finnish combined heat and power (CHP) company, has established a waste-powered district heating system as the first step to a city centre combined heat and power system.

Policy option: provision of sustainability infrastructure

Providing sustainable transport infrastructure (discussed in Chapter 6) is obviously an important way for local economic development activities to promote sustainability. Other forms of physical infrastructure can also play an important role. Examples include:

- heat distribution pipes;

- offices and business units built to high standards of energy efficiency, durability, adaptability and aesthetic quality;

- facilities for environmentally efficient waste management, such as separation and sorting plants, incinerators with energy recovery, and digesters linked to CHP plants.

Policy option: provision
of sustainability
infrastructure

Sustainability of the infrastructure

5.11 Sustainability on industrial sites, Odense, Denmark

The municipality of Odense has prepared 750 hectare of industrial sites for development, separated into zones so that each enterprise can be located appropriately in relation to opportunities for expansion but also to environmental impact. The municipality supplies companies as well as residents with inexpensive heating using waste heat from the Fyn combined heat and power station, and treats industrial waste water. The city has also succeeded in attracting enterprises (such as market gardens) which can use surplus heat commercially. Economic development on this scale is based on partnerships between the municipality and the private sector.

Environmental expertise in the local workforce can both attract sustainable businesses and help existing businesses to become environmentally more aware. Environmental elements in vocational training, links between businesses and higher education establishments and networking opportunities are all of value.

64.

The above has shown that there is in fact considerable scope for action within cities. However it was pointed out that in this area, perhaps more than any other, action at urban level is limited by national and international policies and actions. The following discusses the requirements beyond the urban level to facilitate action.

Local action is limited by national
and international policies and
actions

ECONOMIC ASPECTS OF
SUSTAINABILITY

Policy option: measures
to make environmentally
sustainable business
behaviour commercially
profitable

Policy option: measures to make environmentally sustainable business behaviour commercially profitable

Companies cannot progression toward sustainability is constrained by market conditions. Important market constraints on sustainable behaviour are:

- low costs of energy, materials and waste disposal compared to other factors of production, notably labour, which encourage companies to shed labour even at the expense of higher resource impacts;

- lack of market signals to encourage companies to distinguish between sustainable and unsustainable patterns of resource use;

- high discount rates and rates of return on investments, which discourage investment in resource efficiency measures other than those with very short paybacks, and prevent companies adopting a whole-life resource cost optimisation approach.

Sustainable behaviour should be made commercially viable

Individual businesses will tend to 'free ride' on the environmental consequences of their activity. If pursuing more sustainable activity involves a cost which is not simultaneously imposed on their competitors, companies acting more sustainably would be likely to lose competitive advantage.

68.   Economic development policies which attempt to force companies to go beyond current market 'best practice' will harm the local economy without achieving benefits for the environment. This limitation can only be removed by action to make sustainable behaviour more commercially viable. Such action can often be most easily taken at the level of the whole economy.

Government support for
sustainable development

69.   Four government level responses are particularly important for this:

- environmental tax reform;

- national environmental business partnerships;

- financial institutions;

- market creation for sustainable businesses.

These are discussed in the following sections.

Environmental tax reform

Environmental tax reform

The EU suffers high unemployment, high labour costs compared to industrial competitors, and unsustainable levels of energy use, raw materials depletion and waste production. Yet labour, income and value added are all heavily taxed while energy, resources and wastes are taxed little if at all. As Chapter 3 argued, shifting the burden of taxation away from employment and towards environmentally undesirable impacts could help to address all three of these problems at once. This is therefore arguably the most important integrative tool for an environmentally and socially sustainable economy. Environmental tax reform should not be seen as introducing a 'distortion', but as replacing accidental and undesirable consequences of taxation with planned and beneficial ones.

The White Paper *Growth, Competitiveness and Employment* supports these concepts. It has been argued that the employment goals set out in the White Paper may only be achievable through deliberate *reduction* in the output of the economy and a shift to more labour-intensive activities (Fleming 1994). This may imply a radical revision of EU trade and economic policy.

Any change in taxation will produce winners and losers, and should therefore be introduced slowly, progressiely and with ample forewarning tothose affected. Moreover tax changes alone will often not produce significantly change in behaviour. Increasing the price of petrol has little short term impact on use where people are 'locked in' to patterns of life which depend on car use, or where there is not reliable, affordable and attractive public transport alternative. The wealthy can often afford to ignore financial incentives while the poor can often not afford to respond to them - and may suffer disproportionately where prices of basic necessities are raised.

Tax changes should be accompanied by other policy measures

For all these reasons, ecological tax change must be accompanied by other policy measures which facilitate sustainable behaviour change and protect the disadvantaged. For example, increases in car taxation should be accompanied by investment in public transport and provision for cycling and walking. Increases in domestic energy prices should be accompanied by measures to enable people on low incomes to improve their energy efficiency.

The position on these issues varies greatly between Member States. Denmark has already introduced incentives for a more sustainable economy into the tax system, including, for example:

74.   Ecological taxation varies greatly between Member States

- a carbon dioxide tax, from which biomass fuels are exempt;

- high registration tax for passenger cars, with two elements, based on weight and purchase price;

- charges on CFC's and halons, with exemptions for district heating pipes;

- charges on landfill and incineration of waste, designed to encourage recycling and waste reduction;

- a raw materials charge on extraction and import of materials including sand, gravel, clay and chalk;

- various grant schemes for use of renewable energy including wind, straw, biogas and hydro power;

- advantageous depreciation provisions for environmental investments.

The Dutch government is considering the provision of tax incentives for environmentally-friendly investment and continues to give priority to shifting taxes and charges from earned income to polluting activities. The government is also lobbying for lower VAT rates at EU level on environmentally-friendly products and environmental and energy-saving services. The Government favoured the creation of a European energy tax and adopted a national energy tax.

Economic activity

5

National environmental business partnerships

The importance of partnerships at local level has already been emphasised. Partnership is also a valuable tool at national level.

The Netherlands' 'Nationaal Milieubeleidsplan' (National Environmental Policy Plan, NEPP), the NEPP+ and the NEPP2 established environmental quality objectives over a number of themes and translated these into over 200 quantified targets. It is a fundamental premise of the NEPP that government must devolve responsibility for achieving its objectives on to other groups in society.

One of the main ways the government has achieved this devolution with industry has been through covenants. A covenant is an agreement between the government and an industry sector to reach specified environmental objectives by certain dates. The 'content' of each covenant - called the industry's 'Integrale Milieu Taakstelling' (Integrated Environmental Target Plan) - is established through consultations involving central, provincial and local government, industry representatives (usually drawn from trade associations), employers' and trade union associations.

The Integrated Environmental Target Plan is translated into company environmental plans which indicate targets, timetables, and measures that each company will adopt. The company plans are prepared in close co-operation with the licensing authorities and serve as the basis for the company's permit. By 1995 the government aimed to sign covenants with 15 industry sectors including 12,000 companies, together responsible for over 90% of the country's industrial pollution (Ministry of Housing, Spatial Planning and the Environment, 1994).

Financial institutions

80.   Financial institutions need to promote longer-term investment and strategic company management, and to discourage short-term speculation, asset stripping and the generation of profit through market manoeuvres unconnected with business development.

German investment institutions support long term strategic development, and this is widely believed to have contributed to Germany's economic and industrial strength through the 1980s.

Market management and sustainable businesses

Individual urban areas may be able to promote and attract environmentally friendly businesses, but the amount of environmentally beneficial economic activity which the economy can support is limited by broader economic factors.

For example the amount of recycled materials which can be sold is often limited by the lack of processing capacity or demand for finished products. In these circumstances, one city can only increase its recycling rates at the expense of a reduction elsewhere. In a situation like this, local environmental initiatives can become a 'zero sum game' where initiatives by one city simply shift sustainable activities around in space, unless positive policy action is taken to manage markets.

The Eco-Management and Audit Scheme, with its requirement to publish a Statement on the performance of a company's environmental management system, is a step in the right direction. However its voluntary status means that the companies whose environmental performance is most questionable are those least likely to report their performance to the public. It is more difficult for companies which have already tried hard to improve their environmental performance to show 'continuous improvement' in the future, as registration under the scheme requires, than for companies which start from a poor level of environmental performance. There is therefore a possibility that the scheme will be most useful to 'poor but improving companies', and will neither influence the 'poor and not improving' nor the 'already environmentally-sound'.

In many Member States, the lack of regulatory control of green claims in advertising, or of standardisation of environmental descriptions, means that companies are still able to use advertising to mislead and confuse the public over the environmental performance of products. The EU Eco-Label scheme and the Directive on Freedom of Environmental Information both help the public to exercise informed environmental choices.

'Closure' of city economies

It is difficult to achieve a sustainable city when city economies are almost entirely 'open'. There are of course no economic barriers between cities, so goods, investment, businesses and (to a slightly lesser extent) people can move between them with complete freedom.

EU Single Market and similar policies promote openness for the sake of economic efficiency. EU procurement directives have ruled out one of the last remaining forms of 'closure' at city level, local preference in public procurement. Local economic isolationism is clearly not a viable policy in the current world economy.

It may however be worth remembering that the immense prosperity of many European city states in the Middle Ages, which arguably laid the foundations of all Europe's subsequent development, was achieved through a degree of autonomy between cities and active municipal intervention within them which would be unthinkable today (Girouard 1985).

More freedom for city authorities to insulate the local economy from international market pressures and actively manage the local economy could help move economic activities towards sustainability at local level in the absence of national level policy changes of the sort discussed above.

Levels of local economic autonomy vary greatly between countries. Some of the following measures are already implemented to a greater or lesser extent in some Member States. Significantly, these are often ones where at least some cities are particularly well advanced towards sustainability. Relevant measures include powers to:

• include environmental criteria, such as avoidance of unnecessary travel and transport, in public procurement;

• apply environmental and local developmental criteria to the investment of pension funds and other public funds;

'Closure' of city
economies

86.

87.   'Closure' of city economies
contradicts EU single market
policies

88.

Levels of local economic
autonomy vary greatly between
countries

SUSTAINABLE CITIES

154

SOCIAL ASPECTS OF
SUSTAINABILITY

INTRODUCTION

5   SOCIO-ECONOMIC ASPECTS OF SUSTAINABILITY

- impose local energy, resource and waste charges and/or taxes as mandated by local political processes;

- set up local budgetary feedback loops, such as investment of energy taxes in energy saving measures;

- allow public and quasi-public bodies to raise money in markets and invest in sustainability infrastructure and enterprises with the same freedom as the private sector;

- set local environmental standards in excess of those applying nationally;

- develop regional and local economic instruments, such as tradable permits and road pricing.

As has been emphasised earlier, sustainability in urban areas cannot be achieved by application of any one instrument or type of instrument. Integrated packages of different instruments offer more scope for success. The Helsingor digester project described in chapter 3 section 2 illustrates a successful package. It was made possible by the *combination* of a wide range of different measures including, for example:

- powers for municipalities to lay down the way in which householders sort and present refuse for collection;

- separation of waste collection charges from other local authority funding, and freedom for authorities to choose more expensive disposal options (and charge extra for them) if politically supported;

- high levels of environmental awareness, built up by education over a long term, leading local voters to support investment on environmental grounds;

- substantial municipal investment in heat distribution infrastructure;

- a guaranteed premium price for renewably-generated electricity;

- central government funded research and development of digestion technology;

- government 'soft loans' for sustainable power plants.

2   SOCIAL ASPECTS OF SUSTAINABILITY

2.1   INTRODUCTION

The social debate depends on time and place and is changing constantly. In the 19th century it focused on poverty risks or, in other words, on social class conflicts. During the latter part of the 20th century ecological risks confront us. Ecological risks are no longer tied to their place of origin but by their nature threaten all forms of life on this planet. This is exactly what is meant by the process of globalization of risks: 'risk society in this sense is a world risk society' (Beck, 1992). Ecological risks transcend social class and ignore borders of society: 'poverty is hierarchic, smog is democratic' (Beck, 1992).

Integrated packages of different instruments offer more scope for success

Ecological risks apply to all people

The social dynamic of ecological threats is no longer understood in traditional variables like class, income, or status. Environmental pressure is a function of the number of people, their consumption, and the consumption of resources per product unit (Ester and Mandemaker, 1994).

The social and environmental sustainability agendas have become linked through a common interest in equity. Concern about the present and future distributional consequences of growth and the implications for integration and social cohesion has coincided with the growing concern for environmentally sustainable development. There is no logical link between the principles of equity between generations and equity within the present generation. However, the ethical values which lead to concern for one often also support the other. What started as separate environmental and social equity movements are increasingly converging on a new approach to economic development which questions assumptions about the benefits of indefinite and undifferentiated economic growth from both resource and welfare perspectives.

This Chapter provides a discussion aimed at influencing, from an ecological point of view, the social system in order to transform cities towards sustainability. It identifies policy options leading to principles of social systems or lifestyle changes. It also seeks to reveal the nature and extent of social aspects and, if possible, the variations among countries, cities, and the cities' inhabitants. The analysis offers no dramatic new solutions, but should provide the basis for a better understanding of the relationship between social issues and sustainability.

Not all relevant social issues can be explored in this Chapter. A number of aspects relevant for the social quality of life have been selected: welfare, health impacts, and housing. These issues were chosen because they contain aspects where local authorities have a unique role to play, where the European Commission has relevant expertise, and where both levels can join together in order to tackle the problems.

Influencing behaviour and lifestyle

In the words of the Brundtland Commission it is time to break away from traditional patterns. There is a need for radical changes in all sectors of social life: economy, culture, social structure, industry, traffic and transport, consumption, etc. These radical changes cannot occur without corresponding shifts in the social, economic, and moral character of human society. People must become aware that their everyday existence is threatened. Shifts in the behaviour and lifestyles of politicians and citizens will form a new set of principles, goals and aspirations, with the welfare of future generations at their core.

Environmental concern is widespread in modern society and there is ample reason to believe it will remain high as the environmental dimension becomes a cornerstone of the debate about the future of society.

Subjective norms are related to change of behaviour. For example, using the bus instead of the private car depends on the individual's intention, which in turn is a result of the individual's attitude to the bus and existing norms with respect to taking the bus. There are often many reasons why people's behaviour does not change - to do with individual versus collective interests, and short-term versus long-term effects.

Unlearning old habits, learning
new habits

Changing behaviour and particularly changing patterns of behaviour (lifestyle) is a
much more complex issue for it implies unlearning old habits, learning new habits and
adhering to these new habits. Changing existing values is likely to be the most difficult
task.

Changing behaviour and lifestyle requires environmental marketing. 'One of the major
tasks facing environmental policy and environmental marketing is to communicate that
sustainable lifestyles are normal and not deviant lifestyles; that they reflect responsibility
and care for our planet; that they bring a sense of community; evoke pleasure, harmony,
purity, enrichment, and even excitement' (Nelissen, 1992).

In a study by Environmental Resources Limited (ERL) 'a number of specific 'low cost'
behavioural changes are suggested which are elements of pro-environmental lifestyles and
which can be prompted by environmental marketing such as: tele-shopping, hiring rather
than buying equipment, reusing and recycling goods, making compost out of organic
waste, purchasing services rather than goods, buying goods and services with least
environmental impact, tele-working, tele-conferencing at work, reduced commuting
through living near one's workplace, employment of local school transport service,
increased use of public transport, extended use of motor vehicles, choosing the most
environmentally friendly transport means, choosing less meat and dairy products, and
choosing less heavily packaged foods' (Ester and Mandemaker, 1994).

Lifestyle changes should be
communicated in a positive way

11.   Policy to change behaviour starts with information about the target group, and
disseminates information relevant to the group's behaviour. Above all, lifestyle changes
ought to be communicated in a positive way.

12.   Individual values influence social change. Progress towards sustainability requires a
collective deepening of our sense of responsibility to the earth and to future generations.
Building a sustainable future that satisfies our needs without jeopardising the prospects of
future generations is far from easy and involves re-evaluation of our personal aspirations
and motivation.

Community, future
generations and
involvement of local
people

Community, future generations and involvement of local people

The city is for the people, but it also belongs to the people. Working for a sustainable
future in cities is not only a question of collective enterprise but of ethics in the sense that
there exists a shared responsibility. As formulated in the Fifth Environmental Action
Programme for the Environment (CEC, 1992a), all the parties involved are responsible for
the future of humankind and the planet. Hence the responsibility does not rest only with
government at the different levels, but with industry, agriculture, transport, consumers,
and citizens.

Community involvement is essential for the achievement of sustainability objectives,
principally to ensure 'common ownership' of the issues and solutions, as difficult personal
and political choices must be made. It is important to seek a public debate about what
types of environment the public want and their reactions to limitations on personal
behaviour that may be necessary, such as reducing car use and water consumption.

Natural resources for future
generations

Public participation in spatial planning has often been narrowly defined, for example as choosing between spatial options, or reacting to project proposals. Good practice is discussed in Chapter 3. Improved citizen participation in decision making is one of several components of an action programme initiated jointly by the Portuguese Ministries of Planning and Environment with the participation of several local authorities. This has focused upon the public discussion of Master Plans and the processes of environmental impact assessment.

Social and demographic context

Population size influences sustainability. Population growth in most Western European countries continues to decrease and rates in Germany, the UK, and Belgium are near zero. These population characteristics of the industrial society of Europe are accompanied by the growing prosperity of a consumer society allied with continued environmental degradation and pollution.

Water pollution from sewage provides a classic example of the diseconomies of scale from population growth. If people live at low densities along a large river, their sewage may be dumped directly into the river and natural purification will occur. But if the population increases, the waste-degrading ability of the river becomes strained, and the sewage and the intake water must be treated. In general, the more people living in a catchment area, the higher the per-capita costs in managing water pollution.

Pressures related to the size of the population are already great and are growing rapidly. There is pressure on physical resources (land, food, water, forests, metals), on the ability of the environment to remove and recycle human wastes and to provide other vital services, and on society's ability to dispense services (education, medical care, justice). There are also pressures on societal values such as privacy, freedom from restrictive regulations, and the opportunity to choose from a variety of lifestyles.

Population structure and mix influences the pattern of consumption and behaviour and as a result the sustainability of society. Elements that determine the size and composition of the population includes births, mortality, immigration and emigration. Two trends are of major importance for urban futures:

- A relatively large number of immigrants
  A consequence of the difference in industrial maturity between North-West and Mediterranean regions has been the build-up of a population of Mediterranean 'guest-workers' in the North-West. The prosperity there has also attracted people from Turkey, North-African countries and former colonies (the West-Indies, Indian subcontinent, etc.). Although, the number of immigrants has recently declined in some European countries partly because of stricter immigration rules, the continuing immigration process requires adequate answers to associated problems of segregation, unemployment, overcrowding and homelessness;

WELFARE

The increase in number of one-
and two-person households

5

Policy options for
sustainability

Policy option:
access to basic and clean
environmental amenities

- The increase in number of one- and two-person households
  The increase of one and two-person households results partly from the growing cohort
  of elderly people and partly from changing lifestyles and culture - households are
  getting smaller because of the decrease in the birth-rate and the growing number of
  divorces and single people. This growing number of small households influences
  consumption patterns.

20. It is difficult to disentangle the causes of social urban problems such as poverty,
    unemployment, lack of education, from their demographic and wider urban origins.
    All are important, and often they are linked by an array of cause-and-effect connections.
    If society is to find adequate and rational solutions, it is essential to investigate all the
    factors that interact and cause these problems and to discover the nature and
    consequences of the interactions. Although some of the more subjective aspects of the
    human predicament, such as pressure on values, are equally important, the problems of
    resources and the environment are easier to describe quantitatively.

2.2   WELFARE

1. Movement towards sustainability in society requires transformation of individual and
   collective priorities and values. An important commitment to address these issues was
   made in March 1995 at the UN World Summit for Social Development in Copenhagen.
   The Copenhagen Declaration and Programme of Action together comprise a new social
   contract, with significant political weight, at the global level. The summit pledged to make
   the conquest of poverty, the goal of full employment and the fostering of stable, safe and
   just societies their overriding objectives (UN, 1995).

2. At the European level debate about the establishment of the fundamental social rights of
   citizens as a constitutional element of the European Union is one of the issues discussed
   at the 1996 Intergovernmental Conference. In addition, the Commission is currently
   consulting the European Forum on Social Policy about the possible extension of the Social
   Charter to cover a wider range of individual rights and responsibilities (CEC, 1995g).

Policy options for sustainability

Policy option: access to basic and clean environmental amenities

3. All individuals should have access to clean air, drinking water, and adequate shelter.
   These basic needs must be satisfied in order to provide the foundation for a stable and
   healthy society. In addition, individuals have a right of access to information, to active
   involvement in political processes and to be compensated for damage to their
   environment. These rights should be set in the context of their responsibilities.

Policy option: access to education and training

The development of human resources through education and training is a key factor for social stability in society. This is recognized by the European Union, for example through the adoption of the Leonardo programme for the implementation of a Community vocational training policy, and the Socrates programme on co-operation in the area of education (CEC, 1995g).

Policy option: access to employment

Unemployment is widespread and affecting all European cities. Meaningful and creative employment is one of the keys to the well-being of people and to social integration, whereas unemployment can lead to associated problems such as personal stress, crime, disempowerment and social exclusion. Unemployment also leads to a greater need for welfare provisions, leading to higher social premiums, higher labour costs and in turn to higher unemployment (UN, 1994). Job creation issues are discussed further in section 1 of this chapter.

Policy option: elimination of poverty and social exclusion

Poverty and social exclusion are interrelated. The European Commission has dedicated 1996 to the opening of a European-wide debate on poverty and social exclusion as the basis for identifying the scope for concerted action. This initiative builds upon the Commission's Poverty 1, 2, and 3 Programmes which increased experience and knowledge about the elimination of poverty. The objective of these anti-poverty Programmes (1989 - 1994) was to promote innovative strategies based on the principles of multi-dimensionality, partnership and participation.

'Social exclusion' is a fundamental concept for these programmes and measures to combat social exclusion cannot be implemented in isolation from other aspects of economic and social policy, but must be integrated with, primarily, access to opportunities to earn a living, and measures to enable disadvantaged people to help themselves. Social integration also involves access to, for example, housing, health services, education and transport (CEC, 1994d).

In the Poverty 3 Programme, poverty is considered as a form of social exclusion, rather than an outcome. In other perspectives, it has been stressed that if social exclusion emphasises the mechanisms that lead to exclusion, then the situation of those who are already excluded may be under-estimated, a situation better reflected by the term poverty. Strategies to enable the poor to remove the barriers that entrap them in poverty, and to be involved in the decision-making process of their own communities should be developed (UN, 1994). Particular attention should also be focused on social groups that are marginalised either physically, economically, socially, culturally or politically.

2.3

3.

4.

A healthy environment

Policy option: improvement of the quality of urban space

Urban physical problems such as decay, deterioration and pollution in cities contribute to severe human and social problems, including alienation and violence. Both the physical problems and social symptoms should be addressed. Streets and buildings influence the relationship between the citizen and their city and constitute a framework, an architectural and urban space where urban society and culture can develop. 'Urbanity' is also based upon the citizen's capacity to symbolically recognize themselves in their own city and the greater the sophistication of urban shapes, the more rich and sensitive the effects that they will induce.

HEALTH

Good health depends to a large extent on a healthy environment and the health of an urban population is therefore dependent on physical, social, economic, political and cultural factors related to the urban environment. Furthermore the impact of urban processes on public health is not simply the sum of the effects of the various factors, because these factors are highly inter-related.

Elimination of adverse effects on human health is an important aspect of sustainable development and the World Health Organisation strategy of 'Health for Everyone' to the year 2000 requires public participation and intersectoral action for the improvement of health, especially of the most disadvantaged groups. The 44th World Health Assembly in 1991 recognised that 'in a world of rapid urbanisation, it is up to cities and their elected administrative bodies to take measures in this direction' (European Foundation for the Improvement of Living and Working Conditions, 1992).

In developing and implementing policy for the environment and health, it is important that the effectiveness and affordability of interventions are carefully considered in each case and that, in respect of pollution, priority is always given to interventions aimed at controlling its source.

The role of the European Union in the field of public health is to underpin efforts of the Member States in this field, assist in the formulation and implementation of objectives and strategies and to contribute to the provision of health protection across the Community, setting as a target (where practicable) the highest community standards. Important initiatives in this field include a proposal for a Council Decision aiming to provide the Community and Member States with comprehensive, comparable and reliable data covering areas such as health status, determinants of health, health system components, impact of policies, and needs and priorities. The Commission is also considering the integration of health protection requirements in other Community policies (CEC, 1995g).

Policy options for sustainability

Policy option: adequate provision of basic services

This objective should be integrated with all other policy goals. The environment affects health through water supply, domestic and community sanitation, standing surface water, industrial pollution, working conditions, transport conditions, quality of housing, food supply, and the availability of green and open space. The social difficulties encountered to a greater or lesser extent in all cities, stem largely from the inequalities with which facilities and services are distributed, their availability being too often dependent on the income of the inhabitants. Important examples are lack of, or poor quality of, local schooling, lack of recreational areas, inadequate communications, remoteness from the cultural life of the city, and proximity to polluted areas from industrial activities and disposal of wastes (WHO, 1993, p.33).

WHO considers environmental health as an integral part of urban development. The roleof health authorities is crucial, and ensuring their active involvement in urban development processes may be the most valuable contribution they can make to the WHO strategy 'Health for Everyone'. WHO states that the role of the health authorities is to communicate 'health intelligence' to decision-makers in the public and private sectors.

'In the public sector, health is affected by activities in the following areas: ... industry and labour (protection of workers, disposal of wastes, control of emissions), housing and public works, sanitation, transport, education and communications, crime control, social welfare, energy generation, ..., and environmental management. Activities in the relevant areas of the private sector also need to be addressed; this may be particularly important when they fall outside the scope of government regulations .... To tackle these issues effectively an inter-sectoral approach is needed' (WHO, 1993).

Policy option: adequate provision of health services: prevention and caring

This is partly an issue of financial allocation, partly of spatial planning and partly of accessibility. Sustainable lifestyles cannot be maintained in the absence of suitable health services. Strengthening environmental health can be a powerful strategy for improving human health in the context of sustainable development. Prevention needs to be the highest priority. A deliberate strategy for environmental health must be formulated within the framework of economic and health development.

Ministries of health can support local environmental health services in urban areas by providing health information, stimulating research, linking environmental data with health status, carrying out surveys and information. A general problem in all European cities is the fact that there is no overview of all the factors affecting health.

Policy option: promotion of early warning systems

Early warning systems for major technological accidents are needed. WHO is continuing to collaborate within relevant EU programmes and OECD's Chemical Accidents System co-ordinating activities on early notification of accidents. Early warning is also needed for smog, food contamination, etc. Warning systems with adequate monitoring systems and effective communication within and between countries should be established in all Member States.

5.12 Example of a Healthy City Project initiative in Glasgow, Scotland

Glasgow became a member of the project because the city has a poor health record and wants to improve it. Furthermore Scotland has the fourth highest death rate for men and the second highest for women of 27 major industrialised countries. There is a substantial difference in death rates between social classes. Men living in some of the more deprived areas are three times more likely to die before the age of 65 than their more affluent counterparts. The project has a four-fold strategy:

- policy development, health being a core value in policies and programmes (middle or long term strategy);
- a local action programme, of activities in the most deprived areas (short term focus);
- information and training to explore the relevance of 'health-for-all';
- national and international liaison, to assist other cities in and outside Europe.

Policy option: promotion of healthy lifestyles

5

Policy option: promotion of healthy lifestyles

11.   Education and training programmes should be geared towards the promotion of healthy lifestyles. This should cover not only physical health, but also the promotion of the well-being of the whole human being. There is a need to make the public aware of the issues involved and to obtain practical local data so that interventions can be targeted at the most needy groups (WHO, 1993).

12.   An issue that needs more research and promotion concerns the increasing problems with asthma and allergies, the impact on human health of traffic, pollution, etc. (see also Chapter 6). The European Commission is aiming to present a draft Council Decision in the second half of 1996, on a programme of action on pollution-related diseases, aimed at combatting health problems related to pollution and contributing to their prevention (CEC, 1995g).

2.4   HOUSING

1.   In this context, housing is viewed as a social facility and a social or collective good, as an element in society and in the set of social relations, as well as shelter. Housing also consumes land and demands the provision of physical services such as water and sewage as well as social services to households.

Affordable and decent housing for all should be a key policy goal

2.   Decent housing for all, at an affordable price, should be a key policy goal. Article 11 of the International Pact relating to economic, social and cultural rights (in force since 1976) defines housing as a fundamental right: 'The States signing this Pact recognise the right of everybody to a satisfactory level of life for himself and his family, meaning adequate food, clothing and housing as well as constant improvement in his living conditions' (European

Foundation for the Improvement of Living and Working Conditions, 1992). However, there is little or no support at the level of Member States or the European Commission for a Community housing policy, although some regulations of the internal market affect the housing market.

At the Member State level intervention by local authorities in the housing market to provide subsidised social housing is a major factor in the provision of decent affordable housing. The percentage of the market controlled by the authorities varies significantly between the Member States from 25.7 units of social housing per 1000 inhabitants in Belgium, compared with 66.6 in France, 99.2 in the former West Germany, 104.5 in the United Kingdom and 136.5 in the Netherlands (CEC, 1993d).

The quality of the housing provision in urban areas is essentially conditioned by the qualitative nature of the urban environment. In cities people typically live in close proximity to each other, and activities that generate negative side-effects, for example in the form of industrial pollution and noise traffic tend to occur where population density is greatest affecting those who lack freedom of residential choice and the power or influence to exclude sources of the nuisance. There seems to be no way that market pricing can compensate those who suffer from these negative effects although 'The stolp approach' mentioned in Chapter 7 offers some solutions.

Affordable housing

Policy options for sustainability

National as well as local governments have responsibility for the provision and distribution of housing although private organisations can also exert an influence. Measures that can be taken include:

Policy option: housing for all

Housing shortages based on the relationship between supply, affordability and suitability, exists in all European countries and is particularly great in growth areas and for poorer households. The number of homeless has been growing for several years in many countries. Factors that have contributed to this trend include, according to the European Federation of National Organisations Working with the Homeless (FEANTSA), migration, an increase in home ownership, a reduction in public sector housing and the lack of legal help for the homeless (European Foundation for the Improvement of Living and Working Conditions, 1994).

Overall in the Member States the rate of housing construction is too low and the construction process reacts only with a considerable time lag to changes in demand. In France, 280,000 houses were constructed annually in 1991 and 1992, compared to the demand for 360,000. In the Netherlands, the need for housing construction is underestimated because of the large number of immigrants. In Germany, the decline in housing construction during the 1980s resulted in current housing shortages accentuated by the flow of immigrants from former East Germany and from other East European countries (Ministry of Housing, 1993). Possible measures include:

- increasing the availability of social housing: poorer households should have access to non-profit or cheaper housing. Essentially housing should meet real needs which requires the efficient use of housing stock and relates to issues concerning urban rehabilitation (see Chapter 7);

- giving priority to people in housing need, including households with children, immigrants and refugees, disabled, and single parent families (European Foundation for the Improvement of Living and Working Conditions, 1992);

- improving the quality of social housing in terms of both internal design and comfort (energy efficiency), and the external environment (safety, accessibility to labour market, schools and other facilities). The active involvement of tenants in housing management can contribute to better adaptation of supply to real demand patterns, and to the development of responsibility, self-esteem and creativity among the inhabitants (European Foundation for the Improvement of Living and Working Conditions, 1992);

- improving the living conditions of homeless people. There is a growing social isolation and distinction between homeless people and the rest of the population. However, inadequate statistics make it difficult to estimate the number of homeless people, the underlying causes of their condition, and their health status. It is believed that homeless people represent close to 1% of the population within the European Union (WHO, 1993).

Policy option: creating neighbourhoods instead of just building homes

Policy option: creating neighbourhoods instead of just building homes

8. Generating a sense of community is a relatively intangible goal and difficult to plan for. Certain elements which contribute to 'community' are, however, both tangible and open to influence. Neighbourhoods, as coherent units within the urban system, are one such element. Social investigation needs to combine with spatial analysis in order to identify the conditions which promote good neighbourhoods (see also Chapter 7).

9. Although housing conditions are the prime symbol of the success or failure of social integration, good housing without any other policy measures does not improve labour productivity, school performance, health (except for tuberculosis), nor does it reduce the crime rate (except for sexual crimes committed outside the dwelling). However, if housing is seen as the core of living conditions within a local environment that also consists of improved social and working conditions, then a strong synergy effect can be achieved. Functioning neighbourhoods can not be expected to emerge if the inhabitants feel segregated from society (European Foundation for the Improvement of Living and Working Conditions, 1992).

10. Cities as a whole have a social function and the city centre can be a living room for citizens (Ministry of the Environment, City of Helsinki/Jussi Rautsi, 1993). However, some cities and inner cities are becoming inhospitable because of the absence of people on the streets and the lack of activities at street level and associated problems of worsening crime, social exclusion etc.

Public spaces in cities illustrate some of these issues in performing three distinct functions throughout history: market, moving and meeting. Some cities are 'indoor cities', created specially for commercial activities. The various city activities have been taken indoors to shopping arcades, galleries, atria, and other types of enclosed shopping facilities. Other cities have been turned into 'sky walk cities', where most shops and people have been taken up to an enclosed shopping system on the second floor. Both have seen shops disappear from the streets. Many cities have put a high priority on traffic: the city as a moving place. At the moment the car dominates the streets, but the streets should be reclaimed for pedestrians and bicycles, and public transport systems should be improved.

Policy option: the role of urban rehabilitation

11.

Policy option: the role of urban rehabilitation

Social aspects of urban rehabilitation are an issue of concern and other aspects of urban rehabilitation are covered in Chapter 7. In relation to social sustainable systems urban rehabilitation becomes a quality of life issue and an opportunity for job creation (see section 1). The inefficient use of urban resources reduces the overall quality of urban life and has a directly detrimental effect on the most vulnerable members of society, such as the poor and the least mobile. Conversely, the renewal and reclamation of urban areas increases the overall quality of life and helps to reduce social exclusion.

12.

Flexibility in the permitted use of land should be used to accommodate temporary land uses whilst long-term solutions are sought although this may be more easily secured by the planning systems of some Member States rather than others. Flexible approaches are important because economic situation can frequently delay the pace and process of urban rehabilitation and renewal and land may be abandoned for extended periods of time. During this time the temporary use of the land to prevent the problems of vandalism, crime and based on solutions involving the greening of the land by planting, and other temporary uses should be considered.

13.

Crime and fear are not only problems for residents but also for business. Urban rehabilitation and renewal projects should use the concept of 'public guardianship' of common spaces in their layouts, so that public areas are overlooked. The form of ownership can also be influential in controlling crime. Increased financial participation by the individual who has a stake in the community can be effective in reducing criminal activity.

14.   Public guardianship as a basis for rehabilitation and renewal projects

Policy option: planning for a changing future

15.   Policy option: planning for a changing future

Discernible trends in society include an increase in leisure and increasing demands for open and recreational space. Another trend is that the population is growing older, which requires improved accessibility for dwellings and facilities. The changes in household size mentioned earlier in this section, as well as other demand pictures, such as the tendency of one and two person households to live in central locations while larger households often prefer to live in the periphery of cities, needs to be taken into account in the development of national and local housing policy (European Foundation for the Improvement of Living and Working Conditions, 1992).

3

CONCLUSIONS

Proper management of urban locations can increase the environmental efficiency of economic activities

1. Improving the 'environmental efficiency' of economic activities is an essential component of sustainable development. It is now very clear what general directions of change this will require, although there is plenty of scope for innovation and development.

2. Cities have important roles to play and urban location, if properly managed, has the potential to significantly increase the environmental efficiency of many economic activities. In addition, city authorities can carry out a range of activities to help green the local economy. As leading European cities have already demonstrated, many of these can readily be assimilated into familiar economic development activities such as business development advice, job creation, training, inward investment promotion and the provision of premises and infrastructure.

3. There is an urgent need for better and wider dissemination of good practice and expertise in this field. Sustainability should become a strand running through all local economic development activities and 'toolkit' methods and techniques to achieve this has already been developed among a number of cities. The need now is to make such information more widely available (see Chapter 3).

National and international frameworks limit local action

4. Local action is, however, limited by national and international frameworks. The operation of markets limits the extent to which companies can adopt sustainable methods without losing competitive advantage. Some forms of green business promotion may be `zero sum games' where city gains at the expense of another.

5. Governments must reform the economy at national or international level to bring market price signals into line with sustainability. This will require shifts of taxation from labour to resources, encouragement of longer-term patterns of investment and regulation to encourage more environmentally efficient resource use and production systems. It will also require greater powers for local government to influence the economy at local and regional level to allow cities to promote sustainability in combination with - or in advance of - changes at higher governmental levels.

Government stimulation for changes in behaviour and lifestyle

6. Governments must stimulate contributions to environmental care, environmental technology, and sustainable technology which requires a new 'backcasting' approach.

7. There is an urgent need for changes in behaviour and lifestyle, requiring a changes in individual values in relation to community, ownership, responsibility and participation. This can only be achieved if positive information is disseminated to all citizens, and if national and local governments provide support in the form of awareness raising campaigns and other initiatives.

8. Governments must stimulate opportunities for the development of housing, health care, employment etc. in order to move towards a socially sustainable future. The fulfilment of these basic needs provides the key to social integration and the well-being of citizens. The Commission should take responsibility by stimulating innovation in the form of experiments and comparative studies. The Commission and national governments should promote social sustainability, but initiatives should be taken at the local level too.

9.

Active involvement in decision making processes by all groups in society promotes equality and enables marginalised and disadvantaged groups to help themselves. It enhances the opportunity for all citizens in society to share in its benefits and responsibilities, and to participate fully in economic, social, cultural and political life. Participation processes should be developed using innovative mechanisms to ensure the involvement of all groups in society.

10.

This chapter emphasised the need to integrate social, economic and environmental aims. The Commission has recognised the need for further research into the integration of these three issues, and the European Foundation for the Improvement of Living and Working Conditions has initiated a number of research projects in this area.

11. Cities have proven their ability to develop sustainable urban economies and societies

Despite current limitations European cities have already demonstrated the will and the ability to develop sustainable urban economies and sustainable societies. It is now necessary for Member States and the EU to provide policy frameworks through which these can be implemented.

5

SUSTAINABLE CITIES

170

INTRODUCTION

KEY SUSTAINABILITY
ISSUES   1.

6   1.

SUSTAINABLE ACCESSIBILITY

INTRODUCTION

Analyses of the challenges facing cities in their efforts to achieve a more sustainable development invariably give a high priority to the problems of mobility and access. At the urban level, where transport problems are more acute and concentrated than elsewhere, achieving a sustainable form of mobility is a prerequisite for both improvement of the environment, including social aspects, and enhancement of economic viability.

A great deal of research has been conducted in recent years. The European Commission hasaddressed the issue in research documents and in the Green Paper on Impact of Transport on the Environment (CEC, 1992c). Tackling urban mobility problems is now a priority in the EU's transport and environment policies as outlined in The Future Development of the Common Transport Policy (CEC, 1992b) and the Fifth Environmental Action Programme (CEC, 1992a). The Fifth Environmental Action Programme both identifies the impacts of transport on the environment and specifies measures to reduce them. It sets out a timescale for implementation and identifies the actors involved, including the EU, Member States and local government.

Further steps have been taken by the European Commission through the publication of the Green Paper *Towards fair and efficient pricing policy in transport* (CEC, 1995b) which selects urban areas as a target for a new comprehensive policy response to ensure that prices reflect underlying scarcities which would otherwise not be sufficiently taken into account. The Green Paper *Citizens' Network - Fulfilling the potential of public transport in Europe* (CEC, 1996b) emphasizes the essential role of public transport in improving quality of life and the environment.

KEY SUSTAINABILITY ISSUES

Movement in cities

Movement in cities

Movement in cities has increased and changed substantially in the past decades

Mobility is essential to the livelihood of cities. However, the saturation levels of traffic reached due to the dominance of the private car are impairing the efficient functioning of many cities by reducing accessibility and damaging the environment in the long term. Patterns of urban change in Europe over the past 40 years have led to significant changes in the way people travel and the distances travelled in urban areas. Development and lifestyle changes have encouraged the separation of homes and economic activities. This has resulted in a great increase in traffic flows and a dramatic shift in modes of transport - away from walking, cycling and public transport to the private car. In many cities in the EU the car accounts for over 80% of urban mechanised transport, and in a number, such as Milan and Coventry, the car's share is over 90% (OECD/ECMT 1995).

As for the future, the total annual car kilometrage in the EU is expected to increase by 25% between 1990 and 2010. Road haulage is expected to increase by 42% over the same period with rail freight increasing by only 33% during the same period (CEC, 1992c, cited in OECD/ECMT, 1995). Traffic growth on these scales would jeopardise the Union's ability to meet agreed environmental targets in air quality, greenhouse gas emissions and the protection of landscapes. To achieve a more sustainable form of urban mobility and to improve accessibility it will be necessary to reduce transport in the long term, and, among other things, to minimise or even halt the forecast growth in the number and length of trips and therefore the demand for transport in the shorter term.

Movement in cities

The desire to improve accessibility may itself need to be re-evaluated. Accessibility is usually defined as the ease with which people reach distant but necessary services. It is typically measured by the length of time required to make a particular journey. In consequence, transport planners aim to minimise travel time by reducing congestion and increasing the speed of transport for both private cars and public transport. This in turn can generate greater demand for travel as people find it feasible to live further from their work places or other services and amenities. It is therefore important to ensure that accessibility is not measured exclusively by journey time, but that it reflects people's ability to reach necessary services. This might imply some reversal of the trends towards concentration of certain major services (for example, health services) in a small number of locations rather than developing transport systems capable of reducing journey times.

Existing policies which seek to influence competition between transport modes in urban areas may not encourage individuals to take account of environmental impacts in making decisions about urban travel (it is incorrect to assume that individuals make rational choices based only on their own preferences for particular modes and destinations). The character and availability of competing systems are strongly influenced by the policies of central and local government. Current policies tend to encourage competition but often disadvantage particular modes (for example, where levels of investment in certain modes are insufficient).

As the following sections demonstrate, in certain urban areas the limits of sustainability have already been exceeded from both an environment and a transport point of view. Movement into and within many cities and towns is becoming ever more difficult and sometimes unsafe. Increasing air and noise pollution add to congestion difficulties, making city travel unpleasant, impairing the quality of life and posing health risks to a proportion of the population. Evidence is now emerging to show that, over the long term, unsustainable and inefficient mobility will have a detrimental effect on the economies of our cities.

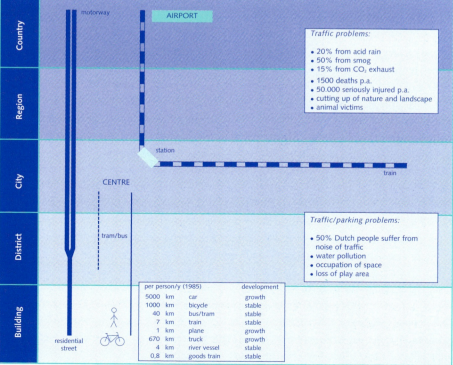

Source: Tjallingii, S. (1995), p.80.

FIGURE - The Traffic Chain, existing systems and environmental problems

Environmental problems   6.

Air pollution is one of the major
environmental problems caused
by transport

7.

8.

Other environmental problems
include energy consumption and
the consequent rise in CO_2
emissions

Health problems

Health problems are linked to   9.
urban traffic

Noise pollution is mainly caused   10.
by road traffic

Environmental problems

Transport is now the major source of the main air pollutants found in European cities. Road traffic is responsible for most of the summer smog formation in Europe, and World Health Organisation guidelines for ozone, NO_x and CO emissions have been breached on numerous occasions. Surveys show, for example, that in 70 to 80 % of the European cities with more than half a million inhabitants, air pollution levels of one or more pollutants exceed these WHO guidelines at least once in a typical year (EEA, 1995a). In some southern European cities levels of air pollution are at times so high that traffic restrictions or bans are introduced on certain days or at certain times of the day.

Although recent and forthcoming legislation on exhaust emissions of cars and lorries will result in substantial reductions in pollution from individual vehicles, the projected increases in vehicles and kilometrage will, over the medium term, largely offset the potential reductions. There is therefore general agreement that technology alone will not solve the air pollution problems caused by transport.

As for energy, the transport sector represents around 30% of total energy consumption in Europe, up from 20% in the early 1970s. Over 84% of energy consumption through transport is from road transport. Fuel consumption from the vehicle fleet has hardly changed over the past 20 years - major developments in engine and vehicle technology have been more than offset by the increases in the fleet, congestion and increases in engine capacities. Increased energy consumption has led to a significant rise in CO_2 emissions from transport - 63% in the EU since the early 1970s. On current trends an additional 25% increase from the transport sector is forecast by the end of the century. This would represent 30% of total CO_2 emissions in the EU compared to today's figure of around 25%. Urban traffic is estimated to be responsible for almost half transport CO_2 emissions.

Health problems

Several studies point to a link between urban traffic and damage to health. Swedish studies found that urban air pollution causes 300 - 2000 new cases of cancer annually. Traffic accounts for 70% of the emissions of carcinogenic substances and substances that may affect the genes of people living in urban areas (Ministry of Environment and Natural Resources, 1992, cited in OECD/ECMT, 1995). A study for the British Government found a link between emission particle levels and cardio-vascular disease, and suggested that up to 10,000 people are killed by exhaust fumes each year in England and Wales (Brown, 1994, cited in OECD/ECMT, 1995). Furthermore, tropospheric ozone which is created by photo-chemical reactions with air containing traces of nitric oxide and hydrocarbons, is a strong oxidiser and can damage the linings of people's lungs (OECD/ECMT, 1995). Whilst it is difficult to find conclusive links, there is widespread evidence of the health effects of major pollutants emitted by transport (TEST, 1991). This is an area where there is a need for more research, especially in local communities.

Road traffic is the main source of noise pollution. Air traffic is also important but affects a much smaller proportion of the population. The report *Europe's Environment: The Dobris Assessment* estimates that about 450m people in Europe are exposed to noise levels over 55 dB(A), while around 113m people are exposed to more than 65 dB(A), unacceptable noise levels that may constitute a risk to health (EEA, 1995a).

An example of a project designed to measure and tackle the environmental and health impacts of transport is the trans-European project involving Kirklees, Berlin, Madeira and Copenhagen. The project, funded under the LIFE programme, is seeking to provide very detailed information on the air pollution, noise and health effects of transport. Geographical information systems will be used to model transport scenarios for the year 2012.

Social issues

Transport has implications for social sustainability. Transport related social problems arise as a result of new patterns of urban development, changing lifestyles and deteriorating public transport services which all contribute to inaccessibility and car dependence (OECD/ECMT, 1995).

Inaccessibility is an increasing problem in urban areas. There is a consistent trend towards decentralisation from inner to outer areas of both people and jobs in most cities, regardless of whether the city is growing or in decline. The location of new development on green field sites in peripheral areas is a trend which generates longer journeys and additional traffic. It serves the car user, but not those dependent on other forms of transport. Such developments are often located in low density areas where the costs of providing satisfactory public transport are generally too high. The social implications of out of town developments would not be so extreme if local facilities were available within the cities. Problems arise when an expansion to green field sites is accompanied by the closing down of local services. The result is that some people are becoming increasingly isolated from the provision of necessary services.

Changing lifestyles is another factor which in itself gives rise to higher car dependency and inaccessibility for those without access to a car or unable to drive. It seems logical that higher densities and mixed developments would increase accessibility. Empirical evidence clearly shows that high densities contribute to reducing the distances travelled, even in the present high-mobility society. However, the contribution of mixed developments is not as clear. Unless heavy restrictions on mobility are imposed, mixed developments seem to be favourable only in inner-city areas (Næss, 1995). For example, it cannot be assumed that people will take advantage of the opportunity to work locally. Evidence from Danish research has shown that it does not happen. If people believe that they can improve their choice, they seem willing to travel longer distances. This often is the case in relation to employment, people are willing to sacrifice personal time and wider environmental, social and economic objectives in order to choose the most interesting, or economically rewarding job. This trend of travelling further to work has been shown to be linked to levels of education. The longer the person's education, the more likely he/she is to gain employment outside the local or neighbouring area (Jorgensen, 1993, cited in OECD/ECMT, 1995).

173

KEY SUSTAINABILITY ISSUES

Noise pollution

Social issues

11.

12.   Transport has implications for social sustainability

13.   Out of town development can isolate people from the provision of necessary services

14.   Changing lifestyles can result in higher car dependence

15. Increased car use not only causes congestion and pollution, but may also lead to a deterioration in the level of public transport provision. The fewer the public transport users, the higher the proportion of operating costs that they have to cover. If subsidies cannot be raised, due to financial constraints, lack of political support, or practical constraints such as private operators, the remaining public transport users will suffer in the form of either higher fares or the withdrawal of services. The social implications for people who are dependent on public transport are significant, in terms of inaccessibility and resulting isolation.

16. However, trends of falling levels of public transport use are not inevitable. There is evidence of a reversal of such trends being achieved through improvements to public transport and to the environment in which it operates. Such measures have been successful in increasing public transport's share of the travel market in Switzerland, where the share of total passenger-km has risen from 18.5% to 20% since the mid 1980s (OECD/ECMT, 1995).

Transport issues

This section examines a range of transport-specific issues including congestion, safety and security. A rather different problem raised is that relating to the take-up of urban land by transport infrastructure.

18. Traffic congestion is causing significant speed reductions of city traffic leading to average speeds not seen since the beginning of this century. A recent study found that traffic speeds declined by 10% over the last 20 years in major OECD cities. In one third of the surveyed cities the early morning speeds in the city centres were below 19 km/h (OECD/ECMT, 1995).

19. Congestion increases polluting emissions and fuel consumption. Current speeds in many large cities are in the most inefficient area of the speed/fuel consumption curve. Congestion also affects road based public transport, making it even less attractive and leading to a reduction in its use. Congestion, defined as 'additional time spent travelling compared with free-flowing travel' is estimated to cost about 2% of GDP (Quinet, 1994, cited in OECD/ECMT, 1995).

20. There is an assumption that transport systems should be designed, and where necessary improved, to meet expectations about travel time between an infinite set of origins and destinations. But those pursuing objectives relating to environmental protection may need to re-evaluate the need for further or continued reductions in journey times. It is reasonable to conclude that, if improving the road network generates traffic, accepting that a limit exists for such improvements could suppress further growth.

21. Attempts to solve urban congestion by additional road investments are, then, environmentally unacceptable in most cases and highly costly due to the price of urban land. Experience confirms that they also generate higher levels of traffic growth. Goodwin et al (1991) have demonstrated that 'all available road construction policies only differ in the speed at which congestion gets worse'.

There is a further dimension to the increase in vehicle speeds which tend to follow from a reduction in road congestion. This relates to the safety of cyclists and pedestrians. In collisions between pedestrians and vehicles travelling at approximately 60 km/h 95% of pedestrians are killed. In collisions with vehicles travelling at half this speed only 5% are killed. It is therefore important to recognise that whilst schemes designed to relieve traffic congestion may reduce environmental damage caused by vehicles operating at 'inefficient' speeds, they can also encourage additional use of motorised transport as journey times fall and increase the danger for cyclists and pedestrians.

Although great efforts have been made by national and local authorities to implement safety measures, road accidents remain a significant problem. In a number of cities the urban road death rate is well above the average national rate - two and a half times the national level in the case of Paris and twice in the case of Reggio Emilia (EEA, 1995a). A large proportion of victims are pedestrians, for whom there has not been the same fall in accidents and deaths as has been observed for car drivers. Children are particularly vulnerable.

In addition to the actual number of accidents, the level of traffic experienced in many cities engenders an impression of danger, particularly on the part of elderly people, cyclists and families with children, and this in turn leads to greater car usage, as Chapter 3 pointed out. For example the percentage of children in the UK travelling to school by their own means fell from 80% in 1971 to 9% in 1990 (Hillman and Adams, 1992). Additionally, the fear of crime in European cities, not least on public transport systems, leads ever more people, especially women, to rely on the private car.

Increasing urban traffic leads to streets acting as barriers, since they are difficult, dangerous and time consuming to cross. In the worst cases, busy streets divide parts of the city. Some attempts have been made to categorise roads according to the degree of their barrier effect. A study of the speed and density of traffic in Aarhus, Denmark shows the strength of this effect. Often children cannot be allowed near the street alone and the crossing facilities are unacceptable for elderly adults (Municipality of Aarhus, 1993).

The proportion of land in cities, particularly public space, taken up by transport-related activities is rising. In Brussels, road and water infrastructure accounted for close on 20% of total area in 1980 compared to under 5% in the 1930s, while in Bilbao the road network alone represents nearly 35% of the total city area. Typically 10 to 15% of the area of large cities in Europe is taken up by road infrastructure.

For transport users the cost of travel is a decisive influence in the choice of transport mode. However, car users impose a number of costs which they do not themselves incur and which they do not therefore take into account in deciding how to travel. Such costs include environmental impacts such as noise and air pollution, accidents, congestion, the use of space and other issues briefly reviewed above. The absence of a charging structure or price for such items is exacerbated by the perceived cost of car use. The car appears cheaper at the point of use than public transport because the fixed costs of its ownership are all 'sunk', while public transport ticket prices include an apportionment of systems costs.

22.   A negative relationship exists between vehicle speed and the safety of other road-users

23.

24.   *Busy streets as barriers*

25.   Busy streets can act as barriers to social interaction in cities

26.

27.   Private car transport does not incur real costs

Economic Issues   28.

Urban congestion defers
investment in cities

Greater urban mobility does not
lead to greater economic activity

Policies at all levels should address
the negative environmental
impacts of transport systems

Economic Issues

In addition to the economic inefficiencies engendered by congestion, the saturation levels of traffic in many cities arguably make them unattractive to investors. This in turn can lead to development locating outside urban areas, on sites which can only be reached by private car and which also often involve longer trips.

29. It is often argued that there is a direct link between economic growth and traffic growth. While it is true that an expansion in economic activity results in traffic growth, such expansion is not dependent upon traffic growth. Traffic is a means to an end. It is a variable cost, and if the same results can be achieved with less traffic then overall costs can be reduced, thus achieving greater economic efficiency.

30. A recent survey of transport professionals throughout Europe (reported in Masser, Sviden and Wegener, 1993) demonstrated a strong consensus of view that the current pursuit of growth in European transport planning is harmful and that it should be replaced by a more ecologically sustainable and equitable approach.

31. There is in any case evidence to show that greater urban mobility in terms of longer trips through private car use does not lead to greater economic or other activity (Department of Transport, 1988 and Brog, 1993). Alternatively, there is some evidence of links between enhanced local economic performance and environmental quality, as indicated by the availability of alternatives to the private car. This particularly applies to the performance of local shopping centres. A study in Germany suggests that retail trade in central city districts increases with policies that encourage 'environmentally friendly' transport modes. Of 38 cities studied, 14 had above average retail growth. Of these 14, 10 had below average provisions of infrastructure for the car (Deutsches Institut für Urbanistik 1991, cited in FOE, 1992).

32. Another dimension to the debate about transport and economic development is that the motor industry is a major source of employment with a significant influence on the performance of regional economies within the EU. The political consequences of policy which aims to increase the cost of car use and reduce its attractiveness should not be underestimated. On the other hand, the fact that social, economic and environmental costs of motorised traffic currently is estimated at 5% of GDP in OECD countries suggests that the benefits of sustainable travel far outweigh the costs suffered by those whose lifestyles would have to change (OECD/ECMT, 1995).

POLICY OPTIONS FOR SUSTAINABILITY

1. Objectives for urban mobility and accessibility need to be seen in the light of national and international policies for transport and the environment. Through the Fifth Environmental Action Programme, the EU and its Member States have set themselves a number of targets to address air quality (NO_x, CO, VOCs, Particulate Matter, SO_2), global warming (CO_2), and noise, amongst others. The concentration of these problems in urban areas means that it is in urban areas where most of the remedial actions will need to take place. The gap between the expected growth of transport and the political targets for stabilisation and reduction of CO_2 creates a tremendous challenge for urban areas. Furthermore, it is often difficult for people living in rural areas to reduce car use, and the implication is, therefore, that cities must provide a greater share of the reduction of CO_2 and other pollutants than their share of population.

There is now broad agreement amongst policy makers from different sectors and environmental organisations on the need to reverse current urban mobility trends by reducing reliance on the private car. Whilst the public readily accept that the environmental consequences of the car are unacceptable, they are not yet willing to accept that a reduction in its use is the only sensible solution. It is increasingly recognised that to reverse these trends will also require a reduction in the demand for urban travel. While reducing reliance on the car could be achieved by actions designed to bring about modal shift, reducing the demand for travel is a much more fundamental shift that requires a reorientation of urban transport planning. As indicated above, it is also necessary to question the assumption that travel opportunities and journey times should be continually improved. The limits placed on travel by increased congestion and recognition of the environmental consequences may represent an opportunity to reverse the growth in the number and length of trips.

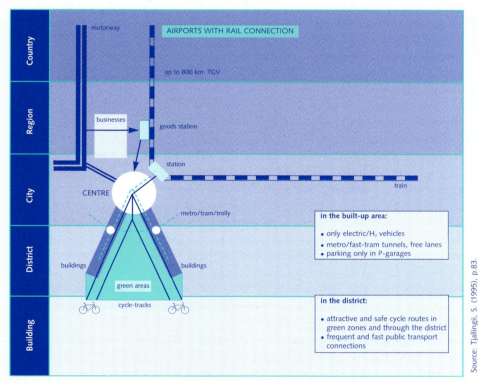

Source: Tjallingii, S. (1995), p.83.

FIGURE - The Traffic Chain, guiding models for the long term

The OECD study Urban Travel and Sustainable Development (1995) sets out three strands of an integrated policy aimed at moving towards sustainability. The first strand involves using best practice in urban policy. The second builds on the first by using innovative land-use and transport measures to reduce the need to travel and converts best practice into a coherent structured policy package. The third strand involves the application of progressive increases in fuel taxation to reduce car kilometres and CO_2 emissions, and to strengthen the other policy measures. It is foreseen that it would take two or three decades to see the full effects of this integrated policy, but that benefits would start to flow as soon as it was implemented.

2.

3.   Policy strands for progression
      towards sustainability

4. The EU's strategy outlined in the Fifth Environmental Action Programme (CEC, 1992a) and the Transport White Paper (CEC, 1992b), and many of the Member States' policies and actions under way in cities, seek principally to improve the urban traffic situation and thereby the urban environment. Among the actions suggested in EU policy documents are:

- land-use planning strategies which reduce the need for mobility and allow for the development of alternatives to road transport;

- promotion of urban transport systems which give priority to public transport, pedestrians and cyclists and provision of adequate link-ups between the different stages of journeys;

- promotion of more environmentally rational use of the private car, along with changes in driving rules and habits.

Specific and measurable targets form the basis of assessment of progress towards sustainability

5. To move towards sustainability it is necessary to go further than these basic objectives by adding, for example, more specific and measurable targets in relation to the reduction in urban traffic to be achieved. Targets can provide a focus for action and also provide a basis against which to measure progress and make any necessary policy adjustments.

6. Targets are also required for funding priorities. The importance that inter-urban initiatives, such as the trans-European networks, have on urban areas should not be underestimated. The overwhelming majority of all trips begin and end in urban areas. Two key points may be made concerning such networks. First we may question the desirability of reducing journey times, encouraging just-in-time manufacturing processes and the pursuit of business and employment opportunities over greater distances. The second point relates to the European Commission's policy of investing in a Trans-European Road Network to assist the regions and facilitate the development of the Single Market but which will in practice give considerable impetus to the use of road transport.

7. The following policy options are based on analyses from action already under way or about to be implemented. They cover short and medium term transport-related action which aims to reduce private car usage and the volume of traffic in urban areas. These are the so-called accompanying actions to technological measures to reduce emissions, fuel use and noise from individual vehicles. Particular emphasis is given to action which highlights environmental and transport objectives aimed at reducing the demand for urban motorised traffic and increasing accessibility with beneficial effects in other areas, such as social welfare, economic development and health.

8. An analysis of more long term spatial planning actions aimed at reducing the need to travel is found in section 7.1. There is overwhelming evidence to show that meeting environmental and transport objectives requires action through an integrated approach combining transport, environmental and spatial planning.

Policy option: integrated multi-modal urban transport systems

There is a need to develop intermodal transport systems where complementarity rather than competition between modes is promoted. Experience has shown, for example, that investment in public transport will not solve the problems unless combined with action to give public transport priority over private cars.

Likewise, restrictions on vehicle access to parts of the urban area and restrictive parking measures require accompanying measures to ensure access through alternatives to the car. Otherwise the restrictions may simply lead to the relocation of businesses and retailers outside the restricted areas to areas only accessible by car.

6.1 Integrated traffic plan for Copenhagen, Denmark

Copenhagen has developed an integrated traffic plan as part of its WHO Healthy Cities programme and has set objectives and specific targets in the areas of road accidents, noise and air pollution. The transport policy has put a strong emphasis on the further development of cycling, which already accounts for 30% of home to work trips in the summer, compared to 37% for public transport and 30% for the private car. Besides improving cycling facilities the programme includes public transport improvements and priority access, restrictions on through traffic by cars and parking measures which give priority to residential parking. The road network itself has remained at the level of 1970 and car traffic measured in terms of kilometres driven per year is some 10% below the 1970 level.

6.2 Integrated traffic policy in Freiburg, Germany

Freiburg's integrated traffic policy is widely regarded as exemplary in Europe and in 1992 the city was voted the 'Federal capital for the protection of nature and the environment'. The policy combines giving priority to public transport and cycling, pedestrian zones and traffic calming, the development of park and ride facilities and reduction of parking inside the city. Since 1976 the car's share of total daily journeys has fallen from 60% to 47%, while the shares of public transport and cycling have risen. A particularly successful innovation, since implemented in other German cities, has been the low price, monthly Eco Ticket, usable throughout the Freiburg region and valid for use on all buses, trams and regional trains.

11. While fully-integrated transport systems are rare, many European cities have established more limited, but still innovative, initiatives. These include elements of integrated systems such as:

- measures to manage traffic demand through access restrictions, reserved lanes for certain vehicle types, road pricing, parking policies, traffic telematics tools and methods to restrict urban goods transport;

- measures which give priority to, or otherwise support, public transport, such as park and ride, the provision of tram, trolley bus and light rail systems and intermodality;

- measures which give priority to cyclists and pedestrians;

- experiments with specialist vehicles and fuels; and

- measures to influence behaviour.

Policy option: traffic demand management

Policy option: traffic demand management

12. An EU wide survey (INRA, 1991) recorded very high support for actions to limit car traffic in town centres. Some 71% of respondents thought it would be effective, and there was equally strong support from both urban and rural residents. The same was true for frequent car users. Pedestrianisation of shopping areas is a measure that has been in existence for over 20 years in many towns and cities, but schemes have tended to cover only a limited area, generally within the central business district. Since the mid-1980s cities have been taking the idea further and reducing or eliminating car access to large parts of the urban area. Lübeck in Germany, for example, has gradually imposed an almost total ban on day-time traffic in the entire city centre. Priority for parking is given to residents and businesses, and service traffic is permitted outside the restricted periods (10.00 - 18.00). Initial objections from traders are no longer heard (FOE, 1992).

Initiatives for car free city centres

13. Furthermore, the European cities forming the 'Car-Free Cities Club' work towards reductions in urban car use and possibly a complete ban on the use of the private car during working hours in inner cities (Car Free Cities Club, 1994). It is important to recognise, however, that despite creating an improved local environment, car free inner cities will only generate a very small share of the required reduction of CO_2, because the greatest part of urban transport and the expected growth are in the urban regions outside the inner cities.

6.3 Neighbourhood without cars, Bremen, Germany

Bremen is developing a neighbourhood without cars (Hollerland). The idea arose from a study of the space requirements of moving and parked cars. Almost a quarter of the entire estate can be used for other purposes as no parking space is supplied. A car sharing scheme is planned for use by the residents. Usually 40% of the road space is required for parking space. With the car free scheme this can be reduced to about 17%.

Car free city center

6.4 Car-free nuclear neighbourhoods, Kuopio, Finland

An attempt to modify the urban structure of a smaller town in order to reduce dependence on the car is exemplified by Kuopio. An analysis of the pattern of urban growth between 1960 and 1990 was conducted within the framework of its structure plan preparation. This showed suburban growth in scattered settlements outside of the historic core, and a low density new town. The new development plan will focus on infilling previously isolated settlements, with car-free nuclear neighbourhoods served by a reorganised bus transit system.

A less severe policy option that may serve either as a permanent policy or as a temporary measure before traffic bans are imposed, is the adoption of speed restrictions in certain areas such as city centres and residential areas. To be effective the speed restrictions should be actively enforced. The installation of traffic calming measures can provide physical support to the enforcement of speed restrictions. However, speed restrictions need to be part of an overall traffic management plan in order to ensure that the positive effects outweigh any negative impacts. Speed restrictions make areas safer and more accessible from the point of view of pedestrians and cyclists, but on the other hand may cause pollution levels to rise as a result of higher inefficiency in fuel consumption. Traffic calming measures should also take into account the needs of emergency services both in terms of the need for speed and comfort for any patients.

14.   Speed restrictions and traffic calming measures

Turning to consider the use of reserved lanes for certain types of vehicle, the introduction of priority access for High Occupancy Vehicles (HOV lanes) has become commonplace in parts of the USA but is a relatively new measure in Europe. Its impact can only be somewhat marginal, being mainly directed at commuter traffic which itself generally accounts for 25 to 35% of trips. The use of public transport and car pooling is promoted in Madrid in Spain through the construction of an HOV lane on a main motorway link. The 'Systems Select' programme in Rotterdam in the Netherlands has introduced lanes reserved for goods vehicles, public transport, service vehicles and high occupancy vehicles on a number of roads giving access to Rotterdam's port facilities as part of an overall package of measures to reduce congestion.

15.   High occupancy vehicles lanes can stimulate public transport and car pooling

Road pricing has been widely advocated both as a disincentive to private car use and as a revenue raiser. A large literature exists on the subject, but as yet few projects have been implemented. Road pricing certainly has advantages. There is some evidence to show that it can provide the push for modal shift, it is a way of internalising costs, and it can also provide funding for alternatives to the car. There are, however, several disadvantages to take into consideration. Road pricing measures could divert traffic and lead to more urban sprawl and out of town developments if they are not integrated with planning policy. There are also equity problems. Those on lower incomes and those who pay all their own motoring costs could bear a disproportionate share of the costs.

16.   Road pricing is an instrument with both advantages and disadvantages

Car sharing

Parking reserved for bicycles

17.

In general, public opinion is hostile to road pricing, as evidenced by the 1991 EU wide survey, in which 65% of those surveyed said it would be ineffective (INRA 1991). However, when the charging is linked to paying for environmental damage there is evidence that opinion is generally more favourable (Jones 1991). Urban road pricing is now being studied and planned in a number of countries and is likely to be put into practice. In order to be effective and acceptable it will need to be linked to using the funds raised to provide alternatives to the car as part of an environmental improvement package.

6.5 Urban toll pricing in Oslo, Norway

Oslo, Norway instituted an urban toll pricing scheme in 1990. Its initial objectives were exclusively financial - to provide for the completion of a highway investment programme. The results were immediate: a reduction from 5-10% of traffic through toll stations, and a stabilisation of public transport flows. Since then the use of the receipts has changed and 20% of the toll receipts are now committed to public transport development.

Local parking policy is an important tool to control traffic volumes

18.

For local authorities parking is an important, and for some the major, tool to control traffic volumes through both price and supply. Parking restrictions, however, do not affect through traffic or, generally, commercial vehicles. However, there are ways in which parking policy can restrict traffic access, for example by giving preference to residents over commuters, limitation of parking provision for offices and other employment sites, *and* priority parking for environmentally friendly vehicles as part of an overall traffic policy. Following the referendum on car traffic in 1992, Amsterdam has chosen parking policy as the main instrument to reduce car journeys. The overall aim of reducing car traffic by 35% will be achieved by reducing commuter parking, giving priority to residents, constructing underground car parks and eliminating on-street parking from many areas or charging at a much higher rate.

6.6 Parking measures in San Sebastian, Spain

In San Sebastian, parking measures are an important element of the city's transport and environmental policy, where a number of objectives in the areas of noise and air pollution have been set. To reduce motorised traffic, priority is given to city residents, while commuters, through a combination of high fees in the centre and free parking at locations connected to the public transport network, are encouraged to use the park and ride system.

Telematics can be used to encourage transfers from car to other modes of transport

19.

Traffic telematic tools such as those tested through the EU DRIVE programme can assist implementation. Such tools need to be used within the framework of a clear definition of the acceptable level of traffic in view of the environmental and planning constraints. In particular they can be used to encourage the transfer from the car to other modes of transport.

6.7 The application of telematics in traffic control, Turin, Italy

The 5T project - Telematic Technologies for Transport and Traffic in Turin - is part of the POLIS project. Telematics will be applied to a variety of traffic control actions, amongst them environmental monitoring of air pollution levels and follow-up action to cut traffic if certain thresholds are breached. Telematics are also applied to give public transport and emergency vehicles priority over private transport depending on traffic levels, and to give real time information to users of public transport and car parks.

Projects of a similar nature are underway in several German cities including, for example, Stuttgart (STORM - Stuttgart Transport Operation by Regional Management), Munich (KVM - Co-operative Traffic management Munich - recently Munich Comfort) and Frankfurt (FRUIT/RHAPIT - Frankfurt Urban Integrated Traffic Management/Rhein-Main Area Project for Integrated Traffic Management).

20.

Access restrictions on heavy goods vehicles have been part of the traffic policies of many cities for some time. These generally involve limitations for part of the day or night. In Sweden the restrictions are based on an environmental index which requires heavy vehicles to be registered in three environmental classes (OECD/ECMT 1994). Some countries and urban areas have begun to look at alternative solutions such as distribution and logistic centres ('transferia'). For example the Netherlands plan to reduce heavy vehicle movements in cities by 50% through the use of such centres.

21.   Access restrictions on heavy goods
vehicles and city distribution
centres

6.8 City distribution centre in Leiden, the Netherlands

Leiden intends to develop a city distribution centre through which the city centre would be supplied by small delivery vans. It is estimated that 70% of the goods supplied to the city could be transferred from heavy vehicles and the current 24,000 daily lorry kilometres that affect the city centre would be reduced by around 80%.

POLICY OPTIONS FOR
SUSTAINABILITY

Policy option: priority

Public transport and accessibility

Accessible public transport

Park and ride is widely used as a
measure accompanying public
transport improvements

Policy option: priority to public transport

22. Public transport has declined considerably in most cities over the past 40 years despite large scale investment. Evidence shows that increased investment and other improvements have not succeeded in reducing car traffic and that often any increased usage has come from a shift from cycling and walking. Action is required on levels of service, comfort, image and safety, and genuine attention needs to be paid to improving the accessibility of public transport so that it can be used in safety and confidence by people with reduced personal mobility. In addition, reserved lanes, links between networks, and operating aid systems (telematics) require improvements, and the measures need to be integrated with those on car restraint in order to give public transport priority over private transport (for example at traffic signals) if it is to flourish.

23. The accessibility of public transport should be improved to take into account the needs of people with reduced mobility - including disabled and elderly people, and parents with children in pushchairs. People with reduced mobility are literally handicapped if the public transport systems are not easily accessible and if they have no alternative transport system. Accessibility is an issue for all public transport users, and besides the specific needs of special user groups, factors such as location of stops and stations, frequency of lines, and both physical and economic accessibility determine the quality of the public transport service. The Commission has drawn up a report on what is needed to achieve a comfortable and accessible public transport system in response to the Council's Resolution of 16 December 1991 and to the White Paper on the future development of the Common Transport Policy. The Commission has outlined the measures which should be taken at Community, national or regional, and local levels.

24. Examples of good, accessible transport systems include the new light railway in Grenoble; low-floor buses, the EU project 'COST 322' will investigate aspects of safety, vehicle design, bus-stop design etc.; the Service-route in Sweden that carries small buses and operates on a flexibly timetabled basis from residential areas to hospitals, town centres, etc.; and the Government and NGO funded wheelchair-accessible taxi developed in Spain and several other Member States.

25. Experience with low-floor buses in Germany indicate an initial price premium of 20 - 25% over existing designs of bus. After six years of production the difference in cost is about 10%, with confident predictions of an ultimate premium of only 2% to 5%. Operating costs can be reduced as a result of the improvement in the waiting time and hence overall running speeds, reducing the requirement for buses and drivers on routes. A current evaluation of low-floor buses in Bremen in Germany, shows that low-floor buses cost an extra 10%, but higher speed and easier operation result in a reduction of 10% in the number of vehicles needed. In any case, only 5% of bus operating costs arise from bus purchase.

26. Park and ride has been widely developed throughout Europe as an accompanying measure to public transport improvements. To be effective park and ride schemes need to include action on signposts, pedestrian links, pricing advantages and security measures for parked cars and drivers, and they need to be accompanied by reductions in parking space in city centres and other dissuasive measures for cars. The city of Oxford estimates that park and ride reduces daily radial traffic to the centre by about 10%. At peak hours the reduction is as much as 24% (Oxford City Council, 1989).

A particular feature of public transport policies in a number of cities in recent years has been the revival or reintroduction of trams and trolley-buses. Other cities have invested in light rail systems. Examples of new tram systems include those in Grenoble, Strasbourg and Nantes in France. In the UK, light rail systems that serve both the town centre and outlying suburbs have been introduced in Manchester and Sheffield . The city of Nancy has been running bi-mode trolley buses since 1983 and estimates that their use has resulted in a 30% drop in energy consumption on the lines where these buses operate. Intermodality schemes are also of some interest.

27.   A range of policy and technical initiatives are deployed to change travel behaviour

6.9 The use of train lines for urban trams, Karlsruhe, Germany

Karlsruhe has implemented a project called 'Stadtbahn' or 'cityline' for the use of train lines for urban trams. Passengers benefit from the direct link, shorter train intervals, more stops and ease of a single fare structure. The number of passengers per day has risen from 2,000 to 8,000, which has helped the different transport companies to recoup their investment. These measures are part of a comprehensive transport plan which also includes inner city parking management and priority lanes for public transport.

Whilst a range of initiatives is being developed to improve public transport and reduce the use of private cars, it is important to recognise that the car is difficult to replace for certain journeys. This is particularly true for trips around urban areas for which fixed route public transport systems are often inappropriate and taxis are relatively expensive.

28.

Partly in response to this challenge, a number of schemes are being developed in Europe to encourage modes intermediate between private and public transport. These include car sharing schemes as, for example, in Berlin and community taxis to service low density areas as, for example, in St Brieux in France, both up to now more familiar in rural than in urban areas. Interesting experiments are in progress in Italy and France to evaluate the potential for 'individual public transport' in urban areas. These experiments involve fleets of small electric vehicles which are self-drive and resemble personal taxis or hire cars.

29.

Policy option: priority to cyclists and pedestrians

In recent years these forms of transport have declined considerably and have tended to be overlooked by policy makers (OECD/ECMT, 1995). However, measures to give priority to cycles and pedestrians should be much more seriously considered, as they have clear benefits, principally low capital cost and very limited impact on the environment. In addition, as a large proportion of urban trips are minimise - around a quarter under 3km in Germany and the UK - there is enormous potential to shift these short trips from the car to cycling and walking.

Policy option: priority to cyclists and pedestrians

30.

Cycling: effective transport for short distances

Cycling and walking are effective
transport alternatives for short
distances

31.   Public transport finds it difficult to cater for short distances, especially when such trips have their origin and destination in suburban areas. The bicycle is closest to the journey time, door-to-door capabilities and flexibility of the private car, and in many ways a more appropriate substitute than conventional fixed route public transport systems. There are some definite signs of a change of attitude in cities beyond those in the Netherlands and Denmark, such as Delft and Copenhagen, which have traditionally been associated with cycling.

32.   Several surveys have shown that when choosing a transport mode, time saving has priority over safety and convenience (Hilpert and Kostwein, 1990, cited in European Federation for Transport and Environment, 1994). Planning for cyclists and pedestrians must therefore meet the need for short and direct connections, without neglecting the elements of safety and convenience.

33.   Cyclist and pedestrian friendly planning therefore requires the prevention of detours and waiting times. The network of cycling and walking routes should be dense to allow direct access to any destination. Connecting paths, shortcuts, passages through buildings, and underpasses or bridges to overcome obstacles such as rivers, rail tracks or motorways can reduce trip length. Waiting times should be kept as short as possible, for example by providing time saving traffic light phases for cyclists and pedestrians, and traffic light bypass options for cyclists turning right (or left in the UK).

34.   Cyclists and pedestrians must also be able to move safely and without fear. Points where conflicts with other transport modes are likely should therefore be removed, and social control along the routes can be used to prevent feelings of fear. Various measures such as traffic calming and speed reduction, emphasis on visibility, prevention of blind areas, safe design of intersections with cycle paths, advanced stoplines for cyclists, and separate lanes for cyclists going straight ahead or turning left (right in the UK) at intersection approach areas can improve traffic safety.

35.   In pursuit of safety objectives many cities have established cycleways separated from the road and following less direct routes. The increase in distance, coupled with the perceived dangers to cyclists travelling in isolated areas at night, have discouraged their use and threatened to undermine the credibility of cycleway policies, as has occurred, for example, in Milton Keynes in UK. The provision of cycle routes along main highways is therefore advocated, using some of the road capacity currently allocated to motorised vehicles. As mentioned above, accompanying action to moderate motor traffic will therefore be of benefit.

36.   This raises an issue which has yet to be resolved in many European cities. A real commitment to the slow modes (walking and cycling) is likely to involve reduction of highway capacity, for example, by narrowing the carriageway for motorised traffic to provide space for a cycle lane or to widen pavements. This may lead in the short term to greater congestion as capacity is reduced and speeds fall. However, such a strategy might be an essential component of a genuinely sustainable long term transport policy.

Cycling and walking should also be made pleasant and convenient. Measures such as wide pavements and separate cycle paths, levelled-off or continuing pavements and cycle paths at intersections, pedestrianisation schemes, removal of obstacles such as kerbstones, smooth surface on cycle paths, and speed humps that do not obstruct bicycle traffic all contribute to increasing the pleasure and convenience of cycling and walking. The development of green corridors based on transport routes, principally footpaths, cycleways and waterways, to form a network of 'greenways', is also a way of enhancing the environmental quality of the cycling and walking environment. Cycling can further be promoted by providing secure bicycle parking facilities near public transport stations, shopping centres, schools, public buildings etc., and by allowing the transport of bicycles on public transport. The provision of washing and changing facilities at work is also important. Employers could also use various incentives to reward employees who cycle, walk or use public transport to get to work.

37.

The creation of functional, safe and attractive conditions for cycling and walking should be supported by so called 'soft policies'. These include not only public relations in terms of advertising, but also creating a cyclist and pedestrian friendly climate. Cyclists and pedestrians should feel that they are respected and welcome as traffic participants (European Federation for Transport and Environment, 1994). The central area of Brussels, for example, illustrates the way in which the emphasis on provision for the motor car has created areas that are not attractive for walking and cycling. Examples of cities making strong provision for cyclists include Erlangen in Germany and Groningen in the Netherlands.

38.   Walking and cycling requires safe and attractive environments

6.10 Promotion of cycling policy in Erlangen, Germany

Erlangen has been promoting a cycling policy for over 20 years by developing a dense network of cycleways accompanied by detailed signalling and parking facilities. Priority is given to cyclists on certain routes. As a result, cycling has doubled its share of city traffic since 1974 (29% from 14%) while the share of private car traffic has remained stable at around 40%. However, the share of pedestrians in the overall number of trips has fallen over the same period. The city plans to reduce the private car share to 30% by the year 2000.

6.11 Favouring use of bicycles and public transport, Groningen, the Netherlands

Groningen has implemented a programme to favour the use of the bicycle and public transport. The idea is to institute restrictive parking policies near facilities, shopping centres and other locations of attraction. As an alternative, the city provides cycle paths and public transport networks near these locations. The city has also improved its bus service through the integration of different networks, the building of separate bus lanes, and ensuring priority for buses at traffic lights. Now Groningen is known to be the world's third ranking city for bicycle use.

Policy option:
experimenting with
specialist vehicles and
fuels

Policy option: experimenting with specialist vehicles and fuels

39. Electric/hybrid vehicles could be introduced, especially for commercial fleets, to cope with air quality problems. As with electric vehicles, alternative/reformulated fuels could be introduced on a regional/urban level to address a particular local air quality problem. These measures do not, of course, contribute towards solving the congestion problem, and in some circumstances simply displace the pollution from the urban area to the area around power stations. Many pilot projects and schemes are being implemented throughout the EU and a network of cities (Citelec) interested in co-operating on common projects has been in existence for several years. Some cities see electric cars playing a different role from the private car and being used more in rental systems. In Florence and many other Italian cities, electric vehicles are the only vehicles permitted in the city on days when the city otherwise is closed to traffic due to high pollution levels. The feasibility of this scheme is in large measure due to the development of a bi-modal scooter by an Italian manufacturer.

6.12 Electric vehicles and other innovative transport forms, La Rochelle, France

As part of its public transport promotion policy 'Autoplus', which includes shared taxi services, 'help yourself' bicycles and sea boats alongside the normal bus services, La Rochelle in France is running several experiments with electric vehicles. Pilot schemes have been in operation since the mid-1980s, especially for city service vehicles, and these are now being expanded to involve both public transport and private vehicles.

Policy option:
influencing behaviour

Policy option: influencing behaviour

40. Public awareness and information campaigns to influence behaviour are vital accompanying measures to the range of actions outlined above. There is also some evidence to show that on their own, campaigns can make a small but significant contribution. Influencing behaviour can be based on pull-factors, but linkages should also be made to healthy lifestyles, economic efficiency and equity. A key element is to make the most of favourable public opinion. There are large majorities in favour of preferential treatment of the more environment friendly modes of transport.

6.13 Transport awareness campaign in Hampshire, United Kingdom

In 1994 Hampshire County Council in the UK launched a transport awareness campaign entitled 'Headstart' with the aim of reducing the rate of growth in car traffic. This is directed at both individuals and a wide variety of groups in the county. The campaign involves both one-off high profile events and medium to long term actions. The feasibility study estimated that an awareness campaign could reduce traffic growth by between 1% and 5% over three years, depending on the level of campaign and financial resources.

The European Commission is acutely aware of the need to act on road safety: 45,000 killed, and 1.5 m injured each year. A useful policy framework has been established with the publication of the Transport White Paper (CEC, 1992b) which combines environmental and mobility objectives. It identified the implementation of a road safety programme including priority actions in the field of driver education and behaviour, vehicle safety and infrastructure, as one of two areas for action. The other area is the strengthening of Community legislation on the carriage of dangerous goods for national and international transport operations.

41.   Road safety must improve

The EU should now develop specific measures to meet the accessibility needs of the urban population whilst protecting the environment. The following actions might be considered:

42.   Actions by the EU to improve accessibility without endangering the environment

- the use of Structural and Cohesion Funds to assist transport which improves accessibility within urban areas whilst reducing the environmental impacts of motorised modes;

- developing an equitable system for evaluating different transport modes which takes effective account of all benefits and costs, including environmental impacts;

- environmental targets (similar to those for CO_2 emissions) should be set and incorporated into the evaluation and funding mechanisms;

- fiscal policy could be employed to reduce the price advantage currently enjoyed by those motorised modes causing the greatest environmental damage (for example carbon tax).

National governments have key responsibility for fiscal policy, the provision of funding and subsidy, methods of evaluating transport investments, and the regulatory regime under which transport operates. They are often directly involved with the provision of national transport infrastructure, producing a network into which urban areas must fit, and the specification of national guidelines for land use and development planning. It is therefore in the following areas that action may be taken:

43.   Actions by national governments

- using economic means, such as additional taxes on the purchase, licensing and use of vehicles to ensure that the full external costs of travel are paid by the road user;

- developing a fiscal policy which encourages the use of transport modes which impose least damage on the environment, for example alteration of company car taxation to put public transport on an equal footing;

- any moneys received from the taxation of environmentally damaging modes to be 'ring-fenced' or 'ear-marked' for the financing or subsidy of environmental improvements or less harmful means of transport;

- the design of a regulatory regime which enables competition where desirable, whilst ensuring control over quality and the environmental impacts of transport.

- the development and use of techniques for evaluating transport modes in an equitable way which takes account of their diverse environmental impacts;

- the specification of a system of land use and transport planning which recognises the important relationships between these two functional areas (as in the Netherlands and more recently in the UK).

Responsibility of local governments   44.

Local government has ultimate responsibility for the 'shape' of the urban environment through control and influence over development and local transport. It will often provide highway and other infrastructure and may control public transport provision. In many countries local authorities retain ownership of transport operators. It is therefore essential to plan strategically to set local objectives on accessibility, environment and economic development. These sometimes contrasting policies will need to be resolved at a political level to ensure the appropriate priority is accorded to each area. Local environmental targets will need to be set alongside those on accessibility and development. Another measure that should be taken by local authorities is to use legal instruments to enforce speed limits.

4

CONCLUSIONS

1.

The importance of travel that takes place in urban areas means that cities must play their part in solving some of the wider environmental problems such as global warming. The relative dependency on cars in rural areas implies that cities must contribute to the reduction of transport by more than their share of the population. In addition, achieving sustainable urban mobility is a vital step in the overall improvement of the urban environment and the maintenance of the economic vitality of cities.

Urban transport contributes to global environmental problems

2.

In the long term, it will be necessary to reduce transport in order to achieve a more sustainable form of urban mobility and to improve accessibility. In the short term, it will be necessary to, among other things, minimise and halt the forecast growth in the number and length of trips and therefore the demand for transport.

3.

Action taken so far towards sustainability in urban mobility and accessibility appears to have been directed overwhelmingly at reducing road traffic and congestion - by encouraging a shift from private cars to public transport and, less often, to cycling and walking. Whilst these actions to reduce traffic clearly have an important impact, few have explicit environmental objectives and they do not in themselves constitute sustainability measures. Rather, they are the means to achieve specified transport-related ends. A better system for monitoring the effectiveness of these actions in relation to specified goals is required. Further development of sustainability goals, indicators, target-setting and monitoring is needed.

Actions by local governments have mainly targeted reduction of private car use

4.

5.

Suburban travel

Further work is needed on suburban travel. Most policies in cities seem to be directed at improving the situation in the central areas, with suburb to suburb traffic being somewhat neglected. However, in recent years, it is in these areas that there has been the most traffic growth. Further consideration could also be given to the enhanced involvement of local communities in formulating transport policies. A fresh look at community-based transport initiatives, not addressed in this report, might also be appropriate.

The development of sustainable urban mobility requires further development of policies aimed at improving accessibility and not simply movement. It is essential to develop measures to reduce demand for travel rather than continuing to emphasise measures which seek to minimise travel time.

6.

The reconciliation of accessibility, economic development and environmental objectives should be the primary objective of a city's transport policy. Setting transport policies within the framework of a city-wide strategy for sustainable development may be one way to enhance policy integration. Within such a strategy, land use and mobility and access issues might be jointly examined through assessment of the mobility and access impacts of new developments.

7.

Affording an equal status to environmental objectives in policies designed to improve accessibility requires a dramatic re-orientation of political and public cultures. Influencing attitudes through democratic consultative processes involving public, private and voluntary sector bodies is therefore prerequisite of more sustainable movement patterns in European cities.

7

SUSTAINABLE SPATIAL PLANNING

SUSTAINABLE AND SPATIAL PLANNING

INTRODUCTION

Consideration of spatial planning is fundamental to the work of the Expert Group on the Urban Environment. Part of the formal remit of the Group is 'to consider how future town and spatial planning strategies can incorporate environmental objectives'. Through the European Sustainable Cities Project the Group is also addressing this issue and extending its work to consider not only environmental but sustainability objectives.

In addition, while the European Sustainable Cities Project has been in progress, work is proceeding at European level on the preparation of a European Spatial Development Perspective (Committee on Spatial Development, 1994). This builds on *Europe 2000+: Co-operation for European Territorial Development* (CEC, 1994a) and stresses the need to develop a polycentric urban system, with cities and towns linked in urban networks, a network of environmentally acceptable infrastructure (including transport infrastructure) and a network of open spaces for the protection of natural resources. Also proposed is a network of research institutes to form a European 'observatory'. One aim of this work, overseen by the Committee on Spatial Development, is to ensure that the imperatives of planning the development of European territory are better taken into account in Member States. Development of the European Spatial Development Perspective is also seen as important in ensuring that all regions and urban areas benefit from the Single Market. Sustainable development within a framework of close co-operation has been fundamental to the proposals so far. It is an important part of the work of the Expert Group to ensure that any proposed Spatial Development Perspective incorporates those principles and mechanisms which offer the best possibilities of achieving sustainable development.

The focus in this chapter is on spatial planning in general, urban regeneration and issues associated with leisure, tourism and cultural heritage.

Role of spatial planning

Spatial planning is designed to regulate the use of land in the public interest. All European countries have systems in place which seek this objective, although the scope and method of operation of each system differs. They are variously termed urban, spatial, physical or territorial planning or space management systems and generally comprise two functions:

- plan-making (providing frameworks through development strategies and plans at different spatial scales from national to local);

- development control (legal or administrative procedures operating at the local level to control the location and form of development, and change of use within buildings).

In some countries, municipalities, through the spatial planning system, are able to take a direct role in promoting certain activities in accordance with development plan priorities. To varying degrees, municipalities are able to purchase or assemble land, to undertake or co-ordinate investment in infrastructure, housing or industrial buildings and to compensate landowners where appropriate. The scope for these kinds of integrated action is strong in, for example, the Netherlands and Norway. It is useful to note the distinction between legally-binding plan-based systems, like that in Denmark and the Netherlands, which give a right to certain kinds of development if they are in conformity with the development plan, and plan-led systems, like that in the UK, where the plan provides only a presumption of the kind of development that will or will not be allowed.

Spatial planning systems are seen by the EU as one of the key mechanisms for working towards sustainable development, the Green Paper on the Urban Environment and the Fifth Environmental Action Programme are both explicit on this point. As such, interest in their capacity both to accommodate innovative approaches to reducing environmental damage and to improve environmental quality has increased recently.

Addressing the new agenda of sustainable development requires environmental professionals to broaden their perspective to consider economic and social sustainability issues as well as environmental aspects of land use (Healey & Shaw, 1993). On the other hand planning professionals should develop more knowledge about the environmental consideration of specific spatial developments.

KEY SUSTAINABILITY ISSUES

Of major concern is the pace at which land, a finite resource, is being consumed by urban development in Europe. Irreversible land use changes, especially those which involve loss of biodiversity, constitute a particular issue for sustainability. Land loss is currently especially acute in Mediterranean countries. More generally, despite a tradition of urban living in many European countries, most cities have been subject to population and employment decentralisation over recent decades leading to the spread of urban peripheries. Rural settlements further down the urban hierarchy and more remote from major cities are also subject to development pressures. In the case of Britain, Green Belt control around major cities has diverted growth to small and medium size towns and villages. Within urban settlements of all sizes, the loss of both public and private green space is a major issue.

Adding to the outward spread of cities have been new forms of commercial and business development. The 1980s saw major investment in new forms of business park and out of town retail centres, seeking to locate at points of high accessibility on the periphery of cities and creating their own environments. These trends have been particularly developed in France, Spain and Britain, partly because the planning systems in these countries have been more responsive to new market pressures. It is apparent that these out of town developments are threatening the vitality and viability of traditional town centres. Some Member States, such as the Netherlands and Germany, have a long tradition in fighting these developments and have taken action to limit them. Nevertheless such developments also occur there.

The trend towards a more land-extensive structure of cities and the increasing separation between activities (home, work, shops) has exacerbated the growth in car-borne traffic, which in turn has increased energy consumption and emissions. It has also affected the viability and patronage of public transport facilities. Planning solutions to the environmental problems of cities earlier this century, especially those emphasising the separation of urban functions, in order to avoid health problems, have contributed to the current generation of environmental problems, primarily from increased dependency on private cars. Rigid zoning systems and institutional funding preferences have all too often encouraged new developments to be single use. Yet European cities have always been valued for their diversity, which results from their complex history and geography, and have typically been collections of diverse neighbourhoods (distinct quarters).

6.

7.

1.2

1.   Threats against urban sustainability

2.   Impact of out-of-town developments

3.   Effects of segregation of functions

Out of town development

Positive and negative effects

4. Every development has some environmental impact, either adverse or beneficial. Spatial planning systems mostly incorporate measures to limit adverse impacts, for example by requiring developers to use environmentally-friendly technology. If adverse impacts cannot be avoided the question is whether to compensate those experiencing the impacts. Clearly the scope for compensation will depend upon the value placed upon the threatened environmental assets. While most European planning systems make some provision for 'planning gain', in which obligations are placed on developers to secure the interests of the local community, extending such procedures to secure ecological or more general sustainability requirements is not straightforward. For example, there are limits as to how far ecological diversity can be protected by such measures. There are also basic ethical questions about how to value the interests of non-human life and these have scarcely begun to be addressed in formal planning systems.

5. Spatial developments do not only affect the local area. The environmental impact is always wider, affecting for example water flows, traffic and air pollution. Spatial development should be considered within the regional context of road infrastructures and ecology.

Some principles of sustainable development

6. Many of the principles of sustainable development are already incorporated into some European planning systems:

- they operate over a range of spatial scales, from local to global, related to the levels at which the environmental issues arise;

- in various ways they allow community involvement, and are open and democratic in operation;

- they seek to take account of future effects and implications on different groups within the population;

- they provide the opportunity to consider economic, social, and environmental objectives.

Sustainability and training of planners

7. Many concepts important for sustainability have been explicit for at least two decades in the training of planners, for example the notion that cities function as a series of interlocking systems in a hierarchy of urban settlements. The new sustainability agenda places new emphasis on the interrelationships between the physical environment and these human and economic systems, acknowledging that there is a capacity beyond which the environment cannot sustain these activity levels. The environment was seen more as an asset or amenity; it is now seen as a functioning system. Hence there is renewed interest in ecology (Healey & Shaw, 1993). Indeed, perhaps the most crucial role for planning is to aim to stay within environmental carrying capacities and to maintain and pass on to future generations the stock of both natural capital and the built heritage. Furthermore, it is essential to move towards models of development for local areas in which problems imported from, or exported to, areas outside the municipality are minimised.

There are many definitions for environmental capacity as a result of different theoretical approaches and differences between Member States. Generally, environmental capacity is related to environmental impacts at local, regional and global level, but estimates of local environmental capacity could be useful indicators against which global and regional environmental concerns should be balanced. The following definition of environmental capacity for spatial planning purposes has been suggested by Breheny (1994):

Planning for environmental capacity requires the identification of the maximum level of development that a local environment (town, city, region) can sustain indefinitely while maintaining critical and constant natural and precious human-made capital within the environment.

Key problems for planners are to define and measure environmental assets and capacity for their local areas, to determine capacity constraints, to identify quantifiable indicators that are sensitive to changes in the status of environmental assets and to determine what kinds, what levels, and what geographical distributions of development are possible without breaching these. These tasks require planners to work with other professionals and with local communities. Choices as to what assets to value and prioritise are ultimately political rather than technical ones.

There is general agreement that embracing sustainable development means increasing the priority given to environmental concerns in formulating development plans and policies and in taking planning decisions. In addition, addressing the sustainability agenda requires that planners consider social and economic dimensions and that they adopt longer time horizons in plan making than has been usual up to now.

POLICY OPTIONS FOR SUSTAINABILITY

Policy option: integrating environmental and spatial planning

The relationship between spatial planning and measures to protect and enhance the physical environment, for example pollution control, varies from system to system. In some countries the functions are combined while in others they are quite separate. Opinions differ as to whether these two essential areas of urban management should be linked by developing integrated environmental plans or by preparing land use plans, with or without an environmental focus, and then subjecting them to environmental appraisal. In practice the approach adopted partly depends upon whether municipalities have responsibility for environmental protection as well as for spatial planning. It also depends upon the extent to which these are effectively integrated at higher levels of government. Denmark and the Netherlands, for example, have strongly integrated hierarchical systems in which national environmental policies provide the context for municipal development planning; and municipal plans are required to incorporate national environmental objectives.

Practical guidance for incorporating environmental aspects into spatial planning is set out in the *Rotterdam Manual for Urban Planning and Environment* (UPE Manual) developed by the city of Rotterdam in the Netherlands. This provides a methodology for implementing environmental policy at a local scale through the spatial planning system. It contains a broad assessment of national environmental regulations, together with

8.   Environmental capacity is related to environmental impacts at local, regional and global level

9.   Sustainability requires planners to work in new ways

10.

1.3

Policy option:
integrating
environmental and
1.   spatial planning

2.

information about possible solutions. Two practical strategies are set out. The first requires that any specific aspect of policy must be located at the appropriate spatial scale. The second provides three clusters of environmental factors which planners must address in decision-making about urban development:

- the sustainability (or 'blue') cluster, which covers matters of relevance to future generations;

- the 'green' cluster, which emphasises ecological quality and refers to the conservation of habitats and species; and

- the 'grey' cluster, which addresses traditional environmental concerns such as noise, safety, odour and soil contamination, all important in relation to the quality of urban life.

Within each cluster specific policy measures are proposed. For example, the sustainability cluster requires economical land use, which may be addressed by multiple use of land, underground construction or compact building (Public Works Rotterdam, 1994).

3.   Public Works Rotterdam have carried out a survey of the extent to which environmental aspects are incorporated into spatial planning in nine European cities and the methods by which this is achieved. While environmental aspects are taken into account in nearly all cases, attention to the different clusters varies. Traditional environmental aspects are routinely incorporated, and 'green' aspects emphasising ecological quality are increasingly used. However, the sustainability aspects are recognised as difficult to address, principally because of a lack of knowledge as to how to tackle them and a lack of suitable standards (Public Works Rotterdam, 1994).

The 'STOLP' method

4.   The Amsterdam Department of Environmental Affairs is developing an integrated district or area oriented policy. This approach is intended to provide answers to:

- the 'paradox of the compact city', the contradictory effects at different levels: positive effects of the compact city at macro levels and negative effects at local levels;

- instruments that contribute to the integration of environmental and city planning;

- problems that are relevant at city level.

5.   This integrated district-oriented policy, called the 'STOLP' method, depicts the current state of the environment in the municipality of Amsterdam. The method is based upon the American 'bubble concept'. The basic idea is that within a defined area certain emissions of pollution are allowed as long as the total pollution decreases. The city stolp is an instrument to measure the total degree of environmental pollution in the city at a given time. This method suits complex situations and contains some new elements:

- combining different type of environmental pollution;

- area or district oriented;

- exchange and compensation.

6.

The Amsterdam Department of Environmental Affairs and the Department of City Planning developed several tools and indicators for this integrated district-oriented policy. An example is the Environmental Matrix, an indicator for environmental effects of urban development, based upon a multi-criteria analysis (Amsterdam Department of City Planning, 1996).

7.   Environmental objectives specified at an early stage in the planning process

A general requirement for more sustainable spatial planning is that environmental objectives should be specified at an early stage in the planning process. However, the scope for giving early consideration to environmental issues varies between planning systems. For example, Marshall (1993) reports difficulties with integrating environmental constraints into the process of preparing the Barcelona sub-regional plan, an exercise largely orientated to accommodating development pressures.

8.

Giving priority to environmental considerations in plan making requires analysis of the local environmental context before development plans are prepared or updated, identifying environmental assets and capacity constraints. A baseline is thus provided against which policies and proposals can be checked to assess the changes they are likely to make. In the UK, local state of the environment reports provide such a basis in some authorities and in addition, the UK government's good practice guide (DOE, 1993b) encourages this form of scoping process as a forerunner to development plan preparation. Environmental atlases have been used in both Denmark and Germany. That for Berlin aims to highlight existing environmental problems, for example the development of open spaces since 1950, in a series of map layers. The French local environmental plans (PLE) also fulfill this diagnostic function.

Surface water network

The dual network
strategy

The dual network strategy

9.

Systems vary in the extent to which ecosystems principles are made explicit in these types of exercise. Emphasis should be placed on transport and water networks in shaping urban form. This has been described as the 'dual network strategy', developed in the Netherlands in work for the Ministry of Housing, Spatial Development and the Environment (Tjallingii et al, 1994). This is an ecologically-inspired planning method in which the transport network is seen as having 'a guiding effect on highly dynamic uses, such as businesses, offices, mass recreation and agriculture', while the water network influences 'less dynamic uses such as water collection, nature and low key recreation' (Van der Wal, 1993). The water network connects all life by the exchange of water nutrients, the transport network connects human activities and exchange of goods. The water network has the potential to be developed into an ecological framework. The transport network may define urban nodes around public transport stops and define boundaries of settlements by the usual radius of cyclists and pedestrians. The combination of both offers a framework to guide urban developments and enables locations suitable for various urban uses to be identified. This approach has been piloted by three municipalities, Breda, Dordrecht, and Zwolle, and the region of Twente. In Twente (Zandvoort Ordening & Advies, 1993), this dual network strategy gives an ecological framework based on the streams and underground water flows to guide the urbanisation (50,000 dwellings) into an urban string of beads along the regional railway.

Practical planning options   10.   This dual-network approach results in a number of practical planning options:

- space for peak and seasonal water storage between the built-up areas of the city;

- the urban area including green zones for clean water, and routes for animals;

- the city including green wedges or green areas for regulation of climate, pedestrian and cycle routes, recreational areas, quiet areas, functional zoning etc.;

- an optimal fringe length of green area has a positive influence on differentiation in types of houses and for land use;

- restriction of car traffic, and car parking in general, and the combination of walking and bicycle routes and public transport routes specifically;

- industrial sites situated alongside road and rail connections and networks.

7.1   Ecological development principles, Breda, the Netherlands

In Breda, the application of ecological development principles, in which the demands of water management, in particular, constrain new development options, has resulted in a polynuclear planning strategy for urban development in the region, set out in the municipal Policy Plan. Breda itself is expected to grow to both the east and west, annexing a number of smaller settlements in the process. Attention is paid to the separation of clean and polluted water courses and, in the city, to the separation of sewage and rainwater systems. The clean water system includes infiltration areas, stream and river basins and polders with seepage, most of which are also designated as nature areas where the original meandering water courses are being restored and wild vegetation encouraged, creating green corridors. The water management requirements do not permit a compact city solution, and large green areas will therefore remain. A compact form, however, is envisaged for the regional sub-centre of Etten-Leur where water management has less of an influence.

11.   Ecological approaches are also being developed in Italy. On a national scale, the Quadroter research project constructed a Territorial Framework of Reference for Environmental Policy based on ecosystems principles. This has resulted in a division of the entire national territory into 'urban ecosystems'. Maps depicting the 'load' of each activity - for example, agricultural land capacity, industrial pollution, tourist areas, transport networks and urban decay - are superimposed to provide an overall land use matrix. This has been used by the Ministry of the Environment in the preparation of a Ten Year Plan for the Environment (Archibugi, 1993).

Early consideration of environmental implications in the planning process   12.   One of the means by which environmental implications can be considered earlier in the planning process is by undertaking environmental assessment of policies while development plans are being prepared. Formal Environmental Impact Assessment can be a powerful tool for anticipating the likely consequences of *projects*, and ensuring that

12.

adequate controls are in place to minimise environmental damage either through planning legislation or parallel pollution control regulations. In fact EIA was the first development control tool to be applied throughout Europe. Although, as section 3.2 stressed the implementation of EIA is variable. Leaving impact assessment until project proposals are brought forward has disadvantages, particularly in European countries where the development plan is the legal framework.

7.2   Ecological approach for the regeneration of water, soil and air, Reggio Emilia, Italy

At city level, Reggio Emilia has developed an ecological approach to spatial planning, categorising areas of the city in terms of their capacity for the regeneration of water, soil and air. Categorisation is based on studies of the main environmental flows and the permeability of different areas of the city. Building is to be most strictly controlled in the most permeable areas. Minimum environmental targets have also been set - relating, for example, to the number of trees along roads. These measures are to be incorporated into the next land use plan for the city, currently in preparation.

13.

The wider adoption of Strategic Environmental Assessment will be dependent upon the development of tools compatible with the method of development plan preparation in each Member State (SEA is described in 3.2). A starting point could be to understand the interactions between objectives for the different sectors to be included within the plan. A recent reference book produced by the German Federal Ministry of Building suggests making such interactions explicit. For example a land use objective of minimising the consumption of space for urban development may support action in other areas such as in nature conservation, whereas the achievement of this objective may be obstructed by insufficient capacity for sewage disposal.

14.

Taking the environment as a starting point is fundamental to sustainability but it is not easy to achieve in practice and taking all aspects of sustainability as a starting point will be still more difficult. Extending the methodologies of EIA and SEA to developing methods of sustainability appraisal in spatial planning may provide a way forward.

Policy option: integrating land use and transport planning

Policy option:
integrating land use and
transport planning

15.

It is widely accepted that urban form, that is the pattern and density of development within and between settlements, influences travel patterns (chapter 6 considers the issue of sustainable accessibility), the ability to maintain biodiversity, and the quality of life. The spatial planning system is a key mechanism influencing urban form. Research conducted by the UK government has suggested that spatial planning policies could reduce projected transport emissions by 16% over a 20 year period (Ecotec, 1993). Other enabling factors such as price mechanisms, and availability of public transport would obviously need to be in place.

Increasing urban densities around
points of high accessibility

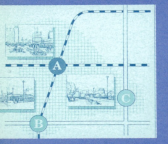

The ABC system

16. There is no unanimity about which urban form is the most sustainable or least unsustainable as discussed in Breheny, 1993. The Green Paper on Urban Environment (CEC, 1990) argues that the 'compact city' form is likely to be the most energy efficient as well as having social and economic advantages. This, however, assumes that it would be possible to reverse the current counter-urbanisation trends evident in all western countries, and concerns have also been expressed about the loss of open space and biodiversity through 'town cramming'. Other urban structures propounded in academic literature include the social cluster city, decentralised concentration, and linear bands.

17. The common feature shared by different solutions is the idea of increasing urban densities around points of high accessibility, and especially points of high accessibility to public transport. Whether this implies the maintenance of a monocentric city structure or the development of a polynuclear structure depends very much on the scale on which this principle is applied and on the characteristics of the local settlement pattern. It is clear that solutions need to be locally based.

18. That urban density is important, not least because it influences the availability of mass transit provision, is not in dispute. Empirical studies have found a strong correlation between high population density coupled with size of city and a shorter average distance travelled (McLaren, 1993), and also between low density and high car usage (Newman, 1993).

19. Increasing densities related to the public transport network is the essence of the Dutch long term policy to achieve 'the right business in the right place', the so-called ABC system. This seeks to match the mobility needs of businesses and other activities with the accessibility characteristics of urban locations. For example an A business with a high worker and visitor intensity should be guided to an A location with high accessibility on the public transport network, while C locations with high accessibility to motorway junctions should be reserved for C businesses with high dependence on road freight.

Some successful examples

20. This Dutch example represents the use of a national policy tool at city level. When applied consistently throughout a country it eliminates any temptation by any individual city to weaken its environmental control regime in favour of employment objectives.

7.3   Right business in the right place, the Hague, the Netherlands

The Hague is an example of a city currently implementing this policy. One A location has so far been identified around the Central Station and this has already attracted the new Ministry of Housing, Physical Planning and Environment with 3,000 employees previously dispersed over several sites in the city. The precise boundaries of this zone are currently being defined by superimposing land use and planning considerations onto transport planning criteria. A second A location has been identified subject to improving bus and tram interchange around the Hollands Spoor Station.

7.4   Site work places at accessibility points, Copenhagen, Denmark

Since its first regional plan (Fingerplan) in 1947, Copenhagen has attempted to restrict new urban development to settlements along five existing railway lines, protecting the green space between them. There is a greater emphasis in the new regional plan produced in 1989, and in the revisions made in 1993, on the location of work places, especially offices and others generating personal transport, at high accessibility points through the identification of priority areas for urban development or renewal near railway stations, especially stations in the radial railway system that provide good bus connections. New investments, including a light rail system to a new urban development of 3000 ha south of the centre, are being co-ordinated with this land use plan. Consistently maintaining such a concept overtime is an essential condition for success.

Many cities throughout Europe are seeking to integrate land use and transport policies through the preparation of updated regional or structure plans. Often such cities have historically had some form of protective policy on open space around the city fringes, or as green wedges extending into the city. There is now a more explicit attempt to guide high movement generating activities to areas of high accessibility.

21.

Ireland provides two examples of attempts to develop city-wide integrated strategies for land use and transport. These are the Cork Land Use and Transport Study and the Dublin Transportation Initiative. The latter strategy, for the Greater Dublin area, seeks to promote the economic health and potential of the city centre through improved public transport, traffic management and commuter parking restraint, reinforced by policies for urban renewal.

22.

As the Dublin Transportation Initiative indicates, success in integrating land use and transport policies seems to be greatest:

23.

• where cities have control of services provided by both public and private transport modes and control of land use policies. Cities lacking influence on land use policies beyond their administrative boundaries have difficulty in providing high quality and accessible public transport systems within their catchment areas;

• where specific targets can be identified; and

• when there exists stable funding and local commitment, because transport and spatial planning interventions require extended implementation times (Steer Davies Gleave 1994).

The importance of vertical integration is demonstrated in strategic sustainability in the Euregion (Zandvoort Ordening & Advies, 1993) where decisions at regional level are decisive for public transport services and environmental quality to be provided at local level.

24.   The importance of vertical integration

Policy option:
open space provision in
land use plans

25.   In 1993, Norway published National Policy Guidelines for co-ordinated transport and spatial planning. Significantly, the guidelines include a section on administrative responsibilities and mechanisms for co-operation between municipalities, county municipalities and representatives of national authorities. The principles are to be embodied in County Plans and followed up in Municipal Master Plans. Counties are expected to take the lead in co-ordination.

Policy option: open space provision in land use plans

26.   The value of open space within the urban fabric is increasingly being rediscovered. Open space comprises a variety of green spaces, including formal and informal parks, remnants of natural systems such as along watercourses, agricultural land, private gardens, urban public spaces such as city squares and the environment around cultural monuments, and habitats which develop on disused land such as industrial sites (Box & Harrison, 1993). Spatial planning systems, through development control powers, are the main mechanism by which these spaces remain open. Local authorities are increasingly exploring the incorporation of minimum targets for open space provision in land use plans. It is essential that all open space is viewed as part of the natural framework within which all built development is set, rather than simply the 'space left over after planning'.

The involvement of the public and
local business is important

27.   There is an important role for public involvement in planning and creating open spaces at the local level. In France, open space is one of the main sectors targeted for action by municipalities. The priorities set out in environmental charters at the municipal level are being converted into action at a more local level through the production of green plans. These are often co-ordinated by an architect with the aim of facilitating public debate about the functions that open areas should serve in a particular neighbourhood. The aim is to try to reach consensus about future uses of open areas.

Functions of open spaces

28.   Local businesses also have an important part to play in the conservation and improvement of open space. In the UK a network of 35 independent local trusts co-ordinated by the Groundwork Foundation, which receives public and private sector funding, involves local industry and residents in environmental improvement projects.

29.   Until now the main justification for retaining open space has been recognition of the social functions that it fulfils, in terms of meeting places, and areas for entertainment, recreation and relaxation, and its amenity value including contribution to quality of life, aesthetic enjoyment, a feeling of security and freedom from the urban noise and pollution. The new emphasis in terms of sustainability is on maximising the ecological role of open spaces within the urban fabric, in addition to maintaining its amenity and social functions, i.e. multi-use of open spaces. Open green space fulfils several ecological functions closely related to the issues of natural resource management discussed in section 4.1, including those related to the management of storm water, increasing biodiversity, and improving air quality. Countries with a long history of spatial planning have been relatively successful in maintaining open space accessible to the majority of their residents. Where development control powers have been weaker, municipalities are now seeking to improve the protection of open space for both its amenity and ecological value.

Open spaces

7.5   Landscape programme, Berlin, Germany

In Berlin, although about 50% of the metropolitan area is open space, it is concentrated in the western part. The new city-wide land use plan is addressing this imbalance. This process is assisted by the parallel production of a landscape programme, which is a strong feature of the German planning system. Landscape programmes formulate goals including the protection of existing green open spaces and the creation of new ones. This parallel process extends down the hierarchy so that a landscape plan is produced in association with the local plan. This ensures that new planting occurs in association with new construction in a co-ordinated way.

Ecological approaches to open space offer considerable scope for innovation and for community participation. Land use systems and planning professionals should allow experimentation on open sites which may in time lead to new approaches to the management of public open space.

30.   Ecological approaches to the management of open spaces

7.6   New approach to the management of open grassed areas, Stockholm, Sweden

In Stockholm a new approach to the management of open grassed areas within the city has recently been adopted. This is not only ecologically beneficial but cheaper and more energy efficient than previous methods of care. In the past the grass was cut several times in a season and the hay left on the ground. Under the new system, which aims to encourage the growth of taller grass and greater diversity of plant species and insects, the grass is cut only once per summer season and the cuttings removed. Removal of cuttings reduces the quantity of nutrients to the soil, preventing certain plants from dominating and encouraging the growth of wild flowers. Residents are encouraged to take an active role in the maintenance of open space through activities such as weeding, mowing and the care of ponds. In partnership with users the city's Real Estate, Streets and Traffic Department prepares a maintenance plan for each area to be cared for, drawing up a user contract. The Department also routinely composts organic waste from city-owned green areas and provides composting facilities in some parks for use by residents.

Most towns and cities in the Netherlands have made considerable progress in the ecological management and development of green space. For example, it is now standard practice to plant native species and to manage green areas without pesticides.

31.

It should be noted that open areas managed according to ecological principles rather than in traditional ways look different to the formal parks which many members of the public still expect to see, and ways need to be found to overcome objections based on, for example, the relatively untidy appearance of natural sites or concerns about personal safety in areas with dense vegetation.

32.

Policy option:
encourage mixed land
use schemes

Varied use at ground and upper floor levels

Mixed use can be important
particularly at local scale

Member State policies to
encourage mixed use development

33.   Ecological approaches to the planning and management of open space also require municipalities to improve their knowledge of ecology. Some authorities, as in the Netherlands, now employ ecologists directly. Others, as in the UK, seek to work in partnership with local environmental organisations or landscape architectural practices where staff have the appropriate expertise.

Policy option: encourage mixed land use schemes

34.   Over-rigid land use zoning has been criticised as one of the causes of new single use development areas within cities. By analogy to ecological systems, mono-use of land, especially over larger areas, tends to lead to deterioration, while mixed uses tend to enhance the vitality of an area. The Green Paper on the Urban Environment (CEC, 1990) strongly recommends the encouragement of mixed use schemes. Mixed use is an urban form which offers the opportunity for reduction in movement overall, particularly if linked to traffic restraint systems. At the city scale it implies seeking a balance of houses, jobs and facilities in each broad sector of the city through whatever broad zoning or land allocation system is used in that particular country.

35.   It is particularly at the neighbourhood or even more local scale that mixed use can be important. Recent research for the EU (Shankland Cox, 1993) identifies four mechanisms to achieve this: formal methods (through the precise allocation of land and building), proximity (encouraging the close relationship between mono-use groupings of blocks), flexible methods (to allow mixed use and change of use within an area subject only to environmental impact) and a blended approach of these three. Owner and user participation are critical in the planning of mixed developments given the potential impact of one use on another. The success of mixed use schemes depends on whether the occupants use them in the way intended by planners. For example, the incorporation of workshop space in residential development does not guarantee that residents will work in them rather than more distant locations. The creation of development packages with economically weaker and stronger land uses will improve the success of mixed land use schemes.

36.   It is to be anticipated that European countries will introduce urban plans and policy guidance that will encourage mixed use development. In the UK, the Department of the Environment's Planning Policy Guidance refers specifically to town and city centres and encourages the creation of a more varied range of uses at ground and upper floor levels. Spatial planning systems, in association with building codes, can also encourage environmental awareness in the design and construction of new neighbourhoods and new buildings.

7.7   Development plans and sustainability, Copenhagen, Denmark

The redevelopment of Copenhagen Docks is an example where a development plan formulated in the 1980s based on a large scale office development has been rejected in favour of a mixed use scheme. A new master plan published in 1990 after extensive public consultation and liaison with Government bodies, seeks a mix of offices, houses, recreation and cultural uses. It also promotes better integration between the surrounding housing areas and the harbour.

7.8   Ecolonia, Alphen aan den Rijn, the Netherlands

Ecolonia is the often quoted demonstration project set up by the Dutch government in the mid-1980s. This relatively small-scale neighbourhood development forms part of the expansion plan for the town of Alphen aan den Rijn, a medium sized Dutch municipality located between Amsterdam, the Hague, Rotterdam and Utrecht. The overall masterplan was designed by a Belgian town planner and nine separate architects were involved in housing designs in order to achieve variety as well as the incorporation of energy saving features. This development provides a good illustration of several themes - mixed use, the avoidance of traffic, emphasis on walking and cycling, the use of open space for rain water retention, and tree planting to influence the microclimate.

SUSTAINABILITY AND URBAN REGENERATION

INTRODUCTION

The importance of urban regeneration has been increasingly recognised from the 1970's. Urban regeneration can involve the rehabilitation of existing structures, redevelopment of existing buildings and sites, or simply the reuse of urban land. The process of regeneration frequently involves derelict or contaminated land. This section explores in more detail the issues relating to urban regeneration, with particular reference to urban rehabilitation and renewal and the treatment of derelict and contaminated land, as well as the various ways to implement regeneration in order to achieve sustainable development.

The EU Green Paper on the Urban Environment sought to identify the full range of problems affecting Europe's conurbations including disused industrial areas and the need to redevelop urban waste land. The report noted that derelict industrial sites provide a strategic opportunity for services and infrastructure linked to urban centres.

Urban regeneration is defined as:

The process of reversing economic, social and physical decay in our towns and cities where it has reached the stage when market forces alone will not suffice (UK's Royal Institution of Chartered Surveyors).

This definition implies that a holistic approach is paramount, that society as a whole should take responsibility and that there is a need for intervention, directly or indirectly, by the public sector. Other definitions, possibly in other European countries, may see urban regeneration as a wider activity in areas of decline, not necessarily requiring public sector intervention. For example, in Germany, urban planning can include guidance based on specific urban redevelopment legislation that encourages regeneration without special need for state intervention.

5.

The restructuring of heavy industry and utilities have left large areas of vacant, and often contaminated, land within cities whilst increasing the pressure for the development of urban open space and countryside. Frequently, this land is so damaged that it is incapable of beneficial use without treatment and represents an actual or potential hazard to health or to the environment. Typically, this land must be prepared, or 'reclaimed', in some way, for example by the removal of buildings, levelling of the site, treatment of contamination or the provision of infrastructure, before it is attractive for redevelopment. Vacant land has often failed to attract investment because of the heavy costs of clean up/decontamination, providing new infrastructure, and the need to secure an attractive image.

A Sustainable Process

Urban regeneration as a sustainable process: reuse and recycling

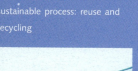

Reuse and recycling of redundant land

A Sustainable Process

6.

There is an urgent need to ensure the reuse of redundant, derelict or contaminated land, which is at a greater scale than during any period in industrial urban history. The recycling of previously developed land, and in some cases existing buildings, of itself can be seen to meet the sustainable objective of the reuse of a resource. In addition, land recycling also has the potential to achieve the sustainable objective of retention of green field sites, protecting the countryside, open space, and wildlife. As well as just reuse, sustainable development requires uses that are supportive of urban life as a whole, and offer opportunities for further sustainable development.

7.

Clearly not all existing buildings and sites can be recycled. Much will depend upon the future contribution that the building makes to the functional fabric of the built environment. The following factors are relevant:

- consideration should be given to the feasibility of reuse of an existing structure. It is probable that urban regeneration will involve the replacement of existing buildings by more modern, flexible and energy-efficient structures, although the qualities of many old buildings for retaining heat and cold are widely misunderstood;

- consideration should be given to the underlying ecological structure of the site;

- consideration should be given to the integration or reintegration of sites into the urban functional fabric in which the former land uses may have formed isolated areas;

- finally, the regeneration of urban areas offers the opportunity to consider the completion and restoration of flows which relate to sustainable development including: water, energy, waste, fresh air, pedestrian and cycle routes and public transport.

2.2

Groundwater and soil are extremely important resources to be protected

KEY SUSTAINABILITY ISSUES

1.

There is potential for contamination to escape from the site and cause environmental damage such as air or water pollution, which may constitute a direct threat to health or safety. Groundwater and soil are extremely important resources to be protected. It is very expensive to provide substitutes for groundwater, and it is expensive and difficult to treat once contaminated. The safeguarding of aquifer water quality is an EU requirement regardless of whether it is currently abstracted (House of Commons Environment Committee, 1990).

The opportunity for new development depends on the scale of the derelict land, and potential for growth. In Germany, huge conversion programmes have been initiated by the Lander in areas such as Brandenburg and Rheinland Pfalz in co-operation with local authorities. In the UK the opportunity and the potential for reuse is equally great. In support of this, the UK Department of the Environment has strengthened its policy requiring developers and local authorities to consider development of derelict and unused urban land before embarking on greenfield site development.

The challenge for sustainability in rehabilitation and renewal areas is to encourage more sensitive and environmentally-sound upgrading and renewal, and to seek a more co-ordinated approach to renewal projects, seeing each as part of the overall structure of the city. Spatial planning policies can assist by encouraging the recycling of derelict land within the urban fabric, and new development at higher densities around public transport nodes. A substantial construction of new buildings and infrastructure may be problematic in relation to sustainability objectives. Therefore, buildings that still serve a function should not be demolished, and neither should new development take place that is not required.

A primary requirement for sustainable approaches to urban rehabilitation and renewal is an overall sustainable development strategy for regeneration related to spatial and economic considerations. Sustainable strategies will make optimal use of existing urban qualities including locational advantages which may be unique. As a consequence these strategies will vary according to the geospatial, economic and social potential, opportunities and problems of cities and the resources available. Rehabilitation and renewal must form part of a holistic planning approach involving city-wide policies relating to such matters as transportation, air quality and pollution. The aim is to strengthen self regenerative capacity rather than contributing to a process in which redevelopment is continuously replaced by periods of decline.

2.

3.   Challenges and requirements for
      sustainable regeneration

4.

POLICY OPTIONS FOR SUSTAINABILITY

2.3

Appropriate policies relating to sustainability must be applied according to future opportunities and the nature of a settlement. Urban regeneration in a sustainable context is a less problematic process if forces in society, including commercial interests, pursue self-regenerative activities. The size of the regeneration area influences the specification of urban regeneration policies. For instance single buildings in need of regeneration in mixed-use environments represent an urban environment which is more conducive to effective policy action. The policy requirements of large scale commercial or industrial areas in need of regeneration are more problematic.

1.   Self-regenerative activities simplify
      the process

Policy option: ecological principles in urban renewal

Urban rehabilitation offers the opportunity to restore former landscapes and establish new green elements or other areas of ecological value. The exchange of resources and nutrients in many cases follows water flows. Regeneration of the original system of surface and underground water should, in order to improve the sustainability of an area, be taken into account while considering landscaping, greening, and planting.

Policy option: ecological
principles in urban
2.   renewal

Solar power in urban renewal

Energy efficiency facilitates urban regeneration

3. Many ecological principles for sustainable building can be applied in rehabilitation and renewal areas, for instance:

- measures to optimise the efficient use of water in buildings;

- systems for the circulation of rainwater with peak and seasonal storage;

- optimalisation of energy use for heating and cooling by insulation;

- application of solar power and of heat-power systems;

- separation of waste.

4. Energy efficiency is important to development as a whole and to urban regeneration projects. It can be applied to the entire town or project if considered at the urban planning level, so as to secure, for example, efficient community-wide heating or cooling systems. The prospects for successful ecological renewal in urban areas seem to be enhanced where municipalities control and manage energy provision and waste.

5. The Ministry of Housing and Building in Denmark has issued advice about buildings and ecology. Systematic environmental assessment of entire building projects, a life cycle approach, is advocated. In all Danish urban renewal schemes, ecological measures - such as better use of resources through energy and water conservation and systems for sorting household waste at source - are encouraged. Both redundant buildings and building materials (cement, wood, slate and brick) are recycled. In addition, all renewal schemes require the provision of adequate open space for outdoor recreation. There is a strong emphasis on planting, which extends to building façades as well as courtyards and other areas of open space. In some areas, public open space has been turned into vegetable gardens. Architects and craftspeople need to be trained in working with recycled materials and in ways of evaluating which building elements are worth preserving.

7.9   Urban ecology in a renewal project, Copenhagen, Denmark

The largest urban renewal project to be implemented in the next few years will be the redevelopment of Vesterbro, a mixed residential and commercial district in Copenhagen. The action plan for Vesterbro adopted in 1991 involved the residents from the outset. The plan involves the renovation of some 4000 dwellings over a 10 to 15 year period. The plan explicitly respects the principles of urban ecology, incorporating water and energy conservation measures and facilities for waste sorting in renovated buildings, along with experimental schemes for low-temperature district heating and passive solar energy.

Policy option: improved accessibility

Typically, former industrial sites are enclosed, forming barriers within the urban fabric. New bus lanes and provision for footpaths and cycle ways through the previously isolated areas reduce distances. In analysing the future use of the regenerated area as a component of the wider city, travel beyond the regenerated area is clearly necessary for many activities. Indeed, such a policy may beneficially reinforce the function of surrounding centres and facilities. This creates a need to ensure adequate dedicated public transport and sustainable transport linkages between the regenerated area and existing or improved off-site facilities and services. If the regenerated area contains dwellings, then linkages to employment zones elsewhere should be considered. Alternatively, if the regenerated area includes public open spaces to serve the wider city, then the linkages by public transport, particularly at leisure times, and also by cycling and walking, to the parkland areas should be carefully considered.

6.   Policy option:
      improved accessibility

7.10 Discouraging heavy vehicles in redevelopment programme, Athens, Greece

In Athens the Queen's Tower Park, currently under construction, is intended to provide economic and environmental regeneration of a peripheral area in the west of the city by means of an environmental awareness and training centre. On a larger scale, the Olive Grove Renewal Programme in Athens focuses on the redevelopment of a 10 km sq. area. The programme includes measures for the removal of all polluting industries, a transport plan to discourage heavy vehicles from using the area, the creation of large green areas for sport and recreation and measures to secure employment. The Olive Grove is intended to be a lever for sustainable development for the entire west Athens region.

Policy option: flexibility of design

It is essential to stimulate the process of urban regeneration through flexibility of design, and through flexibility of permitted use, either temporary or permanent. The flexible design of buildings means that buildings are not restricted to a single function. The same basic structures can serve school, office and factory uses. Changes in technology and the imperatives of ecology will offer the opportunity to make buildings ever more flexible and responsive.

7.   Policy option:
      flexibility of design

The flexible design of buildings can extend the life of structures and in consequence that of neighbourhoods and communities. Buildings have become out moded more quickly than before as a result of rapid technological and social change. Developers and occupiers are forced to write off their investments much earlier than has been the case traditionally. Increased flexibility of design will facilitate longer write-off periods.

8.

Indeed, this issue not only applies to individual buildings, but also to entire blocks of the city. In Berlin, current studies are considering flexible design within large blocks of redevelopment in the city. The need for urban regeneration will decrease if buildings and entire blocks of buildings are constructed to be more flexible, and if planning regimes permit such flexibility of use.

9.

Policy option: policy flexibility

10.   In the UK the Department of the Environment has advised local authorities of the need for more flexible attitudes towards zoning and planning policy, for example, encouraging a greater range of leisure facilities within town centres and use of upper parts of buildings for residential purposes, together with the conversion of out-moded commercial buildings to residential use. Similar policy flexibility is also required in relation to amendments of certain standards in order to assist in supporting the objectives of sustainable renewal and rehabilitation.

7.11 Amending density standards, Munich, Germany

In Munich, a large housing scheme includes a sector of affordable housing where the acceptable density standards have been reduced, thus providing a more compact and potentially more energy-efficient solution.

11.   In the UK, there has been a trend in the last 15 years towards sheltered housing for people in older age groups (generally over 60 years of age) with warden facilities. These normally take a compact form with fewer car parking spaces than for normal housing development. Such accommodation is more energy efficient, concentrates population, and - by reduced parking provision - encourages economic public transport.

Policy option: partnerships and public involvement

12.   A critical issue with mixed use and flexible developments, will be the degree to which they are economically feasible or require to be subsidised. Some features of the design may be capable of inclusion without appreciable increase in costs over current conventional forms, but others may require new areas of subsidy. For example, provision of local services, whether they be retailing or health, may introduce diseconomies of scale which will have to be addressed.

13.   Further constraints concern the ownership of land. Urban development sites in single ownership are much more likely to be favoured by the private sector. Where developers have the certainty of site acquisition, a major hurdle is removed. Multiple ownership makes urban regeneration a complex process, problems can be overcome by the activity of development corporations or similar agencies with the power to assemble large scale regeneration sites. This time-consuming process of negotiation and purchasing requires professional attitudes and flexible co-operation from local authorities.

14.   In general planning schemes should reinforce the mixed use qualities of the city, enhance local self sufficiency and reduce dependency, reintroduce the value of proximity, possibly at the expense of choice. The challenge for local governments therefore concerns the management of change in democratic societies with its limitations on individual choice emphasising the need for public consultation.

15.

The Danish approach exemplifies an increasing emphasis on public participation in renewal schemes. Local authorities lead the urban renewal process, in partnership with non-profit urban renewal companies authorised by the Ministry of Housing and Building, private consultants and residents. Legislation specifically requires the involvement of owners and tenants of buildings in the planning and implementation of urban renewal programmes. Mechanisms for public involvement include meetings with residents' associations, questionnaire surveys, newsletters, and the establishment of shops where residents can obtain information on, for example, energy conservation. Several towns have published technical information in the form of urban renewal catalogues. Such approaches facilitate the public consideration of urban sustainability issues.

7.12 Partnership in a regeneration programme, Longwy, France

Located on the borders of France, Belgium and Luxembourg, declining coal mining and steel production led to a fall in employment in the steel industry from 26,000 to less than 1,000 in an area characterised by industrial dereliction. Regeneration of the area has focused on a European Development Pole (EDP) with three main partners; the EU, the three states, and local authorities at regional, departmental and municipal levels. The regeneration programme established in the mid-1980s involved industrial conversion and the creation of 8,000 alternative jobs over a 10-year period, training programmes including the establishment of a European College of Technology, and assistance through exemptions from EU regulations.

A major feature is the International Business Park developed on contaminated land, utilising recycled concrete for infrastructure and the renovation of former industrial buildings. Progress on job creation is broadly on target and shows what can be achieved when partners in regeneration implement a realistic and well thought-out strategy (European Foundation for the Improvement of Living and Working Conditions, 1994).

7.13 Regeneration of the Ria-area, Bilbao, Spain

The project concerns an extensive area along the 'Ria' (the estuary), that was formerly occupied by industrial and harbour installations. The re-utilisation of that land has strategic significance in relation to the city and to the other urban settlements in the metropolitan area. It is proposed that the area will be transformed into a city of services and into a centre of innovative technologies in order to compete with the other European cities of the Atlantic Arc. It is a long term project, already in progress, that involves the creation of new industrial zones of high technology, office and service buildings, new residential areas and urban elements, all of which will contribute to the improvement of the city's image. The project is managed by the Association Bilbao Metropolis 30, involving almost all the public and private agents active in the development of the city (over 80).

7.14 Regeneration of disused docklands, Old Port, Genoa, Italy

Genoa's port was relocated from an area near the city centre to deep water facilities on the western fringe of the city. To deal with the resultant disused Docklands area, a partnership of the City Council, the Port Authority, the Chamber of Commerce and Regional and Provincial Councils was created. The regeneration programme was focused on the Columbus Fair celebrating the 500th anniversary of the discovery of America. This gave the impetus for renovation of buildings which after the Fair provided space for university, commercial and tourist facilities. Genoa capitalised on a tourist opportunity to regenerate decaying urban fabric, creating construction and other employment and flexible space (European Foundation for the Improvement of Living and Working Conditions, 1994). Policy option: visual upgrading

Policy option:
visual upgrading

Policy option: visual upgrading

16.   The visual upgrading of the physical environment is an important factor in urban rehabilitation and renewal. The rehabilitation of buildings or their redevelopment may appear to be a cosmetic operation, but the treatment of 'eyesore' sites may have a positive effect upon the well-being of local populations. Similarly, the restoration of original waterflows will not only add to local environmental assets but also to the quality of public space.

Policy option:
decontamination

Policy option: decontamination

17.   The attainment of sustainability objectives in the reclamation of contaminated land should be addressed in relation to the ecological and land use context including:

- existing water flows, underground as well as surface water which can be restored;

- quality of soil, which can be improved;

- potential of the area for additional parks and green spaces as required by surrounding inhabitants and/or the new users of the area;

- restoration of the functional urban fabric for example by adding new bus lanes and bicycle provision.

18.   The two approaches to decontamination are:

- end use decontamination; and,

- multi-functionality.

Contaminated land

In the end use approach the extent of clean-up of a given piece of contaminated land depends on its proposed use. It may be possible to dispense with remedial action if the site is to be developed for example as a car park, whereas expensive operations would be required if the site were to be used for housing. There is, therefore, no absolute standard of soil quality which must be achieved in all circumstances; the principle being that soil contaminants are only a danger when sensitive uses are involved, or where there is a risk of groundwater contamination.

19.   End use approach to
decontamination

UK policy is based on end use decontamination approach and contamination is a planning consideration that must be taken into account by local planning authorities in determining planning applications. The Department of Environment provides advisory guidelines on values of contaminants which are acceptable for particular land uses, known as 'trigger values'. UK Government policy sets out to encourage reclamation and development of contaminated land for beneficial use, taking into account the practicable significance of any contamination and the availability of practicable and effective solutions.

20.

The multi-functionality approach means that soil is actually cleaned, to such a degree that the site can be potentially reused for any human activity or land use. This leads on the one hand to very expensive cleansing and reclamation of sites, and on the other hand to the development of sophisticated, mechanical, chemical and bacteriological techniques. Clearly this approach, which is used, for example in the Netherlands, goes furthest towards eliminating risks and restoring ecological balance. The key issue is the extent to which it is widely achievable in practice and economically feasible.

21.   Multi-functionality approach to
decontamination

The most cost-effective solution is that which is tailored to site specific circumstances implemented when a change of use occurs (House of Commons Environment Committee, 1990). However, some consider that by focusing on land use, the pollution dimensions of the problem are underestimated.

22.

7.15   Contamination at Lekkerkerk, the Netherlands

The Dutch policy towards contaminated sites is a response to the very severe case of contamination at Lekkerkerk, in the Netherlands and the unique combination of hydro-geological factors in these lowlands. The policy is based on three elements:

• an integrated environmental approach;

• no problem shifting - contamination is dealt with so far as possible in situ or, if this is not feasible, by removal to secure containment; and,

• multi-functionality.

An integrative approach to spatial planning and decontamination reflects the tension between environmental quality, quality of the built environment and financial consequences. In a study of the Netherlands Ministry of Housing, Spatial Planning and the Environment (Zandvoort Ordening & Advies, 1988), it is established that the integrative approach enables the decontamination of severely polluted urban areas to be funded by

23.   Financial considerations are part of
an integrative approach to spatial
planning and decontamination

urban development. If the urban development is less ambitious, i.e. not utilising the locational opportunities fully, higher costs must be accepted and the quality of the built environment will not be improved so much. The financial feasibility of regeneration projects including decontamination may be enhanced by site assessment based on 'optimal spatial development'. The increased returns resulting from the high land value levels ident- ified with 'optimal spatial development', based on an optimal environmental quality and an optimal quality of the built environment, generally outweigh relatively high regener- ation costs. The study concluded that financial considerations of an integrative approach should be related to the development of a bigger area, thereby permitting the high costs to be offset against urban development elsewhere.

7.16 Transformation of an old military installation, Gijon, Spain

Gijon is an industrial city in northern Spain (autonomous Community of Asturias) that has suffered, over the last 15 years, the consequences of the industrial decline of iron and steel, shipbuilding etc. The city has developed a major scheme to improve the quality of life and the urban environment, and to compensate for the effects of decline. One of the main local projects has been the renovation of an old military installation for the defence of the ancient city and its harbour. The total area, about 68,000 sq. m., has been transformed into an urban park, preserving its natural character with minimal urbanisation. At the top of the hill, in front of the sea, a sculpture has been placed as a symbolic statement of renewal.

7.17 Reuse of contaminated land, Copenhagen, Denmark

The former gasworks, Østre Gasværk, in the area of Østerbro in Copenhagen, have remained undeveloped for a number of years. An overall plan for the area is in preparation, comprising family housing, housing for the elderly and large public service functions. The easternmost part of the area, however, is polluted to the extent that cleaning is impossible as both the cost and health risks involved are prohibitive. Solutions are based on an effective encapsulation of the polluted soil to be developed as a ground for the Copenhagen football club (B93).

Applying the polluter pays
principle to decontamination

24.

Contamination is often seen as a constraint to the reuse of urban land which must be dealt with by future developers and largely funded by them. However, 'the Polluter Pays' principle means that the existing occupier of the land is responsible for contamination. For this reason the occupier must ensure that if necessary the land is decontaminated beforehand or land can be sold at a lower price to facilitate decontamination by the purchaser, for example the local authority. Land can also have a negative value which prevents ownership change and in these cases there is a need for other devices, such as 'clean up' funds financed by fuel taxes, for example.

In the UK, there are a number of grant regimes which provide financial assistance for derelict land. Because of the prevailing 'end use' philosophy, the focus of these grant regimes is on the use of land rather than on environmental quality. In the Netherlands substantial funds are available for decontamination purposes, although in comparison with the scale of proposed schemes they are insufficient. Depending on the magnitude of the project, decisions to allocate funding are made by the National Ministry or the province.

In the Netherlands, every purchase of land or real estate must legally be accompanied by a 'clean soil declaration', stating that all possible pollution has been treated. If pollution appears subsequently, the previous owner may be subject to legal action to ensure compliance.

Apart from new national legislation to reduce the pollution of land and prevent land contamination, actions to encourage the reuse of contaminated land in a sustainable manner should include:

- the preparation of registers of contaminated land;

- dissemination of information about contamination treatments, solutions and costs;

- provision of grants for decontamination;

- provision of information of land transactions as potential purchasers may be unaware of latent problems.

SUSTAINABILITY AND URBAN CULTURAL HERITAGE, LEISURE AND TOURISM

INTRODUCTION

Cultural heritage, leisure and tourism are three main issues that can be identified in relation to the cultural sustainability of a city.

Quality of the urban environment as reflected in the cultural heritage of European cities

The cultural heritage is the expression of the totality of knowledge, beliefs and values, as much artistic as philosophical and moral, which shapes the tradition of people and which underlies its activities expressed in physical terms of time and space, through specific processes and actors (ISOCARP - Mesones, 1992). The city is a cultural subject, a human thing par excellence (Lévi-Strauss, 1987). Cultural identity means the recognition, as a set of values, of the historical evolution of different ethnic groups bounded by language and common social patterns. This identity is closely linked with the territorial areas where such evolution took place (ISOCARP - Malusardi, 1992).

3. UNESCO guidelines confirm that 'man's cultural heritage is essential to his equilibrium and development, as it provides him with a framework that is suited to his lifestyle and enables him to stay in touch with nature and with the witness of earlier civilisations that have been left to him by past generations'J. The importance of cultural heritage is also found in Halbwachs' ideas on 'la mémoire collective'. This concept shows how and why the collective memory is often tied to special places of outstanding importance for the fate of the community as a whole. This is an extremely fragile resource and needs to be maintained for future generations.

4. The identity and effective links between citizen and the city are disturbed, or even eradicated by a dysfunctional urban development. In order to achieve a more attractive city, one must base projects on a qualitative approach that integrates the notion of urban culture (Eidos Maison des Sciences de la Ville - Université de Tours, 1992).

5. Broadly speaking culture is what allows for the development, maturing and evolution of a human community. The qualitative notion of urban culture is not applicable to the city only in its material dimension (the culture of the city) nor to its inhabitants only in their dimension as users (the culture within the city), but to the interaction between the city and its inhabitants. Citizens build cities which in turn build its inhabitants.

6. There are diverse views of the cultural identity of a city, but some coherence can be achieved by considering the city as the site of a specific culture. In these circumstances the citizen seeks for their own personal accomplishment within the city based on a twofold perspective that allows psychological and symbolic appropriation of space, and that improves the minds and characters of citizens. Both are closely related to the concept of citizenship.

7. Literature, media, and politicians are all discovering the same common statement regarding the urban crisis. This crisis, which simultaneously is spatial, economic, social and ecological, will be primarily cultural due to the loss of values of urban civilisation. This demonstrates the paradox which exists today between a functional urban growth rationality dominated by uniformity on the one hand, and on the other citizenship qualitative values, which aim to give a real sense of identity to the urban milieu. It is recommended that political and urban solutions examine the potentially powerful role that cultural identity can perform as a tool of urban management.

8. European culture and cultural heritage is one of the most important in the world, surrounding us in many forms. Historic buildings or archaeological remnants, for example, tell us how and where people lived, and even why they perished or prospered. The richness of cultural heritage is one of the factors that enlivens European diversity. It is the sphere in which regional and local identities find their clearest articulation making people aware that they belong to a community with its own history and values.

9. Cultural heritage also offers real potential in terms of economic development. In a world in which international trade and a globalised economy are the rule, cultural levelling constitutes an impoverishment. Social groups are reacting to this by seeking out cultural products that reflect local and regional identities. The more extensive commercial relations become, the more people feel the need to emphasise cultural and social roots.

Cultural heritage

Furthermore, future transformations in modes of production will create more leisure time which will benefit the development of the cultural sector. These sources of new jobs to be tapped in the development of the sector are fully recognised in the Commission White Paper 'Growth Competitiveness and Employment' (CEC, 1993b). All the above factors emphasize the importance of achieving European cultural sustainability.

10.

Aware of the prime importance of the cultural heritage, the European Commission has for some years been actively supporting policies and actions for its protection. The Community's role in this field is to develop the common cultural heritage while respecting nationally and regionally diverse cultural forms. Initiatives are based on an integrated approach which focuses attention on the conservation of regional and local heritage linked to specific and continuing use, the dissemination of know how and experience, promotion of awareness and support for associated economic development and job creation.

11.

EU funding actions supporting cultural initiatives are drawn from a variety of sources including the Structural Funds. Operational Programmes developed in relation to the latter address conservation of the architectural heritage, restoration of historic sites and monuments, promotion of traditional crafts, creation of regional museums, development of industrial heritage conservation projects and promotion of cultural tourism.

12.

Following the establishment of an appropriate legal base for Community cultural measures in the Treaty on European Union (Article 128), Community action in relation to cultural heritage has been strengthened via the Raphael Programme, which aims to give added impetus to Community activities in the field by redirecting and expanding existing actions and providing a coherent approach to Community actions and policies relating to cultural activities.

13.

Leisure-tourism

In the Fifth Environmental Action Programme, the European Parliament focuses on the cultural aspects of sustainability. In their Resolution the Parliament (Point 35) calls on the Commission to develop a general strategy covering both leisure and tourism. Citizens should be able to spend their leisure time and short breaks in recreational establishments. These should be located either on the outskirts of cities or in urban areas. If the establishments are to be successful, they should be easily accessible.

14.   Leisure and tourism activities put pressure on urban sustainability

Leisure is becoming more and more available and therefore more important in modern society. Leisure results from, and increases as a consequence of, economic growth and the resultant increase in available free time (ISOCARP - Costa Lobo, 1991). In addition to increasing free time, the opportunities for spending leisure time have also expanded. This is due to economic growth as well as different spending patterns. Leisure is becoming a more flexible and unpredictable activity.

15.

Tourism is a subsidiary activity to leisure. Few activities are as directly involved in the process of transforming and developing modern societies as tourism. As tourism becomes a general need at the intellectual, physical, cultural, social and professional level, new or existing economic activities emerge or adapt to serve what they regard as a new market (CEC, 1990).

16.

17. The importance of tourism is recognised on a global level. The 1980 Manila Declaration of the World Tourism Organisation challenged the industry with a concept of tourism that emphasised the social, cultural, environmental, economic, educational and political values. The United Nations World Decade for Cultural Development, operating from 1988 to 1997, is seeking to promote the cultural dimension of development by introducing culture-specific considerations into sectors traditionally managed for economic purposes. Urban rehabilitation and cultural tourism are areas central to this concern. Tourism can be a powerful ingredient of regional and local development. It is a positive force for economic growth and urban regeneration. It is also important to consider that there are changes in the pattern of market demand for tourism, making it more diverse and more discerning than in the past (Shipman Martin, 1993).

The impact of leisure and tourism on the urban cultural heritage

18. To understand the importance and characteristics of the impacts on the quality of the urban cultural heritage environment generated by leisure and tourism activities, it is necessary to define the three basic spaces where the impacts will occur: the historic centre, the new core and the hinterland.

19. The historic centre is the part of the urban environment which has the highest degree of identity, individuality and character. The most important expressions of cultural heritage are normally in this space. The new core or the 20th century developments are the areas that surround the historic centre. Its identity is sometimes clearly defined but there are often few links with the existing city. There are usually some expressions of the cultural heritage, mainly related to the industrial archaeology, often associated with rundown and derelict areas. The hinterland is the area that supports and allows the city's existence. There is no urban environment without its surrounding territory (ISOCARP, 1992), and in this geographical space there are often other cities, villages and rural settlements. Issues of nature conservation are more important in the hinterland than in the other two spaces and cultural and natural heritage issues often require more attention.

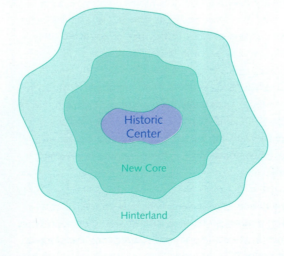

FIGURE The urban cultural heritage environment.

The three spaces identified in this figure should be viewed as areas where the Ecosystems Approach applies to the urban environment. Within this concept, the hard and soft structure and the environment are viewed in an integrated and dynamic interrelation. This requires the consideration of three main fields of interest: impacts of leisure and tourism activities on human, physical and environmental aspects.

Human aspects of leisure and tourism activities

There are four important human aspects which are influenced by leisure and tourism activities: demography, economy, sociology and culture.

Demographic impacts are several. Differences between fixed and seasonal populations are evident and the same applies to employment. Proportions of the municipal housing stock are owned by tourists as summer houses and entrepreneurs make use of local economic opportunities to provide summer cottages and camp sites.

The economic consequences of demographic impacts are both positive and negative. Land values are defined according to tourist demand with property and land prices rising with increased demand. Access by the local population to houses in popular tourist destinations is reduced. Other economic impacts including additional local tax revenue and job creation might be valued more positively. However, tourism activities are reduced outside the main tourist season causing a rise in local unemployment.

Sociological impacts are also severe. The large number of tourists in a local community can make the local population feel alienated from their own city and the seasonal population growth causes related problems, including increased crime. Tourists seen as invaders can also cause stress, phobia and aggression in the local inhabitants.

Cultural identity is under stress as well. Local communities need to change in order to adapt to the external impacts of tourist pressure and imported (international) patterns of culture.

Physical aspects of leisure and tourism activities

Physical aspects which are influenced by leisure and tourism activities relate to traffic density, morphology, cultural heritage and associated conflicts.

New or expanding leisure and tourism activities put pressure on the conservation of cultural heritage. New functions for historic spaces, and new buildings can conflict with local cultural identity. Concentration and congestion of people, buildings and vehicles should be resisted. The adaptability of hard and soft structures, for example hard parking facilities, can prevent and/or lessen negative impacts. The volume and proportions of public spaces should be adapted to the density or demand. Local governments should ensure that new buildings and activities do not contribute to any further alienation of the community. Attention to the non-tourist areas of a city is also required, and degradation should be prevented and degraded areas should be rehabilitated.

Environmental aspects of leisure and tourism activities

28. Environmental aspects influenced by tourism include pollution, conservation and sustainability. Pollution consists, in this context, of several elements: visual (cars, tourist paraphernalia, air, litter, rubbish, signs, etc.), noise (traffic, music, mass groups), vibration, smell (change due to emissions) and water (sea, river, lake, groundwater). Conservation concerns cultural heritage, cultural ambience and identity and landscape. The latter consists of natural features including rivers and hills, and man-made features such as gardens and parks. Sustainability here means safeguarding and sound management of the cultural goods, enhancing the quality of life and prosperity of the city.

29. The relationship between the three fields of interest and their relation to the three categories of urban space identified earlier creates a complex panorama. The best way to understand it is by using a matrix as a working tool. The matrix is identified below and is organised as follows:

FIGURE - Matrix

SPACE / URBAN ENVIRONMENT	FIELDS / SUBFIELDS / SUBSPACE	I-HUMAN					II-PHYSICAL				III-ENVIRONMENT		
		Demography	Sociology	Economy	Culture	Traffic	Density	Morphology	Heritage	Conflicts	Pollution	Agression Destruction Conservation	Sustainability
	HISTORIC CENTER												
	NEW CORE												
	HINTERLAND												

30. The impacts can be evaluated on four levels, varying from (0) no impact to (1) minor impact and (2) medium impact to (3) major impact.

31. Once the boxes in the matrix are completed, the main issues and priorities should become apparent. Further analysis of these will be the first stage in what should be an on-going investigation of leisure and tourism impacts. The significance of the impacts will change depending on the particular context. Each city and its surrounding is a different entity, reacting in a different way within the regional and national framework. Nevertheless, some general points may be made.

32. *Leisure*: The way leisure can affect the urban environment is hard to assess because it is a more habitual activity than tourism. Leisure is also not so concentrated in terms of time and space as tourism. With regard to the historic centre, leisure has a considerable impact because of the concentration of leisure activities and other facilities, and the cultural heritage acting as a magnet. With regard to the new core, leisure does not have a great impact. Even if there are cultural attractions, these are usually not major 'pull factors'.

The hinterland, however, is a major focus for leisure activities. Rural and semi-rural pursuits are particularly evident especially during holiday periods and weekends.

Tourism: Tourist flows are more clearly discernible and have a more direct and visible impact on the quality of the urban environment. The impact is greatest in the historic centre where the cultural heritage attracts tourists. In the new core, the impact of tourism is slight. In the hinterland, the impact is often felt in the same way as in the historic centre, but to a different degree. This is especially so in areas of historic interest but also for outstanding natural features. Impacts in the hinterland are often a consequence of diversification policies, which seek to avoid high concentrations in the historic centres.

HISTORIC CENTRE: KEY SUSTAINABILITY ISSUES

The impacts arising from leisure and tourism are important in each of the three fields of interest: human, physical and environmental.

Human aspects of leisure and tourism in the historic centre

Problems of demographic and social nature include unbalanced population movements at different periods during the year; invasion of living space; loss of privacy, not only in public spaces but sometimes also in residential quarters; segregation of inhabitants due to the priority given to the needs of tourists; changes in activities and increased economic pressure which can lead to the expulsion of the original population thus attracting new social groups and affecting the cultural environment; stress created among the population by the intensity and pressure of mass tourism; changes in the human framework and the visitor flows which can engender insecurity and in the worst cases, may lead to crime.

From an economic point of view there are both positive and negative aspects. This is most clearly illustrated through changes in local employment. Leisure and tourism create new jobs, but more traditional jobs may be lost, thereby disadvantaging certain sectors of the community, such as the old and those unable or unwilling to be retrained. A similar situation arises out of the changes in property and land prices that can occur due to tourist activities. In general, rising prices should benefit the community but may result in some local people being forced out as a result of increased rents. The economic benefits of tourism and leisure may therefore be substantial but they do not come without some social costs.

From the cultural viewpoint impacts vary. Traditional lifestyles may be reinforced and enriched or the local culture may lose its identity and fall victim to the creation of a fake image. There is a danger that international cultural models will change the clear identity of the place and subsume it within a new anonymous character.

33.

3.2

1.

Human aspects of leisure
and tourism in the
historic centre

2.

3.

4.

Tourism causes economic activity

Physical aspects of leisure and tourism in the historic centre

The effects of transportation create some of the best documented problems in relation to the quality of the urban environment. The concentration and congestion resulting from leisure and tourism activities can affect the capacity and adaptability of the hard and soft structures. The structure's capacity to react is put under such pressure that it is sometimes not able to cope and the form and structure of the city is damaged. This is probably the field where impacts are most visible. The cultural heritage itself is also damaged as a result of physical impacts and conflicts arise when the urban environment thresholds are exceeded.

Environmental aspects of leisure and tourism in the historic centre

Problems in this field can be particularly great. In terms of pollution, a subject dealt with extensively in the Green Paper on the Urban Environment, there are still many issues to address. These include destruction, conservation of identity, imageability, values, etc.

HISTORIC CENTRE: POLICY OPTIONS FOR SUSTAINABILITY

Although the problems resulting from leisure and tourism are complex, several policy options exist to reduce the negative impacts in the human, physical and environmental field without endangering the positive effects of leisure and tourism.

Policy options in the human field

The needs and interests of the inhabitants should be considered as a priority. ICOMOS (1990) stated that priority must be given to the long term interests of residents and to their daily life where tourism is going to be developed. Facilities provided should be at the inhabitants disposal and citizens' needs should be harmonised with tourists' aims and needs. Participation of citizens in the decision making process is an important tool for achieving this so that citizens will feel less alienated in their town and less segregated from tourists.

Reorganisation of tourist flows can avoid concentration and congestion of vehicles, people, buildings and functions. Balanced distribution of visitors throughout the historic centre can bring new life to rundown areas or areas of low activity, introducing new uses in mono-functional (residential) areas and lessen the concentration of activities in the central areas. Promoting small and less important cultural resources and less visited areas can help achieve a greater balance of visitor pressure. This should help avoid stress and resultant aggressive attitudes and lead to the creation of new facilities in different parts of the centre.

4.

There should be a balanced programme of job creation, diversification of economic activities and better income distribution to ensure a fair distribution of gains to local communities. Economic activity within the fields of tourism and leisure should contribute to the protection, maintenance and upgrading of the urban environment. It should provide communities and regions with development that offers effective and lasting benefits. To achieve this it is necessary to retain some of the financial resources obtained by the tourist business and related activities within the locality (Zacatecas Declaration, 1988). The investment of resources according to social and environmental as well as economic criteria can be applied specifically to the protection, maintenance, rehabilitation and upgrading of the urban cultural heritage (see also chapter 5).

5.   Leisure and tourism can serve as a new urban economic pillar

Development of new models for combining economic activities with cultural and/or social outputs is necessary. These models should address traditional commercial activities; traditional craft industry; traditional jobs related to the maintenance of the cultural heritage; and genuine local products such as arts, crafts, foods, music, and folklore. Tourism and leisure are a new urban economic pillar used to reinforce the multi-functionality of the historic centres and to recuperate traditional activities and jobs needed for the preservation of the cultural heritage. The new models will differ from place to place, but they have to be developed in order to help cultural/human upgrading for visitors and inhabitants.

7.18 Revitalisation of traditional craft activities, Cordoba, Spain

The Municipal Government in Cordoba supports the revitalisation of the local craft activities combined with marketing promotions. These activities are based on silver jewellery, leather (cordoban) for furniture, interior design and pieces of art, embroideries, ceramics and pottery. The support from the government combines different strategies, rehabilitation of traditional sites in the historic centre for direct sale of products by craftsmen, training courses, promotion of fairs where products can be promoted and compete in a wider market.

7.19 Historical centre rehabilitation, Evora, Portugal

The action programmes developed for Evora are concerned with the improvement of the definition of urban image and function. The projects incorporates three aspects:
- urban travel - the creation of parking spaces at the periphery of the historical centre and establishment of a minibus network, and new traffic plan;
- planning in circles or rings following the shape of the old city, which results in enhancement of urban, social and cultural functions of the wall and the ring;
- strategic plan - the economic, cultural and social positioning of Evora requires a strategic approach creating development options which will foster regional balance.

HISTORIC CENTRE:
POLICY OPTIONS FOR
SUSTAINABILITY

Strategic and spatial planning can reduce land and housing speculation

6. Avoidance of land and housing speculation is important. This can be achieved through strategic and spatial plans. It is essential to avoid using sectoral plans as a short term solution as they do not facilitate integration between problems and interests. Sectoral plans are important tools once the medium and long term planning framework, in which the human, physical and environmental aspects are integrated, is agreed.
Besides the involvement of state, region, and university, the approach is characterized by broad participation of the various public partners.

7. Cultural, aesthetic and 'image' values are equally important to the quality of life and should receive equal priority alongside environmental factors so as to prevent the loss of identity and to conserve the 'genius loci'. It is essential to emphasise the local identity through the preservation and promotion of local traditions and culture.

7.20 Conservation and promotion of local cultural values, Tours, France

Cultural issues are not usually considered in the process of defining guidelines for major urban agglomerations. The Schema Directeur de l'Agglomeration Tourangelle developed a study called 'Identité, Culture, Project Urbain - Le Cas de Tours'. This study attempted to define the specific characteristics of the Tourangelles' identity and culture. This project supports additional proposals which focus on the quality of urban life and future development of the urban area.

Conservation of the real imageability of the historic centre is essential

8. Conserving the real 'imageability' (Lynch, 1968) of the historic centre is essential not only for human behaviour but also from an economic viewpoint. It is this unique character that tourists come to enjoy.

Physical policy options for a sustainable historic centre

Physical policy options for a sustainable historic centre

Reduce pressure on the hard and soft structures

9. Creative solutions are necessary in order to avoid the problems related to visitor pressure. The hard structure cannot be changed, so it has to be used to obtain the greatest benefit. Options include establishing different timetables in order that the same infrastructure can be used for both inhabitants and tourists; extending pedestrian areas, reducing the car domain; introducing new modes of transport; promoting the use of public transport; and creating accessible public transport nodes.

10. Many tourists visit cities by coach, causing long queues and congestion. There is a need to study the human, physical and environmental impacts of coaches in order to identify solutions for this problem. Careful location and layout of coach parks with pedestrian links to the tourist areas should be considered when planning the use of land in relation to the transport model for the city. Transport problems cannot be addressed within the narrow framework of the historic centre only, but should be considered in relation to the entire urban structure in order to develop a balanced transport model for the whole community (see chapter 6 for a discussion about social aspects of transport).

Extending pedestrian areas

11.

It is necessary to avoid over-concentration and congestion. In order to achieve this, management of tourist flows and of tourist use of urban space needs to be reviewed. The most effective use should be made of the hard and soft structures. It is important to enlarge the tourist space and to offer diversity. DG XXIII of the European Commission has proposed research into the regulation of tourist flows which includes examination of the combination of tariffs and revised timetables, and the use of telematics. To achieve a balance between supply and demand and to stimulate the promotion of other sites and cultural patterns, different strategies can seek to reduce, select or increase demand; reduce or increase supply; increase the capacity of sites; achieve a proper balance and complementarity of uses and activities in space and time.

12.   Activities, functions and transport should be spread through the whole city

The tendency to encourage or allow more activities to be focused in the over-used historic centre must be avoided. The dilution of activities, especially those related to leisure which add an extra burden to the functionally exhausted central spaces, should be promoted in order to create a balanced pattern of uses.

13.

Care should be taken, however, to ensure that a dilution of activities does not lead to a mono-functional use of the historic centre. The original urban structure was created to support the complex system of daily community life. To impose a mono-functional use means not only to destroy the real entity of the structure but also to cut the ties between the different parts of a city and thereby cause imbalance. The Green Paper on the Urban Environment recommends the encouragement of mixed uses. The dominance of single functions can result in the historic centre becoming a museum for mass tourism with the consequent emptiness during the off-season periods.

14.

In order to safeguard the cultural heritage it is not advisable to transform the multi-functional spaces of the historic centres into cultural reservoirs (universities, museums, exhibition centres, concert halls, etc.) where the mono-functionality will destroy the city's ambience. This is also an argument of economic sustainability as mono-use may result in a vulnerable situation whereby tourism is reduced and the economic base of the centre is undermined as the image of the centre becomes less popular.

15.

Dilution of activities within a city and multi-functionality of the centre are necessary to re-create balance within the city. The harmony and the quality achieved by the city is directly related to the efficient functioning of each part of it. Planners should take account of the functional role of the whole city.

16.   Local government can reduce the standardisation of townscape

There is a tendency towards standardisation of townscape due to similarities of styles, materials and techniques (CEC, 1992f). Excessive standardisation by large business organisations tends to create a 'could be anywhere' place. Materials, styles and techniques should be studied, rejected or adapted to the local conditions. Universal models should be replaced with respect for the cultural and environmental context, without betraying the different local cultural identities.

17.

Local government should develop rules to establish an appropriate 'fit' between architecture and traditional surroundings. The city's identity should be maintained, for example through urban renewal schemes, by taking account of scale, integrating each new building into its immediate built environment, maintaining and enriching urban form through the relationship between urban fabric and open spaces (piazzas, squares, gardens, etc.), and by acknowledging the cultural heritage. The past should guide the development of the present.

Open spaces are part of the urban identity

18. Identity is not only created by the fabric but also by open spaces. Land use plans should emphasize open spaces, both public and private. Green areas (public and private) are also important in shaping the townscape. The introduction of green elements may also enhance local biodiversity and facilitate the infiltration of storm water into the ground water system as discussed in section 4.1. See section 5.2 for a discussion about the social functions of open space and cultural diversity.

19. Elements that create the cultural heritage, even if made in solid and permanent materials, can be consumed like any other resource. Guidelines are needed to manage the cultural heritage and to ensure its existence. These guidelines should be related to the enlargement and diversification of tourist areas.

Tourists can destroy the place of attraction

20. Economic pressure from tourism can have negative effects on cultural heritage. The requirements of tourists can destroy the cultural heritage which attracts them in the first place. Major international hotels located in historic centres in an open and ugly confrontation with the surroundings is an example of this problem (successfully solved in Amsterdam with the Holiday Inn Hotel). Demand should be carefully managed in order to avoid the destruction of the cultural heritage. This can be achieved by fixing limits to balance demand and supply without endangering either.

Environmental policy options for a sustainable historic centre

Environmental policy options for a sustainable historic centre

Local policies to protect the quality of the urban space

21. Local governments should develop policies to protect the quality of the urban space. These policies must address pollution (visual, noise, water), vibration and conservation. Among the most intrusive elements in the urban scene are traffic and tourist signs. The effects of these and other pollutants are clearly visible in most cities, especially in the deterioration of monuments and buildings. Litter is another problem. Potential solutions include tourist education; increasing the number of litter-bins; and making tour operators responsible for maintaining litter control. Modern designs and the use of new materials and signs on ground floor façades contribute to aesthetic pollution and to the destruction of identity and ambience.

Transport causes visual pollution, noise, and vibration

22. Traffic not only causes visual pollution, it also produces a lot of noise. Vehicles, planes and trains are the most important sources. The Fifth Environmental Action Programme makes special reference to noise as one of the most pressing problems in urban areas. Crowds of people as a result of mass tourism are another source of noise pollution. The level of noise permitted during different times of the day should be fixed.

23. Vibration is a danger to cultural heritage as it can damage buildings and other structures, as well as reduce quality of life of the local population. Sources of vibrations should be identified including road traffic and trains (especially underground).

24. If present, water is an important element of the city's identity. When a river, a lake or the sea form part of the city, it is necessary to protect the purity of these elements. If they are polluted it will affect other parts of the city. Their contribution to the city's cultural identity should be enhanced.

The protection of the cultural heritage depends on the retention of the physical expression achieved through buildings, both large and small. It also depends on the maintenance of intangible cultural ambience and identity and of the townscape as a whole, including natural and human features. Local government should develop policies to promote active conservation and avoidance of the destruction of the urban cultural heritage environment in all its activities.

25.   Application of the precautionary principle in decision and policy making

The extent of environmental impacts of tourism and leisure activities is not easy to predict. The precautionary principle should be applied where there is any uncertainty. This means that the avoidance of risks should be given priority in decision making in order to maintain the balance of the ecosystem. This implies a knowledge of ecological carrying capacity. Brief reference to this issue is made in section 3.1.

26.

Sustainability objectives should be explicitly defined and translated into thresholds, indicators and targets in order to serve as a basis for policy making. Social and physical thresholds should be established to avoid the destruction and deterioration of the 'cultural heritage ecosystem'. There is a clear need to develop sustainability indicators for the cultural heritage environment. This is a task for individual municipalities, Member States and the European Environment Agency, each operating on a different scale but through an integrated approach. Venice in Italy is one of few cities where the city council is considering the introduction of capacity thresholds to control tourist flows. Targets and indicators are considered further in section 3.2.

27.

7.21   Limiting the number of visitors, Alhambra de Granada, Spain

The Alhambra Management Board has established a limit for access to the Alhambra at 800 visitors per hour. It is considered that this level allows for the conservation of the unique world heritage resource of the Alhambra and protects the surrounding districts from traffic congestion.

The human, physical and environmental constraints on tourism and leisure activities outlined above do not imply that growth of these activities is impossible. Balanced growth is possible and policies should ensure that further growth does not exceed thresholds of quality and safety. Spatial development of the tourist industry should ensure continuity and improvement of housing, green spaces and other facilities without threatening the quality of the city. The interaction between different uses should be considered. Exploitation of cultural heritage and tourist developments requires medium and long term planning in order to define the area to be safeguarded and methods to be applied; the residential zones to be rehabilitated; the protection of quality of life of the local population; the number of tourists acceptable; and the upgrading of the urban environment as a whole.

28.   Balanced growth is possible

An Ecolabel scheme could be introduced to reward cities where the relationship between tourism-leisure, cultural heritage and quality of life has reached a balanced and harmonious level. Such a scheme could also serve to promote good practice.

29.

Sustainability of the new core is
necessary for sustainability of the
whole ecosystem

Physical and
environmental policy
options

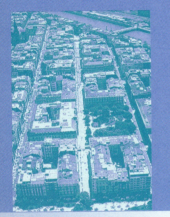

*Accessibility between the historic
centre and the new core*

Multi-functionality and identity in
the new core

3.4   NEW CORE: KEY SUSTAINABILITY ISSUES

The impacts in the new core from leisure and tourism are variable but not as significant as
in the historic centre. The city is a unique organism and acts as an ecosystem: a complex
of interconnected and dynamic systems. The improvement and restructuring of the new
core can create the needed city-wide balance in terms of leisure activities and the
decentralisation of tourist centres. Actions and measures should be taken in the physical
and environmental fields.

3.5   NEW CORE: POLICY OPTIONS FOR SUSTAINABILITY

Physical and environmental policy options

1.   Accessibility between the historic centre and the new core, and among the different areas
in the new core needs to be improved. This improvement should be considered as part of
a wider transport model for the city and should emphasise the role of pedestrians. The
transformation of road design concepts, as with the example of the urban boulevard
(CETUR, 1994), can introduce not only green patterns in the urban layout but also a new
approach to improve the social characteristics of public spaces. It is up to the
neighbourhood with its social and community life to define rules for these spaces in a
self-management setting (Montanari et al, 1993).

7.22 Boulevard linking the new core to the old centre, Manosque, France

The city of Manosque has created a boulevard linking the new core to the old centre.
The boulevard, adapted to the new functions, is defined by two lanes, parking, a
promenade with plants and a park. This creates a linear facility improving the quality of
the space and promoting the linkage between the new and old centres.

2.   New areas of a city tend to be mono-functional. In order for a city to be or become a
dynamic system, each part of the city needs a mix of uses. Each area of the new core
should be treated as a 'small city' where most uses have to be allowed in order to create
a 'self-sufficient cell' enriching the quality of daily life. The interaction between uses
should also be taken into account. It is important to avoid troublesome, unhealthy and
dangerous uses. Community, culture, social life and recreation all contribute to the quality
of human life. Section 7.1 considers the importance of creating mixed land use patterns
that encourage the efficient use of resources and transport infrastructure, and facilitates
the provision of local facilities. Planning is the main tool for achieving multi-functionality.

3.   Most new core areas respond to international models where identity and sense of place
are nearly non-existent. It is necessary to create or promote characteristics that can bring
identity. Citizens participation is essential for the success of this process.

4.   The creation of an identity for the new core implies redefinition of its role. This identity
must relate to the other parts of the city, the centre and the hinterland. The community
in the new core should be aware of this identity and should be proud of it. If citizens are
proud of their neighbourhood and their city they will participate more actively in the
improvement and maintenance of urban environmental quality.

HINTERLAND: KEY SUSTAINABILITY ISSUES

Leisure activities have an important impact within the hinterland, particularly on natural resources but also on small centres. Sometimes these centres have buildings, street layouts and a defined identity that can attract not only people in search of leisure but also tourists. Mass tourism does not normally affect these areas in so far as they are not included in a planned tourist promotion.

However, the impacts can be quite severe because leisure activities are largely uncontrolled. The 'invasion' of the hinterland is often prompted by the media which encourages the discovery of less well known places without taking account of the fragility of certain urban and natural environments.

The biggest impact in the human field is often in terms of work opportunities, where there can be a rapid switch from agriculturally based to service based employment. This can promote out migration when traditional sources of work are rejected in favour of higher paid jobs elsewhere.

HINTERLAND: POLICY OPTIONS FOR SUSTAINABILITY

Policy options in the human field

Tourism and leisure activities and related service sector activities should employ local workers. Retraining is therefore important for the economic development of the region. This process can be facilitated by the educational and training programmes of the EU as developed in the Member States.

It is essential to maintain the ecosystem balance. It is therefore important to avoid abandoning land due to economic pressures of leisure activities and, occasionally, tourist activities. The functional uses of rural and natural areas can be modified, but this should always be considered as part of a regional planning framework. It is also important not to resist change but rather to promote new ways of managing rural and natural areas. Policies to protect and encourage primary sector activities in these areas should be developed.

Physical policy options

The accessibility and mobility of the whole area should achieve and maintain a correct functional balance. Local daily movements as well as tourist movements must be possible without obstructing each other. A traffic pattern should be developed to meet the demands of both kinds of movements. The requirements of new activities should not overload or degrade the existing transport network.

The spatial requirements of leisure activities are extensive and selective. This creates a paradox. If there is a requirement for a substantial amount of land with a high density of uses and location on very special sites, the result can be the destruction of the quality of the site. The development of the leisure structure with a pattern based on the principles of sustainable resource use can prevent such destruction.

HINTERLAND:
KEY SUSTAINABILITY ISSUES

3.6   HINTERLAND:
POLICY OPTIONS FOR
1.   SUSTAINABILITY

Sustainability of the hinterland is affected by leisure and tourism activities

2.

3.

Need for a sustainable traffic pattern

3.7

Policy options in the human field

1.

Local workers are employed in tourism and leisure activities

2.

Maintenance of the ecosystem balance is essential

7

Physical policy options

3.

Development of a sustainable traffic pattern for local and tourist movements

4.

5.   Isolated buildings and settlements create their own particular problems in terms of meeting the requirements of visitors while maintaining the character of the area. One approach to solving this is to develop an integrated plan based on the principles of multiple use. This implies a pattern in which the cultural heritage of these buildings and the small town and village centres can be safeguarded and developed in a balanced way.

Environmental policy options

The above discussion has highlighted the importance of maintaining the links and balance between the city and its hinterland. Protecting and improving the environmental quality of the hinterland is the best way to ensure the overall environmental quality of the city. Policies to ensure this should be developed as a central tenet of policy formulation.

3.8   INSTITUTIONAL ASPECTS

Legal issues

The legal framework for the quality of the cultural heritage environment should be based on certain basic guidelines at the European level. The Member States, in accordance with their own characteristics and regional context, may develop corresponding legal instruments. At the local level the planning framework should promote and facilitate co-ordination, integration, division of responsibility, sustainability, subsidiarity and solidarity.

With regard to tourism, there is a lack of policy guidance at European and Member State level. Following the discussion in this Report it seems necessary to create a European legal framework, to be further developed at regional and local levels, in the fields of tourism related planning and management.

Organisational processes

Heritage protection is part of a decentralised power structure in the European Union (CEC, 1992f). Local initiatives, both from the private and public sector should therefore be stimulated. Power decentralisation should be a goal. State corporations and centralised development agencies should devolve responsibility to new local power structures, provided that local structures are prepared to co-ordinate activities within a regional framework and planning system.

Monitoring is required to assess impacts and to regulate tourist development and flows. Cities should collect more data to provide both indicators of change and measures of capacity. The data should be up-dated regularly in order to facilitate feedback. A local monitoring office with representatives from different functional areas should be created to investigate tourist flows and the impacts of tourism. The monitoring offices should ensure that necessary measures are taken to avoid risks for the cultural heritage environment.

A democratic framework, reflecting the interests of all types of users and tour operators, is the best guarantee for avoiding irreparable damage to the urban cultural heritage environment. Participation facilitates local initiatives and co-operation between the tourism sector and traditional activities.

Knowledge about tourism processes, the urban ecosystem, the carrying capacity of cultural heritage, visitor management in areas of cultural heritage and other important concepts is still limited. It is necessary to co-ordinate and to integrate the many and varied experiences of different European cities, based on a cultural heritage environmental database. Cities should collect more survey data on the various carrying capacity dimensions and perspectives. The European Environmental Agency and the European Environment Information and Observation Network should consider extending their tasks to include an expanded view of the cultural environment.

6.   Co-ordination and integration

CONCLUSIONS

Progress towards the integration of environmental considerations into planning systems differs between countries. It is best integrated into both strategy and instruments in Denmark and the Netherlands. The scope for local innovation is greatest within the German and Dutch systems. The impact of the new environmental agenda on planning systems in southern Europe has remained limited up to now.

4

1.   Integration of environmental considerations and regulations in planning systems

Some basis of regulation must be provided within each planning system in order to respond to environmental concerns and to prevent development migrating to areas of weaker control. Some countries are without these basic measures of development control. Other Member States have systems in place but do not always respect them. Government action is needed to tighten up these control mechanisms in parallel with environmental measures.

2.

Systems with rigid zoning plans need to find ways of becoming more flexible in order to respond to the environmental agenda, such as promotion, where appropriate, of mixed use schemes. Some cities have achieved this with fast-track variations to plans, letting plans lapse, or designating action areas. However, a clear plan framework is important to influence the action of others.

3.

Planning systems, despite their differences, are largely sets of procedures. Their strongest powers relate to the regulation of private development projects. It is the market which determines where proposals/projects will come forward. Planning systems therefore need to work hand in hand with public expenditure programmes and infrastructure/grant regimes to encourage development onto environmentally preferred sites, for example to assist the recycling of vacant land. Greening the market is an important contextual aim for land use planners. Application of the market tools discussed in Chapter 3 to spatial planning remains to be further explored.

4.   Flexible, skilled and powerful planning systems

Contrasts exist between countries in relation to the professional competence and orientation that is applied to town planning. In southern Europe, where local planning previously was dominated by architects and civil engineers, there may be a need for further strengthening of the economic, social and environmental expertise. Countries with a strong tradition of planning and a long established planning profession (Britain, Netherlands, Germany) also need to extend planners' knowledge, for example by increasing their understanding of natural sciences, and to ensure that wider skills, such as negotiation, team building, interdisciplinary working, partnership working and public consultation, are acquired. These need to be addressed in planning education and in relation to continuing professional development.

5.   Partnerships and participation

Analysis of the location in relation
to context

Opportunities offered by urban
regeneration

Impacts of leisure and tourism
activities on the city and the
quality of its cultural heritage

6. Environmental professionals need to form new partnerships with local community representatives and environmental organisations as part of the process of delivering more sustainable land use. They also need to be open to new ideas, for example about town planning and landscape design, and to allow innovative projects space and time to develop.

7. There are no simple, single purpose solutions to the debate on urban form. An analysis of each local situation with consideration of a wider range of environmental issues, needs to precede the formulation of locational strategies. Local proposals need to fit within regional or national strategies.

8. The approach to areas to be regenerated should be based on an analysis of the location of the area in relation to the context, physical as well as social and economic.

9. Urban regeneration allows local communities to restore deficits in their community. This includes the opportunity to fill gaps in the physical urban fabric, allowing new linkages to be made in the infrastructure, and for the provision of additional amenities for surrounding residents.

10. The process of urban regeneration offers opportunities to increase the involvement of the community via public participation processes resulting in the generation of improved living conditions.

11. Urban regeneration also offers opportunities to apply tools of the ecosystems approach to the existing urban settlement. This may result in the conservation of valuable ecological elements, and the restoration of ecological relations.

12. Leisure and tourism activities have both positive and negative impacts on the city and on the quality of its cultural heritage. Three fields are relevant: the human, physical and environmental fields. These impacts can be located at three levels: the historic centre, the new core and the hinterland.

13. Most human impacts vary according to the tourist season. Population size is the most visible and obvious of these impacts. Another is employment, based on seasonal opportunities generated by tourism. Negative effects of tourism include inflated land prices as excess demand makes land unaffordable for the local population. Alienation and loss of identity may result from the influx of 'strangers'. Visitors cause physical impacts and congestion affecting both the hard and soft structures, with consequent degradation of the cultural heritage. Environmental effects are evident in terms of pollution expressed in terms of visual, noise, smell, vibration and water pollution. Transport is a major causal factor.

14. Solutions can be found in a more balanced use of the whole city. All levels, including the historic centre, the new core and the hinterland should include multiple uses rather than the mono-functional ones. A balance should be struck between local daily movements and tourist movements. The existence of the cultural heritage and its use as a resource is another balance to be struck. A cultural identity, a proudness in the neighbourhood and an awareness of the function of the neighbourhood within the urban system should be created through participation.

As a non-renewable resource, cultural heritage should be maintained and enhanced
through the integration of cultural heritage management with spatial and environmental
planning.

15.

7

Cities and sustainability

CONCLUSIONS, RECOMMENDATIONS AND RESEARCH AGENDA

INTRODUCTION

1. This report of is intended as a contribution, on the part of the Expert Group of the Urban Environment, to the growing debate about cities and sustainability in Europe. It draws together a wide range of thinking and practical experience in addressing questions of urban management for sustainability. Despite a growing raft of legislation, directives and regulations, European cities continue to face economic and social problems and environmental degradation. New ways of managing the urban environment need to be found so that European cities can both solve local problems and contribute to regional and global sustainability.

2. This report recognises and celebrates the diversity of European cities. Clearly the legal and organisational basis for urban environmental action varies between Member States, in part reflecting differences in the responsibilities assigned to different tiers of local government. In addition, cities differ in their geographical circumstances and city administrations vary in terms of the sophistication of local responses, processes and techniques. Approaches to sustainable development are likely to be different in different cities.

3. This report, therefore, does not suggest blanket solutions or recipes for all cities. Instead it advocates the provision of supportive frameworks within which cities can explore innovative approaches appropriate to their local circumstances, capitalising on traditions of local democracy, good management and professional expertise. Whatever their responsibilities and competencies, local governments throughout Europe, through the many and varied roles which they perform, are now in a strong position to advance the goals of sustainability.

4. The report and its conclusions are aimed at a wide audience. Elected representatives in cities, city managers/administrators and urban environment professionals have key roles to play in urban management for sustainability. However, successful progress depends upon the active involvement of local communities and the creation of partnerships with the private and voluntary sectors within the context of strong and supportive government frameworks at all levels. Political leadership and commitment are critical if progress is to be made.

5. The remainder of this chapter describes the principal approaches advocated in the report, and makes conclusions and recommendations for policy, practice and research.

2   ISSUES OF KEY CONCERN

1. This report envisages the sustainable city in process terms rather than as an end point. Accordingly, it highlights policy processes as well as policy content. Both emphases are significant when it comes to the transfer of good practice from one locality to another. The city is seen as a complex system requiring a set of tools which can be applied in a range of settings. Although the system is complex, it is appropriate to seek simple solutions which solve more than one problem at a time, or several solutions that can be used in combination.

Urban Management

Sustainable development will only happen if it is explicitly planned for. Market forces or other unconscious and undirected phenomena cannot solve the serious problems of sustainability. Agenda 21 specifies a thorough process of considering a wide range of issues together, making explicit decisions about priorities, and creating long term frameworks of control, incentives and motivation, combined with specified targets in order to achieve stated aims. Sustainable urban management should be based on the above process.

The process of sustainable urban management requires a range of tools addressing environmental, social and economic concerns in order to provide the necessary basis for integration. There are various tools, some addressing environmental, social, or economic concerns of urban management separately, others attempting to combine these concerns. The Sustainable Cities Project focuses on the environmental tools available to urban management processes.

Five main groups of environmental tools are advocated. These are collaboration and partnership; policy integration; market mechanisms; information management; and measuring and monitoring. Each tool is considered as an element within an integrated system of sustainable urban management. There can be no prescriptions for how to use or combine these tools; there are many ways of moving towards sustainability. Institutional and environmental contexts are different in different Member States and in different cities, and each therefore requires a unique approach. The fundamental goal is to achieve an integrated urban management process, but the elements in that process will evolve through the interplay of different interests.

The approach to these tools implies a need for a broader and more active view of the role of government, especially municipal government, than has become current in parts of Europe. Management for sustainability is essentially a political process which has an impact on urban governance. The tools advocated in this report are all means of modifying or constraining the operation of professions, performance monitoring, and markets within sustainability objectives set from outside. By applying these tools, urban policy making for sustainability can become much broader, more powerful and more ambitious than has hitherto been generally recognised.

The political process of democratic choice can legitimate both sustainability objectives and the means to achieve them - provided people are educated and accurately informed about the consequences of their choices. Many of the problems related to unsustainability are only soluble if the people accept limits on their freedoms. These limitations can only be acceptable if the people affected choose or at least consent to them. The 'social contract' model of politics, in which civil society is created through individuals voluntarily agreeing to collective limitations on their own actions in order to make them all better off, may hold the solution to sustainable urban management.

Policy integration

Ecosystems thinking

Policy Integration

7. The need for co-ordination and integration is emphasized in Chapter 8 of the Fifth Action Programme on the Environment. This is to be achieved through the combination of the subsidiarity principle with the wider concept of shared responsibility. In setting out the recommendations which emerge from the Sustainable Cities Project, the Expert Group is seeking to achieve both horizontal and vertical integration.

8. Horizontal integration is necessary in order to realise the synergies of further integration of social, environmental, and economic dimensions of sustainability and therefore strongly stimulate the process towards sustainability. Horizontal integration requires integration between the policy fields within municipalities, within regional and national authorities and within the European Union. This latter is required across the European Commission's activities as well as within each Directorate General.

9. At local, regional and national level a movement towards integration between policy fields or sectors has started. Projects, research programmes etc. are, at least in some Member States, being developed, stimulated and disseminated through horizontal structures in organisations. There is, however, a need to further develop the capability and experience of professionals to work in an interdisciplinary manner, and to increase their understanding of policy fields and sectors other than their own. Professional education and training programmes should therefore be adapted to provide for this wider dimension that interdisciplinary working requires.

10. Vertical integration across all levels at European Union, Member States and regional and local governments is equally important. Vertical integration might result in greater coherence of policy and action, so that the development of sustainability at local level is not undermined by decisions and actions by Member State governments and the EU.

Ecosystems thinking

11. Ecosystems thinking emphasizes the city as a complex system which is characterized by continuous processes of change and development. It regards aspects such as energy, natural resources and waste production, as flows or chains. Maintaining, restoring, stimulating and closing the flows or chains contributes to sustainable development. The regulation of traffic and transport is another element of ecosystems thinking.

12. The dual network approach is based on the principles of ecosystems thinking and provides a framework for urban development at regional or local level. This framework consists of two networks: the hydrological network and the infrastructure network. The hydrological network defines ecological cohesion by managing water quantity and flows. The infrastructure network provides opportunities to minimize car mobility and to stimulate the use of public transport systems, walking and cycling. Attention in the planning process should be paid to aspects including:

• water quality and quantity, main flows, ecological values;

• existing or potential public transport, employment and amenities in relation to residential areas, integration of pedestrian and cycle routes in residential areas.

Analysing these aspects will result in basic principles for urban sustainability from a physical ecosystems point of view. Ecosystems thinking also includes a social dimension, which considers each city as a social ecosystem. The protection and development of niches and diversity form the elements of the social ecosystem.

Co-operation and Partnership

Co-operation and partnerships between different levels, organisations, and interests are essential parts of moving towards sustainability. It reduces the tendency of individual organisations and agencies to pursue their own agendas in isolation from the broader public interest. Furthermore, most problems can only be solved through co-ordinated action by a range of actors and agencies, in line with the principle of shared responsibility as advocated by the Fifth Action Programme on the Environment.

The Sustainable Cities Project emphasizes the importance of 'learning by doing'. Involvement in decision making and management means that organisations and individuals engage in a process of mutual betterment. Viewing sustainable urban management as a learning process both reinforces the point made earlier about taking the first step towards sustainability and highlights the importance of experimentation.

Much can be learned from sharing experiences between cities. However, it must be acknowledged that transferring lessons on physical matters, such as river basin management and recycling initiatives, is currently easier than with spatial planning initiatives because of the extra complication imposed by the variety of legal and cultural issues on which planning systems are based. The possible emergence of a European Spatial Development Perspective over the coming years offers considerable potential for the application of sustainability approaches to spatial planning.

Two categories of co-operation are specifically promoted in this report. The first category is focused on the operations of local authorities and include professional education and training; cross-disciplinary working; and partnerships and networks. This latter includes public-private partnerships, the involvement of NGOs, as well as city and other networks. The second category is focused on the relationship between a local authority and its community and includes community consultation and participation; and innovative educational mechanisms and awareness raising. Whatever the type of co-operation, it implies a need for changes in traditional methods of working and for the adoption of innovative approaches.

A key goal is to create the conditions that enable co-operation and partnership to take place. This is important for the above mentioned reasons, as well as because co-operation promotes equivalence between actors, rather than hierarchy, thus facilitating increased understanding and sense of responsibility among different actors.

SUSTAINABLE CITIES

242

CONCLUSIONS AND
RECOMMENDATIONS FOR
EACH THEMATIC CHAPTER

Conclusions - Chapter 3:
Sustainable urban
management

Progress towards sustainability

CONCLUSIONS AND RECOMMENDATIONS FOR EACH THEMATIC CHAPTER

Conclusions - Chapter 3: Sustainable urban management

1. The challenge of urban sustainable development is to solve both the problems experienced within cities and the problems caused by cities, recognising that cities themselves provide many potential solutions. City managers must seek to meet the social and economic needs of urban residents while respecting local, regional and global natural systems, solving problems locally where possible, rather than shifting them to other spatial locations or passing them on to future generations.

2. An ecosystems approach to urban sustainability requires a commitment to certain patterns of organisational management. This in turn implies the adoption of organisational patterns and administrative systems which address issues in a holistic way. What is needed, therefore, is the definition of core institutional principles which should help guide the type of approach which is most appropriate to the pursuit of sustainable development. Drawing on the ecosystems metaphor and the goals of sustainable development, the principles of integration, co-operation, homeostasis, subsidiarity and synergy are advocated.

3. Section 3.2 elaborated a range of tools for environmental policy integration. Existing tools developed in relation to environmental action need to be re-appraised and extended to address the economic and social dimensions of sustainability. Urban management for sustainability is facilitated through the application of these tools within city-wide policy frameworks and action plans, as exemplified by environmental charters and strategies in which policy goals, responsibilities and timetables for action are explicitly set out.

4. Progress towards sustainability may be measured using indicators and targets. Indicators have much to offer but their use is not straightforward. For example, there is a tension between ease of measurement and policy significance. While the main emphasis in work to date has been on indicators of physical sustainability, indicators of the availability of more sustainable lifestyle options are likely to be important in reconciling physical sustainability with social welfare. Another group of tools is concerned with bringing market mechanisms and price signals into line with the requirements of sustainability.

5. The final part of Section 3.2 focused on the political processes through which cities gain political and public support and begin to apply the mechanisms introduced earlier. Key messages include the importance of democracy and new forms of public involvement, the need for partnerships, and the need for diversity and experiment.

6. This report strongly advocates the development of city-wide strategies for sustainable urban management. However, the Sustainable Cities Project is also considering the application of this approach in a range of key policy areas. Ultimately the aim must be to facilitate integration across the policy areas themselves. The policy areas selected as priorities for this report are management of natural resources, socio-economic aspects, accessibility and spatial planning, examined, respectively, in Chapters 4, 5, 6 and 7.

243

CONCLUSIONS AND
RECOMMENDATIONS
FOR EACH THEMATIC
CHAPTER

7.   Recommendations -
Chapter 3: Sustainable
Urban Management

Recommendations - Chapter 3: Sustainable Urban Management

In setting out the recommendations which emerge from the Sustainable Cities Project, the Expert Group is seeking to achieve:

- further integration of the economic, social and environmental dimensions of sustainability across all policy sectors at European Union, Member State, and regional and local government levels;

- improved capacity for managing urban areas for sustainability;

- greater coherence of policy and action, so that the development of sustainability at local level is not undermined by decisions and actions by Member State governments and the EU;

- measures to avoid wasteful duplication of work and to enhance the productive exchange of experience; and

- both the enhanced application of existing policies, programmes and mechanisms and, where necessary, the development of new ones.

The problems of non-integration of environmental policies into other areas identified in cities in Section 3.1 apply equally, if not more so, to higher levels of government. All governmental and public agencies should:

- apply the principles and tools for policy integration to themselves;

- promote the development of sustainability appraisal through appropriate applied research and ultimately include sustainability appraisal in the decision making process for all significant changes in action or policy; and

- establish formal management procedures for declaring environmental aims; deciding on, resourcing and implementing actions to work towards aims; and monitoring and reporting on progress.

Action by the European Union

The most urgent responsibility for the **European Union** is to integrate its own policies and actions. This is required across the European Commission's activities as well as within each Directorate General. In addition, the EU should consider the following:

- providing guidance on sustainability appraisal informed by ecosystems thinking;

- providing guidance for environmental management systems approaches in the public sector;

- continuing to develop a European urban policy with sustainable urban management as a central concern;

SUSTAINABLE CITIES

244

CONCLUSIONS AND
RECOMMENDATIONS FOR
EACH THEMATIC
CHAPTER

8   CONCLUSIONS, RECOMMENDATIONS AND RESEARCH AGENDA

- paying greater attention to assessing applications to the Structural Funds against sustainability criteria;

- requiring projects receiving funding through the URBAN initiative to contain explicit objectives for sustainable development and, where appropriate, seek to apply the principles and policy tools explored in this report;

- increasing the funding opportunities available to urban initiatives for sustainable development and requiring submissions for urban projects to be prepared to a high standard;

- continuing to provide policy and financial support for networking between cities and towns in the pursuit of sustainability. However, steps should be taken to avoid duplication of effort by formal city networks;

- supporting the maintenance of an information system about local environmental initiatives, providing examples of good practice, reference literature and access to experts on environmental issues to European local authorities;

- together with Member States, providing assistance to inter-municipal projects to further develop and test the tools for sustainable urban management. Comparative projects are needed at international, national and local levels; and

- together with Member States, networks and international organisations, encouraging and facilitating exchanges and secondments of the staff of city and county administrations (such as those arranged through the European Municipal Officials Exchange Programme 1993-94).

Action by Member States, regional and local governments

10. In relation to the commitments made at Rio the Expert Group calls upon Member State governments to be explicit on the urban dimension of sustainable development, in particular in their reports to the CSD and in action on Agenda 21. Member States with specialist urban policies should build sustainable development goals into their main programmes.

11. Regional and local governments within the EU need to ensure that they are addressing the Fifth Environmental Action Programme. In particular, local authorities need to work with a range of partners in order to implement the Programme.

The links between the Fifth Environment Action Programme and Agenda 21 are significant and EU Member States and cities have a complementary role in responding positively to the environmental objectives contained in the two programmes. The approach adopted in the Sustainable Cities Project is broadly in line with the Local Agenda 21 process. The following are recommended:

- that local governments receive enhanced funding and support to enable them to fulfill their obligations under the Fifth Environment Action Programme and Agenda 21;

- that Member States and European cities encourage positive North-South links to implement Local Agenda 21, as developed at Global Forum, Manchester;

- that central and local government forums or steering groups be established in all Member States to take forward urban environmental issues specifically in relation to the Fifth Environmental Action Programme, Agenda 21 and Local Agenda 21.

At **local government** level measures are recommended to foster city-wide, strategic approaches to sustainable urban development involving application of the principles and tools discussed in Chapter 3 of this report. Local governments should be encouraged to establish appropriate cross-cutting administrative arrangements and to employ specialist staff such as environmental policy co-ordinators and animators.

The development of strategic approaches also requires the establishment of public-private-NGO partnerships which can enhance the effectiveness of the activities of all concerned and create a sense of mutual trust and mutual purpose. The creation of such partnerships typically requires professionals from different backgrounds to work together and requires local government staff to work with NGOs and with the public.

Successful development and application of these approaches have long term implications for the education and training of professionals and politicians involved in city management. Sustainability issues and their management should be included in the curriculum for all professional and technical education and training and qualifications.

In the short term the preparation of video and training packs for basic awareness raising for city staff, local politicians and the public in general is recommended. In the long term, all levels of government need to consider the development of educational and information programmes for the public (including children) to underpin policy changes and project innovations.

Member States and cities should work towards an adequate structure of regional and local government in urban regions. Often there is a gap between functional and administrative structures, with negative impacts for environmental protection, spatial planning and transport planning. In many European urban regions there is a need to establish metropolitan governments with a strong planning competence at the strategic level. The provision of smaller democratic units within these strategic urban frameworks is in some Member States seen as an important feature of this re-organisation.

It is recommended that, in the longer term, cities are given increased freedom to experiment and to devise and implement their own policies and actions for sustainable development.

246

CONCLUSIONS AND
RECOMMENDATIONS FOR
EACH THEMATIC
CHAPTER

Conclusions - Chapter 4:
Sustainable management
of natural resources

Conclusions - Chapter 4: Sustainable management of natural resources

19.   Chapter 4 identifies the problems of consumption of non-renewable or slowly renewable natural resources that exceeds the capacity of the natural system. It links this problem to the related waste accumulation that is characteristic of today's lifestyles in European cities.

20.   The functioning of urban systems is compared to natural systems, where equilibrium is maintained by circulating resources and wastes internally. The difference between the functioning of the natural and the urban system lies in the way the latter is dependent on importing natural resources and energy into the city and exporting waste and pollution out to the surrounding areas. Cities are highly dependent open systems rather than closed systems, where natural resources are used in an economical way to provide energy, and any unused material is reused, recycled or processed for re-entering the circulation process. By depending on surrounding areas for the provision of natural resources and energy, and for the disposal of waste, cities impose their problems on these areas. Depletion of natural resources, pollution and environmental degradation with their resulting social, economic and environmental consequences affects the rural population as well as urban systems.

21.   The chapter emphasizes that a more sustainable functioning of urban systems requires a move towards management of cities that makes use of the lessons that nature can teach about ecological and economical flow management.

22.   An integrated approach to closing the cycles of natural resources, energy and waste should be adopted within cities. The objectives of such an approach should include minimising consumption of natural resources, especially non-renewable and slowly renewable ones; minimising production of waste by reusing and recycling wherever possible; minimising pollution of air, soil and waters; and increasing the proportion of natural areas and biodiversity in cities. These objectives are often easier to achieve on a small scale, which is why local ecological cycles can be ideal for introducing more sustainable policies for urban systems. However, the appropriate level at which cycles ideally should be closed is not fixed, but could be the neighbourhood level, local or regional levels depending on circumstances.

Recommendations - Chapter 4: Sustainable management of natural resources

23.   The issues of natural resources, energy and waste are closely interconnected. Cities are places of high energy intensity, and energy plays an increasingly important role in the operation of urban systems. The more energy that is consumed, the higher the need for natural resources to support the energy production. Similarly, the higher the consumption of natural resources and energy, the more waste is accumulated. Because of this inter-relationship it is logical that several of the relevant policy options have multiplier effects. So by addressing one particular problem, the policy options may simultaneously solve one or more other problems.

The key goal of sustainable management in relation to air is to ensure quality and supply.

24.

- The EU should continue to define and adopt stringent emission standards in relation to air quality.

- The EU, Member States and regional and local governments should adopt regulatory instruments and technical measures to reduce pollution sources and quantities. They should also develop policies and mechanisms to promote air generation and filtering, for example through the provision of more green elements in cities.

- It is recommended that the measures designed to improve air quality and supply are developed within an overall framework of an action plan for air quality. This will, in effect, be a requirement once the EU's 'Directive on Ambient Air Quality Assessment and Management' becomes operational.

The general aim in relation to soil, flora and fauna is to increase the proportion of natural and human-made eco-systems within cities.

25.

- Regional and local governments should facilitate the development of green corridors linking country-side to the various green elements within cities. This provides the best ecological frameworks for habitats, thus combining an increase in biodiversity with recreational value. A move from mono-culture towards increased biodiversity is important in the sustainable management of cities.

Sustainable water management

- It is also recommended that green elements are used to provide a ground for education and awareness raising in relation to the way ecosystems function and how urban functions can be integrated into the natural system.

The principles of sustainable water management are related to water conservation and minimising the impact of all water related functions on the natural system.

26.

- Regional and local governments should utilise measures to green cities to improve the water system. Maximising the use of permeable surfaces facilitates the infiltration and cleansing of storm water, while creating ponds, ditches and wetlands facilitates the retention of storm water, purifies the water and enriches the flora and fauna.

- It is also recommended that water use efficiency is included as part of sustainable water management. Taking into account the end use of the water in determining the required quality is a means that aids water conservation. Collecting storm water for secondary uses and recycling grey water are important measures.

- The EU, Member States and regional and local authorities are also urged to promote the implementation of more environmentally friendly sewerage solutions. Biological treatment plants and passive water treatment methods based on ecological functions should be more widely utilised.

SUSTAINABLE CITIES

248

CONCLUSIONS AND
RECOMMENDATIONS FOR
EACH THEMATIC
CHAPTER

8   CONCLUSIONS, RECOMMENDATIONS AND RESEARCH AGENDA

27.   The basic aim of sustainable energy management is concerned with energy conservation. The key to energy conservation lies in behaviour of individuals and organisations, but also in energy production and distribution.

- The EU should continue to support the setting up of urban energy agencies to tackle energy management and thus contribute to the environmental protection and sustainable development of cities. The EU should also consider the extension of other initiatives within the field of energy conservation, especially those targeted particularly towards local authorities.

- National governments should provide the necessary frameworks for facilitating the implementation of energy conservation policies. Such frameworks may include fiscal measures, regulatory changes, new powers for municipalities etc.

- The EU and Member States should facilitate decentralisation of energy management and production wherever appropriate, in order to increase the possibility for co-ordinating actors, for working actively towards reducing energy demand and increasing efficiency of production and distribution.

- The EU, Member States and regional and local governments should create the right conditions to replace non-renewable energy sources with renewable ones wherever possible.

- Regional and local governments should apply sustainable design principles which facilitate energy conservation. Densities, siting, layout, bio-climatic architectural design, materials, insulation, orientation of buildings, micro-climate, green elements etc. should be used in land use planning and required in development control to minimise energy consumption.

- Regional and local governments should undertake an energy audit of both internal and external activities, and of the city's own building stock, in order to move towards adopting suitable energy efficiency measures, thus contributing to energy conservation while reducing running costs. Greening the city's activities in such a way, also provides a valuable example for other organisations and individuals to follow. It adds credibility to any awareness raising initiatives undertaken by cities.

28.   Various solutions that utilise waste for energy production serve the dual purpose of conserving natural resources and making efficient use of waste products. The ultimate aim of sustainable waste management is, however, to minimise production of waste.

- The EU should take steps to provide policy guidance for an integrated system of waste management, that allows for context specific implementation in all Member States.

- The EU, Member States and regional and local governments should promote the reduction of packaging, and the increased use of reusable and recyclable packaging.

- Regional and local governments should promote maximum separation at source and composting to minimise waste production, reduce the level of contamination of waste, and turn some of the waste into useful forms, such as topsoil or biogas.

Other recommendations for waste management coincide with those for water management, especially those for liquid waste management.

Finally, the EU, Member States and regional and local governments should bear in mind that influencing behaviour through education, information and practical evidence is a key factor in achieving more sustainable urban systems. The relationship between influencing behaviour and sustainable management of natural resources is particularly evident. It is an area where people's behaviour affects the level of sustainability directly, and where people can see the results of changed behaviour in a transparent way.

Conclusions - Chapter 5: Socio-economic aspects of sustainability

Chapter 5 identified the socio-economic problems in current societies and links socio-economic aspects with sustainability. Section 5.1 located European cities in their international context and stressed the key role of cities in the European and global economy.

Population shifts and economic restructuring within the European urban system have impacted differently upon cities. Greater economic integration through the Single European Market, developments in Central and Eastern Europe and the expansion of the EU as new Member States join are having far-reaching effects upon the economies, social structures and environments of cities.

The Fifth Environmental Action Programme refers to the use of economic instruments in delivering sustainable development and sets industry as one of the five target sectors. Section 5.1 examined the potential for local government action in this area. Greening local economies involves building sustainability goals into conventional policy approaches as well as exploring new forms of action.

Further work is required to link the greening of economic development to social sustainability concerns through a consideration of local labour markets and examination of the scope for community-based initiatives in line with the Fifth Environmental Action Programme.

Section 5.2 addressed social aspects of sustainability. A recent trend has been to ignore environmental and social risks and to concentrate on accumulating material wealth. From a social perspective, a key question is whether the poor and the wealthy citizens are affected by risk to the same degree. The underlying questions are: will a risk society replace the social class structure, or will a risk society be integrated in the current class society? Wealth and risk differs between the Member States, between regions in Member States, between cities in regions and within cities.

Resting these trends implies changes to the underlying values in society, as well as to the basics of economic systems. Shifts in the behaviour and lifestyles of politicians and citizens will be required, and these need to consider the welfare of future generations. This, in turn, may require a change in individual values in relation to communities, ownership, responsibility and individual involvement.

Recommendations-
Chapter 5: Socio-
economic aspects of
sustainability

37.   Access to basic services and amenities, education and training, health care, housing and employment form the basis for the well-being of people, and for the enhancement of equality and social integration. Physical aspects such as the quality of urban space also affect social sustainability.

38.   In addition, as the chapter pointed out, issues of economic and social sustainability cannot be considered in isolation from issues relating to land use planning and transport systems.

Recommendations- Chapter 5: Socio-economic aspects of sustainability

39.   There is a need for the EU and Member States to create the conditions in which businesses can profit by operating in more environmentally-sound ways, since the extent to which cities can encourage local businesses to be greener is very much constrained by the operation of market economics.

40.   The EU and Member States should consider active economic management to promote sustainable behaviour for business development through, for example:

- promotion of the environmental business sector, for example by creating markets for environmental products and services through the use of regulation, taxation, incentives and investment;

- the development of environmental standards for products and processes;

- regulatory frameworks for utilities which encourage demand management and tariff structures which reward lower use;

- management of the relationships between fixed and variable costs to make sustainable behaviour more attractive at point of decision (for example, shifting car taxation from ownership to use); and

- promotion of longer term investment institutions.

41.   Governments should further consider shifting taxation away from socially desirable activities such as employment towards environmentally undesirable activities such as energy use, resource depletion and the production of waste.

42.   All policies need to encourage energy efficiency, since improved energy efficiency is now recognised as a key means of achieving both economic development and environmental quality objectives.

43.   Member State initiatives involving the private sector should be encouraged. However, wherever services significant for sustainability are privatised the regulatory framework must be designed to ensure that sustainability-enhancing policy choices are more profitable, and that unsustainable policy choices are prevented.

44. The use of pilot projects should be increased, but these should be more systematic in their approach so that a co-ordinated set of objectives in employment and environment can be pursued and results measured.

45. It is recommended that **regional and local authorities**:

- explore ways of creating employment through environmental measures;

- encourage better environmental performance in existing businesses in their areas;

- target inward investment strategy towards types of economic activity which are more favourable in terms of sustainability; and

- seek to build competitive advantage in relation to inwards investment by developing and promoting the environmental and quality of life attributes of their areas.

46. The scope for more radical action depends upon cities having powers to manage their local economies in more sustainable ways, subject to local democratic mandate. For example, cities should be enabled:

- explicitly to consider local environmental, social and economic consequences in decisions about purchasing, tendering and company support; and

- to invest their resources according to social and environmental as well as economic criteria.

47. In the field of social sustainability there is a need for the EU and Member States to strengthen their commitment and actions in striving towards the achievement of just societies that provide the necessary conditions for the well-being of all citizens. This includes the elimination of poverty and social exclusion, access for all to basic services, education, health care, housing and employment, and the facilitation of active involvement in decision making by all groups of the society.

48. The Expert Group recognises the EU's initiatives in the establishment of the fundamental social rights of citizens as a constitutional element of the European Union, and the extension of the Social Charter to cover a wider range of individual rights and responsibilities, particularly if these may aid social sustainability.

49. In addition, the EU should continue to develop and implement initiatives that support the development of human resources through education and training, and especially the integration of young people into the labour market. At the national and local levels, Member States and regional and local authorities should:

- facilitate the adaptation of the workforce to changing needs and conditions of the labour market through the implementation of national and local training initiatives and programmes;

- focus specifically on groups of society that are disadvantaged or segregated from society, and help them to help themselves through education and training as a key means of getting access to meaningful employment opportunities.

SUSTAINABLE CITIES

252

CONCLUSIONS AND
RECOMMENDATIONS FOR
EACH THEMATIC
CHAPTER

8   CONCLUSIONS, RECOMMENDATIONS AND RESEARCH AGENDA

50.   The EU and Member States should actively contribute to improving the health of their citizens through the integration of health protection measures in legislation and policy, and together with regional and local authorities through:

- adequate provision of health services;

- education and training programmes;

- the collection of statistical data;

- the reduction of traffic and other polluting activities; and

- awareness raising campaigns.

51.   In the absence of a Community housing policy, the EU should promote the principle of adequate housing for all through pilot projects and initiatives focusing on promoting co-operation between agencies, exchanging information and experiences, and financial support to innovative experiments that further social aspects of housing and reduces homelessness. Member States should:

- create the legal and financial frameworks for the implementation of innovative housing schemes building on public-private partnerships and aimed at providing good quality housing well integrated within the existing urban structures to be available for rental at affordable prices.

52.   Regional and local authorities should:

- widen schemes aimed at enabling the allocation of social housing in accordance with urgency criteria, to take into account other aspects than mainly financial ones, for example racial prejudice and other reasons which might prevent people from gaining access to decent housing;

- promote the conversion and use of derelict land and buildings for the development of social housing schemes or temporary shelters for the homeless through spatial planning, development control and creative use of housing finance.

53.   In recognition of the social role that public places play, the EU and Member States should financially support public space and conservation strategies and projects, and regional and local authorities should facilitate:

- the enhancement of the quality of public spaces, including the prevention of physical deterioration and the implementation of greening measures;

- the reclamation of those spaces for people rather than cars; and

- the creation of safe environments, for example by applying the 'public guardianship' concept.

Conclusions - Chapter 6: Sustainable accessibility

Achieving sustainable urban accessibility is a vital step in the overall improvement of the urban environment and maintenance of the economic viability of cities.

Under 'key sustainability issues' Chapter 6 considered the general importance of accessibility in the way the city functions and the linked problem of traffic growth, projected to continue. Associated environmental problems, health related problems, and social issues were reviewed, drawing on the latest available research evidence, along with traffic-specific issues such as congestion, safety and the proportion of public space in cities occupied by transport-related activities.

Meeting environmental and transport objectives requires integrated approaches combining transport, environmental and spatial planning. However, relatively few cities have fully integrated systems. Current actions towards sustainability in this field mainly seek to reduce road traffic and congestion, essentially by encouraging a modal shift from private cars to public transport and, less often, to cycling and walking. Whilst these actions are important, they do not in themselves constitute sustainability measures.

Achieving sustainable urban accessibility requires the development of sustainability goals and indicators, target setting and monitoring, along with policies aimed at improving accessibility and not simply movement. Reconciliation of accessibility, economic development and environmental objectives should be the primary objective of a city's transport policy.

Recommendations - Chapter 6: Sustainable accessibility

A useful policy framework for mobility and access has been established with the publication of the White Paper 'Common Transport Policy' and the subsequent Green Papers 'Towards fair and efficient pricing policy in transport' and 'Citizens' Network - Fulfilling the potential of public transport in Europe'. The EU, Member States and regional and local governments should now develop transport policies which seek to minimise energy consumption and the environmental and social impacts of motorised travel. The following paragraphs summarise the principal measures required.

In drafting transport policies targets should be set covering all aspects of the environment (for example, land take, noise and visual intrusion), and in the longer term all aspects of sustainability. These targets can be incorporated into evaluation and funding mechanisms.

There should be an equitable system for evaluating different transport modes which takes effective account of all benefits and costs, including environmental impacts.

Car pooling

57.

Recommendations -
Chapter 6: Sustainable
accessibility

58.

59.

60.

61.   It is essential to develop measures to reduce the need to travel rather than continuing to emphasise measures which seek to minimise travel time.

- At city level there is a need for strategic planning in the management of urban transport systems, moving towards long-term time horizons and away from ad hoc, incremental responses to demand. Sustainability goals need to be developed for transport planning.

- Reducing demand for travel clearly requires close linkage between the management of urban transport systems and the strategic planning of future settlement patterns. As indicated above, transport and land use plans are intrinsically interlinked. All transport plans should be assessed within a land use framework.

62.   Policies to ensure a transfer from private to mass transit are essential. The accessibility of mass transit should be improved to take into account the needs of people with reduced mobility in particular. Existing tram and trolley systems should be maintained and optimised, and alternative means of transport developed, including walking and cycling. Attention should also be given to the role of restraint and pricing measures as essential elements of reducing private car travel through increased costs. Alongside this, new methods of communication - including telecommunications - should be fostered and promoted.

- The use of the Structural and Cohesion Funds to assist transport which improves accessibility within urban areas whilst reducing the environmental impacts of motorised modes is recommended.

- All programmes for funding under the EU support framework should be assessed to ensure that they set out policies and actions which will reduce rather than increase the dependence on private motorised transport in cities.

- Support should be given to all projects which increase cycling and walking in cities. More space should be given to the only truly environmentally friendly modes of transport.

63.   The full social and environmental costs of urban transport need to be appreciated and absorbed by users, as agreed by European Transport Ministers. This requires the creation of new accounting mechanisms which would form the basis for improving both the price structure and the provision of transport infrastructure. The following are recommended for Member States:

- the development of fiscal policy to reduce the relative price advantage currently enjoyed by those motorised modes causing the greatest environmental damage (for example, a carbon tax);

- adding taxation on usage to taxation on ownership, for instance, fuel taxes, road pricing and road licensing arrangements, in order that transport users acknowledge and pay for the urban environmental costs which they generate as a result of the frequency and extension of their transport habits, ultimately being persuaded to change their behaviour;

- 'ring fencing' or 'ear marking' of monies received from the taxation of environmentally damaging modes for the financing or subsidy of less harmful means of transport. However, hypothecation is not at present acceptable to all Member State governments.

Member States should seek to design regulatory regimes which enable competition where desirable, whilst ensuring control over quality, access and the environmental impacts of transport.

64.

Accomplishing these policy changes requires the establishment of appropriate administrative arrangements. Greater co-ordination is required between public and private transport (for example through creation of a separate joint administrative agency to manage urban transport in totality).

65.

- City transport should be under the aegis of one authority only, preferably the same authority that has the remit for land use and development within the city.

Local governments should develop measures to facilitate the effective involvement of local communities in the formulation of transport policies. Similarly, local governments should encourage community-based solutions to urban mobility problems, for example, through modes intermediate between private and public transport, as happens in rural areas.

66.

Incentives are needed to encourage employees of organisations in all sectors to use environmentally friendly alternatives to the car.

67.

Conclusions - Chapter 7: Spatial planning

Conclusions - Chapter
7: Spatial planning

Spatial planning systems are essential for the implementation of city-wide policies for sustainable development. In developing policy and practice recommendations for land use in cities the Expert Group acknowledges the diversity of local problems and solutions and seeks to strengthen existing spatial planning systems, especially by encouraging ecologically-based approaches.

68.

Land use plans should advocate mixed uses rather than separation of uses through rigid zoning. Spatial planning systems which currently rely on zoning will need to become more flexible to accommodate this.

69.

The concept of 'green building' should be promoted and expanded in order to ensure not only the resource-conscious use of all building materials but also the design of buildings for durability, adaptability and multiple use.

70.

SUSTAINABLE CITIES

256

CONCLUSIONS AND
RECOMMENDATIONS FOR
EACH THEMATIC
CHAPTER

8   CONCLUSIONS, RECOMMENDATIONS AND RESEARCH AGENDA

71.   Planning should not always seek to 'balance' the benefits of development against costs to the environment. Instead, planners should increasingly define environmental capacities and prevent them from being breached. This may mean ruling out some kinds of development, whatever their current benefits. Planning should be 'supply limited' rather then 'demand driven'.

72.   The restructuring of heavy industry and utilities have left large areas of vacant and often contaminated land within cities whilst increasing the pressure for the development of urban open space and countryside. There is an urgent need to ensure the reuse of redundant, derelict or contaminated land, which is at a greater scale than during any period in industrial urban history. The recycling of previously developed land, and in some cases existing buildings, of itself can be seen to meet the sustainability objective of the reuse of a resource. In addition, land recycling also has the potential to achieve the retention of green field sites, and protection of countryside, open space and wildlife.

73.   Decontamination of polluted soil is a major concern in many urban regeneration projects. Cleansing techniques are often expensive operations. Decontamination should not be seen as a separate project requiring subsidy, but rather as part of an integrative approach - this provides a financially advantageous position. The integrative approach is based on two components:

   • the regeneration site should be considered in relation to its context of a wider area in which urban regeneration activities are envisaged;

   • consideration of the future development opportunities of the site should not be constrained by its existing negative image, but should reflect its realistic potential within the entire urban context.

74.   Both components require a development vision that covers the wider area and takes into account the potential strengths of specific sites. The proceeds of financially sound developments should be utilized to finance decontamination costs. The inclusion of a wide area within the development vision provides the possibility for achieving such cross-subsidy between sites. These principles should be incorporated into the various planning systems in order to create better frameworks for sustainable development.

75.   Cultural heritage, which is the expression of knowledge, values and beliefs, forms the cultural identity of a city and its inhabitants. The city itself is a cultural subject, a collection of places with cultural values and different lifestyles. Cultural heritage is expressed in many different spaces: historic centres, the new core and the hinterland, and consequently in many different ways.

76.   Leisure and tourism activities can have significant impacts on the quality of a city's cultural heritage. A historic city or a city with special architecture is attractive for tourists, which has positive economic and social effects on the one hand, but on the other can be a threat, specifically in social and environmental respects, for the sustainable development of a city.

257

CONCLUSIONS AND
RECOMMENDATIONS
FOR EACH THEMATIC
CHAPTER

77.   Recommendations -
Chapter 7: Spatial
planning

78.

79.

80.

81.

Recommendations - Chapter 7: Spatial planning

Sustainability requires a move to planning systems in which environmental carrying capacities at local, regional and global levels are accepted as guiding principles within which other considerations may be traded off. Capacity-based approaches are already being applied in certain Member States and should be encouraged.

Member States should seek to provide a coherent framework for spatial planning, such that plans prepared at municipal level fit within regional and national environmental policy frameworks. Where such overarching frameworks do not exist, Member States should allow municipalities increased scope to devise local solutions.

Planning should seek to be objectives-led. Objectives should formulate strategic directions and specific levels of environmental quality, economic growth and social progress. Through them, plans should describe intended states of the environment. Plans should include both national and locally-derived targets related to sustainability, and indicators should be developed to measure both the extent of problems and the degree of success in addressing them.

In order to reduce the need to travel, spatial planning needs to be complemented by fiscal and restraint measures such as road pricing and traffic calming, which are capable of producing results in the short term. Use of the planning system to influence urban form is a long term mechanism since new development is a relatively small proportion of the total urban stock, but it is essential for the development of more radical measures in the future.

Urban regeneration should be used to meet goals of sustainable development as follows:

• to strengthen social cohesion by involving residents of deprived residential areas in the regeneration process;

• to ensure the restoration of ecological links and the strengthening and conservation of ecological values, as part of an integrated ecosystem;

• to improve accessibility of existing areas. New infrastructure should be designed to complete the fabric of footpaths, cycle lanes and bus lanes, and public transport provision should be encouraged in order to provide opportunities for more sustainable transport patterns;

• urban regeneration sites near railway stations should be used for high density developments which concentrate activities.

Planning for cultural heritage

General themes

Europe-wide research

82.   In relation to tourism-leisure and cultural heritage, the following is recommended:

- planning for tourism, leisure and cultural heritage should be integrated in national guidelines and regional policies dealing with economic, social, environmental and cultural aspects;

- tourism, leisure and cultural heritage issues should be an integral part of the spatial planning process;

- cultural and environmental policies require long term planning - planners and decision makers should avoid the use of planning procedures that are inspired by short term gains where they reduce opportunities for the achievement of long term objectives;

- a balanced urban structure should be created so that the historic centre and the new core support mixed uses which complement their roles, and protect and maintain existing elements with architectural or traditional values. The balance between human features and local environmental conditions should be kept.

4   RESEARCH AGENDA

General themes

1.   The theme of cities and sustainability is a broad one, and much remains to be explored. This section highlights research requirements ranging from the academic to the practical. Some relate to the policies and activities of the European Union, some to Member States. Others are specific to regional and local government levels. Since, in addition to city-wide action, this report has discussed four particular policy areas - natural resource management, socio-economic issues, accessibility and spatial planning - research recommendations specific to these topics are also proposed. All, however, have a common focus: the search for sustainable development in European urban settings.

2.   General research requirements include the measurement of the ecological footprint of European cities and towns at both regional and global scales and exploration of the lifestyle changes which are at the heart of the search for a more sustainable urban Europe.

Europe-wide research

3.   At **European Union** level the following are proposed:

- assessment of the implications of new Member States on EU policy development for sustainability;

- examination of relationships and apparent contradictions between the requirements and impact of the Single Market and the scope for progress towards sustainable development in a range of European urban settings. The limitations on the greening of local economies imposed by the Single Market deserve particular attention;

- identification of a set of strategies to move towards a new development model where economic growth can be promoted in a sustainable way which contributes to higher intensity of employment and lower intensity of energy and natural resources consumption;

- examination of the integration of sustainable development objectives, principles and mechanisms into regional policy initiatives, including projects funded under the new URBAN initiative;

- assessment of the lessons learned from attempts to integrate policy in other settings. Integrated rural development programmes, for example, stress the importance of partnerships and networking, community identification of needs and solutions, the role of animaters, the pooling of finance and a focus on small areas;

- assessment of the implications of the forthcoming European Spatial Development Perspective for the implementation of sustainable development in national and local contexts.

Projects for Member States

At **Member State** level the following are proposed:

- a review of existing urban policy as developed by certain Member States (examples are 'City Challenge' in the UK and the 'Contrats de Villes' in France) to establish the extent to which sustainable development objectives are being pursued and the policy shifts that would be required to move towards sustainability;

- reviews of the extent to which sustainable development objectives are being pursued in sectoral policy areas of relevance to the urban environment, such as housing and tourism.

4.   Projects for Member States

Comparative research on regional and local government

At **regional and local government** level it is apparent that the major goal of policy integration still remains elusive. Progress towards this goal may be advanced by further development of the principles and mechanisms for sustainable urban management outlined in this report. In particular there is scope for exploring the links between ecosystems approaches and current thinking about good management in local government. It will be important to take account of the findings of OECD's The Ecological City project in specifying further work in this area.

Comparative research on regional and local government

5.

Although information is available about individual initiatives - as the many examples mentioned in this report demonstrate - much of this evidence is fragmentary or even anecdotal. And while descriptions of existing 'success stories' from practice are valuable, it is important to derive more rigorous means of measuring success and to learn more about the processes by which success is achieved in practice.

6.

To what extent are cities sustainable?

8

Application of principles
and tools for urban
management in different
policy areas

7. An important next step is systematically to establish how far the principles and mechanisms discussed in this report have already been taken up by European municipalities and regions and to evaluate the relevance of this approach for local government practice in Member States. For example, how far do politicians and professionals in European cities consider the principles of environmental limits, demand management, environmental and welfare efficiency and equity, as discussed in this report, to be of relevance in the day to day work of city management.

8. To what extent, and in what ways, are European cities establishing strategic approaches to sustainable development, preparing charters and action programmes, engaging in state of the environment reporting, setting up environmental management systems, establishing partnerships, seeking more effective citizen participation and developing sustainability indicators to measure their progress? Similarly, to what extent are market-based tools being applied? What scope is there for their further application? Does environmental action of this type remain on the agenda of city governments as economic conditions fluctuate?

9. To what extent does the take-up of these principles and tools depend upon organisational and political culture within regional and local governments? How far is the adoption of these principles and mechanisms leading to organisational change - to the establishment of new administrative and political arrangements and to the creation of new roles for urban managers?

10. The relationship between policy and action needs further exploration in relation to sustainable development in cities. As in many other areas of public policy, it is important to understand more fully why apparently similar cities respond differently to similar problems or external pressures, why some cities innovate and others do not, why there is variation in priorities at the operational level, and why some cities succeed in developing an integrated and co-ordinated approach and others do not. It is important to confront issues of power and dependence, vested interests, motivations, behaviour and the frameworks for action at different levels of government.

11. Further work is needed on the relationships between systems of regional and local government and the prospects for more sustainable urban management. What type of local government arrangements (including, for example, legal powers, structure, and geographical coverage) are most likely to deliver sustainable development? Is it necessary to establish municipal governments of a certain area and population size in order, for example, to achieve the effective integration of transport and spatial planning systems?

Application of principles and tools for urban management in different policy areas

12. Turning to consider the four policy areas, immediate priorities are the systematic examination of how far the principles and tools for sustainable urban management developed in Chapter 3 of this report are currently being applied in the management of natural resources, urban economies and policy for social systems, policy for accessibility and in spatial planning. An evaluation of their effectiveness in practice, and an estimation of the scope for their further application, are required. Some tools seem to deserve

particular attention. Examples are the mechanisms for partnership and citizen participation in policy formulation and implementation - and in particular processes of environmental mediation through which key issues, conflicts and solutions are identified - and the development and application of indicators of, and targets for, sustainable action in all four policy fields.

Research on natural resource management

Both scientific and empirical research is needed into the theory and practice of closing flows and creating ecological cycles within the urban system. The implications of circulating materials and energy within closed cycles on spatial planning and the special design requirements that such an approach might give rise to should be investigated.

13.

It is also recommended that the research agenda in relation to natural resource management should include:

14.

- the identification and further development of successful energy policies;

- the examination of various types of energy management systems as well as the conditions in which they can best be implemented;

- the identification of frameworks that enhance the implementation of least cost planning strategies;

- the continued development of technological applications for use of renewable resources and implementation of other energy conservation measures;

- empirical evaluations of the range of benefits of different types of ecological housing, from inner city residential areas to rural eco-villages;

- studies to advance and generalise the expertise regarding the design and implementation of ecological housing schemes so that construction would become less specialised and more viable;

- systematic scenario based comparison of the 'compact city' and the 'short cycles' models for sustainable cities, focusing on advantages and disadvantages of each model.

The further development of environmentally friendly waste water treatment and disposal methods should be supported. It is especially important that the implementation in urban settings of passive methods which make use of ecological functions is investigated, but it is also necessary to develop new technological solutions for biological treatment of waste water.

15.

The educational gains from short cycles for waste and sewage treatment (on-site and neighbourhood) should be examined more closely. To what extent is the environmental awareness higher among residents living in areas where refuse is treated locally, and is any difference in awareness created by the system for local waste and sewage treatment?

16.

Research on socio-
economic issues

17. In relation to air quality and the reduction of pollution sources, there is a need for empirical research into the effects of pollution 'licences' and the trading of such licences. In particular distributional aspects in terms of both the equity and geographical consequences of being able to 'buy' rights to pollute more than a pre-allocated share implies. The effects of these issues on local populations and urban economies should be investigated.

Research on socio-economic issues

18. It is recommended that the research agenda in relation to economy and the urban environment is expanded to include the following:

* identification of the most effective combinations of policy tools (including regulatory and economic instruments) to deal with specific sustainability issues;

* empirical work on tariff and price structures to establish how these affect the decisions of different social groups and to devise some general rules for tariff and pricing structures to promote sustainability;

* work in the field of utility regulation, especially since some utilities (such as energy, water, waste and transport) are responsible for a large proportion of the environmental damage in cities;

* examination of the differential effect on economies and employment in cities and regions resulting from environmental actions on the part of Member States;

* exploration of the employment implications of environmentally sound actions in different industrial sectors;

* the identification of needs for particular skills (often in the context of training provision). For example, as pollution control processes are becoming integrated rather than end-of-pipe, so are the jobs that run the processes;

* systematic examination of the extent of green local economic development action in European urban settings, the means by which it is achieved and the means by which it is monitored and evaluated;

* linking current research on social exclusion in urban settings more closely to work on the greening of local economies;

* empirical research on peoples' perception of quality of life, and on the extent to which it is at all possible to construct a widely applicable definition of quality of life. The extent to which cultural factors influence such definitions;

- empirical studies on the links between the physical environment, social conditions and behavioural problems related to crime and vandalism. The development of preventative policies;

- linking current knowledge on pollution related health problems to transport and spatial planning; and

- analysis of methods of promoting the active involvement of people from all groups of society in decision making processes, and engaging people through the devolvement of responsibilities and ownership.

Research on accessibility

In the field of mobility and access, re-examination of the concept of accessibility is a basic requirement. A shift in focus away from the search for further reductions in journey time towards ways of limiting travel growth must be a priority.

- At all levels there is a need to develop better systems for monitoring transport-related actions in relation to specific sustainability goals.

- Support should only be given to transportation studies which consider land use, and the implications of land use, in their overall proposals.

- Further research is needed to establish exact linkages between declining air quality associated with motorised traffic and health problems in urban communities.

- Suburban travel, and alternative approaches to it, remains an under-researched area.

At EU level, examination of the impact of the Trans-European Road Network on city environments and local economies is required.

More generally, the employment and environmental effects of shifting funding currently provided by the EU and Member States for road building into public transport systems deserve examination. Is it indeed the case that investment in roads creates fewer jobs per ecu than other means of transport?

Support should also be given for the following:

- research into road pricing programmes;

- further development of low emission vehicles; and

- further development to improve accessibility to public transport vehicles for people with reduced mobility;

- technological research and development leading to the provision of improved access to information to assist sustainable transport, especially mode transfers.

23.   At city level the following are suggested:

- systematic reporting and evaluation of the initiatives of towns and cities in the Car Free Cities Club;

- examination of community-based transport schemes (such as car sharing and community buses) developed in rural areas to establish what lessons these might provide for cities; and

- examination of the scope for enhanced involvement of local communities in the formulation of transport policies.

24.   There is a need for further examination of the education and training of transport professionals and engineers so as to ensure that they have the necessary competence to contribute towards the achievement of sustainability in cities and towns.

Research on spatial planning

25.   In relation to spatial planning the key research question would seem to be the identification of the necessary attributes of a spatial planning system offering the best hope of achieving sustainable development. A comparative examination of spatial planning systems and policies in the different Member States will be published by DGXVI of the European Commission in the near future. This will provide a useful basis for in-depth comparative analysis of national and local frameworks for implementing sustainability.

26.   Secondly, systematic research is needed on current attempts to integrate transport and spatial planning in cities, with an emphasis on the mechanisms through which such integrative strategies are developed and implemented.

27.   In the context of debates about self-sufficiency and the ecological footprint of cities, research into the space requirements of urban living (for example, food production, energy generation, waste sink capacity) might allow cities to identify and plan to accommodate more of these land uses.

28.   In addition, there is a need for research into methodologies for identifying the sustainability impacts of development proposals, together with further development of existing limited work on measures for mitigation and compensation.

29.   Urban regeneration as a process of reversal of urban economic, social and physical decay has a key role to perform in the attainment of urban sustainability. Research into alternative pan-European models of the processes by which partnership and community participation can assist in securing long-lasting sustainable urban regeneration should be actively pursued.

Cultural heritage and the interrelationships with urban leisure and tourism provide a prime focus of research into sustainable urban development. Key questions include the extent to which an integrated approach linking cultural heritage conservation to opportunities for urban tourism and leisure activities can be achieved whilst generating new sources of urban economic potential.

30.

There is a need for further examination of the education and training of urban environment professionals, for example town planners, in Europe so as to ensure that they have the necessary competence to contribute towards the achievement of sustainability in cities and towns.

31.

EPILOGUE

In the preface to this report we pointed to the global urban challenges that need to be urgently addressed by European cities and towns as we enter the next millennium. The report goes some way in comprehensively identifying problems, providing ideas and recommending actions to support policy communities across Europe in their continuing goal of seeking sustainability in urban settings.

The finalisation of this report provides the foundation for the other components of the Sustainable Cities Project which will be completed in time for the Lisbon conference - the good practice guide and European Good Practice Information System, the targeted studies and the dissemination conferences. In addition the Sustainable Cities and Towns Campaign and the 'network partners' (CEMR, Eurocities, ICLEI, UTO and WHO) are actively engaged in the sharing of information and experience between cities and towns and in the development of advice based on experimental and demonstration projects at the local level.

In the next stages of the Sustainable Cities Project after the Lisbon conference we can speculate on the priorities for action. These may include:

- consolidation and implementation of the thinking in this report through a range of mechanisms
- continuation of the other outputs and the network projects
- further development of the European Sustainable Cities and Towns Campaign
- evaluation of progress in a more measured evaluative research programme
- focus on Southern and Central and Eastern Europe
- dialogue with international agencies to explore ways of encouraging European cities to enhance their links with cities in the South.

Whatever the priorities emphasis must be placed on the 'sustainability transition'. In general it is easier both to diagnose what is wrong with present ways of doing things and to describe desired future states than to establish how to move from the current position to the desired future. The 'sustainability transition' - how to make this step should be emphasised in policy development, research and practice.

The sustainable city process is about creativity and change. It is about the substance of policy as well as policy methods. It challenges the legitimacy of traditional governmental responses and seeks new institutional and organising capacities and relationships. The notion of sustainability is dynamic and evolving and will change over time as understanding of the local and global environment becomes more sophisticated and shared. This report and its recommendations represent a contribution to this dynamic process, to be refined and consolidated as the Sustainable Cities Project progresses.

BIBLIOGRAPHY

ADRIAANSE A. (1993) *Environmental Policy Performance Indicators: A Study on the Development of Indicators for Environmental Policy in the Netherlands.* Sdu Uitgeverij Koninginnegracht.

AMSTERDAM DIENST RUIMTELIJKE ORDENING (1996) *Milieumatrix Structuurplan; signalering van milieu-effecten van ruimtelijke ordeningsvoorstellen op structuurplan-niveau.*

ARCHIBUGI F. (1993) *'Ecological Equilibrium and Territorial Planning: The Italian Case'.* Paper to the VII AESOP Congress Planning and Environment in Transforming Europe Lodz, Poland July 14-17.

ASSOCIATION FOR THE CONSERVATION OF ENERGY (1991) *Lessons from America?*

BARRAQUE B. (1994) 'Le gouvernement local et l'environnement' in Biarez S. & Nevers J.: *Gouvernement Local et Politiques Urbaines.* Actes du colloque international, Grenoble, 2-3 Fevrier 1993.

BECK U. (1992) *Risk society - Towards a new modernity.* Sage Publications, London.

BIGG T. (1993) *The United Nations and the Commission on Sustainable Development.* UNEP/United Nations Association UK.

BLOWERS (ed) (1994) *Planning for a Sustainable Environment.* Town and Country Planning Association.

BOX J. & HARRISON C. (1993) *'Natural spaces in urban places'.* In Town & Country Planning Sept pp 231-235.

BRADLEY K. (1993) *Integration of environment within Community Regional Policy.* Mimeo.

BREHENY M. (1993) *'Planning the sustainable city region'.* In Town & Country Planning April pp 71-75.

BREHENY M. (1994) *Planning for environmental capacity: the case of historic towns.* Paper to the International Symposium on Urban Planning and the Environment, Seattle, March.

BROG W. (1993) *Social data Munich.* Paper to the Velocity Conference, Nottingham, UK September.

BROWN L.R. (1991) *A sustainable future.* In Resurgence no.147.

BRUGMANN J. (1992) *Managing Human Ecosystems: Principles for Ecological Municipal Management.* ICLEI, Toronto.

CAR FREE CITIES CLUB (1994) *Car Free Cities Charter.* Brussels.

CETUR (1994) *METROPOLIS - Urbanisme/Planification Regionale/Environnement.* Entrées de Ville. Trimestriel N° 101/102. Paris.

CLAYTON A. & RADCLIFFE N. (1993) *Sustainability: A Systems Approach*. WWF Scotland.

CLRAE (1992) *The European Urban Charter*. Standing Conference of Local and Regional Authorities of Europe. Council of Europe, Strasbourg.

COMMISSION OF THE EUROPEAN COMMUNITIES (undated) *Energy and Economic and Social Cohesion*. DGXVII. Supporting document on: Energy and the Urban Environment. Brussels.

COMMISSION OF THE EUROPEAN COMMUNITIES (1985) *Directive on the Assessment of the Effects of Certain Private and Public Projects on the Environment (85/337/EEC)*. Official Journal of the European Communities L175, 5.7.1985. Brussels.

COMMISSION OF THE EUROPEAN COMMUNITIES (1990) *Green Paper on the Urban Environment*. COM(90) 218 CEC, Brussels.

COMMISSION OF THE EUROPEAN COMMUNITIES (1991a) *Europe 2000: Outlook for the Development of the Community's Territory*. COM(91) 452 CEC, Brussels.

COMMISSION OF THE EUROPEAN COMMUNITIES (1992a) *Towards Sustainability: A European Community Programme of Policy and Action in Relation to the Environment and Sustainable Development*. COM(92) 23, Brussels 27 March.

COMMISSION OF THE EUROPEAN COMMUNITIES (1992b) *The Future Development of the Common Transport Policy: A Global Framework for Sustainable Mobility*. COM (92) 494 Final, Brussels 2 December.

COMMISSION OF THE EUROPEAN COMMUNITIES (1992c) *Green Paper on the Impact of Transport on the Environment*. COM(92) 46 Final, Brussels 20 February.

COMMISSION OF THE EUROPEAN COMMUNITIES (1992d) *Treaty on European Union*. Brussels.

COMMISSION OF THE EUROPEAN COMMUNITIES (1992e) *State of Europe's Environment*. Brussels.

COMMISSION OF THE EUROPEAN COMMUNITIES (1992f) *Encouragement de la CEE a la Protection des Villes Historiques*. DGXI. Rapport Final. Novembre.

COMMISSION OF THE EUROPEAN COMMUNITIES (1993a) *Community Action in Urban Matters*. Brussels.

COMMISSION OF THE EUROPEAN COMMUNITIES (1993b) *Growth, Competitiveness, Employment - The Challenges and Ways Forward into the 21st Century, White Paper*. COM(93) 700 Final Brussels, 5 December.

COMMISSION OF THE EUROPEAN COMMUNITIES (1993c) *Report from the Commission of the Implementation of Directive 85/337/EEC on the Assessment of the Effects of Certain Public and Private Projects on the Environment.* COM (93) 28 Final Vols 1-13 Luxembourg.

COMMISSION OF THE EUROPEAN COMMUNITIES (1993d) *Statistics on Housing in the European Comunity.* DGV.

COMMISSION OF THE EUROPEAN COMMUNITIES (1994a) *Europe 2000+: Cooperation for European Territorial Development.* Brussels.

COMMISSION OF THE EUROPEAN COMMUNITIES (1994b) *Community Initiative Concerning Urban Areas (URBAN).* COM(94) 61 Final. Brussels, 2 March.

COMMISSION OF THE EUROPEAN COMMUNITIES (1994c) Report from the Commission under Council Decision 93/389/EEC - *First Evaluation of Existing National Programmes under the Monitoring Mechansim of Community CO2 and Other Greenhouse Gas Emissions.* COM(94)67 Final. Brussels, 10 March.

COMMISSION OF THE EUROPEAN COMMUNITIES (1994d) *Poverty 3, The lessons of the Poverty 3 Programme.* DGV/E/2.

COMMISSION OF THE EUROPEAN COMMUNITIES (1994e) *Proposal for a Council Directive amending Directive 85/337/EEC on the assessment of the effects of certain public and private projects on the environment. 16.3.1994.* COM(93) 575 final. Brussels.

COMMISSION OF THE EUROPEAN COMMUNITIES (1994f) *Directions for the EU on environmental indicators and green national accounting: the integration of environmental and economic information systems.* Communication from the Commission to the Council and European Parliament. COM(94) 670 Final. 21.12.1994. Luxembourg.

COMMISSION OF THE EUROPEANCOMMUNITIES (1994g) *City and environment.* Brussels.

COMMISSION OF THE EUROPEAN COMMUNITIES (1995a) *Communication from the Commission to the Council, the European Parliament, the Economic and Social Committee and the Committee of the Regions - The Common Transport Policy Action Programme 1995-2000.* COM(95)302 Final. Brussels, 12 July.

COMMISSION OF THE EUROPEAN COMMUNITIES (1995b) *Towards Fair and Efficient Pricing in Transport - Policy Options for Internalising the External Costs ofTransport in the European Union.* COM(95)691. Brussels.

COMMISSION OF THE EUROPEAN COMMUNITIES (1995c) *Structural Funds Innovatory Measures 1995-1999 - Guidelines for the Second Series of Actions under Article 10 of the ERDF Regulation.* Doc. XVI/261/95. Brussels.

COMMISSION OF THE EUROPEAN COMMUNITIES (1995d) *Cohesion Policy and the Environment* - Communication from the Commission to the Council, the European Parliament, the Economic and Social Committee and the Committee of the Regions. COM(95)509 Final. Brussels, 22 November.

COMMISSION OF THE EUROPEAN COMMUNITIES (1995e) *Report from the Commission on the State of Implementation of Ambient Air Quality Directives.* COM(95)372 Final. Brussels, 26 July.

COMMISSION OF THE EUROPEAN COMMUNITIES (1995f) *Amended proposal for a Council Directive on Ambient Air Quality Assessment and Management presented by the Commission pursuant to Article 189 a (2) of the EC-Treaty.* COM(95)312 Final. Brussels, 6 July.

COMMISSION OF THE EUROPEAN COMMUNITIES (1995g) *The Medium Term Social Action Programme 1995-1997.* DGV. Adopted by the Commission 12.4.1995.

COMMISSION OF THE EUROPEAN COMMUNITIES (1995h) *Local Development and Employment Initiatives - An Investigation in the European Union.* COM (95)564. Brussels, March.

COMMISSION OF THE EUROPEAN COMMUNITIES (1995i) *A review of the European Commission Research on Environmental Protection and Conservation of the European Cultural Heritage.* DGXII, Brussels.

COMMISSION OF THE EUROPEAN COMMUNITIES (1995j) *Tourism and the Environment in Europe.* DGXXIII, Brussels.

COMMISSION OF THE EUROPEAN COMMUNITIES (1995k) *Community Action Plan to assist tourism.* DGXXIII, Brussels.

COMMISSION OF THE EUROPEAN COMMUNITIES (1995l) *The role of the Union in the field of tourism.* Green Paper COM(95)97. Brussels.

COMMISSION OF THE EUROPEAN COMMUNITIES (1996a) *Progress Report from the Commission on the Implementation of the European Community Programme of Policy and Action in relation to the Environment and Sustainable Development "Towards Sustainability'.* COM(95)624 Final. Brussels, 10 January.

COMMISSION OF THE EUROPEAN COMMUNITIES (1996b) *The Citizens' Network - Fulfilling the potential of public passenger transport in Europe.* Green Paper. Brussels.

COMMITTEE ON SPATIAL DEVELOPMENT (1994) *Principles for a European Spatial Development Policy.* Paper to the Informal Council of Spatial Planning Ministers, Leipzig 21-22 Sept 1994.

DEPARTMENT OF TRANSPORT (1988) *National Travel Survey 1985/86 Report.* HMSO, London.

DEPARTMENT OF THE ENVIRONMENT (1993a) *Guide to the Eco-Management and Audit Scheme for UK Local Government.* HMSO, London.

DEPARTMENT OF THE ENVIRONMENT (1993b) *The Environmental Appraisal of Development Plans: A Good Practice Guide.* Prepared by Baker Associates and University of the West of England. HMSO, London.

DEPARTMENT OF THE ENVIRONMENT (1994) *Assessing the Impacts of Urban Policy.* HMSO, London.

DRAPER R,. CURTICE L., HOOPER J. & GOUMANS M. (1993) *WHO Healthy Cities Project: Review of the First Five Years (1987-1992).* WHO, Copenhagen.

DRI (1994) *The Potential Benefits of Integration of Environmental and Economic Policies.* Study for the European Commission, DG XI.

DRYZEK J. (1987) *Rational Ecology: Environment and Political Economy.* Oxford, Basil Blackwell.

ECOTEC (1993) *Reducing Transport Emissions through Planning.* Report to the Department of the Environment. HMSO, London.

ECOTEC (1994) *The Potential for Employment Opportunities from Pursuing Sustainable Development.* Report to the European Foundation for the Improvement of Living and Working Conditions, September.

EIDOS MAISON DES SCIENCES DE LA VILLE-UNIVERSITÉ DE TOURS (1992) *Identite, Culture, Projet Urbain. Le cas de Tours.* Mai.

ENERGIE CITÉS (1994) *Urban Energy Planning Guide.* Besancon.

ESTER, P. AND MANDEMAKER T. (1994) *Socialization of environmental policy objectives: tools for environmental marketing.* In the environment towards a sustainable future, Dutch Commission for Long-term Environmental Policy, Samsom H.D. Tjeenk Willink, Alphen aan den Rijn/Kluwer Academic Publishers, Dordrecht, Boston, London.

EUROPEAN SUSTAINABLE CITIES AND TOWNS CAMPAIGN (1994) *Charter of European Cities and Towns Towards Sustainability.* Aalborg. May.

EUROPEAN ENVIRONMENT AGENCY (1995a) *Europe's Environment: The Dobris Assessment.*

EUROPEAN ENVIRONMENT AGENCY (1995b) *Statistical Compendium for the Dobris Assessment.* European Commission.

EUROPEAN ENVIRONMENT AGENCY (1995c) *Environment in the European Union 1995.* European Commission.

EUROPEAN FEDERATION FOR TRANSPORT AND ENVIRONMENT (1994) *Pedestrian and cycling policy.* (T&E 94/6), Brussels.

EUROPEAN FOUNDATION FOR THE IMPROVEMENT OF LIVING AND WORKING CONDITIONS (1992) *The Improvement of the Built Environment and Social Integration in Cities.* Selected Papers and Conclusions. Berlin 9-11 October 1991.

EUROPEAN FOUNDATION FOR THE IMPROVEMENT OF LIVING AND WORKING CONDITIONS (1993) *Innovations for the Improvement of the Urban Environment. A European Overview.*

EUROPEAN FOUNDATION FOR THE IMPROVEMENT OF LIVING AND WORKING CONDITIONS (1994) *Urban Innovations and Employment Generation - Environmental, Social and Economic Initiatives in European Towns and Cities.* Shankhill, Co. Dublin.

EUROPEAN INSTITUTE OF URBAN AFFAIRS (1992) *Urbanisation and the Functions of Cities in the European Community.* Regional Development Studies No 4, CEC Directorate-General for Regional Policies. Prepared by the European Institute of Urban Affairs, Liverpool John Moores University.

FLANDER, J.P. (1994) *"Ekologia Kaupungissa'.* In Suomen Arkkitehtiliitto: Kohti Kestävää Kaupunkia - Seminaariraportti. Helsinki.

FLEMING D. (1994) *Towards the low-output economy: the future that the Delors White Paper tries not to face.* Green College, Oxford.

FRIENDS OF THE EARTH (1992) *Less Traffic Better Towns: Friends of the Earth's Illustrated Guide to Traffic Reduction.* Friends of the Earth Trust Ltd.

FRIENDS OF THE EARTH. MEDNET (1994) *Sustainable tourism in the Mediterranean.* Sponsored by our Joint Future: DGXI for the quality of life. Mednet. Friends of the Earth, Europe. Madrid.
GIROUARD M. (1985) *Cities and People.*

GLASSON J. & HEANEY D. (1993) *'Socio-economic impacts: the poor relations in British Environmental Impact Statements'.* In Journal of Environmental Planning & Management Vol 36 (3) pp 335-343.

GLASSON, J., THERIVEL, R., CHADWICK, A. (1994) *Introduction to Environmental Impact Assessment.* UCL Press, London.

GOLDENBERG J., JOHANSSON T.B., REDDY A.K.N. & WILLIAMS R.H. (1985) *'An end-use oriented global energy strategy'.* In Annual Review of Energy 10 pp 613-688.

GOODWIN P., HALLETT S., KENNY F. & STOKES G. (1991) *Published report to the Rees Jeffreys Road Fund for discussion at the 'Transport: New Realism* Conference, Church House, London 21 March.

GREEN, G. (1995) *"Housing, Energy, Health and Poverty'*. In Case Studies and Sub-Plenary Presentations, Volume I, pp. 149-159. International Healthy and Ecological Cities Congress, Madrid, 22-25 March 1995.

HAHN, E. (1993) *"Ecological Urban Restructuring'*. In Ministry of the Environment: The European City Today - The Helsinki Roundtable on Urban Improvement Strategies. Helsinki.

HEALEY P. & SHAW T. (1993) *'Planners, plans and sustainable development'*. In Regional Studies Vol 28(8) pp 769-776.

HEALEY P. & WILLIAMS R. (1993) *'European urban planning systems: diversity and convergence'* Urban Studies Vol 30 (4/5) pp 701-720.

HEINO, E. (1994) *"Tulevaisuuden Jätehuolto'*. In Suomen Arkkitehtiliitto: Kohti Kestävää Kaupunkia - Seminaariraportti. Helsinki.

HILLMAN M., ADAMS J. & WHITELEGG J. (1990) *One False Move : A Study of Children's Independent Mobility*. Policy Studies Institute, London.

HILLMAN M. & ADAMS J. (1992) *'Safer Driving - Safer for Whom?'* Paper to conference on Eurosafe - Safer Driving in Europe July. The Association of London Borough Road Safety Officers.

HILLMAN M. (Ed) (1993) *Children, Transport and the Quality of Life*. Policy Studies Institute, London.

HOGARTH T., GREEN A. & FLANAGAN H. (1993) *'Analysing the impact of the Single European Market and European integration upon local economies: A case study of Gloucestershire'* . In Local Economy Vol 8(3) Nov pp 231-246.

HOUSE OF COMMONS ENVIRONMENT COMMITTEE (1990) Contaminated Land: first report, session 1989-90. Vol 1. Great Britain, Parliament. HMSO, London.

INRA (1991) *Eurobarometer 35.1 European Attitudes Towards Urban Traffic Problems and Public Transport*. July.

INSTITUTION OF ENVIRONMENTAL HEALTH OFFICERS (1993) *Sustainable Development and the Environmental Health Profession*. IEHO, London.INTERNATIONAL COUNCIL FOR LOCAL ENVIRONMENTAL INITIATIVES (1993) *The Local Agenda 21 Initiative - ICLEI Guidelines for Local and National Local Agenda 21 Campaigns*. ICLEI, Toronto.

INTERNATIONAL COUNCIL FOR LOCAL ENVIRONMENTAL INITIATIVES (1994) *Local Agenda 21 Participants Handbook - Local Agenda 21 Model Communities Programme*. Local Environmental Initiatives. ICLEI, Toronto.

INTERNATIONAL COUNCIL ON MONUMENTS AND SITES - ICOMOS (1990) *European Conference on Heritage and Tourism*. March. Canterbury, United Kingdom.

ISOCARP (INTERNATIONAL SOCIETY OF CITY AND REGIONAL PLANNERS) (1991) *Planning for Leisure. The Challenge of Tourism*. Final Report. 19-24 September, Guadalajara-Mexico.

ISOCARP (INTERNATIONAL SOCIETY OF CITY AND REGIONAL PLANNERS) (1992) *Cultural Identities in Unity -Towards Planning for Sustainable Development at a Supra-National Level*. 1-6 October, Córdoba-Spain.

ISOCARP (INTERNATIONAL SOCIETY OF CITY AND REGIONAL PLANNERS) (1993) *City Regions and Well-Being -What can planners do to promote the health and well-being of people in city regions?* 31 Aug.-4 September, Glasgow-Great Britain.

JACKSON, T. (1992) *Efficiency without Tears - 'No-Regrets' Policy to Combat Climate Change*. Friends of the Earth. London.

JACOBS M. (1991) *The Green Economy: Environment, Sustainable Development and the Politics of the Future*. Pluto Press, London.

JACOBS M. (1994) *Green Jobs? The Employment Implications of Environmental Policy*. A report for WWF. CAG Consultants, London.

JANSEN, J.L.A. (1994) *"Towards a sustainable future, en route with technology!'* In The Environment Towards a Sustainable Future, pp. 497 - 526. Dutch Commission for Long-term Environmental Policy, Samsom H.D. Tjeenk Willink Alphen aan den Rijn/Kluwer Academic Publishers. Dordrecht, Boston, London.

JONES (1991) *Assessing Traveller Responses to Urban Road Pricing*. Transport Studies Unit, University of Oxford, December.

JORGENSEN, G. (1993) *Ecological Land-use Patterns - Which Strategies for Redevelopment?* OECD Expert Meeting on the Ecological City, 12 May 1993, OECD, Paris.

KENNEDY M. & HAAS D., with GNAD F. (1993) *Forward-looking Building of Ecological Estates in Europe*. European Academy for the Urban Environment, Berlin December.

LEVI-STRAUSS, C. (1987) *L'identité: seminaire interdisciplinaire dirige par Claude Levi-Strauss professeur au College de France 1974-1975*. 2nd edition. Quadrige/Presses Universitaires de France.

LOCAL GOVERNMENT MANAGEMENT BOARD (1992a) *A Statement on Behalf of UK Local Government*. UNCED, February.

LOCAL GOVERNMENT MANAGEMENT BOARD (1992b) *Agenda 21: A Guide for Local Authorities in the UK*. Earth Summit Rio '92 Supplement No 2. LGMB, Luton.

LOCAL GOVERNMENT MANAGEMENT BOARD (1993a) *A Framework for Local Sustainability*. LGMB, Luton.

BIBLIOGRAPHY

LOCAL GOVERNMENT MANAGEMENT BOARD (1993b) *Greening Economic Development.* LGMB, Luton.

LOCAL GOVERNMENT MANAGEMENT BOARD (1993c) *The UK's Report to the UN Commission on Sustainable Development.* An Initial Submission by UK Local Government. May.

LOCAL GOVERNMENT MANAGEMENT BOARD (1994a) *Local Agenda 21 - Principles and Process - A Step by Step Guide.* LGMB, Luton.

LYNCH, K. (1968) *The Image of the City.* MIT Press.

MARSHALL T. (1993) *'Regional environmental planning: progress and possibilities in Western Europe'.* In European Planning Studies Vol 1(1) pp 69-90.

MASSER I., SVIDEN O. & WEGENER M. (1993) *'Transport planning for equity and sustainability'.* In Transportation Planning and Technology Vol 17 pp 319-330.

MCLAREN D. (1993) *'Compact or dispersed? Dilution is no solution'* In Built Environment Vol 18(4) pp 268-284.

MILLS L. (1994a) *'Gouvernement local au Royaume-Uni : le role de la politique de l'environnement'* in Biarez S. & Nevers J.: Gouvernement Local et Politiques Urbaines Actes du colloque international, Grenoble, 2-3 Fevrier 1993.

MILLS L. (1994b) *'Economic development, the environment and Europe: arenas of innovation in UK local government'.* In Local Government Policy Making Vol 20 (5) May pp 3-10.

MINISTERE DE L'ENVIRONNEMENT (1994) *Mission Emploi - Emplois Verts.* Circulaire du 10 mars 1994 & documents divers.

MINISTRY OF THE ENVIRONMENT/CITY OF HELSINKI/RAUTSI J. (1993) *Paper on the European City Today - The Helsinki Round Table on Urban Improvement Strategies.* Ministry of the Environment and City of Helsinki, Helsinki.

MINISTRY OF THE ENVIRONMENT AND NATURAL RESOURCES (1992) *Eco Cycles - The Basis of Sustainable Urban Development.* SOu 1992:43. Stockholm.

MINISTRY OF HOUSING (Boverket) (1993) Housing in Sweden; in an international perspective, Sweden, Rapport 1993:2 e.

MINISTRY OF HOUSING, SPATIAL PLANNING AND THE ENVIRONMENT (1994) *Working with Industry : Environmental Policy in Action.* Ministry of Housing, Spatial Planning and the Environment, The Hague.

MOLLENKOPF J.H. & CASTELLS M. (Eds) (1991) *Dual City: Restructuring New York.* Russell Sage, New York.

MONTANARI A., CURDES G., FORSYTH L (1993) *Urban Landscape Dynamics. A Multi-Level Innovations Process.*MORPHET J., HAMS T., JACOBS M., LEVETT R., LUSSER H. & TAYLOR D. (1994) *Greening Your Local Authority.* Longman, London.

MUNICIPALITY OF AARHUS (1993) *Transport and Environmental Quality. A Planning Theme.* Aarhus, Denmark.

NÆSS P. (1995) *Urban Form and Energy Use for Transport - A Nordic Experience.* Thesis for the doctorate Dr. Ing. Thesis No. 1995:20. Norwegian Institute of Technology, Trondheim.

NELISSEN, N.J.M. (1992) *Afscheid van de vervuilende samenleving?* Kerckebosch, Zeist.

NEWMAN P. (1993) *'The compact city: an Australian perspective'.* In Built Environment Vol 18(4) pp 285-300.

OECD (1990) *Environmental Policies for Cities in the 1990s.* OECD, Paris.

OECD (1993) *The Social Costs of Transport. Evaluation and Links with Internalisation Policies.* Group on Economic and Environmental Policy Integration. OECD, Paris.

OECD (1994) *OECD-Sweden International Seminar on the Ecological City Draft Summary Record.* Project Group on the Ecological City 1st Sept 1994.

OECD - ECMT (1995) *Urban Travel and Sustainable Development.* Paris.

OVE-ARUP (1993) *Environmental Capacity and Development in Historic Cities: A Study with particular reference to Chester* Report to Cheshire County Council, Chester City Council, English Heritage and Department of the Environment.

OXFORD CITY COUNCIL (1989) *Park and Ride in Oxford.* Internal report.

PARKINSON M. (1992) *Leadership and Urban Regeneration; Britain and the Rise of the Entrepreneurial European City.* Institutions and Cities - Anglo-Dutch conference on Urban Regeneration, The Hague, March 1992. Centre for Urban Studies, University of Liverpool, Liverpool.

PUBLIC WORKS ROTTERDAM (1994) *Survey of the Integration of Environmental Aspects in Land Use Plans in Nine European Cities.* Public Works Rotterdam, Department of Environmental Policy.

REES W.E (1992) *'Ecological footprints and appropriated carrying capacity; what urban economics leaves out'* In Environment & Urbanisation Vol 4 (2) pp 121-130.

SANTALA, E. (1994) *Mitä on Kestävä Kehitys Vesihuollossa?* In Suomen Arkkitehtiliitto: Kohti Kestävää Kaupunkia - Seminaariraportti. Helsinki.

SHANKLAND COX (1993) *Mixed Uses in Buildings, Blocks and Quarters.* Report to the Commission of the European Communities DG XI.

SHEATE W. (1993) Review of CEC (1993) in EIA Newsletter 8, Winter EIA Centre, Department of Planning and Landscape, University of Manchester.

SHIPMAN MARTIN, B. (1993) *Urban Environment: The Problems of Tourism*. Final report. DGXi, Commission of the European Communities. January.
STEER DAVIES GLEAVE (1994) *Dublin Transportation Initiative Phase 2 Draft Final Report.* January.

STORKSDIECK M. & OTTO-ZIMMERMAN K. (1994) *Local Environmental Budgeting.* Paper presented at the First International Expert Seminar: Advanced Environmental Management Tools and Environmental Budgeting at the Local Level, Freiburg, Germany 14-16 March.

TEST (1991) *Wrong Side of the Tracks : Impacts of Road and Rail Transport on the Environment.* Transport and Environmental Studies, London.

THERIVEL, R. et al (1992) *Strategic Environmental Assessment.* Earthscan, London.

TJALLINGII, S. (1992) *Ecologisch Verantwoorde Stedelijke Ontwikkeling.* Rijksplanologische Dienst 's-Gravenhage en Instituut voor Bos- en Natuuronderzoek Wageningen, the Netherlands.

TJALLINGII, S., HACCOU, H. & ZONNEVELD, W. (1994) *Econiveaus; een discussie over schaalniveaus en strategieën voor duurzame ontwikkeling van stedelijke systemen.* Instituut voor Bos- en Natuuronderzoek, Heidemij Advies, Zandvoort Ordening & Advies, the Netherlands.

TJALLINGII S. (1995) *Ecopolis - Strategies for Ecologically Sound Urban Development.* Institute for Forestry and Nature Research, Wageningen.

UNITED NATIONS (1994) *Social development - Notes for speakers.* United Nations, New York.

UNITED NATIONS (1995) *The Copenhagen Declaration and Programme of Action - World Summit for Social Development 6-12 March 1995.* United Nations, New York.

UNITED NATIONS CENTRE FOR HUMAN SETTLEMENTS (1990) *Sustainable Cities.* Press Release 29 August.

UNITED NATIONS ECONOMIC COMMISSION FOR EUROPE (1992) *Application of Environmental Impact Assessment Principles to Policies, Plans and Programmes.* UNECE, Geneva.

UNITED NATIONS ENVIRONMENT PROGRAMME (1994) *Environmental Data Report 1993-94.*

UNITED NATIONS ENVIRONMENT PROGRAMME. INDUSTRY AND ENVIRONMENT (1995) *Environmental codes of conduct for tourism.* Technical Report Nr. 29. Paris.

VAN DER BIE M. (1993) *Environmental Twinning: A Status Report of the First Phase of the Environmental Twinning Project.* Stichting Milieu Educatie/Institute of Environmental Communication, Utrecht, July.

VAN DER WAL L.J.J. (1993) *Ecological Planning in an Urban Region.* INRO-TNO 93 NP-116, INRO-TNO, Delft.

VAN WEESEP J. & DIELEMAN F.M. (1993) *'Evolving urban Europe*: editors' introduction to the special issue' in Urban Studies Vol 30(6) pp 877-882.

VILLE DE RENNES (1995) Les Indicateurs au service d'une politique de la ville. Resumés. Conference 3-4 Avril 1995, Rennes, France.

WELFORD R. (1993) *'Local economic development and environmental management: an integrated approach'.* Local Economy.

WERRETT M. (1994) *'Discovering a forgotten people in impact assessment'.* In Planning 1055 11 Feb pp 22-23.

WHITELEGG J. (1993) *Transport for a Sustainable Future.* Belhaven, London.

WILSON E. & RAEMAEKERS J. (1992) *An Index of Local Authority Green Plans.* 2nd Edition Edinburgh College of Art/Heriott Watt Research Paper No 44.

WORCESTER R. (1994) *The Sustainable Society : What we Know About What People Think and Do.* Paper for World Environment Day Symposium 2 June.

WORLD BANK (1993) *Toward Environmental Strategies for Cities* Review Draft. Urban Development Division, Washington.

WORLD COMMISSION ON ENVIRONMENT AND DEVELOPMENT (1987) *Our Common Future.* Oxford University Press, Oxford.

WORLD CONSERVATION UNION, UN ENVIRONMENT PROGRAMME, WORLD WIDE FUND FOR NATURE (1991) *Caring for the Earth.* IUCP/UNEP/WWF, Gland.

WORLD HEALTH ORGANISATION (1993) *WHO Global Strategy for Health and Environment.* WHO, Geneva.

ZACATECAS DECLARATION (1988) Zacatecas Declaration. Congress, November, City of Zacatecas, Mexico.

ZANDVOORT ORDENING & ADVIES (1988) *Integratie stadsvernieuwing en milieubeleid; een methode.* Ministerie van Volkshuisvesting Ruimtelijke Ordening en Milieubeheer, the Netherlands.

ZANDVOORT ORDENING & ADVIES (1993) *Ruimtelijke verkenning Aggloraillijn Twentse Stedenband*, the Netherlands.

GLOSSARY

Backcasting - directing and determining the process that technological development must take and possibly also the pace at which this development process must be put into effect.

Capacity Building - the processes and means for national governments and local communities to develop the skills and expertise needed to manage their environment and natural resources in a sustainable manner.

Closure versus Openness - a key ecosystems concept which refers to the degree to which a system is insulated from, or vulnerable to, external changes.

Community Profiling - gauging the public's perceptions of the environment and needs in relation to health, social services and community development.

Cross-disciplinary Working - working across professional boundaries through the grouping of technical specialisms into multidisciplinary, task-oriented teams.

Demand Management - the management, that is reduction or redirection, of certain demands rather than the meeting of them in order to reconcile the principles of sustainable development with the aspirations of human societies to develop, progress and improve wealth and living standards.

Dual Network Strategy - a strategy within the Ecosystems Approach and a planning concept where particular emphasis is placed on transport and water networks.

Ecological Footprint - the impact of an entity, for example a city or country, on local, regional and global ecosystems.

Ecosystems Approach - a framework for considering the city as an ecosystem and understanding the problems of urban sustainability and choosing approaches to solving them using ecological concepts.

Emergence - a key ecosystems concept which refers to the ability of a complex system to develop characteristics and behaviour which are 'greater than the sum of its parts' and cannot necessarily be predicted or managed in terms of the behaviour of its constituent elements.

Environmental Capacity - the ability of a particular environment to perform, and continue to perform, its various natural functions.

Environmental Impact Assessment - a formal procedure for the assessment of the effects of a proposed new activity or development on the environment.

Environmental Threshold - the earth's carrying capacity.

Environmental Efficiency - the achievement of the maximum benefit for each unit of resources used and wastes produced.

Environmental Carrying Capacity - a notion of environmental thresholds to be considered in urban management and planning.

Environmental Tax Reform - shifting the burden of taxation away from employment and towards environmentally undesirable impacts.

Environmental Audit - a review of environmental conditions and environmental impact of the activities of a particular enterprise or institution. At city level, the environmental audit may be divided into the external audit (State of the Environment Report) and the internal audit (review of policies and practices).

Environmental Performance Indicators - secondary and tertiary indicators used to measure the influence of human activities on the environment.

Environmental Quality Indicators - primary indicators used to measure the condition of key environmental features.

Environmental Management System - standardised approaches to the preparation and implementation of environmental strategies.

Environmental Budgeting - applying techniques of financial accounting and budget management to manage a city's environmental 'wealth', 'income' and 'expenditure'.

Equity - social solidarity in terms of fairness to people living now and in the future.

Expert Group on the Urban Environment - established by DGXI of the European Commission in 1991 to facilitate the incorporation of environmental objectives in spatial planning, the development of the urban environment dimension within Community environment policy, and the improvement of the urban environment by the Community.

Green Consumerism - where both corporate and individual consumers identify and value products and services generated more sustainably.

Greenhouse Gases - a group of gases, including carbon dioxide and methane, which trap long-wave radiated energy in the earth's atmosphere.

Homeostasis - a key ecosystems concept where feedback loops keep the overall system much the same while elements within it alter considerably (change within stability).

Hypothecation - earmarking money raised by a tax directly for spending on measures to counter the damage, rather than treating the money as general revenue.

Least Cost Planning - an approach whereby a utility provides and charges for a service to the consumer, for example warmth or light for a room, rather than units of energy. This motivates the utility to provide the specified service level using as little natural resources and energy as possible, while it allows the utility to still make profits.

Local Agenda 21 - a strategic process of encouraging and controlling sustainable development.

Municipal Twinning - a long-established framework for cooperation between individual local authorities for the exchange of experiences.

Natural Ecosystem - a system that maintains its equilibrium by circulating resources and wastes internally.

Negative Feedback - a key ecosystems concept where the system reacts to change in such a way as to limit or contain it.

Networking - the sharing through both formal and informal contact between agencies of ideas and experience in the development, management and implementation of policies and projects for cities and towns.

Positive Feedback - a key ecosystems concept where the system reacts to change in such a way as to reinforce it.

Precautionary Principle - where significant environmental damage may occur, but knowledge on the matter is incomplete, decisions made and measures implemented should err on the side of caution.

Quality Indicators - indicators which translate 'technical' environmental indicators into visible and emotive indicators which will help generate and facilitate community involvement.

Quality of Life - composed of several aspects including material living standards, public health and safety, access to education, health care, fulfilling occupations, opportunities for personal development and advancement, community, culture, social life and recreation, environmental amenities and aesthetic qualities.

Residuarity Principle - the counterpart to the subsidiarity principle, stating that where one level of government is unable or unwilling to take action appropriate to it, other levels have a responsibility to try to fill the gap.

State Transition - a key ecosystems concept where the way the components of a system mesh together alters fundamentally and irreversibly ('step' change).

State of the Environment Report - the external element of an Environmental Audit.

Strategic Environmental Assessment - a formal procedure for the assessment at the strategic level of the effects of a proposed policy, programme or plan on the environment.

Subsidiarity - the principle that decisions should be taken at European level only where this adds value.

Sustainability Indicators - definable, measurable features of the world whose absolute levels or rate and direction of change are intended to reveal whether the world (or a city) is becoming more or less sustainable.

Sustainable development - "development that meets the needs of the present without compromising the ability of future generations to meet their own needs" (World Commission on Environment and Development, 1987, p. 43).

Urban System - a system where problems of supply and waste disposal have generally been solved by increasing both supply and discharge and thus the flows into and out of the system, exacerbating both internal and external environmental problems.

Welfare Efficiency - the achievement of the greatest human benefit from each unit of economic activity.

Whole Life Asset Management - seeking the best ratio of benefits to costs over the whole life of an asset rather than a quick payback.

INDEX

ILLUSTRATIONS

Provided by/photographer:Illustration(s) on page:

Ayuntamento de San Sebastián	33, 56, 204, 218, 226, 230, (cover)
Enviplan	25, 30, 41, 242, 260
Generalitat de Catalunya, Departament de Medi Ambient	75, 92, 180, 223, 238, 258, (cover)
Ministerie van VROM	49, 119, 202, 210, (cover)
Ministerie van VROM/Oerlemans van Reeken Studio	130, 139, 142, 170, 184, 195, 206, 231, 253, (cover)
Rijks Planologische Dienst/R.H.H. Poelenjee	61, 68, 145, 152, 191
Stattauto	181
S. Tjallingii	42, 58, 67, 85, 90, 100, 102, 107, 115, 121, 128, 156, 160, 185, 199, 247, (cover)
Zandvoort Ordening & Advies	6, 8, 13, 18, 104, 111, 149, 163, 172, 175, 182, 208, 214, (cover)

European Commission

European Sustainable Cities

Luxembourg Office for Official Publications of the European Communities

1996-303 pp.-21 x 29,7

ISBN 92-827-8259-X
Price (excluding VAT) in Luxembourg: ECU 24

Copies of the European Sustainable Cities report, copies of a database with examples of good practices of urban policy leading towards sustainability, or further information on the work of the Expert Group on the Urban Environment can be obtained from:

The European Commission
DG XI - Environment, Nuclear Safety and Civil Protection
Unit D.3 - Urban Environment, Air Quality, Transport, Noise, Energy
Boulevard du Triomphe 174/Triomflaan 174
B-1160 Bruxelles/Brussel
Fax: (32-2) 296 9554

Electronic versions of the report and the database are available:

The address of the report can be found on the homepage of DGXI:
http://europa.eu.int

The address of the database is:
http://cities21.com/europractice

Local Authorities interested in implementing policies for sustainable development at local level can join the Sustainable Cities and Towns Campaign. Further information available from:

The Sustainable Cities and Towns Campaign
Rue du Cornet 22/Hoornstraat 22
B-1040 Bruxelles/Brussel
Fax: (32-2) 230 5351